DATABASE SYSTEMS

Introduction to Databases and Data Warehouses

Nenad Jukić

Loyola University Chicago

Susan Vrbsky

The University of Alabama

Svetlozar Nestorov

Loyola University Chicago

Prospect Press

Cover Design: Maddy Lesure
Cover Photo: © istock.com/mapichai
Editor: Beth Lang Golub
Production Management: Kathy Bond Borie
Text Font: Palatino

Founded in 2014, Prospect Press serves the academic discipline of Information Systems by publishing innovative textbooks across the curriculum including introductory, emerging, and upper level courses. Prospect Press offers reasonable prices by selling directly to students. Prospect Press provides tight relationships between authors, publisher, and adopters that many larger publishers are unable to offer. Based in Burlington, Vermont, Prospect Press distributes titles worldwide. We welcome new authors to send proposals or inquiries to Beth.golub@prospectpressvt.com.

CIP Data for this title is available on file at the Library of Congress

10 9 8 7 6 5 4 3 2 1

eTextbook ISBN: 978-1-943153-18-3
Available from Redshelf.com and VitalSource.com

Paperback ISBN: 978-1-943153-19-0
Available from Redshelf.com

In memory of my mother, Ruža. To my father, Drago, and to Linda and Lee Albritton. To my wife, Maria, and our kids, Maja, Niko, and Boris.

—Nenad

To Austin, who teaches me new things every day. To my students, who continually remind me of the joy of learning. To Brian, who recognizes my need for both.

—Susan

To my parents, Atanaska and Evtim.

—Svetlozar

BRIEF CONTENTS

CONTENTS

PREFACE

Database Systems: Introduction to Databases and Data Warehouses is an introductory yet comprehensive database textbook intended for use in undergraduate and graduate information systems database courses. Even though it is likely that students taking a course based on this book will have already been exposed to an introductory information systems course, the book itself can also be used with no prerequisite course taken. The book contains all necessary introductions, followed by a detailed coverage of database topics. Its goal is to provide a significant level of database expertise to its readers and users.

COVERAGE OF OPERATIONAL AND ANALYTICAL DATABASES

The current job market in fields such as information systems, business data analysis, and decision support requires both operational and analytical database systems competence. *Database Systems: Introduction to Databases and Data Warehouses* covers operational and analytical database systems in a comprehensive fashion, providing a theoretical foundation and meaningful hands-on experiences. Students in database courses based on this textbook will learn how to design and use operational *and* analytical databases and will be prepared to apply their knowledge in today's business environments, which require a solid understanding of both of these types of databases.

Both operational and analytical databases are now mainstream information systems topics. A responsible educational approach is to teach both of these topics in a meaningful way, even when the curriculum allows for only one database-related class. In our opinion and experience, it is pedagogically straightforward to teach a course based on this book. We have been teaching database courses (both in semester and quarter versions at both the graduate and undergraduate levels) based on the material presented in this book for several years. In every instance, we were able to cover all of the intended topics. Our courses based on this book have received overwhelmingly positive evaluation scores. In addition, we have received numerous written testimonies from former and current undergraduate and graduate students and their hiring companies (both in internship and full-time job scenarios) reporting the high level of preparedness of our students for jobs that require database competence.

FEATURES

Our coverage of fundamental topics related to the design and use of operational and analytical databases is divided into 10 chapters and 10 appendices.

Chapters 1 through 6 focus on operational database topics and include coverage of standard database issues, including *database requirements, ER modeling, relational modeling, database constraints, update anomalies, normalization, SQL, the database front-end,* and *data quality.*

Chapters 7 through 9 focus on analytical database topics and include coverage of data warehouse and data mart-related topics, including *data warehousing concepts, dimensional modeling (star schemas), data warehouse/data mart modeling approaches, the extraction/transformation/load (ETL) process, online analytical processing (OLAP)/business intelligence (BI) functionalities,* and *the data warehouse/data mart front-end.*

Chapter 10 presents a higher-level (less-detailed) overview of *database administration.*

Appendices (A, B, C, D, E, F, G, H, I, and **J)** contain brief overviews of additional database and database-related topics, including *enhanced ER modeling (EER), further normal forms (beyond 3NF), enterprise resource planning (ERP), data governance and master data* *management, object-oriented databases, distributed databases, parallel databases, cloud comput-ing, data mining, XML, NoSQL databases,* and *Big Data.*

Suggestions on how to efficiently cover the presented topics in both semester and quarter versions of courses are included in the instructor's resources accompanying this book.

The book's Web site includes access to the free Web-based data modeling suite **ERDPlus** (*erdplus.com*), designed and developed in conjunction with the book. Students and instructors can use this data modeling suite, specifically designed for use in academic settings, to create ER diagrams, relational schemas, and dimensional models (star schemas). We encourage instructors and students to give this provided data modeling suite a try, and experience its simplicity, ease of use, portability, and fit for academic use. Of course, instructors and students are also welcome to use other tools for the purpose of creating ER diagrams, relational schemas, and dimensional models. Coverage of the included exercises is possible either by using the provided data modeling suite ERDPlus or by using other modeling tools and means for creating these diagrams (such as Visio, ERwin, ER/Studio, MS Word, MS Excel, MS PowerPoint, free drawing, etc.).

SUPPLEMENTS

Database Systems: Introduction to Databases and Data Warehouses is accompanied by a comprehensive set of supplementary materials for instructors and students. The supplements include:

A companion Web site (*dbtextbook.com*), which includes:

- Link to ERDPlus, a data modeling software suite (developed in conjunction with the book)
- SQL scripts and data sets
- Instructions for free access to DBMS and OLAP/BI software

- E-mail access to the authors

For Instructors

The Instructor Resource Center, which includes:

- PowerPoint slides (versions for *quick coverage, typical coverage,* and *complete coverage*)
- An Instructor's Manual that includes:
  - Solutions for the end-of-chapter questions, exercises, and mini cases
  - Additional exercises (with solutions)
  - Sample syllabi and topic coverage plans
  - Project ideas
- A Test Item File that includes a comprehensive set of test questions in multiple-choice, true/false, and essay format, each with a page reference and difficulty level.

PEDAGOGICAL APPROACH

Database Systems: Introduction to Databases and Data Warehouses combines clear descriptions of theoretical concepts, easy-to-understand examples, and comprehensive hands-on components, wherever appropriate and useful. For every skill that students acquire, multiple hands-on exercises and mini cases are given at the end of corre-sponding chapters.
Most of the chapters end with sections whose titles contain the phrase "A Note About . . .". These sections represent topics that can be studied as additional optional readings or be covered in the same fashion as the other content (depending on the level of class and the time available). More about the pedagogy of each chapter is given in the following outline.

OUTLINE

Chapter 1: Introduction

MAIN TOPICS The introductory chapter gives a quick overview of basic database-related terms, concepts, and components, such as data and information, database management system (DBMS), database system development steps, and operational versus analytical databases.

PEDAGOGY The introductory topics are covered using short descriptions and brief introductory examples. This chapter is designed to be covered in a quick and to-the-point fashion, setting the stage for the following chapters.

Chapter 2: Database Requirements and ER Modeling

MAIN TOPICS This chapter provides comprehensive coverage of entity-relationship (ER) modeling as a conceptual method for formalizing user database requirements. A varia-tion of Chen ER notation is used throughout the chapter, but other notations and con-ceptual data modeling methods are mentioned as well. The purpose of ER modeling as a method for collecting and visualizing requirements is stressed. The chapter covers ER constructs—entities (including weak entities); attributes (regular, unique, composite, multivalued, derived); and 1:1, 1:N, and M:N relationships (binary and unary).

ADDITIONAL NOTES Notes at the end of this chapter discuss several additional issues related to ER modeling (M:N relationships with multiple instances between the same entities, associative entities, and ternary and higher-degree relationships).

PEDAGOGY This chapter is example-driven and presents comprehensive examples of the collection of requirements and the creation of ER models. Exercises, mini cases, and free software (ERDPlus—*ER diagram feature*) reinforce the introduced concepts. This chapter is designed to be covered in depth by first describing concepts relating to ER modeling and requirements visualization to the students, and then reinforcing the concepts through multiple hands-on exercises.

Chapter 3: Relational Database Modeling

MAIN TOPICS This chapter provides comprehensive coverage of the relational database model, including relational concepts, relational schema, integrity constraints, and user-defined constraints. It covers the process of mapping ER diagrams (entities, attributes, binary and unary 1:1, 1:N, and M:N relationships) into relational schemas.

ADDITIONAL NOTES Notes at the end of this chapter discuss several additional issues related to relational database modeling (mapping associative entities, mapping ternary relationships, designer-created primary keys and autonumber option, and the necessity of both ER and relational modeling).

PEDAGOGY This chapter is example-driven and presents comprehensive examples of the mapping of ER constructs and the creation of relational schemas. Exercises, mini cases, and software (ERDPlus—*relational schema feature*) reinforce the concepts that have been introduced. This chapter is designed to be covered in depth by first relating the relational database modeling concepts to the students, and then reinforcing the concepts through multiple hand-on exercises.

Chapter 4: Update Operations, Update Anomalies, and Normalization

MAIN TOPICS This chapter describes update operations (insert, delete, and modify) and provides coverage of normalization and update anomalies (as justification for normalization). It introduces and discusses the concept of functional dependencies. It covers first normal form (1NF), second normal form (2NF), and third normal form (3NF) (other normal forms are covered in Appendix B).

ADDITIONAL NOTES Notes at the end of this chapter discuss several additional issues related to normalization (normalization exceptions, denormalization, normalization versus ER modeling, adding tables for streamlining database content).

PEDAGOGY This chapter is example-driven and presents comprehensive examples of update operations, update anomalies, and the normalization process. It provides exercises to reinforce the introduced concepts. This chapter is designed to be covered in depth by first relating the update and normalization concepts to students and then reinforcing the concepts through multiple hand-on exercises.

Chapter 5: SQL

MAIN TOPICS This chapter provides comprehensive coverage of SQL (Structured Query Language). It covers SQL statements for creating, updating, and querying relational databases. Coverage of commands for retrieval of data includes the SELECT statement (with multiple conditions using AND, OR, and NOT operators), aggregate functions (SUM, COUNT, AVG, MIN, MAX), GROUP BY, ORDER BY, HAVING, nested queries, UNION and INTERSECT operators, IN, EXISTS, various joins, and an overview of other SQL statements and functionalities.

ADDITIONAL NOTES Notes at the end of this chapter discuss several additional issues related to SQL (inappropriate use of observed values in SQL, SQL standard, and SQL syntax differences in various popular RDBMS packages).

PEDAGOGY This chapter is example-driven and presents comprehensive examples of concepts that have been introduced. It is designed to explain the process of building, populating, and querying a relational database using SQL statements. It contains examples of SQL commands doing this, executed in their natural consecutive order. The companion Web site (*dbtextbook.com*) presents scripts containing all SQL statements from this chapter for six popular DBMS packages (Oracle, MySQL, Microsoft SQL Server, PostgreSQL, Teradata, and IBM DB2). Instructors can use these scripts to copy, paste, and execute SQL statements directly in an RDBMS (of their choice) during the lectures based on this chapter. By doing so, instructors can *introduce students to SQL commands* and, at the same time, *demonstrate created, populated, and queried databases*. Data sets, exercises, and mini cases reinforce the concepts that have been introduced. In addition, the companion Web site (*dbtextbook.com*) provides instructions on how to obtain free, unlimited access to state-of-the-art relational DBMS software. This chapter is designed to be covered in depth by first relating the SQL concepts to the students and then reinforcing the concepts through multiple hands-on exercises.

Chapter 6: Database Implementation and Use

MAIN TOPICS This chapter includes coverage of data quality issues—accuracy, completeness, consistency, uniqueness, timeliness, and conformity of data. These topics are covered in the context of data stored within database systems. This chapter also covers the design and use of database front-end interfaces (database forms, reports, and applications), referential integrity options (delete and update options: cascade, restrict, set-to-null, and set-to-default), indexes, and the implementation of user-defined constraints.

ADDITIONAL NOTES An additional note at the end of this chapter discusses assertions and triggers.

PEDAGOGY This chapter is designed to provide quick but meaningful coverage of the most fundamental database implementation issues and those database use issues not covered in Chapter 5. It presents examples of concepts that have been introduced. Hands-on exercises reinforce the concepts that have been introduced.

Chapter 7: Basic Data Warehousing Concepts

MAIN TOPICS This chapter defines the terms data warehouse and data mart and introduces basic data warehouse components and concepts (source systems, ETL-extraction/transformation/load, integrated analytical data repository, subject-oriented databases, and OLAP/BI front end). It also gives an overview of data warehouse system development steps.

PEDAGOGY The introductory data warehousing topics are covered using short descriptions and brief introductory examples. This chapter is designed to be covered in a quick and to-the-point fashion, setting the stage for the following two chapters.

Chapter 8: Data Warehouse and Data Mart Modeling

MAIN TOPICS This chapter covers dimensional modeling, a conceptual and logical data design technique used for designing analytical databases (e.g., data warehouses or data marts). It describes concepts such as fact and dimension tables, star schema, snowflake schema, constellations, and slowly changing dimensions. It also covers ER modeling as a technique for modeling analytical databases (as opposed to ER modeling as a technique for modeling operational databases, covered in Chapter 2). This chapter also gives an overview of different development approaches to data warehousing projects: data warehouse bus architecture (a.k.a. the Kimball approach), including a discussion of conformed dimensions, normalized data warehouse (a.k.a. the Inmon approach), and independent data marts.

ADDITIONAL NOTES An additional note at the end of this chapter compares dimensional modeling and ER modeling as data warehouse/data mart design techniques.

PEDAGOGY This chapter is example-driven and presents comprehensive examples of dimensional models (star schemas) based on single and multiple sources, detailed and aggregated fact tables, slowly changing dimensions, and other dimensional modeling related topics. This chapter also presents examples of ER modeled/normalized data warehouses. Exercises, mini cases, and free software (ERDPlus—*star schema feature*) reinforce the concepts that have been introduced. This chapter is designed to be covered in depth by first relating the data warehouse and data mart modeling concepts to the students and then reinforcing the concepts through multiple hands-on exercises.

Chapter 9: Data Warehouse Implementation and Use

MAIN TOPICS This chapter gives an overview of the ETL process, including the creation of infrastructure and procedures for the tasks of extracting analytically useful data from the operational sources, transforming such data so that it conforms to the structure of the target data warehouse model, ensuring the quality of the transformed data through processes such as data cleansing or scrubbing, and loading the transformed and quality assured data into the target data warehouse. This chapter defines the terms "online analytical processing (OLAP)" and "business intelligence (BI)," which are commonly used to refer to front-end use of analytical databases. It also presents functionalities that are common for all OLAP/BI tools.

ADDITIONAL NOTES Additional notes at the end of this chapter discuss different database models for OLAP/BI tools and different OLAP/BI architectures.

PEDAGOGY This chapter is example-driven and presents examples of concepts that have been introduced. The companion Web site (*dbtextbook.com*) gives instructions for obtaining free unlimited access to state-of-the-art OLAP/BI software, data sets, and exercises. This chapter is designed to provide quick but meaningful coverage of the most fundamental data warehouse implementation and use issues.

Chapter 10: Overview of DBMS Functionalities and Database Administration

MAIN TOPICS This chapter gives an informative overview of the DBMS functionalities and components. It also gives an overview of database administration issues, such as data security, backup, recovery, performance, and optimization.

PEDAGOGY This chapter presents a quick overview of the introduced topics. It is designed to familiarize readers with DBMS functionalities and database administration topics without covering them in a great level of detail.

Appendices: Overview of Additional Topics

MAIN TOPICS The appendices give an overview of additional database-related topics, including enhanced ER modeling (EER), further normal forms (beyond 3NF), enterprise resource planning (ERP), data governance and master data management, object-oriented databases, distributed databases, parallel databases, cloud computing, data mining, XML, NoSQL databases, and Big Data.

PEDAGOGY The topics in the appendices are covered in the form of short notes and examples. They are designed to familiarize readers with additional database-related topics without covering them in a great level of detail.

ACKNOWLEDGMENTS

We wish to thank the following reviewers for their thoughtful comments and suggestions during the development of this book:

Gary Baram, Temple University
Jeff Hassett, University of Utah
Emily Kelly, Loyola University Chicago
Barry King, Butler University
Mark Llewellyn, University of Central Florida
Brian Mennecke, Iowa State University
Sree Nilakanta, Iowa State University
Janet Renwick, University of Arkansas
John Russo, Wentworth Institute of Technology
Julian Scher, New Jersey Institute of Technology
Linda Zhou, University of Maryland

We are truly grateful for the generous contribution of time, effort, advice, and expertise by a number of individuals. We wish to thank industry experts Benjamin Korallus (PricewaterhouseCoopers), Robin Edison and Douglas Marcis (OptumInsight), Stan Ozenbaugh and Kevin Little (Teradata), Mark Watson and Abhishek Sharma (Federal Reserve Bank of Kansas City), Ryane Bohm (General Electric), Alexander Rukhostkiy (Boeing), Creighton Lang (NTT DATA, Inc.), Zachary Relli (Booz Allen Hamilton), and Gregory Roszczybiuk (Leo Burnett). We are also thankful to our colleagues Stefan Lessmann (University of Hamburg), Mary Malliaris and Faruk Guder (Loyola University Chicago), Michael Goul (Arizona State University), Hugh Watson (University of Georgia), Boris Jukić (Clarkson University), and Miguel Velasco (University of Minnesota). Our thanks also go to the following students at Loyola University Chicago: Melanie Ruiz, Jordan Braun, Subash Pant, Sarah Shea, Adam Chorazy, Anton Dokov, and Karan Desai.

Special thanks to world-class DBA/database designer/programmer Zoran Avramović for persistently keeping us grounded by providing forthright and detailed scrutiny of the manuscript, and to Ivan Bare for providing extensive logistical and technical support during the preparation of this manuscript.

Nenad would also like to express his gratitude to the excellent information technology teachers he was fortunate to have in his life: Professor Zoran Vlašić, Professor Damir Kalpić, Professor Allen Parrish, and Professor Susan Vrbsky.

In the process of writing this book we received kind and thoughtful advice and encouragement from Dr. Paul Gray, who passed away in 2012. Paul was one of the founding pioneers of information systems education and research, and he is truly missed.

Nenad Jukić

Susan Vrbsky

Svetlozar Nestorov

ABOUT THE AUTHORS

NENAD JUKIĆ is a professor of information systems and the director of the Graduate Certificate Program in Business Data Analytics at the Quinlan School of Business at Loyola University Chicago.

Dr. Jukić has been teaching undergraduate, graduate, and executive education classes in the Information Systems and Operations Management Department at the Quinlan School of Business since 1999. Between 2005 and 2007, Dr. Jukić was also a visiting professor of information systems in the Beijing International MBA Program at the China Center for Economic Research at Peking University, Beijing, China. Between 1997 and 1999, he taught at the School of Computing and Information Systems at Grand Valley State University in Allendale, Michigan.

Dr. Jukić received his undergraduate degree in computer science and electrical engineering from the School of Computing and Electrical Engineering at the University of Zagreb in Croatia. He received his M.S. and Ph.D. in computer science from the University of Alabama in Tuscaloosa, Alabama.

Dr. Jukić conducts active research in various information technology–related areas, including database modeling and management, data warehousing, business intelligence, data mining, e-business, and IT strategy. His work has been published in numerous management information systems and computer science academic journals, conference publications, and books. In addition to his academic work, his engagements include providing expertise to database, data warehousing, and business intelligence projects for corporations and organizations that vary from startups to *Fortune* 500 companies to U.S. government and military agencies.

SUSAN V. VRBSKY is an associate professor and graduate program director of computer science at the University of Alabama in Tuscaloosa, Alabama.

Dr. Vrbsky has been teaching undergraduate and graduate courses in the Department of Computer Science at the University of Alabama since 1992. She is the director of the Cloud and Cluster Computing Laboratory at the University of Alabama. She also taught in the Computer Science Department at Southern Illinois University from 1983 to 1986.

Dr. Vrbsky received her B.A. from Northwestern University in Evanston, IL, and her M.S. in computer science from Southern Illinois University in Carbondale, IL. She received her Ph.D. in computer science from the University of Illinois, Urbana-Champaign.

Dr. Vrbsky's research is in the area of databases and cloud computing, including data intensive computing, real-time databases, database security, mobile databases, and green computing. She has co-authored over 100 peer-review publications in computer science academic journals, conference publications, and books. She has received funding from such sources as the National Science Foundation.

SVETLOZAR EVTIMOV NESTOROV is an assistant professor of information systems at the Quinlan School of Business at Loyola University Chicago.

Previously, he was a senior research associate at the Computation Institute at the University of Chicago, and he was an assistant professor in computer science at the University of Chicago, where he taught databases and computer systems to undergraduate and graduate students. While on leave, he co-founded *Mobissimo*, a venture-backed travel search engine that was chosen as one of the 50 coolest Web sites by *Time* magazine in 2004.

Dr. Nestorov received his undergraduate degrees in computer science and mathematics from Stanford University and his M.S. in computer science from Stanford University. He received his Ph.D. in computer science from Stanford University with a dissertation titled "Data Mining Techniques for Structured and Semistructured Data." His advisor was Professor Jeffrey Ullman.

Svetlozar led the design and development of the data warehouse project at the Nielsen Data Center at the Kilts Center for Marketing, which is part of the Chicago Booth School of Business. His research interests also include data mining, high-performance computing, and Web technologies.

Chapter 1

Introduction

INITIAL TERMINOLOGY

In the contemporary world, daily interaction with databases is a fact of life. It occurs in many everyday situations, such as when we make purchases, view content on the Internet, or engage in banking transactions. Databases are vital for the functioning of modern companies and organizations. This book will provide coverage of the most fundamental issues and topics related to the development and use of databases and database systems. We will start with an overview of the basic database-related terms.

The term **data** refers to facts that are recorded and can be accessed. In addition to text and numbers, data can also appear in other formats, such as figures, graphics, images, and audio/video recordings. Whatever the format is, the data is recorded and kept because it is considered to be of use to an intended user.

The term **information** refers to the data that is accessed by a user for some particular purpose. Typically, getting the needed information from a collection of data requires performing an activity, such as searching through, processing, or manipulating the data in some form or fashion.

To illustrate the terms "data" and "information," let us consider a phone book. A phone book is a collection of data—the phone numbers of people, restaurants, banks, and so on. Within the appropriate context, these phone numbers become information. For example, if a person in possession of a phone book becomes hungry and decides to make a phone call and have a pizza delivered to his or her house from the nearest pizza delivery place, e.g., Pizza Adria, the phone number of Pizza Adria becomes the information that this person needs. Searching for and finding the phone number of Pizza Adria in the collection of data in the phone book is the necessary action that will yield the information from the data.

In another example, let us assume that a manager in a large retail company, ZAGI, needs information about how good the sales of apparel in the current quarter are. Let us assume that every single sales transaction within this retail company is recorded in a computer file available to the manager. Even though such data captures the needed information about the apparel's sales performance, examination of each individual record in such an enormous file by the manager is not a feasible method for producing the needed information. Instead, the data has to be processed in a way that can give insight to the manager. For example, the data about apparel sales in the current quarter can be summarized. This summary can then be compared to the summarized sales of apparel in the previous quarter or to the summarized sales of apparel in the same quarter from last year. Such actions would yield the needed information from this collection of data.

The terms "data" and "information" are often interchanged and used as synonyms for each other. Such practice is very common and is not necessarily wrong. As we just explained, information is simply the data that we need. If the data that an organization gathers and stores has a purpose and satisfies a user's need,

0001	B	2	11:01
0001	F	3	11:01
0002	S	2	11:02
0002	B	1	11:02
0003	F	2	11:03
...	...	...	...

FIGURE 1.1 Data without metadata.

then such data is also information.[1] In this book, we will frequently use the terms "data" and "informa-tion" as interchangeable synonyms.

Metadata is the data that describes the structure and the properties of the data. Metadata is essential for the proper understanding and use of the data. Consider a data sample shown in Figure 1.1. It is difficult to make sense of the data shown in Figure 1.1 without the understanding of its metadata. The columns of numeric and textual data as presented in Figure 1.1 have no meaning.

The data from Figure 1.1 is shown again in Figure 1.2, now accompanied by its metadata. It is now clear what the meaning of the shown data is. The metadata explains that each row represents a sale of a product in Store 101 of the restaurant chain Burger Prince on September 1, 2013. The first column represents a transaction identifier; the second column refers to a product bought within a purchase transaction; the third column indicates how many items of the particular product were bought in a purchase transaction; and the fourth column shows the time of purchase.

A **database** is a structured collection of related data stored on a computer medium. The purpose of a database is to organize the data in a way that facilitates straightforward access to the information captured in the data. The structure of the database is represented in the database metadata. The **database metadata** is often defined as the data about the data or the database content that is not the data itself. The database metadata contains the following information:

- names of data structures (e.g., names of tables, names of columns)
- data types (e.g., column Product—data type Character; column ItemsSold—data type Integer)
- data descriptions (e.g., "column ItemsSold represents the quantity of sold items")
- other information describing the characteristics of the data that is being stored in a database

A **database management system (DBMS)** is software used for the following purposes:

- creation of databases
- insertion, storage, retrieval, update, and deletion of the data in the database
- maintenance of databases

For example, the relationship between a DBMS and a database is similar to the relationship between the presentation software (such as MS PowerPoint) and a presentation.

METADATA —

Burger Prince Store 101, Sales Data for Sept 1, 2013
(Product Codes: B – Burger, F – Fries, S – Soda)

PURCHASE TRANSACTIONS TABLE

TransactionId	Product	ItemsSold	Time
0001	B	2	11:01
0001	F	3	11:01
0002	S	2	11:02
0002	B	1	11:02
0003	F	2	11:03
...	...	...	...

FIGURE 1.2 Data with metadata.

---

[1]On the other hand, there are situations when the portion of the stored data that is of little or no use in the organization is so significant that it obscures the data that is actually useful. This is often referred to as a "Too much data, too little information" scenario.

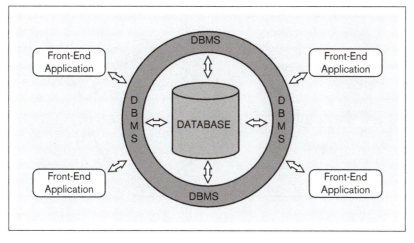

FIGURE 1.3 Typical database system architecture.

Presentation software is used to create a presentation, insert content in a presentation, conduct a presentation, and change or delete content in a presentation.

Similarly, a DBMS is used to create a database, to insert the data in the database, to retrieve the data from the database, and to change or delete the data in the database.

A **database system** is a computer-based system whose purpose is to enable an efficient interaction between the users and the information captured in a database. A typical architecture is shown in Figure 1.3.

The three main components of a database system[2] are the database, the DBMS, and the front-end applications. At the heart of a database system is the database. All interaction with the database occurs via the DBMS. **Front-end applications** are created in order to provide a mechanism for easy interaction between the users and the DBMS. Consider the following example of a user interacting with the DBMS by using a front-end application.

An ATM screen showing options to the user, such as "Withdrawal from checking account" or "Withdrawal from savings account," is an example of a front-end application. When a user makes a choice by selecting from the options on the screen, a communication between the front-end application and the DBMS is triggered, which subsequently causes a communication between the DBMS and the database. For instance, selecting from the ATM screen options, a user can request a withdrawal of $20 from the checking account. As a result, the front-end application issues several commands to the DBMS on the user's behalf. One command tells the DBMS to verify in the database if the user has enough money in the checking account to make the withdrawal. If there is enough money, the ATM releases the money to the user, while another command is issued to the DBMS to reduce the value representing the amount of money in the user's checking account in the database by $20.

Users using a database system to support their work- or life-related tasks and processes are often referred to as **end users (business users)**. The term "end user" distinguishes the actual users of the data in the database system from the technical personnel engaging in test-use during the implementation and maintenance of database systems.

The type of interaction between the end user and the database that involves front-end applications is called **indirect interaction**. Another type of interaction between the end users and the database, called **direct interaction**, involves the end user directly communicating with the DBMS. Figure 1.4 illustrates direct and indirect interaction.

---

[2]Another commonly used term for the system whose architecture is shown in Figure 1.3 is "information system." The terms "information system" and "database system" often have the same meaning, but they are used in different contexts. Since databases are the focus of this book, we will use the synonym "database system."

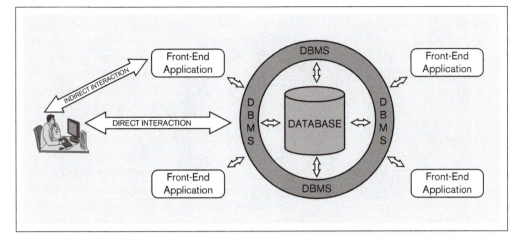

FIGURE 1.4   Direct and indirect interaction between the end user and the database.

Whereas indirect interaction typically requires very little or no database skill from the end user, the level of expertise and knowledge needed for direct interaction requires database-related training of the end users. The direct interaction requires that the end user knows how to issue commands to the specific DBMS. This typically requires that the end user knows the language of the DBMS.

The database and DBMS are mandatory components of a database system. In an environment where every person who needs access to the data in the database is capable of direct interaction and has the time for it, the front-end component is not necessary and the database system can function without it. However, in the vast majority of cases in everyday life and business, database systems have a front-end component, and most of the interactions between the end users and the database occur via front-end applications as indirect interactions.

STEPS IN THE DEVELOPMENT OF DATABASE SYSTEMS

Once the decision to undertake the database project is made and the project is initiated, the predevelopment activities, such as planning and budgeting, are undertaken. Those activities are followed by the actual process of the development of the database system. The principal activities in the process of the development of the database system are illustrated in Figure 1.5.

Next, we give a brief discussion and description of each of the steps shown in Figure 1.5.

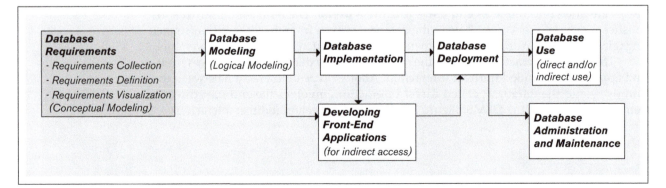

FIGURE 1.5   Steps in the development of database systems.

Database Requirements Collection, Definition, and Visualization

The first and most critical step in the development of the database is **requirements collection, definition, and visualization**. If this step is successful, the remaining steps have a great chance of success. However, if this step is done incorrectly, all of the remaining steps, and consequently the entire project, will be futile. In Figures 1.5 and 1.6 we highlight this step with a gray background in order to underscore its critical nature.

This step results in the end user requirements specifying which data the future database system will hold and in what fashion, and what the capabilities and functionalities of the database system will be. The requirements are used to model and implement the database and to create the front-end applications for the database.

The collected requirements should be clearly defined and stated in a written document, and then visualized as a **conceptual database model** by using a conceptual data modeling technique, such as entity-relationship (ER) modeling.[3] "Conceptual data modeling" is another term for requirements visualization.

The guidelines and methods for database requirements phase call for an iterative process. A smaller beginning set of requirements can be collected, defined, and visualized, and then discussed by the database developers and intended end users. These discussions can then lead into another iteration of collecting, defining, and visualizing requirements that gradually increases the first set of requirements.

Even when a set of requirements is agreed upon within the database requirements collection, definition, and visualization step, it can still be subject to change initiated by the other steps in the database development process, as illustrated by Figure 1.6.

Instead of mandating the collection, definition, and visualization of all database requirements in one isolated process, followed by all other steps in the development of the database systems, the common recommendation is to allow refining and adding to the requirements after each step of the database development process. This is illustrated by the white dashed lines in Figure 1.6.

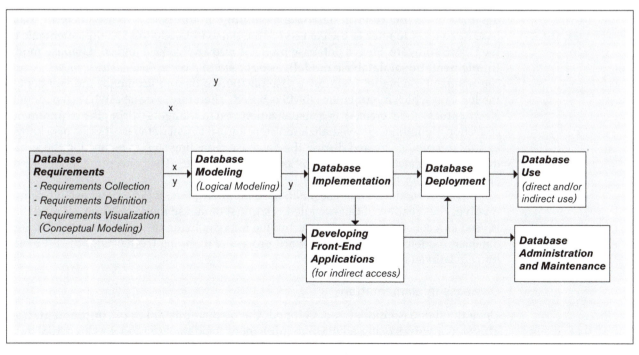

FIGURE 1.6 Iterative nature of the database requirements collection, definition, and visualization process.

[3]Entity-relationship (ER) modeling is covered in the next chapter.

For example, a common practice in database projects is to collect, define, and visualize an initial partial set of requirements and, based on these requirements, create and implement a preliminary partial database model. This is followed by a series of similar iterations (marked by letter x in Figure 1.6), where the additional requirements are added (collected, defined, and visualized) and then used to expand the database model.

The requirements can also be altered iteratively when other steps, such as the creation of front-end applications or actual database use, reveal the need for modifying, augmenting, or reducing the initial set of requirements.

Every time the set of requirements is changed, the conceptual model has to be changed accordingly, and the changes in the requirements must propagate as applicable through all of the subsequent steps: modeling, creating the database, creating front-end applications, deployment, use, and administration/maintenance.

No implicit changes of requirements are permitted in any of the database development steps. For example, during the database implementation process (middle rectangle in Figure 1.6) a developer is *not* allowed to create in an ad hoc way a new database construct (e.g., a database table or a column of a database table) that is not called for by the requirements. Instead, if during the database implementation process it is discovered that a new construct is actually needed and useful, the proper course of action (marked by letter y in Figure 1.6) is to go back to the requirements and augment both the requirements document and the conceptual model to include the requirement for the new construct. This new requirement should then be reflected in the subsequently augmented database model. Only then should a new database construct actually be implemented.

Forming database requirements is widely recognized as the most critical step in the database system development process. The outcome of this step determines the success of the entire database project. If this step is not done correctly, the requirements will be off-target and, consequently, the resulting database will not properly satisfy the needs of its end users.

Database Modeling

The first step following requirements collection, definition, and visualization is **database modeling (logical database modeling)**. In this book, we use the term "database modeling" to refer to the creation of the database model that is implementable by the DBMS software. Such a database model is also known as a **logical database model (implementational database model)**, as opposed to a *conceptual database model*. A conceptual database model is simply a visualization of the requirements, independent of the logic on which a particular DBMS is based. Therefore, a database has two models: a conceptual model created as a visualization of requirements during the requirements collection, definition, and visualization step; and an actual database model, also known as a logical model, created during the database modeling step to be used in the subsequent step of database implementation using the DBMS. The conceptual model serves as a blueprint for the actual (logical) database model.

In most modern databases, database modeling (i.e., logical database modeling) involves the creation of the so-called relational database model.[4] When ER modeling is used as a conceptual modeling technique for visualizing the requirements, relational database modeling is a straightforward process of mapping (converting) the ER model into a relational model.

Database Implementation

Once the database model is developed, the next step is **database implementation**. This step involves using a DBMS to implement the database model as an actual database that is initially empty. Database implementation is a straightforward process that involves database developers using the DBMS functionalities and capabilities to implement the database model as an actual functioning database, much in the same way a

---

[4]The relational database model is covered in Chapters 3 and 4.

construction crew uses construction equipment to implement a blueprint for a building as an actual building. As we mentioned, most modern databases are modeled as relational databases, and for that reason they are implemented using relational DBMS (RDBMS) software. SQL (Structured Query Language)[5] is a language used by most relational DBMS software packages. Among its features, SQL includes commands for creating, modifying, and deleting database structures. These commands are used during database implementation.

Developing Front–End Applications

The process of **developing front-end applications** refers to designing and creating applications for indirect use by the end users. Such applications are included in most database systems. The front-end applications are based on the database model and the requirements specifying the front-end functionalities of the system needed by the end users. Front-end applications usually contain interfaces, such as forms and reports, accessible via navigation mechanisms, such as menus. Figure 1.5 illustrates that the design and creation of front-end applications can commence and proceed in parallel with database implementation. For example, the look and feel of the front-end applications, as well as the number of particular components (e.g., forms and reports) and their individual functionalities, can be determined before (or while) the database is implemented. Of course, the actual creation of a front-end application also involves connecting it to the database. Connecting a front-end application to the database can only be done once the database is implemented.

Database Deployment

Once the database and its associated front-end applications are implemented, the next step is **database deployment**. This step involves releasing the database system, i.e., the database and its front-end applications, for use by the end users. Typically, this step also involves populating the implemented database with the initial set of data.

Database Use

Once the database system is deployed, end users engage in **database use**. Database use involves the **insertion, modification, deletion, and retrieval** of the data contained within the database system. The database system can be used indirectly, via the front-end applications, or directly via the DBMS. As we mentioned, SQL is the language used by most modern relational DBMS packages. SQL includes commands for insertion, modification, deletion, and retrieval of the data. These commands can be issued by front-end applications (indirect use), or directly by the end users themselves (direct use).

Database Administration and Maintenance

The **database administration and maintenance** activities support the end users. Database administration and maintenance activities include dealing with technical issues, such as providing security for the information contained in the database, ensuring sufficient hard-drive space for the database content, and implementing backup and recovery procedures.

THE NEXT VERSION OF THE DATABASE

In most cases, after a certain period of use, the need for modifications and expansion of the existing database system becomes apparent, and the development of a new version of the existing database system is initiated. The new version of the database should be created following the same development steps as the initial version. This is illustrated in Figure 1.7.

---

[5]SQL is also sometimes referred to as "Sequel." SQL is covered in Chapter 5.

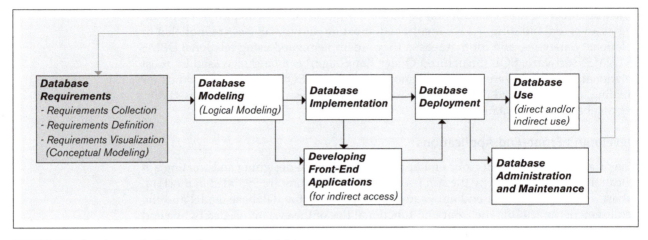

FIGURE 1.7   Development of the next version of the database.

As with the initial version of the database system, the development of subsequent versions of the database system will start with the requirements collection, definition, and visualization step. Unlike with the initial version, in the subsequent versions not all requirements will be collected from scratch. Original requirements provide the starting point for additions and alterations. Many of the additions and modifications result from observations and feedback by the end users during the use of the previous version, indicating the ways in which the database system can be improved or expanded. Other new requirements may stem from changes in the business processes that the database system supports, or changes in underlying technology. Whatever the reasons are, change is inherent for database systems. New versions should be expected periodically and handled accordingly.

DATABASE SCOPE

Databases vary in their scope, from small single-user (personal) databases to large enterprise databases that can be used by thousands of end users. Regardless of their scope, all databases go through the same fundamental development steps, such as requirements collection, modeling, implementation, deployment, and use. The difference in the scope of databases is reflected in the size, complexity, and cost in time and resources required for each of the steps.

PEOPLE INVOLVED WITH DATABASE SYSTEMS

The creation and use of database systems involve people in different types of roles. The roles and titles given to the people involved in the creation, maintenance, and use of databases can vary from project to project and from company to company. There are a number of ways in which these roles could be classified. Here, we divide the roles of people involved with the database projects and systems into the following four general categories:

- database analysts, designers, and developers
- front-end applications analysts and developers
- database administrators
- database end users

These categories reflect in which part of the database lifecycle the different people are involved and in what capacity.

Database Analysts, Designers, and Developers

Database analysts are involved in the requirements collection, definition, and visualization stage. **Database designers (database modelers or architects)** are involved in the database modeling stage. **Database developers** are in charge of implementing the database model as a functioning database using the DBMS software. It is not uncommon for the same people to perform more than one of these roles.[6] These roles are related to converting business requirements into the structure of a database that is at the center of the database system. An ideal characteristic of the people in these roles is technical and business versatility or, more specifically, the knowledge of database modeling methodologies and of business and organizational processes and principles.

Front–End Applications Analysts and Developers

Front-end applications analysts are in charge of collecting and defining requirements for front-end applications, while **front-end applications developers** are in charge of creating the front-end applications. The role of front-end applications analysts involves finding out which front-end applications would be the most useful and appropriate for indirect use by the intended end users. This role also involves determining the features, look, and feel of each front-end application. The role of the front-end applications developer is to create the front-end applications, based on the requirements defined by the front-end applications analysts. The role of the front-end applications developer often requires knowledge of programming.

Database Administrators

Once the database and the associated front-end applications are designed, implemented, and deployed as a functioning database system, the database system has to be administered. Database administration encompasses the tasks related to the maintenance and supervision of a database system. The role of **database administrator (DBA)** involves managing technical issues related to security (e.g., creating and issuing user names and passwords, granting privileges to access data, etc.), backup and recovery of database systems, monitoring use and adding storage space as needed, and other tasks related to the proper technical functioning of the database system. A database administrator should have the technical skills needed for these tasks as well as detailed knowledge of the design of the database at the center of the database system.

Database End Users

Arguably, database end users are the most important category of people involved with database systems. They are the reason for the existence of database systems. The quality of a database system is measured by how quickly and easily it can provide the accurate and complete information needed by its end users. End users vary in their level of technical sophistication, in the amount of data that they need, in the frequency with which they access the database system, and in other measurements. As we mentioned before, most end users access the database in an indirect fashion, via the front-end applications. Certain end users that are familiar with the workings of the DBMS and are authorized to access the DBMS can engage in the direct use of the database system.

The four categories we highlighted here represent the roles of people who are directly involved with the database system within an organization or company. In addition to these four categories, other people, such as the developers of the DBMS software or the system administrators in charge of the computer system on which the database system resides, are also necessary for the functioning of database systems.

OPERATIONAL VERSUS ANALYTICAL DATABASES

Information that is collected in database systems can be used, in general, for two purposes: an operational purpose and an analytical purpose.

---

[6]In fact (especially in smaller companies and organizations), the same people may be in charge of all aspects of the database system, including the design, implementation, administration, and maintenance.

The term **operational information (transactional information)** refers to the information collected and used in support of the day-to-day operational needs in businesses and other organizations. Any information resulting from an individual transaction, such as performing an ATM withdrawal or purchasing an airline ticket, is operational information. That is why operational information is also sometimes referred to as "transactional information."

Operational databases collect and present operational information in support of daily operational procedures and processes, such as deducting the correct amount of money from the customer's checking account upon an ATM withdrawal or issuing a correct bill to a customer who purchased an airline ticket.

The term **analytical information** refers to the information collected and used in support of analytical tasks. An example of analytical information is information showing a pattern of use of ATM machines, such as what hours of the day have the most withdrawals, and what hours of the day have the least withdrawals. The discovered patterns can be used to set the stocking schedule for the ATM machines. Another example of analytical information is information revealing sales trends in the airline industry, such as which routes in the United States have the most sales and which routes in the United States have the least sales. This information can be used in planning route schedules.

Note that analytical information is based on operational (transactional) information. For example, to create the analytical information showing a pattern of use of ATM machines at different times of the day, we have to combine numerous instances of transactional information resulting from individual ATM withdrawals. Similarly, to create the analytical information showing sales trends over various routes, we have to combine numerous instances of transactional information resulting from individual airline ticket purchases.

A typical organization maintains and utilizes a number of operational databases. At the same time, an increasing number of companies also create and use separate **analytical databases**. To reflect this reality, this book provides coverage of issues related to both operational and analytical databases. Issues related to the development and use of operational databases are covered in Chapters 2–6, while the topics related to the development and use of analytical databases are covered in Chapters 7–9.

RELATIONAL DBMS

The relational database model is the basis for the contemporary DBMS software packages that are used to implement the majority of today's operational and analytical corporate databases. Examples of relational DBMS software include Oracle, MySQL, Microsoft SQL Server, PostgreSQL, IBM DB2, and Teradata. Among these DBMS tools, Teradata was developed specifically to accommodate large analytical databases, whereas the others are used for hosting both operational and analytical databases. In Chapter 10, we will provide an overview of some of the basic functionalities of contemporary relational DBMS packages and illustrate how those functionalities are used for administration and maintenance of both operational and analytical databases.

BOOK TOPICS OVERVIEW

This book is devoted to the most fundamental issues and topics related to the design, development, and use of operational and analytical databases. These topics and issues are organized as follows.

Chapter 1 introduced basic terminology, listed and briefly described the steps in the development of database systems, provided an overview of database scope and the roles of people involved with database systems, and defined operational and analytical databases.

Chapter 2 covers the topics of collection and visualization of requirements for operational databases by giving a detailed overview of ER modeling, a conceptual data modeling technique.

Chapter 3 covers the topics of modeling operational databases by giving a detailed overview of the basics of relational modeling, a logical data modeling technique.

Chapter 4 continues the coverage of modeling operational databases, discussing additional topics related to the relational database model.

Chapter 5 provides detailed coverage of SQL and its functionalities for creating and using relational databases.

Chapter 6 gives an overview of basic topics related to the implementation and use of operational database systems.

Chapter 7 introduces basic terminology and concepts related to analytical databases, which are also known as data warehouses and data marts.

Chapter 8 covers the topics of modeling analytical databases by giving an overview of data warehouse/data mart modeling techniques.

Chapter 9 gives an overview of basic topics related to the implementation and use of data warehouses/data marts.

Chapter 10 provides a concise overview of DBMS functionalities and the database administration topics that are universal for both operational and analytical databases.

The **appendices** provide brief overviews of selected additional database and database-related issues.

Key Terms

Analytical databases *10*
Analytical information *10*
Conceptual database model *5*
Data *1*
Database *2*
Database administration and maintenance *7*
Database administrator (DBA) *9*
Database analysts *8*
Database deployment *7*
Database designers (database modelers or architects) *8*

Database developers *9*
Database implementation *6*
Database management system (DBMS) *2*
Database metadata *2*
Database modeling (logical database modeling) *6*
Database system *3*
Database use *7*
Developing front-end applications *7*
Direct interaction *3*
End users (business users) *3*

Front-end applications *3*
Front-end applications analysts *9*
Front-end applications developers *9*
Indirect interaction *3*
Information *1*
Insertion, modification, deletion, and retrieval *7*
Logical database model (implementational database model) *6*
Metadata *2*
Operational databases *10*

Operational information (transactional information) *10*
Requirements collection, definition, and visualization *5*

Review Questions

Q1.1   Give several examples of instances of data.

Q1.2   Give several examples of converting data to information.

Q1.3   Create your own example that shows a collection of data, first without the metadata and then with the metadata.

Q1.4   Describe the relationship between the database and DBMS.

Q1.5   What are the main components of a database system?

Q1.6   Give an example of an indirect use of a database system.

Q1.7   What are the steps in the development of a database system?

Q1.8   Explain the iterative nature of the database requirements collection, definition, and visualization process.

Q1.9   What is the purpose of conceptual database modeling?

Q1.10   What is the purpose of logical database modeling?

Q1.11   Briefly describe the process of database implementation.

Q1.12   Briefly describe the process of developing the front-end applications.

Q1.13   What takes place during database deployment?

Q1.14   What four data operations constitute database use?

Q1.15   Give examples of database administration and maintenance activities.

Q1.16   What are the similarities and differences between the development of the initial and subsequent versions of the database?

Q1.17   How does the scope of the database influence the development of the database system?

Q1.18   What are the main four categories of people involved with database projects?

Q1.19   What is the role of database analysts?

Q1.20   What is the role of database designers?

Q1.21   What is the role of database developers?

Q1.22   What is the role of front-end application analysts?

Q1.23   What is the role of front-end application developers?

Q1.24   How is the term "quality of a database system" related to the end users?

Q1.25   Give an example of operational (transactional) information.

Q1.26   Give an example of analytical information.

Q1.27   List several relational DBMS software packages.

Chapter 2

Database Requirements and ER Modeling

INTRODUCTION

The first and most critical step in the process of developing a database is determining the **database requirements** and creating the conceptual database model that represents and visualizes those requirements.

Database requirements are statements that define the details and constraints of the data and metadata for the database that is being developed. Requirements can be derived from interviews with business members, business documentation, business policies, or a combination of these and other sources.

Properly collected requirements should clearly state what the future database will keep track of and in what fashion. **Entity-relationship (ER) modeling**, a widely used conceptual database modeling method, is a technique that enables the structuring and organizing of the requirements collection process and provides a way to graphically represent the requirements.

In this chapter, we will explain how to properly collect database requirements and visually represent them using the ER modeling technique.

BASIC ER MODELING CONSTRUCTS

The result of ER modeling is an **ER diagram (ERD),** which serves as a blueprint for the database. Two basic ER diagram constructs are the **entity** and the **relationship**. There is no universally adopted ER notation to which all database projects conform. Instead, there is a variety of available ER notations currently in use. Depending on which ER notation is used, entities and relationships can be represented differently, but they always have the same meaning. In this book, we will use a modified version of the standard Chen ER notation, and all of the constructs will be described in the context of the chosen notation. We have chosen this notation for the following reasons:

- Pedagogical value: easy for novices to learn and use
- Completeness: all the basic ER concepts are represented
- Clarity and visibility: all the concepts are graphically represented and every concept is easily distinguished
- Compatibility with software: this book provides access to the database modeling software tool ERDPlus (available at erdplus.com), which uses the same ER notation

Upon learning one ER notation, adapting to alternative ER notations is quick and straightforward. At the end of this chapter, we will describe several other ER notations. We will also illustrate how easy and intuitive it is for a developer who is familiar with one ER notation to comprehend and use other ER notations.

FIGURE 2.1   Two entities.

ENTITIES

Entities are constructs that represent what the database keeps track of. They are the basic building blocks of an ER diagram. Entities[1] represent various real-world notions, such as people, places, objects, events, items, and other concepts. For example, an ER diagram for a retail company may contain entities such as CUSTOMER, STORE, PRODUCT, and SALES TRANSACTION.

In an ER diagram, entities are represented as rectangles, with the name of the entity inside the rectangle. Within one ER diagram, each entity must have a different name. Figure 2.1 shows examples of two entities, CUSTOMER and STORE.

Each depicted entity contains a number of **entity instances (entity members)**. For example, entity CUSTOMER may contain entity instances such as customer Joe, customer Sue, and customer Pat. Entities themselves are depicted in the ER diagrams, while entity instances are not. However, entity instances will eventually be recorded in the database that will be created based on the ER diagram.

ATTRIBUTES (UNIQUE AND NON–UNIQUE)

Each entity in an ER diagram has attributes. An **attribute (of an entity)** describes a characteristic of an entity. While entities are constructs that represent what the database keeps track of, attributes represent the details that will be recorded for each entity instance. For example, for entity CUSTOMER, we may decide to keep track of the following attributes: CustID (customer's identification number), CustName (customer's name), CustBdate (customer's birth date), and CustGender (customer's gender). Figure 2.2 illustrates how attributes are depicted in the ER diagram. Each attribute is represented by an oval containing the attribute name. Within one entity, each attribute name must be different. Every attribute oval is connected by a line to its entity. A **unique attribute** is an attribute whose value is different for each entity instance. Every regular entity must have at least one unique attribute. In an ER diagram, the name of a unique attribute is underlined, as shown in Figure 2.2. The requirements for the database illustrated in Figure 2.2 specify that each customer in the database will have a unique customer identification number (CustID), while we could have more than one customer with the same birth date, name, and/or gender.

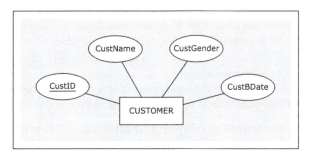

FIGURE 2.2   An entity with attributes.

---

[1]Entities are also sometimes referred to as "entity types." In this book, we will simply use the term "entity."

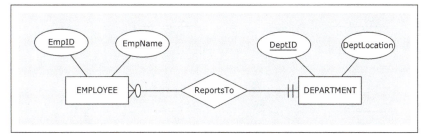

FIGURE 2.3   A relationship between two entities.

RELATIONSHIPS

Within an ER diagram, each entity must be related to at least one other entity via a construct called a relationship. Relationships[2] are shown in an ER diagram as a diamond, with a word or phrase naming the relationship inside the diamond. The diamond is connected with lines to the entities that take part in the relationship.

Cardinality Constraints

The lines connecting the relationship to the entities include symbols depicting how many instances of one entity can be associated with instances of another entity. These symbols are known as **cardinality constraints**. Consider the ER diagram shown in Figure 2.3. The diamond with the phrase "ReportsTo" depicts the relationship between EMPLOYEE and DEPARTMENT. Cardinality constraints are marked on an ER diagram as symbols placed next to an entity rectangle on the line connecting the entity rectangle to the relationship diamond.

Each cardinality constraint symbol is composed of two parts:

- **Maximum cardinality**—the part of the cardinality constraint symbol closer to the entity rectangle
- **Minimum cardinality (participation)**—the part of the cardinality constraint symbol farther away from the entity rectangle

Maximum cardinality can either be *one* (represented by a straight bar: |) or *many* (represented by a crow's foot symbol: ⊁).

Participation can be either *optional* (represented by a circular symbol: 0) or *mandatory* (represented by a straight bar: |).

Figure 2.4 shows all four possible cardinality constraints for Entity A in a Relationship B.

We will use the example ER diagram containing the relationship ReportsTo (shown in Figure 2.3) to clarify the concept of cardinality constraints. These are the requirements that are used as the basis for the ER diagram shown in Figure 2.3:

- *The database will keep track of employees and departments.*
- *For each employee, we will keep track of his or her name and unique employee ID.*
- *For each department, we will keep track of the unique department ID and the location.*
- *Each employee reports to exactly one department. A department may have many employees reporting to it, but it does not have to have any.*

First, consider the cardinality constraint symbol "||" on the right side of the ReportsTo diamond in Figure 2.3. The *mandatory participation* symbol (left straight bar, in this case) indicates that an employee must report to at least one department. In other words, the minimum cardinality of entity EMPLOYEE in ReportsTo relationship is *1*. The maximum cardinality symbol *one* (right straight bar, in this case) indicates that each employee can report to one department at most. In other words, the maximum cardinality of entity EMPLOYEE in ReportsTo relationship is *1*. Therefore, those two symbols together indicate that each employee reports to exactly one department.

---

[2]Relationships are also sometimes referred to as "relationship types." In this book, we will simply use the term "relationship."

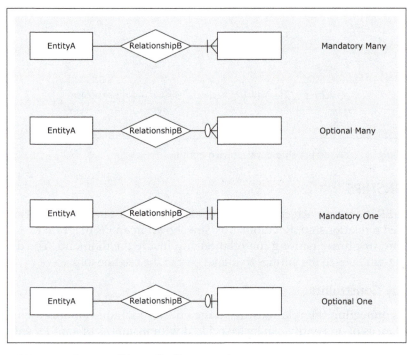

FIGURE 2.4   Four possible cardinality constraints.

Next, consider the cardinality constraint symbol "⇸" on the left side of the ReportsTo diamond. The *optional participation* symbol (circular symbol) indicates that a department does not have to have any employees reporting to it. In other words, the minimum cardinality of entity DEPARTMENT in the ReportsTo relationship is *0*. The maximum cardinality symbol *many* (⇸) indicates that a department may have many employees reporting to it. In other words, the maximum cardinality of entity DEPARTMENT in the ReportsTo relationship is *many*. Therefore, those two symbols together indicate that a particular department may have many employees reporting to it, but it does not have to have any. In other words, a department has a minimum of *0* employees and a maximum of *many* employees.

Note that the proper way of interpreting a relationship in any ER diagram is to consider it *twice* (once in each direction) by applying the following rule: *rectangle – diamond – cardinality constraint – rectangle*. For example, observe how we interpret the "ReportsTo" relationship:

- One direction: rectangle (an employee) – diamond (reports to) – cardinality constraint (exactly one) – rectangle (department)
- Opposite direction: rectangle (a department) – diamond (has reporting to it) – cardinality constraint (between zero and many) – rectangle (employees)

To recap the concept of relationship and cardinality constraint, observe a few of the various possible versions of the relationship ReportsTo shown in Figure 2.5 (entity attributes are omitted for brevity).

The following are requirements for each of the versions shown.

Version A:

- *Each employee reports to exactly one department. A department may have many employees reporting to it, but it does not have to have any.*

Version B:

- *An employee can report to one department or to no departments at all. A department may have many employees reporting to it, but it does not have to have any.*

Version C:

- *Each employee reports to exactly one department. A department must have at least one employee reporting to it, but it may have many employees reporting to it.*

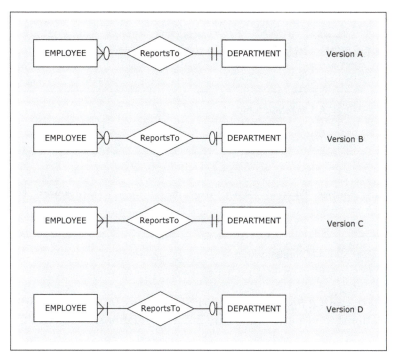

FIGURE 2.5 Several possible versions of the relationship ReportsTo.

Version D:

- *An employee can report to one department or to no departments at all. A department must have at least one employee reporting to it, but it may have many employees reporting to it.*

TYPES OF RELATIONSHIPS (MAXIMUM CARDINALITY–WISE)

The maximum cardinality on either side of the relationship can be either *one* or *many*. Therefore, when considering maximum cardinality without participation, we can classify each relationship between two entities into one of the following three types:

- **one-to-one relationship (1:1)**
- **one-to-many relationship (1:M)**
- **many-to-many relationship (M:N)**

Figure 2.6 illustrates these three types of relationships, maximum cardinality-wise (participation is omitted for clarity, since it does not affect the maximum cardinality).

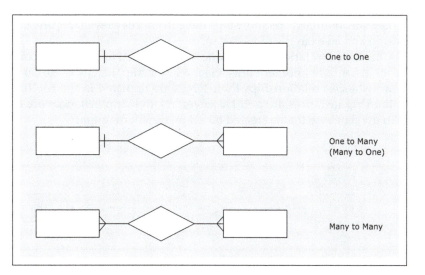

FIGURE 2.6 Three types of relationships (maximum cardinality-wise).

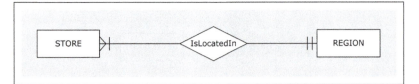

FIGURE 2.7   A 1:M relationship.

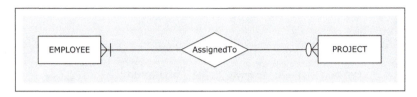

FIGURE 2.8   A M:N relationship.

Figures 2.3 and 2.5 show examples of a 1:M relationship. Another example of a 1:M relationship is shown in Figure 2.7. This relationship reflects the following requirements:

- *Each store is located in exactly one region. Each region must have at least one store located in it, but it may have many stores located in it.*

Figure 2.8 shows an example of an M:N relationship. This relationship reflects the following requirements:

- *An employee may be assigned to a number of projects, but he or she can also be assigned to none of the projects. A project must have at least one employee assigned to it, but it may have many employees assigned to it.*

Figure 2.9 shows an example of a 1:1 relationship. This relationship reflects the following requirements:

- *Each employee is allotted either one vehicle or no vehicles. Each vehicle is allotted to exactly one employee.*

RELATIONSHIPS AND RELATIONSHIP INSTANCES

Recall that each entity has its instances. For example, entity EMPLOYEE can have entity instances employee Bob, employee Lisa, employee Maria, and so forth. Entities themselves are depicted in the ER diagrams, while the entity instances are not. However, entity instances are eventually recorded in the database that will be created based on the ER diagram. Similarly, relationships have instances as well. Figure 2.10 illustrates a relationship and an example of its instances.

As illustrated, **relationship instances** occur when an instance of one entity is related to an instance of another entity via a relationship. Just as is the case with entities and their instances, relationships themselves are depicted in the ER diagrams, while the relationship instances are not. However, relationship instances are eventually recorded in the database that is created based on the ER diagram.

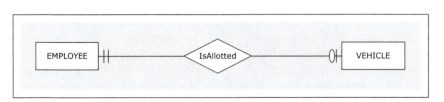

FIGURE 2.9   A 1:1 relationship.

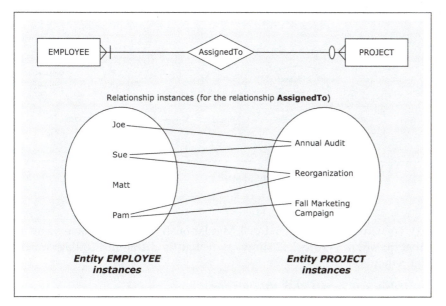

FIGURE 2.10   A relationship and its instances.

Note in Figure 2.10 that entity EMPLOYEE has optional participation in the relationship AssignedTo. That is why, in the bottom part of this figure, it is possible to have some of the actual employees (e.g., Matt) without lines connecting them to actual projects. However, because entity PROJECT has mandatory participation in the relationship AssignedTo, every instance of entity PROJECT is connected to at least one instance of entity EMPLOYEE.

Also note that AssignedTo is an M:N relationship. That is why there are instances of both EMPLOYEE and PROJECT entities with multiple lines connecting them to the instances of the other entity.

RELATIONSHIP ATTRIBUTES

In some cases, many-to-many relationships can actually have attributes of their own, which are referred to as **relationship attributes**. Figure 2.11 illustrates such a case. The requirements for this ER diagram are as follows:

- *The database will keep track of students and campus organizations.*
- *For each student, we will keep track of his or her unique student ID, and his or her name and gender.*
- *For each organization, we will keep track of its unique organization ID and the location.*
- *Each student in the database belongs to at least one organization and can belong to multiple organizations.*
- *Each organization in the database has at least one student belonging to it and can have multiple students.*
- *For every instance of a student belonging to an organization, we will record the student's function in the organization (e.g., president, vice president, treasurer, member, etc.).*

Note that the last requirement (*For every instance of a student belonging to an organization, we will record the student's function in the organization*) implies that a student can have several functions, one for each organization he or she belongs to. If we include function as an attribute (or several attributes) of the entity STUDENT, we would not know in which organization the student has what function. Similarly, an organization can have multiple functions, one for each student who belongs to it. If we include function as an attribute (or several attributes) of the entity ORGANIZATION, we would not know which students hold which functions in the organization. Therefore, the only appropriate place to include the Function attribute is in the relationship BelongsTo, as shown in Figure 2.11.

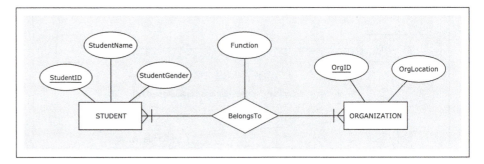

FIGURE 2.11 A M:N relationship with an attribute.

Next, we consider whether 1:1 or 1:M relationships can also have an attribute. To answer that question, Figure 2.12 shows two slightly different ER diagrams based on these requirements:

- *The database will keep track of students and colleges.*
- *For each student, we will keep track of his or her name and unique student ID.*
- *For each college, we will keep track of its unique name and its location.*
- *Each student in the database attends exactly one college.*
- *Each college in the database has multiple students.*
- *For each student, we keep track of the date he or she started attending his or her college.*

The top diagram in Figure 2.12 shows a 1:M relationship with an attribute. The bottom diagram is based on the exact same requirements, but with the student's college start date as an attribute StudentCollSdate of the entity STUDENT, rather than the attribute DateStarted of the relationship Attends. Since a student attends only one college, his or her start date at that college can be an attribute of the entity STUDENT itself. As illustrated by this example, an attribute of a 1:M relationship can be assigned to an entity whose maximum cardinality in the relationship is 1 (in this case the entity STUDENT). More generally, a relationship attribute can be assigned to an entity whose maximum cardinality in the relationship is 1. Therefore, an attribute of a 1:M relationship or a 1:1 relationship is not necessary. On the other hand, as we illustrated by the example shown in Figure 2.11, attributes are necessary for some M:N relationships.

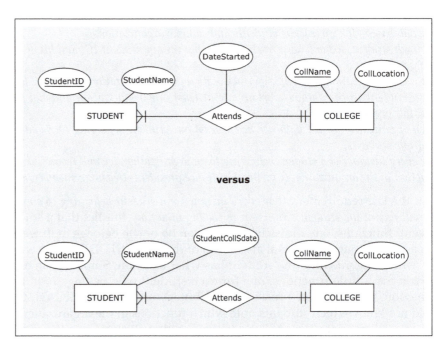

FIGURE 2.12 A 1:M relationship with and without an attribute.

EXAMPLE: SET OF DATABASE REQUIREMENTS AND ER DIAGRAM

The following retail-related example illustrates a collection of database requirements and the subsequent ER diagram.

The sales department of the ZAGI Retail Company has decided to create a database that contains the details of its sales process. After conducting interviews within the company and studying the company documentation, the database team extracted the following requirements for the future database:

ZAGI Retail Company Sales Department Database will capture data about the following:

- For each **product** being sold: a product ID (unique), product name, and price
- For each **category** of product: category ID (unique) and category name
- For each **vendor**: vendor ID (unique) and vendor name
- For each **customer**: customer ID (unique), name, and zip code
- For each **store**: store ID (unique) and zip code
- For each **region**: region ID (unique) and region name
- For each **sales transaction**: transaction ID (unique) and date of transaction
- Each product is supplied by exactly one vendor.
  Each vendor supplies one or more products.
- Each product belongs to exactly one category.
  Each category contains one or more products.
- Each store is located in exactly one region.
  Each region contains one or more stores.
- Each sales transaction occurs in one store.
  Each store has one or more transactions occurring at it.
- Each sales transaction involves exactly one customer.
  Each customer can be involved in one or more sales transactions.
- Each product is sold via one or more sales transactions.
  Each sales transaction includes one or more products.
- For each instance of a product being sold via a sales transaction, the quantity of sold products is recorded.

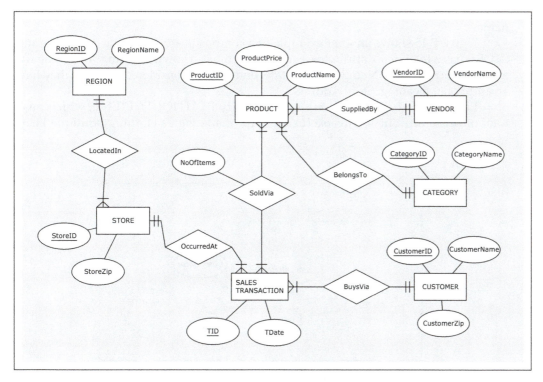

FIGURE 2.13   An ER diagram example: ZAGI Retail Company Sales Department Database.

The ER diagram based on these requirements is shown in Figure 2.13. Note that the knowledge of ER notation helps database requirements collectors gather structured and useful requirements for the future database. In other words, knowing that an ER diagram has to be developed upon the completion of the database requirements process helps database requirements collectors focus on asking the right questions. Examples of such questions (posed during the requirements collection process for the diagram shown in Figure 2.13) are listed here:

- *What in particular would you like to record for each customer?* (customer ID, name and zip code)
- *Is customer ID value unique for each customer?* (Yes)
- *Is customer name value unique for each customer?* (No)
- *Does each product belong to one or multiple categories?* (One)
- *Does each product come from only one vendor?* (Yes)
- *Would you ever record a vendor who does not supply any products?* (No)
- *Do you keep track of customers that did not buy anything yet (i.e., customers that were not involved in any sales transactions yet)?* (No)

COMPOSITE ATTRIBUTES

In addition to the regular attributes shown thus far, ER diagrams can depict several other types of attributes. One additional attribute type is a **composite attribute**, an attribute that is composed of several attributes. Figure 2.14 shows a composite attribute.

In Figure 2.14, attribute CustFullName (customer's full name) is composed of two components: attribute CustFName (customer's first name) and attribute CustLName (customer's last name). The purpose of a composite attribute is to indicate a situation in which a collection of attributes has an additional meaning, besides the individual meanings of each attribute. In Figure 2.14, the depicted entity CUSTOMER has *five* attributes: CustID (depicting customer's unique identification number), CustGender (depicting customer's gender), CustBdate (depicting customer's birth date), CustFName (depicting customer's first name), and CustLName (depicting customer's last name). CustFullName is not an additional attribute of the entity CUSTOMER. Instead, CustFullName simply states that when CustFName and CustLName are combined together, that combination results in the customer's full name.

Figure 2.15 shows another example of a composite attribute. The depicted entity STORE has a total of six attributes, each of which has its own meaning. When the five attributes Street, StreetNumber, City, State, and Zip are considered together they have an additional meaning: Store Address.

Figure 2.16 shows an example of an entity BOUTIQUECLIENT, which has a total of seven attributes. This exclusive tailor-made men's clothing boutique keeps

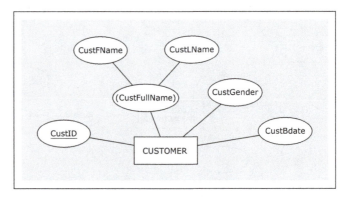

FIGURE 2.14   An entity with a composite attribute.

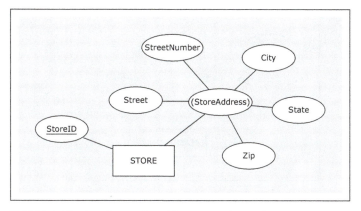

FIGURE 2.15   Another entity with a composite attribute.

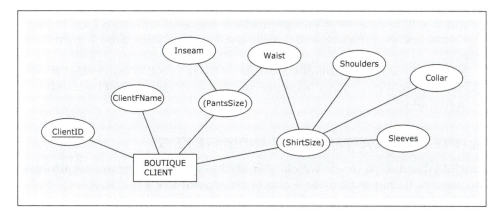

FIGURE 2.16   Composite attributes sharing components.

track of the client's unique identifier and client's first name. Also, the boutique keeps track of the client's five clothing measurements: inseam (length of the leg), waist, sleeves (length of the arm), shoulders (shoulder width), and collar (neck size). This example illustrates how the same simple attribute can be used as a component of more than one composite attribute. In this case, waist is used by two different composite attributes. The combination of inseam and waist is used for the pants size, while the combination of waist, shoulders, collar, and sleeves is used for the shirt size.

COMPOSITE UNIQUE ATTRIBUTE

Figure 2.17 illustrates the case of an entity that has a **composite unique attribute**. In entity CLASSROOM shown in Figure 2.17, none of the three attributes (Building, Room Number, and Number of Seats) are unique. The requirements for this entity indicate the following:

- *There can be multiple classrooms in the same building (e.g., multiple classrooms in Building A).*
- *There can be multiple classrooms with the same room number (e.g., Room 111 in Building A versus Room 111 in Building B).*
- *There can be multiple classrooms with the same number of seats (e.g., multiple classrooms with 40 seats).*

Since none of the three attributes are unique, this entity does not have a regular (single-component) attribute that can serve as its identifier. However, the combination of two attributes, Building and Room Number, is unique (there can be only one classroom in

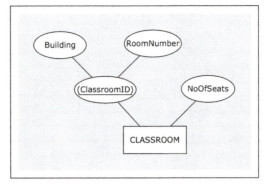

FIGURE 2.17   An entity with a composite unique attribute.

the entire resulting database with a particular combination of values for Building and Room Number), and therefore, a composite attribute combining these two attributes is unique.

Note that the unique composite attribute ClassroomID ensures that the entity CLASSROOM is in compliance with the rule that each entity must have at least one unique attribute.

MULTIPLE UNIQUE ATTRIBUTES (CANDIDATE KEYS)

Figure 2.18 illustrates a case in which an entity has more than one unique attribute. In such cases, each unique attribute is also called a **candidate key**. The term "candidate key" comes from the fact that a candidate key is a "candidate" to be chosen as the primary identifier (also known as a primary key) when implementing the resulting database. In other words, one of the candidate keys will be chosen later as the primary key for the table corresponding to the entity that contains the candidate keys. Primary keys will be discussed in Chapter 3.

In Figure 2.18, attributes Employee ID and SSN uniquely identify individual instances of the EMPLOYEE entity. Therefore, both Employee ID and SSN are candidate keys. Note that both of these unique attributes are underlined. Attribute Salary is not unique and is therefore not underlined.

An entity can have regular (single-component) and composite candidate keys at the same time. The example in Figure 2.19 shows entity VEHICLE whose attribute VIN (vehicle identification number) is unique, as is the composite attribute License Plate, which is composed of attributes State and License Plate Number.

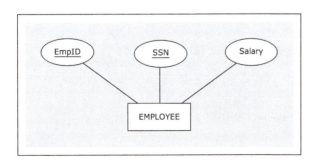

FIGURE 2.18   An entity with multiple unique attributes (candidate keys).

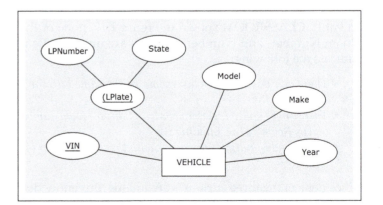

FIGURE 2.19   An entity with a regular and composite candidate key.

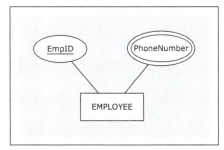

FIGURE 2.20   A multivalued attribute.

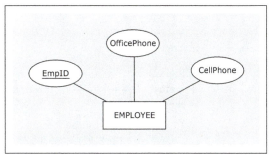

FIGURE 2.21   A scenario that does not use multivalued attributes.

MULTIVALUED ATTRIBUTES

A **multivalued attribute** is used in cases where instances of an entity can have multiple values for the same attribute. Figure 2.20 depicts an entity that contains a multivalued attribute. The multivalued attribute is depicted by a double line around the oval. The ER diagram in Figure 2.20 shows that we want to keep track of employees' multiple phone numbers.

The multivalued attribute is used in cases in which there is a variable number of values that can be assigned to the particular attribute of the entity. The example in Figure 2.20 is applicable to a situation in which employees have a varying number of phone numbers for which we want to keep track. For example, some employees may have two phone numbers, other employees may have more than two phone numbers, and yet other employees may have fewer than two phone numbers.

If for every employee, we want to keep track of *exactly* two phone numbers (e.g., office phone number and cell phone number) we would *not* use a multivalued attribute. We would simply use two separate attributes, as shown in Figure 2.21.

DERIVED ATTRIBUTE

A **derived attribute** is an attribute whose value will not be permanently stored in a database. Instead, the value of a derived attribute will be calculated from the stored values of other attributes and/or additional available data (such as the current date). Figure 2.22 shows a small example that illustrates a derived attribute in an ER model.

A derived attribute is depicted by a dashed oval line. In this case, attribute OpeningDate is a regular attribute whose value will be stored in the resulting database. Attribute YearsInBusiness is a derived attribute whose value will not be stored in the resulting database. Instead, the value for YearsInBusiness will be derived from the value of the store's OpeningDate and from the current date. If attribute YearsInBusiness was a regular attribute, its value in the resulting database would be stored and it would have to be reentered manually as time goes by (once a year for each store), or the database would contain inaccurate information. By depicting YearsInBusIness as a derived attribute, we assure that the subsequent database will implement this attribute as a formula that will always present an accurate value of the YearsInBusiness attribute to the users of the database.

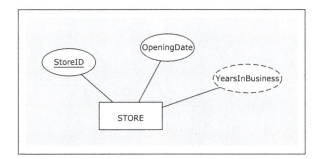

FIGURE 2.22   A derived attribute example.

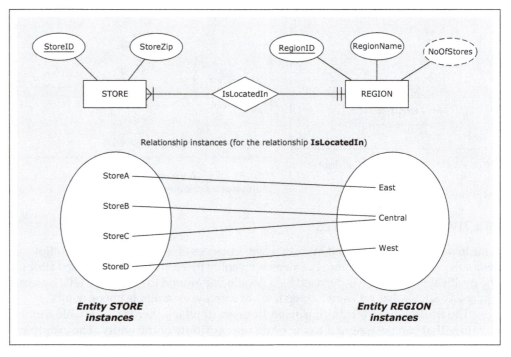

FIGURE 2.23   Another derived attribute example.

Figure 2.23 shows another example that illustrates a derived attribute. In this case, the values for the derived attribute NoOfStores will be derived by counting how many instances of entity STORE are connected to each instance of the entity REGION via the instances of the relationship IsLocatedIn.

In this example, for regions *East, Central,* and *West,* the values of the NoOfStores attribute will be *1, 2,* and *1,* respectively. If, for example, the entity STORE gets a new instance StoreE, and if this new store is connected with entity REGION instance West via a new instance of the relationship IsLocatedIn, then the value for the derived attribute NoOfStores for the *West* region will automatically increase from *1* to *2.*

OPTIONAL ATTRIBUTE

Most of the attributes in an entity will have a value for each entity instance, but some of the attributes may be allowed to not have a value. Such an attribute is called an **optional attribute**. Figure 2.24 illustrates the example of an optional attribute. The example is based on the following requirements:

- *For each employee, we keep track of his or her unique employee ID, and his or her salary and annual bonus. Not every employee will have an annual bonus.*

The depicted entity has one optional attribute, while the rest of the attributes are required attributes. The optional attribute is depicted by a capital letter O in parentheses at the end of the attribute's name.

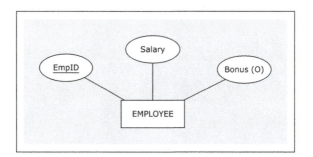

FIGURE 2.24   An optional attribute.

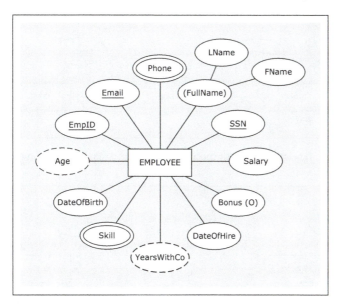

FIGURE 2.25   An entity with various types of attributes.

EXAMPLE: ENTITY CONTAINING VARIOUS TYPES OF ATTRIBUTES

To recap the various types of attributes, Figure 2.25 shows an entity that contains a number of different types of attributes. This entity reflects the following requirements:

- *The database will keep track of employees.*
- *For each employee, we will keep track of the following: an employee's unique ID, unique e-mail, first name, last name (first and last name can be combined into a full name), multiple phone numbers, date of birth, age (which will be calculated from the date of birth and the current date), salary, bonus (optional), multiple skills, unique Social Security number, the date the employee was first hired, and the number of years he or she has worked in the company (which will be calculated from the date of hire and the current date).*

EXACT MINIMUM AND MAXIMUM CARDINALITY IN RELATIONSHIPS

In some cases, the **exact minimum and/or maximum cardinality** in relationships is known in advance. In our notation, we use pairs of numbers in parentheses placed on the relationship lines to depict the exact values for minimum and maximum cardinality. The first number in the pair, the number next to the open parenthesis, indicates minimum cardinality. The second number, the number next to the closed parenthesis, indicates maximum cardinality. These pairs of numbers can be placed on either side or on both sides of the relationship, depending on which exact mini-mum and maximum cardinalities are known in advance.

For example, the requirements for the relationship EnrollsIn, shown Figure 2.26, state the following:

- *Each student must enroll in at least 2 and at most 6 classes, while a class must have en-rolled in it at least 5 students and at most 40 students.*

Specific maximum and minimum cardinalities are depicted by the pairs of numbers between the diamond and the cardinality constraint symbols.

In this notation, when we are depicting minimum–maximum cardinality as a pair in parentheses, we must show both values (min and max), even if one of them is

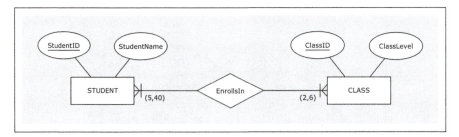

FIGURE 2.26   A relationship with specific minimum and maximum cardinalities.

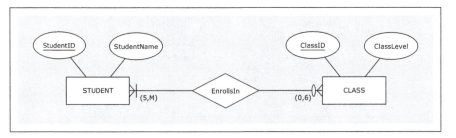

FIGURE 2.27   A relationship with a mixture of specific and non-specific cardinalities.

non-specific. For example, the requirements for the relationship EnrollsIn, shown in Figure 2.27, state:

- *Each student enrolls in at most 6 classes but does not have to enroll in any. A class must have at least 5 students enrolled in it but can have more than 5 students.*

In this case, the optional participation of the entity STUDENT in the relationship EnrollsIn is depicted twice: once by the optional participation symbol for minimum cardinality and again by the number 0 as the minimum cardinality in the number pair that appears between the relationship and cardinality constraint symbol. Also, the multiple (but without a specific number) maximum cardinality of the entity CLASS is depicted twice: once by the crow's foot symbol for maximum cardinality and again by the letter M as the maximum cardinality in the number pair that appears between the cardinality symbol and the relationship.

UNARY RELATIONSHIPS AND RELATIONSHIP ROLES

The **degree of a relationship** indicates how many entities are involved in a relationship. So far, every relationship we have examined involved two entities. A relationship between two entities is called a **binary relationship** or a relationship of degree 2 (because it involves two entities). Even though the vast majority of relationships in business-related ER diagrams are binary relationships, there are relationships of other degrees that can occur as well. A relationship of degree 1, also known as a **unary relationship (recursive relationship)**, occurs when an entity is involved in a relationship with itself. Figure 2.28 shows examples of three unary relationships: 1:M, M:N, and 1:1.

The requirements for Figure 2.28, Example A are:

- *A client can refer many clients but does not have to refer any. Each client is either referred by one other client or is not referred at all.*

The requirements for Figure 2.28, Example B are:

- *An employee can advise many employees but does not have to advise any. An employee can be advised by many employees but does not have to be advised by any.*

The requirements for Figure 2.28, Example C are:

- *In a database for a gift-giving event (Secret Santa), each person gives a gift to exactly one person and each person receives a gift from exactly one person.*

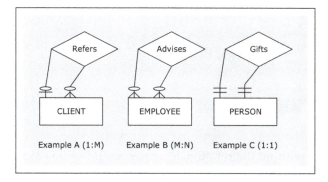

FIGURE 2.28   Unary relationship examples.

A **relationship role** represents additional syntax that can be used in ER diagrams at the discretion of a data modeler to clarify the role of each entity in a relationship. Relationship roles can be used in relationships of any degree, but their usefulness is most apparent when they are used in unary relationships. Relationship roles are represented by the text placed next to the relationship lines. Figure 2.29 shows unary relationships with specified relationship roles.

Diagrams in Figure 2.29 can now be additionally interpreted as follows.

Figure 2.29, Example A:

- *A client can be a referring party and as such can refer many clients. A client does not have to be a referring party.*
- *A client can be a referred party and as such can be referred by only one client. A client does not have to be a referred party.*

Figure 2.29, Example B:

- *An employee can be an advisor for many employees or for no employees at all.*
- *An employee can be an advisee of many employees or of no employees at all.*

Figure 2.29, Example C:

- *A person must be a giver of a gift for exactly one person.*
- *A person must be a recipient of a gift from exactly one person.*

Figure 2.30 shows an example of relationship roles in a binary relationship.

As we already mentioned, usage of relationship roles is at the discretion of the ER diagram modeler. Relationship roles can certainly provide clarification in some cases. However, if overused, they can also represent unnecessary clutter. For example, in Figure 2.30, a competent observer would most likely not need the explicitly stated relationship roles to interpret the "Ships" relationship. Therefore, the

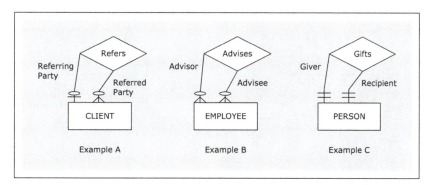

FIGURE 2.29   Unary relationships with role names.

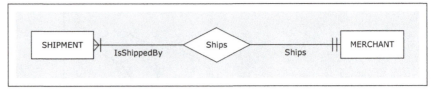

FIGURE 2.30   A binary relationship with role names.

same ER diagram without the relationship roles would be just as informative, while containing less verbiage.

MULTIPLE RELATIONSHIPS BETWEEN SAME ENTITIES

It is not unusual for the same entities in an ER diagram to be related via more than one relationship. Figure 2.31 shows an example of such a scenario. The example is based on the following requirements.

- *A shipping company wants to create a database to keep track of its employees and packages.*
- *Each package is picked up by exactly one employee.*
- *Each employee picks up multiple packages.*
- *Each package is delivered by exactly one employee.*
- *Each employee delivers multiple packages.*

WEAK ENTITY

Recall that each regular entity has to have at least one unique attribute. A **weak entity** is a construct in an ER diagram used to depict entities that do not have a unique attribute of their own. A weak entity is represented by a double line depicting a frame of its rectangle. Within an ER diagram, each weak entity must be associated with its **owner entity** via an **identifying relationship**. This type of relationship is represented as a double-framed diamond.

Figure 2.32 illustrates an example of a weak entity. The example is based on the following requirements.

- *An apartment rental company wants to create a database to keep track of its buildings and apartments.*
- *For each building, we will keep track of a unique building ID and the number of floors in the building.*
- *For each apartment, we will keep track of the apartment number and the number of bedrooms in the apartment.*

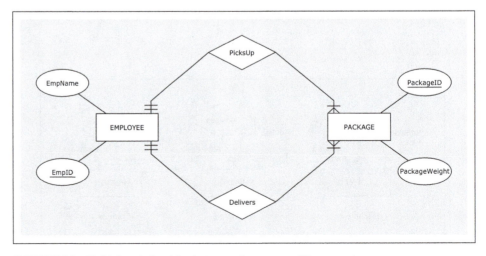

FIGURE 2.31   Multiple relationships between the same entities.

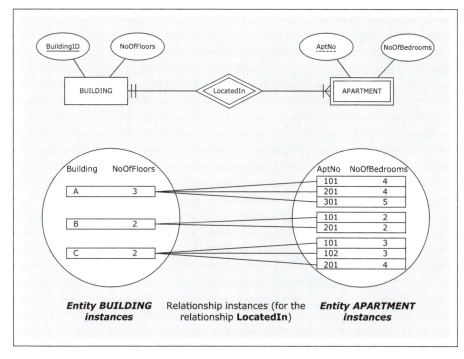

FIGURE 2.32   A weak entity example with entity instances.

- *Each building has multiple apartments, and each apartment is located in one building.*
- *We can have multiple apartments with the same apartment number in our database, but within one building each apartment will have a different apartment number.*

As indicated by the requirement, there is no unique attribute for the entity APART-MENT. However, the apartment number attribute is unique within each building. Such an attribute is called a **partial key**, and it is depicted in the ER diagram by a dashed underline. A combination of the partial key and the unique attribute from the owner entity uniquely identifies every instance of the weak entity. For example, instances of the weak entity APARTMENT are uniquely identified by combining the value of their partial key AptNo and the primary key BuilidingID of their owner entity BUILDING, as follows:

A 101, A 201, A 301, B 101, B 201, C 101, C 102, C 201.

The concept of a weak entity is actually similar to the concept of a multivalued composite attribute. Figure 2.33 illustrates this point.

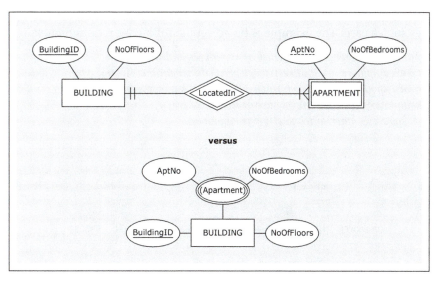

FIGURE 2.33   A weak entity versus a multivalued composite attribute.

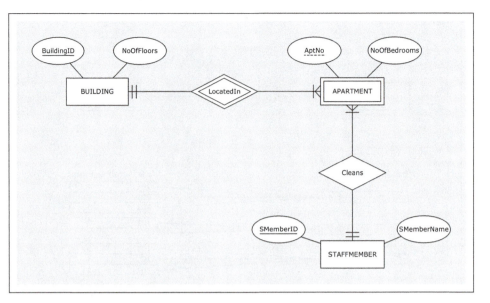

FIGURE 2.34   A weak entity with an identifying and regular relationship.

Both diagrams in Figure 2.33 represent the same requirements. However, the weak entity notation is capable of depicting a partial key, while there is no such option for the multivalued composite attribute. For example, in the top part of Figure 2.33, we can depict that each apartment number is unique for apartments within one building, while in the bottom part of Figure 2.33 we cannot.

A weak entity can have regular (non-identifying) relationships with other entities. If we used a multivalued composite attribute instead of a weak entity, we would not be able to depict such a relationship. An example of a weak entity engaged in a non-identifying relationship is given in Figure 2.34.

Even though weak entities and multivalued composite attributes are similar at first glance, there are meaningful differences between these two concepts, as we have just illustrated.

Each weak entity always has the mandatory one-cardinality constraint in the identifying relationship with its owner. This ensures that each instance of a weak entity is associated with exactly one instance of its owner. The owner entity, on the other hand, can have a mandatory or optional participation in the identifying relationship, as it is possible to have owner entities with instances that do not have weak entity instances associated with them.

In the majority of cases, an identifying relationship is a 1:M relationship. However, it is possible to have a 1:1 identifying relationship, in which case a partial identifier attribute in the weak entity is not necessary. The example shown in Figure 2.35 illustrates such a case. The example is based on the following requirements:

- *In our database, we will keep track of employees and their spouses.*
- *For each employee, we will keep track of his or her unique ID and name.*
- *For each spouse, we will keep track of his or her name and birthdate.*
- *An employee either has one spouse or no spouse.*
- *Each spouse is married to exactly one employee.*

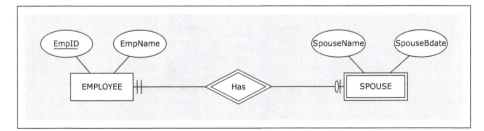

FIGURE 2.35   A weak entity with a 1:1 identifying relationship.

Note that the weak entity SPOUSE does not have a partial identifier, because each employee can be associated with only one spouse; therefore, we do not need a partial identifier to distinguish one spouse from the other.

NAMING CONVENTIONS FOR ENTITIES, ATTRIBUTES, AND RELATIONSHIPS

In the process of ER modeling, a good practice is to adopt certain guidelines for naming entities, relationships, and attributes. In this book, the convention is to use all uppercase letters for naming entities and a combination of uppercase and lowercase letters for naming attributes and relationships.

For naming entities and attributes, a common guideline for keeping ER diagrams as legible and clear as possible is to use singular (rather than plural) nouns. For example, entity names *STUDENT, STORE,* and *PROJECT* are better choices than *STUDENTS, STORES,* and *PROJECTS.* Similarly, the attribute name *Phone* is a better choice than the attribute name *Phones,* even in the case of a multivalued attribute. Plurality of instances in the case of entities and multivalued attributes is understood by the nature of these constructs, without having to use a word in plural form.

For naming relationships, it is common to use verbs, or verb phrases, rather than nouns. For example *Inspects, Manages,* and *BelongsTo* are better choices for names of relationships than *Inspection, Management,* and *Belonging.*

When naming entities, attributes and relationships, it is advisable to be as brief as possible, without being so condensed as to obscure the meaning of the construct. For example, in the case of an ER diagram for a university, the entity name *STUDENT* would be a better choice than *UNIVERSITY STUDENT,* which is unnecessarily wordy, since it is clear that that in this context *STUDENT* refers to university students. Likewise, using *US* as an abbreviation that stands for "University Stu-dent" may be too cryptic for the average user of the future database based on this ER diagram. That is not to say that in some cases multiple words or abbreviations are not a good choice. For example, *SSN* is a perfectly valid choice for a name of an attribute, due to the widespread understanding of the meaning of this abbrevia-tion as a Social Security number. Also, the multiword phrase *NoOfFloors* is a better choice for naming the attribute that indicates the number of floors for the entity *BUILDING,* than the single word *Floor,* which is too ambiguous, or abbreviation *NoF,* which is not recognizable by most users.

As we mentioned at the beginning of this chapter, one of the basic rules of ER modeling is that every attribute within the same entity must have a different name. A good style rule of ER modeling is to give all attributes in the entire ER diagram dif-ferent names. For example, instead of using the word *Name* to represent two different attributes of two different entities *EMPLOYEE* and *CUSTOMER,* we would use two different words, *EmpName* and *CustName.*

The guidelines stated here are not mandatory and are subject to exceptions. How-ever, when applied consistently, these conventions usually result in ER diagrams that are more legible and clearer than ER diagrams created without them.

MULTIPLE ER DIAGRAMS

In an ER diagram, each entity is always connected to all of the other entities, either via a direct relationship or indirectly via other entities and relationships. In other words, within each ER diagram, there is a path from one entity to every other entity.

If an ER schema contains entities that are not connected to other entities in the schema, such schema actually represents multiple ER diagrams for multiple separate databases. For example, in Figure 2.36, entities A, B, and C are not connected to entities D, E, F, and G. Therefore, entities A, B, and C are components of one ER diagram, while entities D, E, F, and G are components of another ER diagram.

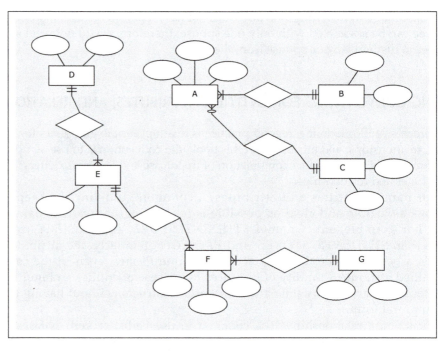

FIGURE 2.36 A schema with two separate ER diagrams (potentially misleading).

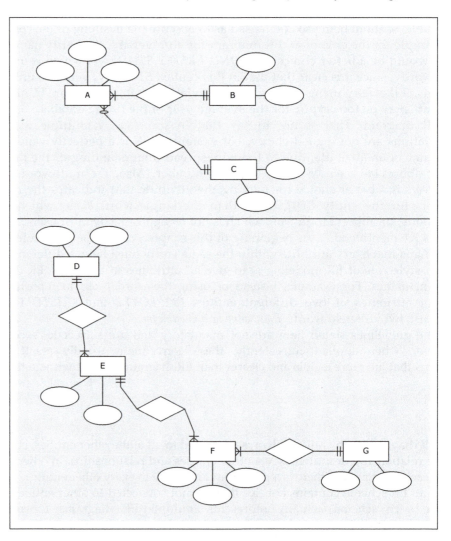

FIGURE 2.37 Separate ER diagrams in separate schemas.

In general, when depicting multiple ER diagrams, each diagram should be *visualized separately*. Instead of two diagrams in one schema, as shown in Figure 2.36, a better choice would be to present each ER diagram individually, as shown in Figure 2.37. This eliminates the possibility of confusion for any viewer that does not notice that the schema contains multiple (non-connected) ER diagrams.

EXAMPLE: ANOTHER SET OF DATABASE REQUIREMENTS AND AN ER DIAGRAM

In order to recap the introduced ER modeling concepts, we will look at another example of an ER diagram in Figure 2.38, based on the following requirements:

HAFH ("Home Away from Home") Realty Company leases apartments to corporate clients. HAFH Realty Company Property Management Database will keep track of HAFH buildings, apartments, corporate clients, building managers, cleaning staff members, and building inspectors.

The property management database for the realty company HAFH will capture data about the following:

- *For each building: BuildingID (unique) and BNoOfFloors (number of floors in the building)*
- *For each apartment: AptNo (partially unique, i.e., unique within a building) and ANoOfBedrooms (number of bedrooms in the apartment)*

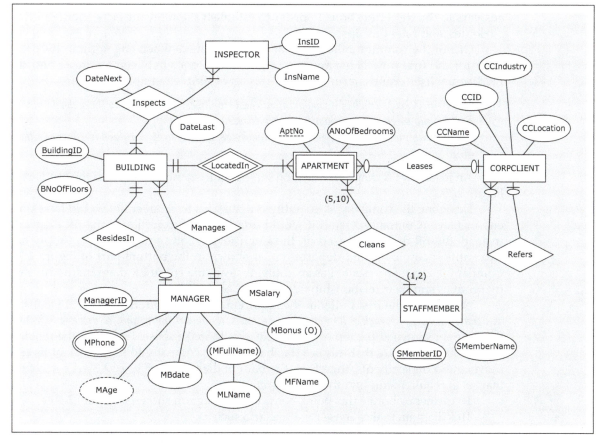

FIGURE 2.38   Another ER diagram example: HAFH Realty Company Property Management Database.

- *For each corporate client: CCID (unique), CCName (unique), CCLocation, and CCIndustry*
- *For each manager: ManagerID (unique), MFullName (composed of MFName and MLName), multiple MPhones, MBDate, MAge (derived from MBdate and current date), MSalary, and MBonus (not every manager will have a bonus)*
- *For each staff member: SMemberID (unique) and SMemberName*
- *For each inspector: InsID (unique) and InsName*
- *Each building has one or more apartments.*
  Each apartment is located in exactly one building.
- *Each apartment is either leased to one corporate client or to no one.*
  Each corporate client leases one or many apartments.
- *Each corporate client can refer many corporate clients but does not have to refer any.*
  Each corporate client can be referred by one corporate client or is not referred by any.
- *Each apartment is cleaned by either one or two staff members.*
  Each staff member cleans between 5 and 10 apartments.
- *Each manager manages one or many buildings.*
  Each building is managed by exactly one manager.
- *Each manager resides in exactly one building.*
  Each building either has one manager residing in it or no managers residing in it.
- *Each inspector inspects one or many buildings.*
  Each building is inspected by one or many inspectors.
- *For each building that a particular inspector inspects, the dates of the last inspection by the inspector and of the next future inspection by the inspector are kept.*

DATABASE REQUIREMENTS AND ER MODEL USAGE

ER modeling provides a straightforward technique for collecting, structuring, and visualizing requirements. An understanding of ER modeling is crucial, not just for creating ER models based on the requirements, but is also important during the requirements collection process itself. It helps keep the focus on asking or seeking answers to the right questions in order to establish the relevant facts about entities, attributes, and relationships.

One of the common mistakes that beginners make when engaging in ER modeling for the first time is not recognizing the difference between an entity and the ER diagram itself. For example, consider this set of simple requirements:

- *Company X keeps track of its departments and employees who report to those departments.*
- *Each employee reports to exactly one department.*
- *Each department can have many employees reporting to it but does not have to have any.*

An incorrect ER diagram based on these requirements is shown in the top part of Figure 2.39.

Depicting the company as an entity is a mistake. Such an entity would have only one instance (Company X) and it would unnecessarily complicate the ER diagram. Instead, the ER diagram, based on the small set of requirements above, simply has two entities: employee and department, as shown in the bottom part of Figure 2.39. Company X is not represented as an entity. Instead, the entire ER diagram (in this case two entities and their relationship) represents Company X.

Note that if the first bullet in the requirements were different, e.g., "*An industry association is keeping track of its member companies, its departments and its employees,*" then the diagram shown at the top of Figure 2.39 would make sense. However, the requirements clearly indicate that this is a database for one company to keep track of its employees and departments; therefore, the bottom diagram in Figure 2.39 is correct for that set of requirements and the top diagram is not.

To further elaborate this point, consider the diagram shown in Figure 2.40.

This diagram makes sense for a scenario such as:

- *A non-profit foundation keeps track of the scholarship recipients that it is funding.*
- *For each student (scholarship recipient), it keeps track of his or her unique student ID, name, and the date he or she started college.*

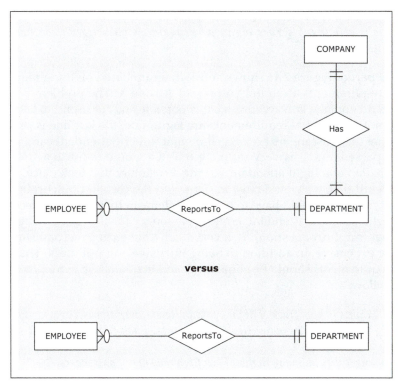

FIGURE 2.39 An ER diagram incorrectly and correctly interpreting requirements.

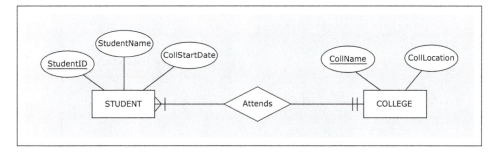

FIGURE 2.40 An ER diagram containing student and college entities.

- *For each college attended by its scholarship recipients, the foundation keeps track of the unique college name and college location.*
- *Each scholarship recipient attends exactly one college. Each college in the database has at least one of the scholarship recipients attending.*

Note that the diagram in Figure 2.40 would not make sense for a database for one individual college keeping track of its students. In that case, entity COLLEGE would be unnecessary, just as the entity COMPANY was unnecessary in Figure 2.39.

Another common database requirements collection and ER modeling mistake made by novices is not distinguishing between:

modeling of the data that is wanted and can be kept track of

versus

modeling of everything that takes place in an organization

For example, the following set of requirements fails to make such a distinction:

- *Airline X wants to keep track of flights, flight attendants, and passengers.*
- *Each flight is staffed by many flight attendants. Each flight attendant staffs many flights.*

- *Each passenger flies on many flights. Each flight has many passengers.*
- *Each flight attendant serves many passengers. A passenger is served by many attendants.*

The top part of Figure 2.41 shows an ER diagram based on these requirements. All of these requirements accurately represent Airline X. The problem is that these requirements do not take into account what is possible and/or useful to keep track of. While the first three lines of requirements are legitimate, the last line is problematic. While it is true that passengers are served by many flight attendants and attendants serve many passengers, it is very unlikely that we would want to actually record every combination of a flight attendant serving a customer that took place. Even if we wanted to record this, we would have to figure out the cost and practicality of doing so. In this example, we would have to have a mechanism that somehow records every occurrence when a flight attendant serves a passenger for the first time (e.g., brings a drink, answers a short question). It is very likely that such a mechanism would be prohibitively expensive, in addition to being intrusive and pointless. Therefore, the last row of requirements should be eliminated, and the database requirements should be listed as follows:

- *Airline X wants to keep track of flights, flight attendants, and passengers.*
- *Each flight is staffed by many flight attendants. Each flight attendant staffs many flights.*
- *Each passenger flies on many flights. Each flight has many passengers.*

Subsequently, the diagram should be constructed as shown in the bottom part of Figure 2.41.

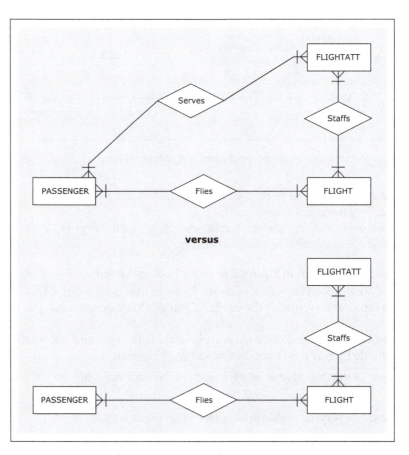

FIGURE 2.41 An ER diagram based on unfeasible and proper requirements.

VARIOUS ER NOTATIONS

As we mentioned earlier, there is no universally adopted ER notation to which all database projects conform. Instead, there is a variety of available ER notations currently in use. However, if a designer is familiar with one ER notation, other alternative ER notations are easy to understand and use, if need be.

Figure 2.42 illustrates the same exact ER diagram in three different notations. The top diagram in Figure 2.42 illustrates the ER notation that is used in the ER diagrams in this book.

The middle diagram in Figure 2.42 uses a notation in which attribute names are listed in the same rectangle with the entity name, while the relationship is represented as a dashed line connecting the entities with a relationship name embedded in the line. Cardinality constraints are represented by numbers in parentheses. In this notation, cardinality constraints are *reversed* (when compared to the notation used in this book) and the rule for interpretation of relationships is entity – cardinality constraint – relationship – entity. For example, each instance of entity EMPLOYEE participates exactly once in the relationship ReportsTo with the instances of entity DEPARTMENT, while each instance of entity DEPARTMENT can participate between zero and many times in the relationship ReportsTo with the instances of entity EMPLOYEE.

The bottom diagram in Figure 2.42 uses UML (Unified Modeling Language) notation to represent the same ER diagram. This notation uses a similar visualization of entities and relationships as the middle notation, but the rules for interpretation of cardinality constraints are the same as for the notation in the top diagram. Cardinality constraints are represented by two numbers separated by two dots when participation is optional, and by just one number when participation is mandatory.

There are many other ER notations in existence, in addition to the ones shown here. Fortunately, they all depict the same concepts: entities, relationships, and attributes. A designer who is familiar and comfortable with those concepts can quickly adapt to any ER notation.

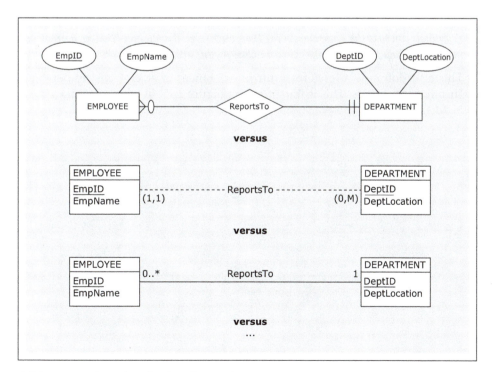

FIGURE 2.42 Examples of various ER notations.

ENHANCED ER (EER)

The term **enhanced ER (EER)** modeling refers to an expanded ER notation that depicts additional concepts beyond standard ER modeling. We give a brief overview of EER in Appendix A. While the EER extensions of traditional ER concepts have value and use, most common business-related databases can be modeled in large part by the standard ER notation introduced in this chapter. A competent ER modeler can learn and apply EER extensions easily, if and when needed.

This chapter has presented the most fundamental issues related to database requirements and ER modeling. The following notes cover several additional issues related to ER modeling.

A Note About M:N Relationships with Multiple Instances Between the Same Entities

In some cases, M:N relationships can have multiple occurrences between the same instances of involved entities. The following example illustrates such a case. Observe the requirements listed below:

- *The database will keep track of students and classes.*
- *For each student, we will keep track of his or her unique student ID and name.*
- *For each class, we will keep track of the unique class ID and the class level.*
- *Each student in the database can complete multiple classes, but does not have to complete any.*
- *Each class in the database was completed by at least one student and could have been completed by multiple students.*
- *For every instance of a student completing a class, we will record the class grade and the semester.*

Figure 2.43 shows an ER diagram based on these requirements.

Figure 2.44 illustrates some of the possible instances of the relationship shown in Figure 2.43.

If we now add a small but critical addition to the above requirements, we will fundamentally change the nature of the depicted M:N relationship:

- *A student can take the same class more than once (e.g., if a student receives a grade below a minimum grade, he has to take the same class again, until the minimum grade is achieved).*

This addition now allows for multiple instances of a relationship between the same instances of entities. This is illustrated by Figure 2.45, in which *Pat* takes the same class *IS101* three times.

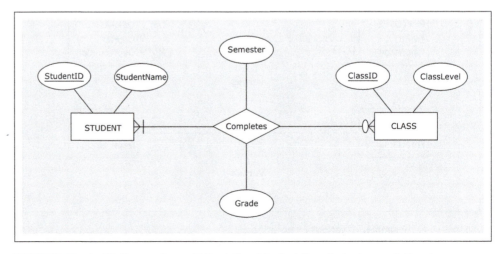

FIGURE 2.43 An ER diagram for an M:N relationship depicting students completing classes.

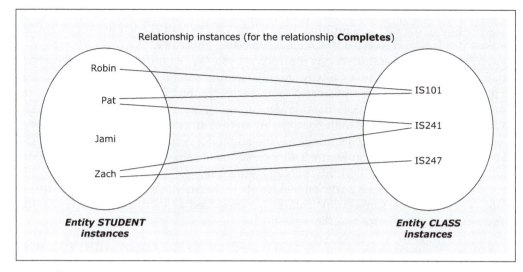

FIGURE 2.44   Instances of the M:N relationship shown in Figure 2.43.

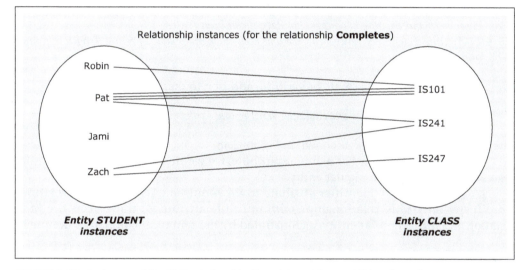

FIGURE 2.45   Instances of the M:N relationship Completes with an additional requirement.

We cannot depict these expanded requirements in an ER diagram as an M:N relationship. Instead, we will use a weak entity with two owners as shown in Figure 2.46.

The reason we used a weak entity is to depict the attribute Semester as a partial identifier. Two or more occurrences of the same student taking the same class can now

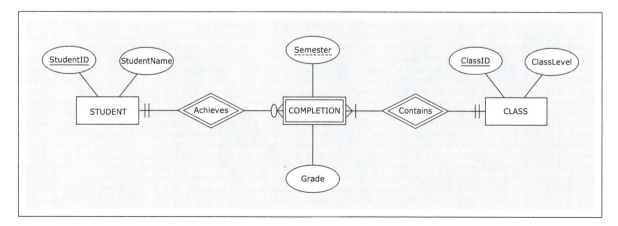

FIGURE 2.46   An ER diagram for an M:N relationship represented as a weak entity.

be distinguished, even if the same grade is given more than once. For example, suppose a student takes a class multiple times, earns a grade of *D* each time, then finally retakes the class, and receives the minimum passing grade of *C*.

When an M:N relationship is represented as a weak entity, the cardinality constraints of the weak entity are always mandatory-one, and the cardinality constraints of the M:N relationship are transferred to the corresponding non-weak entity. Consider Figures 2.43 and 2.46. The optional-many relationship of STUDENT Completes CLASS in Figure 2.43 corresponds to the optional-many relationship of STUDENT Achieves COMPLETION in Figure 2.46. Similarly, the mandatory-many relationship of CLASS Completed by STUDENT in Figure 2.43 corresponds to the mandatory-many relationship of CLASS Contains COMPLETION in Figure 2.46.

Figure 2.47 shows an additional example of an M:N relationship with multiple instances between the same entity instances, represented as a weak entity. The requirements for this example are as follows.

- *A rental car company wants to keep track of its cars and the customers who rent the cars.*
- *For each customer, we will keep track of his or her unique ID and name.*
- *For each car, we will keep track of its unique VIN and its make.*
- *A customer can rent many cars, but has to rent at least one. A car may be rented by many customers, but we may have cars that have never been rented.*
- *Every time a customer rents a car, we will keep track of the date of rental, length of rental, and price per day.*

Note that if we add a small, but critical, addition to these requirements:

- *Each rental that involves one customer renting one car has its own unique rental ID.*

the ER diagram would look as shown in Figure 2.48.

Since each rental now has a unique attribute, we would no longer depict the rental as a weak entity, but as a regular entity.

Adding a unique identifier attribute to the requirements for an M:N relationship (especially M:N relationships with multiple attributes) transforms the M:N relationship into a regular entity, as illustrated by the rental car company example in

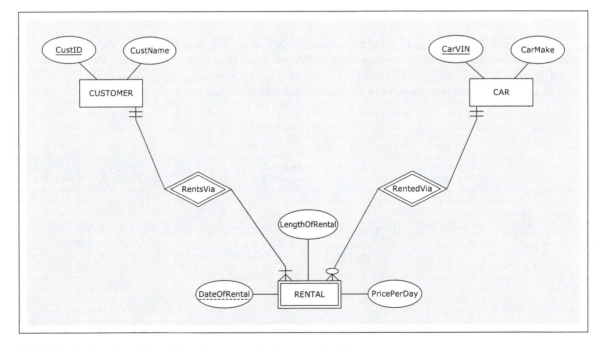

FIGURE 2.47   Another M:N relationship represented as a weak entity.

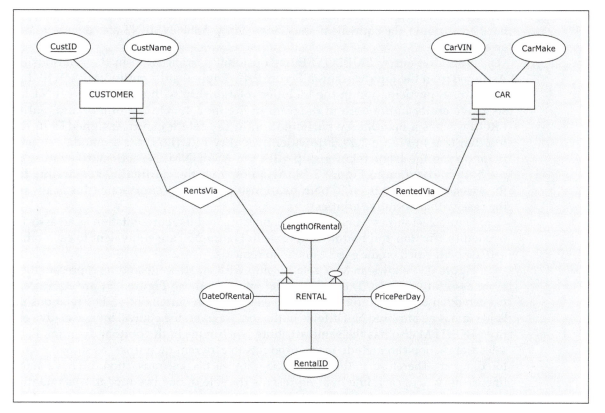

FIGURE 2.48   A regular entity, instead of an M:N relationship represented as a weak entity.

Figure 2.48. Adding the unique identifier in such fashion is a commonly used technique for streamlining ER diagrams and the subsequent resulting databases.

A Note About Associative Entities

An **associative entity** is a construct used as an alternative way of depicting M:N relationships. An associative entity is represented by a rectangle with a diamond inside of it. Associative entities do not have unique or partially unique attributes, and often do not have any attributes at all.

Figure 2.49 shows an M:N relationship and its representation as an associative entity. The top and bottom diagrams in Figure 2.49 are equivalent to each other and

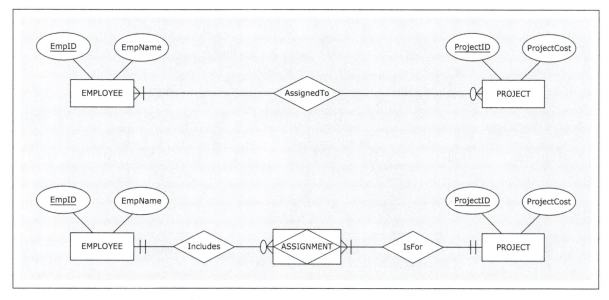

FIGURE 2.49   An identical relationship represented as a M:N relationship and as an associative entity.

are both based on the exact same requirements. Since relationship AssignedTo does not have an attribute, the equivalent associative entity ASSIGNMENT also does not have an attribute.

Note that entity EMPLOYEE has optional participation in the relationship AssignedTo in the top diagram in Figure 2.49. Equivalently, entity EMPLOYEE has an optional participation in the Includes relationship with the ASSIGNMENT associative entity in the bottom diagram in Figure 2.49. On the other hand, entity PROJECT has a mandatory participation in the relationship AssignedTo in the top diagram in Figure 2.49. Equivalently, entity PROJECT has a mandatory participation in the IsFor relationship with the ASSIGNMENT associative entity in the bottom diagram in Figure 2.49. Also note that the cardinality constraints for the associative entity itself in both relationships are mandatory-one (this is always the case with associative entities).

Figure 2.50 shows a unary M:N relationship and its representation as an associative entity. The top and bottom diagrams in Figure 2.50 are equivalent to each other and are both based on the exact same requirements.

Figure 2.51 shows an M:N relationship with an attribute and its representation as an associative entity. The top and bottom diagrams in Figure 2.51 are equivalent to each other and are both based on the exact same requirements. Since relationship SoldVia has an attribute NoOfItems in the top diagram, the equivalent associative entity LINEITEM also has the same attribute NoOfItems in the bottom diagram. Each sales transaction can include many products in different quantities, as shown by the top diagram. Therefore, in the bottom diagram, each sales transaction can have many line items, where each line item represents the sale of one product and its quantity within one sales transaction.

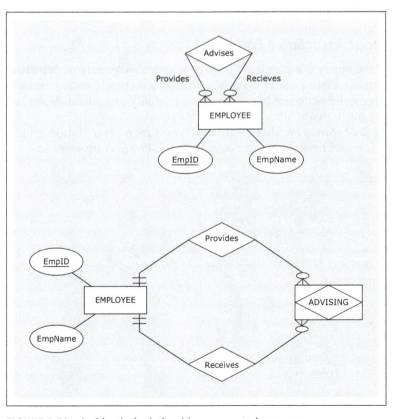

FIGURE 2.50 An identical relationship represented as a unary M:N relationship and as an associative entity.

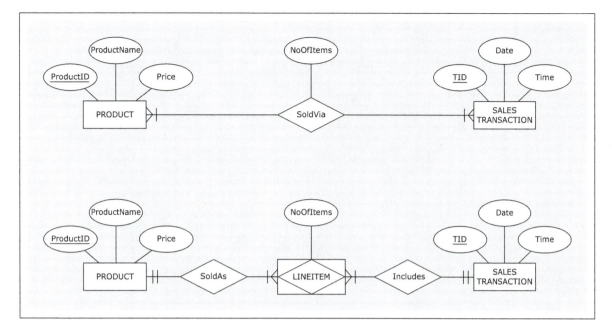

FIGURE 2.51 An identical relationship represented as an M:N relationship with an attribute and as an associative entity with an attribute.

Associative entities are not necessary constructs for depicting binary or unary relationships. As we illustrated in the above examples, for binary or unary relationships, associative entities are simply another way of depicting a relationship that can just as easily be depicted without using an associative entity. However, as we show in the next note, for relationships with a degree higher than 2 such as ternary relationships, associative entities provide a way to eliminate potential ambiguities in the ER diagrams.

A Note About Ternary (and Higher Degree) Relationships

A relationship of degree 3, involving three entities, is also known as a **ternary relationship**. To illustrate a ternary relationship, we will use the following example:

Company MG (Manufacturing Guru) wants to keep track of its suppliers, components, and products.

In particular, Company MG wants to keep track of which supplier provides which component for which product. During the requirements collections process, Company MG provided the following specifics:

- *We have multiple products.*
- *We have multiple suppliers.*
- *We have multiple components.*
- *We will keep track of which suppliers provide which components for which product.*
- *Every product contains one or more components, each of which is provided by one or more suppliers.*
- *Every supplier can provide many components for many products, but they also do not have to provide any components for any products.*
- *Every component is provided for one or many products by one or many suppliers.*

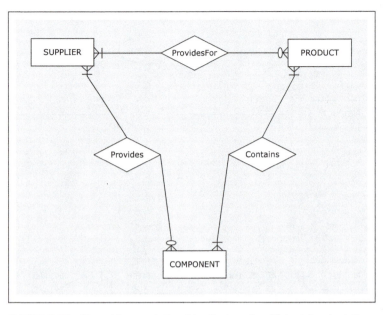

FIGURE 2.52   Three binary relationships that are insufficient for depicting Company MG requirements.

Simply creating three binary relationships between the three entities *will not* fully depict the above requirements. Figure 2.52 shows three relationships depicting which product is associated with which supplier, which supplier is associated with which component, and which component is associated with which product (for brevity, all figures in this section are shown without entity attributes). However, the database based on the diagram in Figure 2.52 *would not* keep track of which suppliers provide which components for which product.

For example, in the database resulting from the diagram, we could depict that suppliers A1 and A2 are the providers of component B, and that component B is one of the components for product C. However, let us assume that supplier A1 provides component B for product C and that the supplier A2 does not provide component B for product C (i.e., supplier A2 provides component B, but not for product C). The database resulting from diagram 2.52 could not depict such a scenario.

In order to accommodate such perfectly plausible scenarios, all three entities must be connected with one relationship, i.e., a ternary relationship has to be created.

One problematic issue with ternary relationships is that it is not possible to unambiguously show cardinality constraints in a ternary relationship. Observe Figure 2.53, showing the ternary relationship Provides that involves entities SUPPLIER, PRODUCT, and COMPONENT. The reason there are no cardinality constraints in this figure is that it is not possible to assign cardinality constraints unambiguously.

It is not clear in the ER diagram in Figure 2.53 where we would put a symbol indicating that we may record some suppliers who do not provide any components for any products. If we put an optional symbol on the component side of the relationship, it is simply not clear if we are saying that we want to keep track of suppliers that do not provide any components for products *or* if we are saying that we want to keep track of products for which no components are provided by any suppliers.

In other words, we simply cannot depict cardinalities unambiguously in a ternary relationship. However, if we use an associative entity instead, as shown in Figure 2.54, then we can depict the ternary relationship with all of its necessary cardinality constraints unambiguously.

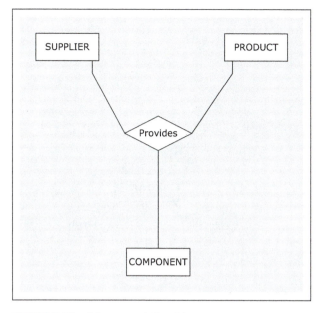

FIGURE 2.53   A ternary relationship.

Notice that the diagram shown in Figure 2.54 depicts which supplier supplies which component for which product. If we wanted to keep track of actual deliveries of components for products from suppliers, we would have to add additional attributes, such as quantity. However, we cannot simply just add attribute Quantity by itself to the associative entity shown in Figure 2.54. The same supplier may deliver the same

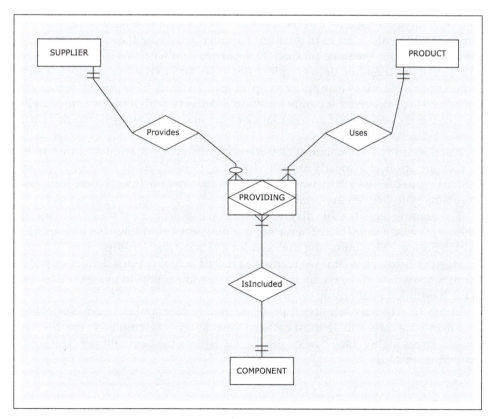

FIGURE 2.54   A ternary relationship via associative entity.

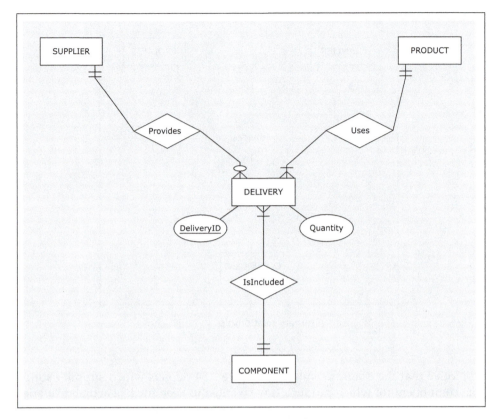

FIGURE 2.55   A regular entity replacing a ternary relationship.

quantity of the same component for the same product on more than one occasion. If we added only attribute Quantity to the associative entity, there would be no way of distinguishing different instances of the same supplier delivering the same quantity of the same component for the same product. One way to deal with this situation is to create another attribute, a unique delivery identifier. If we add to the requirements a stipulation that each instance of a supplier supplying a particular component for a particular product is considered a separate individual delivery with its own unique delivery identifier, we no longer need an associative entity and can now use a regular entity as shown in Figure 2.55.

Another thing to note about ternary relationships is that, in addition to being rare, they are applicable mostly as many-to-many-to-many relationships. To illustrate, consider Figure 2.56, which instead of a many-to-many-to-many relationship, shows a many-to-many-to-one ternary relationship.

The requirements for this diagram state that *each component is exclusively supplied by one supplier for one product*. Therefore, the diagram could have been simplified as shown in Figure 2.57, eliminating the need for a ternary relationship.

However, do note that if we wanted to record actual various deliveries and their quantities, we would still have to use the same diagram as shown in Figure 2.55, except that the IsIncluded relationship would be 1:1.

In practice, ternary relationships are relatively rare, and relationships of degree higher than 3 are rarer still. In most cases when a designer is tempted to create relationships of degrees higher than 2, he or she should explore the possibility of creating additional entities instead.

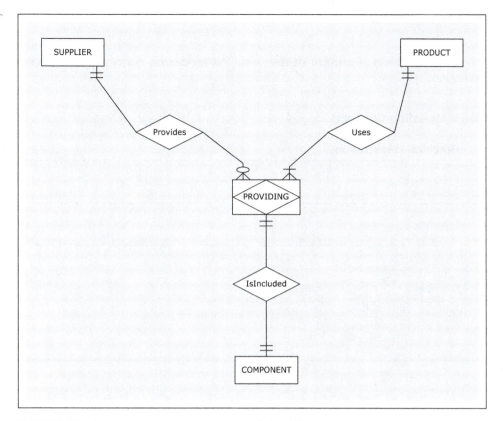

FIGURE 2.56   A many-to-many-to-one ternary relationship.

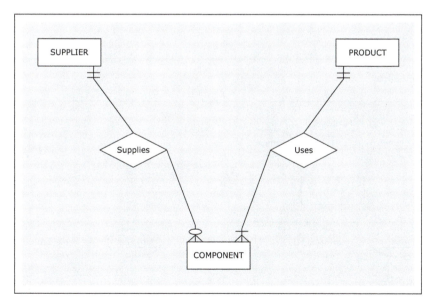

FIGURE 2.57   A many-to-many to-one ternary relationship eliminated.

Summary

Table 2.1 provides a summary of the basic ER modeling concepts introduced in this chapter.

TABLE 2.1   Summary of the Basic ER Modeling Concepts

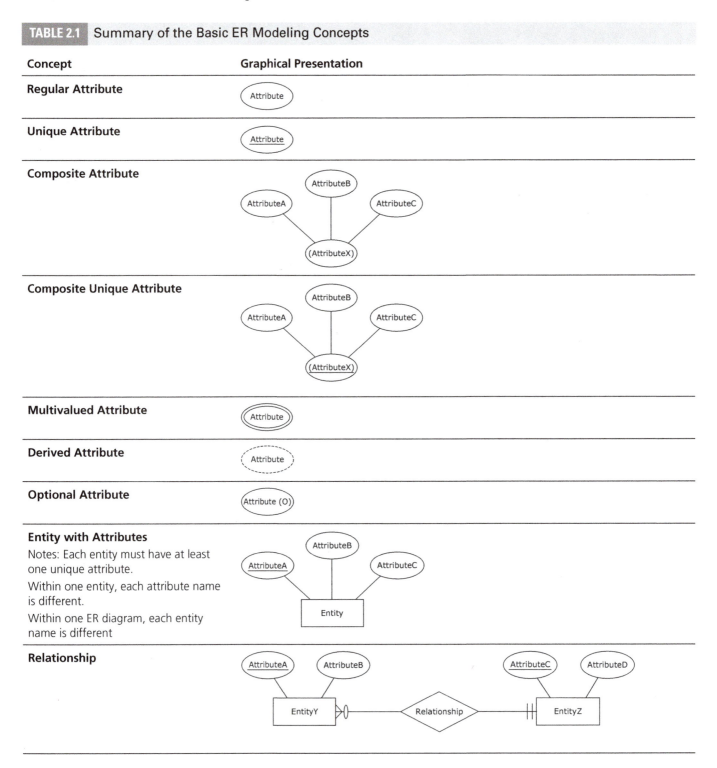

Concept	Graphical Presentation
Regular Attribute	
Unique Attribute	
Composite Attribute	
Composite Unique Attribute	
Multivalued Attribute	
Derived Attribute	
Optional Attribute	
Entity with Attributes Notes: Each entity must have at least one unique attribute. Within one entity, each attribute name is different. Within one ER diagram, each entity name is different	
Relationship	

TABLE 2.1   Summary of the Basic ER Modeling Concepts (*Continued*)

Concept	Graphical Presentation
Cardinality Constraints	
Four Possible Cardinality Constraints	
Three Types of Relationships (Maximum Cardinality-Wise)	
Relationship with an Attribute Note: Applicable for many-to-many relationships	
Relationship with Specific Minimum and Maximum Cardinalities	
Unary Relationship Degree of a Relationship: 1 (one entity involved)	
Binary Relationship Degree of a Relationship: 2 (two entities involved)	

(*Continued*)

TABLE 2.1   Summary of the Basic ER Modeling Concepts (*Continued*)

Concept	Graphical Presentation
Ternary Relationship Degree of a Relationship: 3 (three entities involved) Notes: Mostly applicable as many-to-many-to-many relationships. Ternary relationships are rare (relationships of a degree higher than 3 are even rarer).	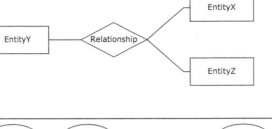
Weak Entity Notes: Always associated with its owner via an identifying relationship (which is either 1:M or 1:1). If identifying relationship is 1:M, then weak entity must have a partially unique attribute.	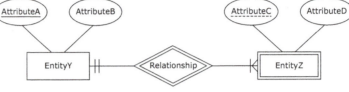
Associative Entity Note: Alternative method for depicting M:N relationships; particularly useful for depicting ternary relationships.	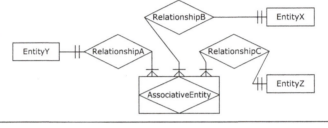

Key Terms

Associative entity *43*
Attribute (of an entity) *14*
Binary relationship *28*
Candidate key *24*
Cardinality constraints *15*
Composite attribute *22*
Composite unique attribute *23*
Database requirements *13*
Degree of a relationship *28*
Derived attribute *25*
Enhanced ER (EER) *40*

Entity *13*
Entity instances (entity members) *14*
Entity-relationship (ER) modeling *13*
ER diagram (ERD) *13*
Exact minimum and/or maximum cardinality *27*
Identifying relationship *30*
Many-to-many relationship (M:N) *17*
Maximum cardinality *15*

Minimum cardinality (participation) *15*
Multivalued attribute *25*
One-to-many relationship (1:M) *17*
One-to-one relationship (1:1) *17*
Optional attribute *26*
Owner entity *30*
Partial key *31*
Relationship *13*

Relationship attributes *19*
Relationship instances *18*
Relationship role *29*
Ternary relationship *45*
Unary relationship (recursive relationship) *28*
Unique attribute *14*
Weak entity *30*

Review Questions

Q2.1   What is the purpose of ER modeling?
Q2.2   What are the basic ER modeling constructs?
Q2.3   What is a unique attribute?
Q2.4   What is depicted by cardinality constraints?
Q2.5   What are the four possible cardinality constraints?
Q2.6   What are the three types of relationships (maximum cardinality-wise)?
Q2.7   What is a composite attribute?
Q2.8   What are candidate keys?
Q2.9   What is a multivalued attribute?

Q2.10   What is a derived attribute?
Q2.11   What is an optional attribute?
Q2.12   How are exact minimum and maximum cardinalities depicted in a relationship?
Q2.13   What is a binary relationship?
Q2.14   What is a unary relationship?
Q2.15   What is a weak entity?
Q2.16   What is an associative entity?
Q2.17   What is a ternary relationship?

Exercises

E2.1 Create an example of an entity with several attributes.

E2.2 Create requirements and the ER diagram for a scenario with two entities (both with several attributes) involved in the following relationship:

E2.2a 1:M relationship, where participation on the 1 side is mandatory and participation on the M side is optional.

E2.2b 1:M relationship, where participation on the 1 side is optional and participation on the M side is mandatory.

E2.2c 1:M relationship, where participation on both sides is mandatory.

E2.2d 1:M relationship, where participation on both sides is optional.

E2.2e M:N relationship, where participation on one side is mandatory and participation on the other side is optional.

E2.2f M:N relationship, where participation on both sides is mandatory.

E2.2g M:N relationship, where participation on both sides is optional.

E2.2h 1:1 relationship, where participation on one side is mandatory and participation on the other side is optional.

E2.2i 1:1 relationship, where participation on both sides is mandatory.

E2.2j 1:1 relationship, where participation on both sides is optional.

E2.3 Create requirements and the ER diagram for a scenario with two entities (both with several attributes) involved in a many-to-many relationship that has a relationship attribute.

E2.4 Create an example of an entity with a composite attribute.

E2.5 Create an example of an entity with a composite unique attribute.

E2.6 Create an example of an entity with candidate keys (multiple unique attributes).

E2.7 Create an example of an entity with a multivalued attribute.

E2.8 Create an example of an entity with a derived attribute.

E2.9 Create an example of an entity with an optional attribute.

E2.10 Create requirements and the ER diagram for a scenario with two entities (both with several attributes) involved in a relationship with exact minimum and maximum cardinalities.

E2.11 Create requirements and the ER diagram with several attributes for the scenario with an entity involved in a unary relationship.

E2.12 Create requirements and the ER diagram for the scenario with two entities (both with several attributes) involved in two separate relationships.

E2.13 Create requirements and the ER diagram for the scenario with two entities (both with several attributes), one of which is a weak entity and the other its owner entity, involved in an identifying relationship.

Mini Cases

MC1 Investco Scout

Investco Scout is an investment research company. Create the ER diagram for the Investco Scout Funds Database, based on the following requirements.

- *The Investco Scout Funds Database will keep track of investment companies, the mutual funds they manage, and securities contained in the mutual funds.*
- *For each investment company, Investco Scout will keep track of a unique investment company identifier and a unique investment company name as well as the names of multiple locations of the investment company.*
- *For each mutual fund, Investco Scout will keep track of a unique mutual fund identifier as well as the mutual fund name and inception date.*
- *For each security, Investco Scout will keep track of a unique security identifier as well as the security name and type.*
- *Investment companies can manage multiple mutual funds. Investco Scout does not keep track of investment companies that do not manage any mutual funds. A mutual fund is managed by one investment company.*
- *A mutual fund contains one or many securities. A security can be included in many mutual funds. Investco Scout keeps track of securities that are not included in any mutual funds.*

- *For each instance of a security included in a mutual fund, Investco Scout keeps track of the amount included.*

MC2 Funky Bizz

Funky Bizz is a rental business that rents musical instruments to bands. Create the ER diagram for the Funky Bizz Operations Database, based on the following requirements.

- *The Funky Bizz Operations Database will keep track of instruments, bands, repair technicians, and shows.*
- *For each instrument, Funky Bizz will keep track of a unique instrument serial number as well as the instrument model and brand, the year when the instrument was made, and the age (measured in years) of the instrument.*
- *The customers of Funky Bizz are bands. For each band, Funky Bizz will keep track of the unique band name and unique band identifier as well as the band's address, contact person's name, and multiple phone numbers.*
- *Repair technicians maintain the instruments. For each technician, Funky Bizz will keep track of a unique SSN as well as a name, address, and multiple phone numbers.*
- *Funky Bizz will record information about shows that its customer bands perform in. For each show, it will keep track of a unique show identifier composed of the show venue name and date. For*

each show, it will also keep track of show type and show name (a show may or may not have a name).

- A band does not have to rent any instruments, but may rent up to 30. Each instrument may be rented by one band or by no bands at all.
- A repair technician may repair many or no instruments, and an instrument may be repaired by many or no technicians.
- A band may perform in many shows, but does not have to perform in any. Each show must have at least one band performing, but may have many bands performing.
- For each band, Funky Bizz keeps track of the number of shows that each band performs in.

MC3 Snooty Fashions

Snooty Fashions is an exclusive custom fashion designer business. Create the ER diagram for the Snooty Fashions Operations Database based on the following requirements.

The Snooty Fashions Operations Database will keep track of the following:

- For each designer: a unique designer identifier and unique SSN as well as the name (composed of first and last name)
- For each customer: a unique customer's identifier as well as his or her name and multiple phone numbers
- For each tailoring technician: a unique SSN as well as his or her name (composed of first and last name)
- For each outfit: a unique outfit's identifier as well as the outfit's planned date of completion and its unreasonable price
- For each fashion show: a unique show identifier as well as the date of the show and location
- Each designer designs many outfits. Each outfit has only one designer.
- Each outfit is sold (in advance) to exactly one customer. Customers can buy one or many outfits (Snooty Fashions will not keep track of customers that have not made any purchases yet).
- Each tailoring technician must work on at least one outfit but can work on many. Each outfit has at least one tailoring technician working on it but can have many.
- Snooty Fashions will keep track of the date when a tailoring technician started working on a particular outfit.
- Each designer can participate in a number of fashion shows, but does not have to participate in any. Each fashion show can feature one or two Snooty Fashions designers (Snooty Fashions will not keep track of fashion shows that do not feature Snooty Fashions designers).

MC4 Signum Libri

Signum Libri (SL) is a publishing company. Create the ER diagram for the SL Operations Database based on the following requirements.

SL Operations Database will keep track of the following:

- For each book SL publishes: a book name, genre, date of publication, and number of pages
- For each writer: a unique writer identifier as well as the writer's name
- For each agent: a unique agent identifier as well as the agent's name
- For each editor: a unique editor identifier as well as the editor's name
- Each SL book is written by one writer, and each writer can write many SL books. SL will not keep track of writers who did not write a book for SL. All books written by the same writer have a different book name. However, two writers can write two different books with the same book name.
- Each writer is represented by one agent. Each agent represents at least one writer, but can represent many.
- Each book has one editor. Each editor edits at least one book, but can edit many books.
- Each editor can mentor one or more other editors, but does not have to mentor any. Each editor can have at most one mentor editor, but does not have to have any.

MC5 ExoProtect

ExoProtect is an insurance company. Write out all requirements for the ER diagram for the ExoProtect Employees' Computers Database shown in Figure 2.58.

MC6 Jones Dozers

Jones Dozers is a construction equipment company. Write out all requirements for the ER diagram for the Jones Dozers Sales and Rentals Database shown in Figure 2.59.

MC7 Midtown Memorial

Midtown Memorial is a hospital. Write out all requirements for the ER diagram for the Midtown Memorial Patients Drug Dispense Database shown in Figure 2.60.

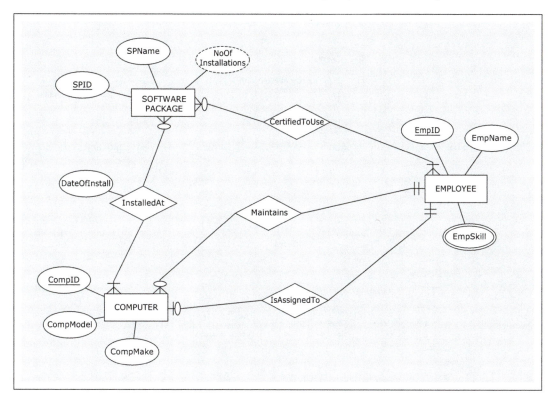

FIGURE 2.58   An ER diagram for the ExoProtect Employees' Computers Database.

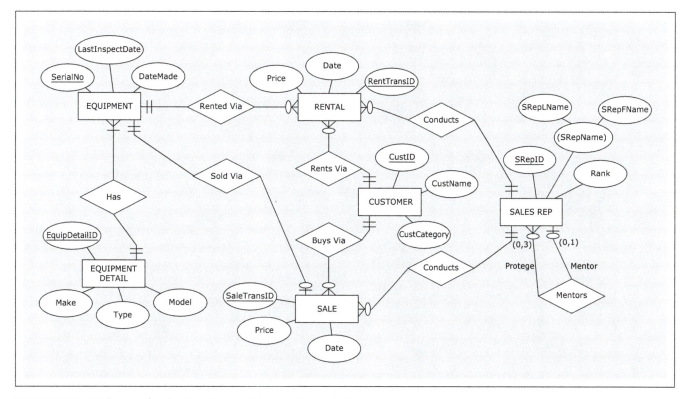

FIGURE 2.59   ER diagram for the Jones Dozers Sales and Rentals Database.

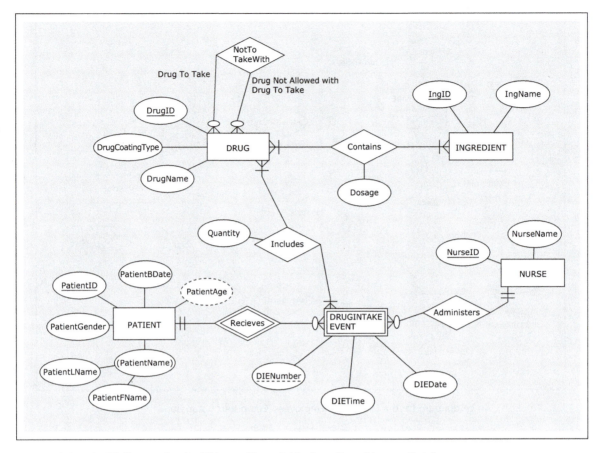

FIGURE 2.60   An ER diagram for the Midtown Memorial Patients Drug Dispense Database.

Chapter 3

Relational Database Modeling

INTRODUCTION

Recall from Chapter 1 that the term "logical database model" refers to the database model that is implementable by the DBMS software. The most commonly used logical database model is the **relational database model**. A database that is modeled using the relational database model is known as a **relational database**.

Once database requirements are collected and visualized as an ER diagram, the next step in creating a relational database is to map (convert) the ER diagram into a logical database model represented as a **relational schema**. A relational schema is a visual depiction of the relational database model.

Most contemporary commercial DBMS software packages, such as Oracle, MySQL, Microsoft SQL Server, PostgreSQL, Teradata, IBM DB2, and Microsoft Access, are **relational DBMS (RDBMS)** software packages. They are based on the relational database model and are used to implement relational databases.

In this chapter, we will describe the basic concepts of the relational database model and explain how to properly map an ER diagram into a relational schema.

RELATIONAL DATABASE MODEL: BASIC CONCEPTS

The main construct in the relational database model is a **relation**, which is a table containing rows and columns. A relational database is a *collection of related relations within which each relation has a unique name.*

A relation is also sometimes referred to as a **relational table** or even just a **table**. A **column** in a relation is sometimes referred to as a **field** or **attribute (of a relation)**. A **row** in a relation is sometimes referred to as a **tuple** or **record**. Table 3.1 summarizes the synonyms used in relational database terminology.

TABLE 3.1	Synonyms Used in the Relational Database Model				
Relation	=	Relational Table	=	Table
Column	=	Attribute	=	Field
Row	=	Tuple	=	Record

As shown in Table 3.1, it is common practice to refer to a relation as a table. However, it is important to keep in mind that although every relation is a table, not every table is a relation. In order for a table to be a relation, the following conditions must hold:

1. *Each column must have a name. Within one table, each column name must be unique.*
2. *Within one table, each row must be unique.*

Relational Table (Relation)

EmpID	EmpName	EmpGender	EmpPhone	EmpBdate
0001	Joe	M	x234	1/11/1985
0002	Sue	F	x345	2/7/1983
0003	Amy	F	x456	4/4/1990
0004	Pat	F	x567	3/8/1971
0005	Mike	M	x678	5/5/1965

Not a Relational Table

EmpID	EmpInfo	EmpInfo	EmpPhone	EmpBdate
0001	Joe	M	x234	1/11/1985
0002	Sue	F	x345	2/7/1983
0001	Joe	M	x234	1/11/1985
0004	Pat	F	x567, x789	3/8/1971
0005	Mike	M	x678	a long time ago

A Relation

EmpID	EmpName	EmpGender	EmpPhone	EmpBdate
0001	Joe	M	x234	1/11/1985
0002	Sue	F	x345	2/7/1983
0003	Amy	F	x456	4/4/1990
0004	Pat	F	x567	3/8/1971
0005	Mike	M	x678	5/5/1965

Exact Same Relation (order of rows and columns is irrelevant)

EmpName	EmpID	EmpGender	EmpBdate	EmpPhone
Joe	0001	M	1/11/1985	x234
Amy	0003	F	4/4/1990	x456
Sue	0002	F	2/7/1983	x345
Pat	0004	F	3/8/1971	x567
Mike	0005	M	5/5/1965	x678

FIGURE 3.1   Example of relational and non-relational tables.

FIGURE 3.2   Example of a relation with rows and columns appearing in a different order.

3. *Within each row, each value in each column must be single valued. Multiple values of the content represented by the column are not allowed in any rows of the table.*
4. *All values in each column must be from the same (predefined) domain.*

We will illustrate these rules with the example shown in Figure 3.1, in which two tables keep track of employee information. Assume that in the table containing the employee information, the predefined domain for each of the columns is as follows:

Employee ID – four digits

Employee Name – up to 20 characters

Employee Gender – character M or F

Employee Phone – letter x (stands for extension), followed by three digits

Employee Bdate – a date (day, month, year)

The top part in Figure 3.1 shows a relational table that satisfies the above listed conditions: each column has a unique name, each row is different, all rows per each column have single valued entries, and all values in each column are from the same domain.

The bottom part in Figure 3.1 shows a non-relational table (i.e., a table that is not a relation) that violates all of the above listed conditions: two columns have the same name, two of the rows are identical, one of the rows contains multiple entries in the phone column, and one of the entries has a value for age column that is not from the same predefined domain as the other values in the age column.

Note that both of these tables could have been implemented as shown in a spreadsheet tool, such as MS Excel. However, only the top table could have been implemented with a relational DBMS. A relational DBMS package would not allow the implementation of the bottom table. Instead, during an attempt to implement the bottom table, a relational DBMS would display error messages for the violations.

In addition to the four conditions for relational tables listed above, two additional properties hold for every relational table:

5. *Order of columns is irrelevant.*
6. *Order of rows is irrelevant.*

These two properties simply state that no matter which way the rows and/or columns of a relational table are sorted, resorted, or unsorted, the table contains the same information and is still considered to be the same table. When both rows and columns

EMPLOYEE

EmpID	EmpName	EmpGender	EmpPhone	EmpBdate
0001	Joe	M	x234	1/11/1985
0002	Sue	F	x345	2/7/1983
0003	Amy	F	x456	8/4/1990
0004	Pat	F	x567	3/8/1971
0005	Mike	M	x678	5/5/1965
0010	Mike	M	x666	8/1/1974
0007	Barbara	F	x777	4/5/1980
0011	Ivan	M	x777	3/4/1981
0009	Amy	F	x777	1/11/1985

FIGURE 3.3   Relation with the primary key underlined.

of an existing table are resorted, each row still contains the same information (just in different order) and the table still contains the same rows (just in different order). The example in Figure 3.2 illustrates this point. It shows the same relation whose columns and rows appear in a different order.

PRIMARY KEY

Every relation has a column (or a set of columns in some cases) that serves as a **primary key**. The purpose of the primary key is to distinguish one row from another in a relation. The following is a definition of a primary key.

Primary Key

Each relation must have a primary key, which is a column (or a set of columns) whose value is unique for each row.

In the relation EMPLOYEE shown in Figure 3.3, column EmpID serves as a primary key. Note that the name of the primary key column is underlined in order to distinguish it from the other columns in the relation.

In this example, each employee is assigned a unique EmpID value. Other columns in this relation could not serve as a primary key due to the fact that, as illustrated by Figure 3.3, multiple employees can have the same name, same gender, same birthdate, or the same phone number assigned to them.

MAPPING ENTITIES INTO RELATIONS

As we mentioned, once an ER diagram is constructed, it is subsequently mapped into a collection of relations. This process starts by mapping entities into relations. Each regular entity becomes a relation, and each regular attribute of a regular entity becomes a column of the newly created relation. If an entity has a single unique attribute, then that attribute becomes the primary key in the resulting mapped relation.[1]

An example of an entity mapped into a relation is shown in Figure 3.4. A relation is depicted as a rectangle containing the names of all columns of the relation. Note that the column name CustID is underlined, to indicate that CustID is the primary key of the relation CUSTOMER.

---

[1]Later in this chapter, we will show how entities with multiple unique attributes are mapped into relations.

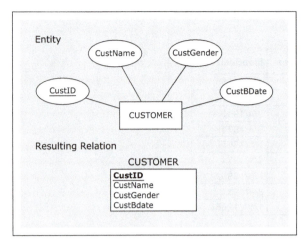

FIGURE 3.4   Entity mapped into a relation.

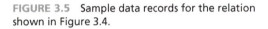

CUSTOMER

CustID	CustName	CustGender	CustBdate
1111	Tom	M	1/1/1965
2222	Jenny	F	2/2/1968
3333	Greg	M	1/2/1962
4444	Sophia	F	2/2/1983

FIGURE 3.5   Sample data records for the relation shown in Figure 3.4.

Once the mapped relation is created as a part of an implemented relational database, it can be populated with data, as shown in Figure 3.5, which shows sample data for the relation CUSTOMER.

MAPPING ENTITIES WITH COMPOSITE ATTRIBUTES INTO RELATIONS

If an entity contains composite attributes, each component of a composite attribute is mapped as a column of a relation, while the composite attribute itself does not appear in the mapped relation.

Figure 3.6 shows an example of mapping an entity with a composite attribute. Note that the name of the composite attribute does not appear in the mapped relation.

Once the mapped relation is created as a part of an implemented relational database, it can be populated with data, as shown in Figure 3.7.

Even though the name of the composite attribute is not a part of the relational schema, it can appear as a part of a front-end application based on the

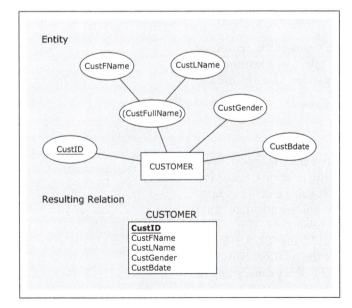

FIGURE 3.6   Entity with a composite attribute mapped into a relation.

CUSTOMER

CustID	CustFName	CustLName	CustGender	CustBdate
1111	Tom	Lendrum	M	1/1/1965
2222	Jenny	Jones	F	2/2/1968
3333	Greg	Newton	M	1/2/1962
4444	Sophia	Danks	F	2/2/1983

FIGURE 3.7   Sample data records for the relation shown in Figure 3.6.

CUSTOMER

CustID	CustFName	CustLName	CustGender	CustBdate
	CustFullName			
1111	Tom	Lendrum	M	1/1/1965
2222	Jenny	Jones	F	2/2/1968
3333	Greg	Newton	M	1/2/1962
4444	Sophia	Danks	F	2/2/1983

FIGURE 3.8   The relation shown in Figure 3.7 as presented to a user in a front-end application.

created relational database. For example, a front-end application component based on the database that contains the CUSTOMER relation shown in Figure 3.7 may include an additional caption above the CustFName and CustLName columns indicating that they are components of the composite attribute CustFullName. This is illustrated by Figure 3.8, which shows how this relation could be presented to a user in a front-end application[2] for this database.

MAPPING ENTITIES WITH UNIQUE COMPOSITE ATTRIBUTES INTO RELATIONS

Recall from Chapter 2 that an entity can have a unique composite attribute. Figure 3.9 illustrates how an entity whose only unique attribute is a composite attribute is mapped into a relation.

Note that in the resulting relation, both the Building and RoomNumber column names are underlined because *combined together, they form the primary key* of the relation CLASSROOM. A primary key that is composed of multiple attributes is called a **composite primary key**. Figure 3.10 shows the relation CLASSROOM with sample data records depicting four different classrooms and their seating capacity. Note that none of the columns contain unique values. However, for every row, the combination of Building and RoomNumber values is unique.

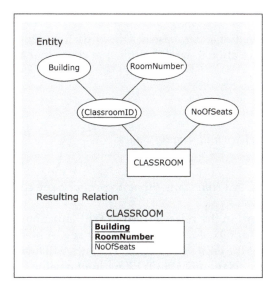

FIGURE 3.9   Entity with a unique composite attribute mapped into a relation.

CLASSROOM

Building	RoomNumber	NoOfSeats
Maguire	110	100
Maguire	210	50
Houser	110	50
Houser	210	50

FIGURE 3.10   Sample data records for the relation shown in Figure 3.9.

---

[2]Front-end applications are discussed in Chapter 6.

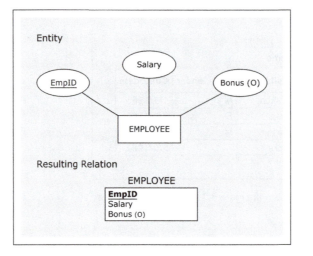

FIGURE 3.11 Entity with an optional attribute mapped into a relation.

EMPLOYEE

EmpID	Salary	Bonus
1234	$75,000	
2345	$45,000	$10,000
3456	$55,000	$4,000
1324	$70,000	

FIGURE 3.12 Sample data records for the relation shown in Figure 3.11.

MAPPING ENTITIES WITH OPTIONAL ATTRIBUTES INTO RELATIONS

Recall from Chapter 2 that entities can contain optional attributes—attributes that are allowed to be without a value. When optional attributes are mapped into relations, the resulting optional columns is marked as (O), as illustrated by the example shown in Figure 3.11.

Once the relation shown in Figure 3.11 is implemented as a part of a relational database, it can be populated with data, as shown in Figure 3.12. The Bonus attribute is optional and, accordingly, the rows without a value in the Bonus column are permitted.

Note that the first and last rows in the table EMPLOYEE shown in Figure 3.12 do not have any values entered in the Bonus column. In database terminology, an unfilled entry is also referred to as "null," which means "no value." Therefore, we can say that the first and last records have null values in the Bonus column.

ENTITY INTEGRITY CONSTRAINT

The term "constraint" refers to a rule that a relational database has to satisfy in order to be valid. The **entity integrity constraint** is a relational database rule that states that all primary key columns must have values.

Entity Integrity Constraint

In a relational table, no primary key column can have null (empty) values.

In other words, the entity integrity constraint is a rule stating that no primary key column can be optional. Every RDBMS enforces this rule.

For example, in Figure 3.13, every record in the relation EMPLOYEE must have a value in the EmpID column, because the EmpID column is the primary key. A missing value for EmpID constitutes a violation of the entity integrity constraint. A RDBMS would not allow a record to be inserted in the relation EMPLOYEE without a value for the EmpID column.

Similarly, in Figure 3.14, every record in the relation CLASSROOM must have a value in both the Building and RoomNumber columns, because both of these columns form a composite primary key.

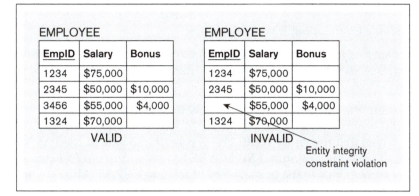

FIGURE 3.13   Entity integrity constraint—compliance and violation.

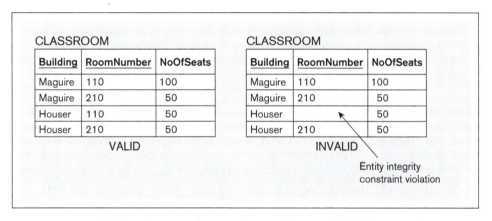

FIGURE 3.14   Entity integrity constraint—another compliance and violation example.

FOREIGN KEY

During the process of mapping ER diagrams into relational schemas, in addition to mapping entities, relationships also have to be mapped. The **foreign key** is a mechanism that is used to depict relationships in the relational database model. A foreign key is defined as follows:

Foreign Key

A foreign key is a column in a relation that refers to a primary key column in another (referred) relation.

For every occurrence of a foreign key, the relational schema contains a line pointing *from* the *foreign key to* the *corresponding primary key.*

Examples in this chapter will illustrate the foreign key concept, its depiction in the relational schema, and how it is used to implement the one-to-many (1:M), many-to-many (M:N), and one-to-one (1:1) relationships in the relational database model.

MAPPING RELATIONSHIPS INTO RELATIONAL DATABASE CONSTRUCTS

As we showed, entities in the ER diagram are mapped as relations. The following describes how the relationships are mapped into relational schema.

Mapping 1:M Relationships

Observe the rule for mapping 1:M relationships:

*The relation mapped from the **entity on the M side** of the 1:M relationship **has a foreign key** that corresponds to the primary key of the relation mapped from the 1 side of the 1:M relationship.*

The example in Figure 3.15 illustrates how this rule is applied. In the 1:M relationship ReportsTo, entity EMPLOYEE is on the M side and entity DEPARTMENT is on the 1 side. Given that the entity EMPLOYEE is on the M side of the 1:M relationship ReportsTo, the resulting relation EMPLOYEE has an additional foreign key column DeptID that corresponds to the primary key of relation DEPARTMENT. The relational schema in Figure 3.15 contains a line pointing from the foreign key column DeptID in the relation EMPLOYEE to the corresponding primary key column DeptID in the relation DEPARTMENT.

Once the relational schema shown in Figure 3.15 is implemented as a relational database, it can be populated with data, as shown in Figure 3.16.

Notice how the foreign key value (value of the column DeptID in the relation EMPLOYEE) connects each employee to the department he or she reports to.

We will now discuss the effect of optional and mandatory participation on the one and many side of a relationship in a resulting relational database.

MANDATORY PARTICIPATION ON THE 1 SIDE   Observe the effect of mandatory participation on the 1 side of a relationship. Note in Figure 3.15 that because the entity EMPLOYEE has a mandatory participation in the ReportsTo relationship, the DeptID foreign key column in relation EMPLOYEE is a required (non-optional) column. Therefore, in Figure 3.16, every row in relation EMPLOYEE has a value in the DeptID column. In other words, there are no null values in the DeptID column of the EMPLOYEE relation.

MANDATORY PARTICIPATION ON THE M SIDE   Observe the effect of mandatory participation on the M side of a relationship. Because of the mandatory participation on the M side of the ReportsTo relationship by the entity DEPARTMENT in Figure 3.15, in Figure 3.16 all the departments shown in the relation DEPARTMENT are referred to by at least one value in the DeptID column of the relation EMPLOYEE. In other words, there is no record in the DEPARTMENT relation that is not referred to by a record in the EMPLOYEE relation. Department (*1, Suite A*) is referred to by employees (*1234, Becky*) and (*3456, Rob*), while department (*2, Suite B*) is referred to by employees (*2345, Molly*) and (*1324, Ted*).

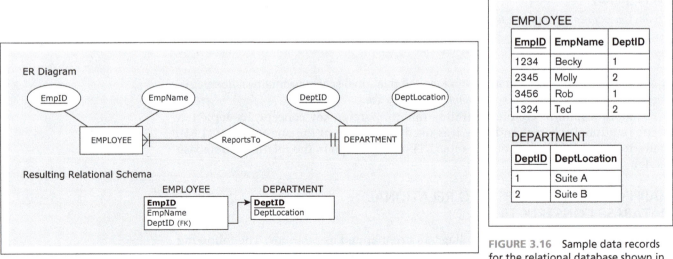

FIGURE 3.15   Mapping a 1:M relationship.

FIGURE 3.16   Sample data records for the relational database shown in Figure 3.15.

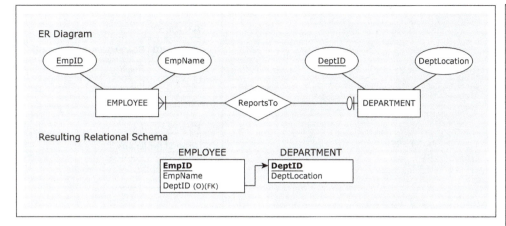

FIGURE 3.17   Mapping a 1:M relationship with optional participation on the 1 side.

EMPLOYEE

EmpID	EmpName	DeptID
1234	Becky	1
2345	Molly	2
3456	Rob	
1324	Ted	2

DEPARTMENT

DeptID	DeptLocation
1	Suite A
2	Suite B

FIGURE 3.18   Sample data records for the relational database shown in Figure 3.17.

OPTIONAL PARTICIPATION ON THE 1 SIDE   The effect of optional participation on the 1 side of a relationship is illustrated by the example in Figure 3.17. In this example, the entity EMPLOYEE has an optional participation in the ReportsTo relationship, and therefore, foreign key column DeptID in relation EMPLOYEE is an optional column.

Once the relational schema shown in Figure 3.17 is implemented as a relational database, it can be populated with data, as shown in Figure 3.18.

Notice that the EMPLOYEE table in Figure 3.18 differs from the EMPLOYEE table in Figure 3.16 because not every record has a value for the foreign key column DeptID. Employee (*3456, Rob*) does not have a DeptID value. DeptID is an optional column in relation EMPLOYEE due to the optional participation of the entity EMPLOYEE in the ReportsTo relationship in Figure 3.17.

OPTIONAL PARTICIPATION ON THE M SIDE   Let us now observe the case in which the participation on the M (many) side of a relationship is optional. This case is illustrated in Figures 3.19 and 3.20.

Once the relational schema shown in Figure 3.19 is implemented as a relational database, it can be populated with data, as shown in Figure 3.20.

Notice in Figure 3.20 that relation DEPARTMENT contains a department that no employee reports to—department (*3, Suite C*) has no one reporting to it. This is possible because of the optional participation on the M side of the ReportsTo relationship by the entity DEPARTMENT in Figure 3.19.

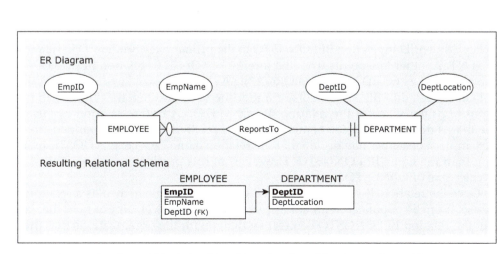

FIGURE 3.19   Mapping a 1:M relationship with optional participation on the M side.

EMPLOYEE

EmpID	EmpName	DeptID
1234	Becky	1
2345	Molly	2
3456	Rob	1
1324	Ted	2

DEPARTMENT

DeptID	DeptLocation
1	Suite A
2	Suite B
3	Suite C

FIGURE 3.20   Sample data records for the relational database shown in Figure 3.19.

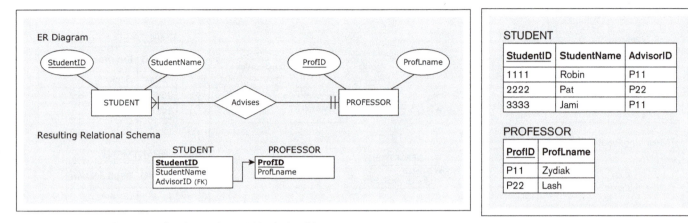

FIGURE 3.21   Another example of mapping a 1:M relationship.

FIGURE 3.22   Sample data records for the relational database shown in Figure 3.21.

RENAMING THE FOREIGN KEY   Figure 3.21 shows another example of mapping a 1:M relationship into a relational schema. Note that in this example, foreign key AdvisorID in relation STUDENT is renamed and no longer the same as the name of the primary key ProfID in the corresponding table PROFESSOR. Renaming a foreign key is perfectly legal. In this case, we renamed the foreign key to better illustrate the role of the professor's ID in the STUDENT relation in this scenario.

Once the relational schema shown in Figure 3.21 is implemented as a relational database, it can be populated with data, as shown in Figure 3.22.

Mapping M:N Relationships

Observe the rule for mapping M:N relationships:

*In addition to the two relations representing the two entities involved in the M:N relationship, **another relation** is created to **represent the M:N relationship itself**. This new relation has **two foreign keys**, corresponding to the primary keys of the two relations representing the two entities involved in the M:N relationship. The **two foreign keys form the composite primarykey** of the new relation.*

The example in Figure 3.23, showing an M:N relationship BelongsTo between entities STUDENT and ORGANIZATION, illustrates how this rule is applied. When the ER diagram in Figure 3.23 is mapped into a relational schema, in addition to relations STUDENT and ORGANIZATION, another relation BELONGSTO is created to represent the M:N relationship BelongsTo. The relation that represents an M:N relationship, such as relation BELONGSTO, is sometimes referred to as the **bridge relation**. The relation BELONGSTO has two foreign keys, each depicted by the lines pointing from each of the foreign keys to its source. One line points from the foreign key StudentID in relation BELONGSTO to the primary key StudentID in relation STUDENT. Another line points from the foreign key OrgID in relation BELONGSTO to the primary key OrgID in relation ORGANIZATION. Foreign keys StudentID and OrgID in the relation BELONGSTO are underlined because together they form the composite primary key of the relation BELONGSTO. (A bridge relation can use a name that is different than the name of the M:N relationship it was mapped from. For example, a designer may decide that the relation name PARTICIPATION is more fitting than the name BELONGSTO. However, in this particular case we will stay with the name BELONGSTO.)

Once the relational schema shown in Figure 3.23 is implemented as a relational database, it can be populated with data, as shown in Figure 3.24. Notice how the values in the relation BELONGSTO connect students with the organizations that they belong to.

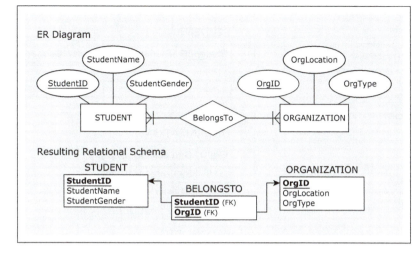

FIGURE 3.23 Mapping an M:N relationship.

If the entity STUDENT had optional participation in the BelongsTo relationship, then there could be additional students in the relation STUDENT whose IDs would not appear in the StudentID column of the BELONGSTO table. Similarly, if the entity ORGANIZATION had optional participation in the BelongsTo relationship, then there could be additional organizations in the relation ORGANIZATION whose IDs would not appear in the OrgID column of the BELONGSTO table. Such a scenario is illustrated by Figures 3.25 and 3.26. Figure 3.25 shows a BelongsTo relationship with optional participation on both sides. Once the relational schema shown in Figure 3.25 is implemented as a relational database, it can be populated with data, as shown in Figure 3.26. Notice that student (*4444, Abby*) does not belong to any organization. Also notice that organization (*O50, Damen Hall, Politics*) has no students. Such occurrences are possible because of optional participation on both sides of the relationship BelongsTo in Figure 3.25.

Recall from Chapter 2 that an M:N relationship can have its own attributes. When an M:N relationship with its own attributes is mapped into the relational model, the relation representing the M:N relationship includes a column for every attribute of the M:N

STUDENT

StudentID	StudentName	StudentGender
1111	Robin	Male
2222	Pat	Male
3333	Jami	Female

ORGANIZATION

OrgID	OrgLocation	OrgType
O11	Student Hall	Charity
O41	Damen Hall	Sport
O47	Student Hall	Charity

BELONGSTO

StudentID	OrgID
1111	O11
1111	O41
2222	O11
2222	O41
2222	O47
3333	O11

FIGURE 3.24 Sample data records for the relational database shown in Figure 3.23.

STUDENT

StudentID	StudentName	StudentGender
1111	Robin	Male
2222	Pat	Male
3333	Jami	Female
4444	Abby	Female

ORGANIZATION

OrgID	OrgLocation	OrgType
O11	Student Hall	Charity
O41	Damen Hall	Sport
O47	Student Hall	Charity
O50	Damen Hall	Politics

BELONGSTO

StudentID	OrgID
1111	O11
1111	O41
2222	O11
2222	O41
2222	O47
3333	O11

FIGURE 3.26 Sample data records for the relational database shown in Figure 3.25.

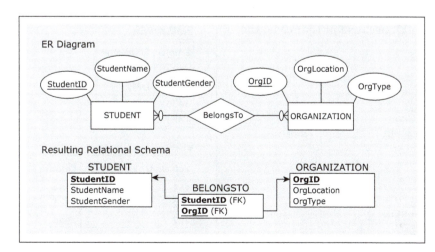

FIGURE 3.25 Mapping an M:N relationship (optional participation on both sides).

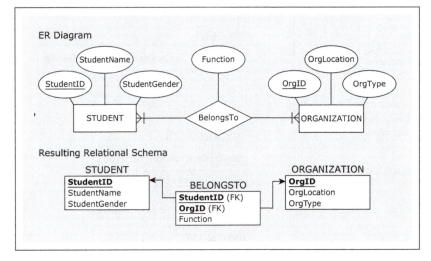

FIGURE 3.27   Mapping an M:N relationship with an attribute.

relationship being mapped. Figure 3.27 illustrates such a scenario.

Once the relational schema shown in Figure 3.27 is implemented as a relational database, it can be populated with data, as shown in Figure 3.28.

Mapping 1:1 Relationships

1:1 relationships are mapped in much the same way as 1:M relationships. One of the resulting relations has a foreign key pointing to the primary key of the other resulting relation. When mapping 1:M relationships, we have to follow the rule that states that the primary key of the relation mapped from the 1 side becomes a foreign key of the relation mapped from the M side. In a 1:1 relationship, maximum cardinalities of both entities are 1. Therefore, we simply choose one of the mapped relations to have a foreign key referring to the primary key of the other mapped relation.

In cases when there is no particular advantage in choosing which resulting relation will include a foreign key, the choice can be arbitrary. In other cases, one choice can be more efficient than the other. For example, whenever there is a choice between an optional and a mandatory foreign key, choosing the mandatory foreign key is recommended. Consider Figures 3.29 and 3.30, which illustrate mapping of a 1:1 relationship. We chose the relation VEHICLE to include the foreign key EmpID, because in that case, the

STUDENT

StudentID	StudentName	StudentGender
1111	Robin	Male
2222	Pat	Male
3333	Jami	Female

ORGANIZATION

OrgID	OrgLocation	OrgType
O11	Student Hall	Charity
O41	Damen Hall	Sport
O47	Student Hall	Charity

BELONGSTO

StudentID	OrgID	Function
1111	O11	President
1111	O41	Member
2222	O11	V.P.
2222	O41	Member
2222	O47	Treasurer
3333	O11	Member

FIGURE 3.28   Sample data records for the relational database shown in Figure 3.27.

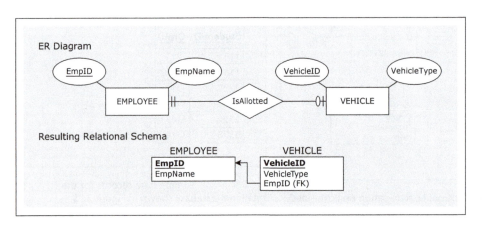

FIGURE 3.29   Mapping a 1:1 relationship.

EMPLOYEE

EmpID	EmpName
1234	Becky
2345	Molly
3456	Rob
1324	Ted

VEHICLE

VehicleID	Vehicletype	EmpID
111	Sedan	1234
222	Van	2345
222	Van	3456

FIGURE 3.30   Sample data records for the relational database shown in Figure 3.29.

foreign key will be required. The only other option would have been to have relation EMPLOYEE include the foreign key VehicleID, and in that case the foreign key would have been optional, and as a result the foreign key column may contain a number of null values. Optional foreign keys are legal (as illustrated by Figures 3.17 and 3.18), but if we have a choice between creating a relation with an optional or required foreign key (as illustrated in Figure 3.29), the required foreign key is a preferred choice.

REFERENTIAL INTEGRITY CONSTRAINT

The term **referential integrity constraint** refers to the relational database rule that defines values that are valid for use in foreign keys.

Referential Integrity Constraint

*In each row of a relation containing a foreign key, the value of the **foreign key EITHER matches** one of the values in the **primary key** column of the referred relation **OR** the value of the **foreign key is null** (empty).*

The above definition allows for the possibility of a foreign key value not being entered. Such cases are allowed when the relationship being implemented with the foreign key has optional participation by the entity whose resulting mapped relation contains the foreign key. To illustrate the referential integrity constraint definition, we will use the example relational schema shown in Figure 3.17.

In the ER diagram in Figure 3.17, the entity EMPLOYEE has an optional participation in the relationship with the entity DEPARTMENT. In the resulting schema relation EMPLOYEE has a foreign key DeptID. Figure 3.31 illustrates several cases of compliance with and violation of referential integrity constraints for the scenario presented in Figure 3.17.

In the top example in Figure 3.31, all foreign key values in the EMPLOYEE relation refer to existing primary key values in the relation DEPARTMENT, and therefore, there is no violation of the referential integrity constraint.

In the middle example in Figure 3.31, all entered foreign key values in the EMPLOYEE relation refer to existing primary key values in the relation DEPARTMENT. One of the foreign key values is null, which is also in compliance with the referential integrity constraint (and with the optional participation of the EMPLOYEE entity in the relationship shown in Figure 3.17).

In the bottom example in Figure 3.31, one of the entered foreign key values in the EMPLOYEE relation (DeptID = 4) does not refer to any of the existing primary key values in the relation DEPARTMENT, which is a violation of the referential integrity constraint.

Recall that the relational schema is composed of the relations and the lines connecting the relations by pointing from the foreign keys to the corresponding primary keys. Because each line pointing from the foreign key to the corresponding primary key indicates an instance that is regulated by a referential integrity constraint, it is common to refer to such lines in the relational schema as **referential integrity constraint lines**.

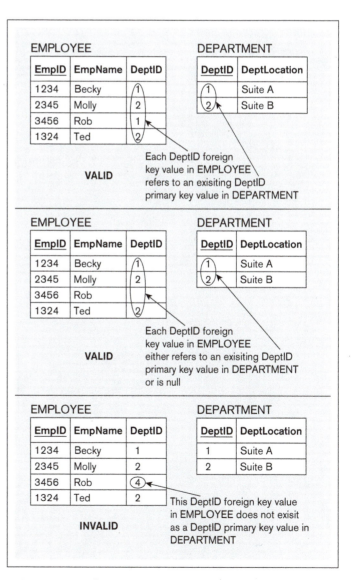

FIGURE 3.31 Referential integrity constraint—compliance and violation examples.

EXAMPLE: MAPPING AN ER DIAGRAM INTO A RELATIONAL SCHEMA

We now present an example that summarizes the rules we have covered so far for mapping ER diagram constructs into relational database constructs. Figure 3.32 shows a relational schema resulting from mapping the ZAGI Retail Company Sales Department Database ER diagram (shown in Figure 2.13 in the previous chapter, repeated here for convenience).

The ER diagram has seven entities and one M:N relationship. Consequently, the relational schema has eight relations, one for each of the entities and one for the M:N relationship.

Once the relational schema shown in Figure 3.32 is implemented as a relational database, it can be populated with data, as shown in Figure 3.33.

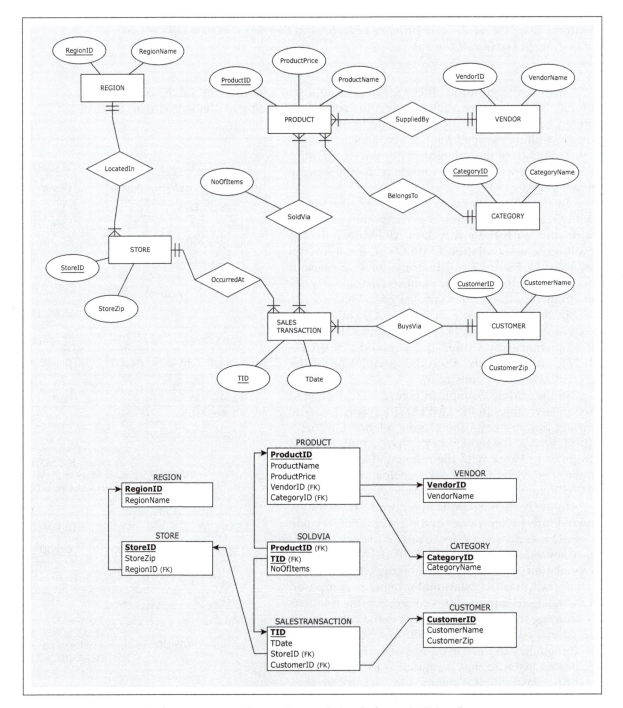

FIGURE 3.32   An example of mapping an ER diagram into a relational schema: ZAGI Retail.

REGION

RegionID	RegionName
C	Chicagoland
T	Tristate

STORE

StoreID	StoreZip	RegionID
S1	60600	C
S2	60605	C
S3	35400	T

PRODUCT

ProductID	ProductName	ProductPrice	VendorID	CategoryID
1X1	Zzz Bag	$100	PG	CP
2X2	Easy Boot	$70	MK	FW
3X3	Cosy Sock	$15	MK	FW
4X4	Dura Boot	$90	PG	FW
5X5	Tiny Tent	$150	MK	CP
6X6	Biggy Tent	$250	MK	CP

VENDOR

VendorID	VendorName
PG	Pacifica Gear
MK	Mountain King

CATEGORY

CategoryID	CategoryName
CP	Camping
FW	Footwear

SALES TRANSACTION

TID	CustomerID	StoreID	TDate
T111	1-2-333	S1	1-Jan-2013
T222	2-3-444	S2	1-Jan-2013
T333	1-2-333	S3	2-Jan-2013
T444	3-4-555	S3	2-Jan-2013
T555	2-3-444	S3	2-Jan-2013

SOLDVIA

ProductID	TID	NoOfItems
1X1	T111	1
2X2	T222	1
3X3	T333	5
1X1	T333	1
4X4	T444	1
2X2	T444	2
4X4	T555	4
5X5	T555	2
6X6	T555	1

CUSTOMER

CustomerID	CustomerName	CustomerZip
1-2-333	Tina	60137
2-3-444	Tony	60611
3-4-555	Pam	35401

FIGURE 3.33 Sample data records for the ZAGI Retail Company Sales Department Database shown in Figure 3.32.

MAPPING ENTITIES WITH CANDIDATE KEYS (MULTIPLE UNIQUE ATTRIBUTES) INTO RELATIONS

Recall from Chapter 2 that an entity can have more than one unique attribute. In such cases, each unique attribute is also called a "candidate key." The term "candidate key" comes from the fact that one of the candidate keys has to be chosen by the database designer as a primary key during the entity-to-relation mapping process, while the other candidate keys are mapped as non-primary-key columns. An example of mapping an entity with candidate keys is shown in Figure 3.34.

In a relational schema, only the primary keys are underlined, while the other columns are not underlined. In the mapped relation in Figure 3.34 only EmpID is underlined, because it was chosen as the primary key. Consequently, SSN is not underlined because it is not a primary key of this relation. However, we can still mark the non-primary key columns as unique by showing the letter U in parentheses next to the names of unique non-primary key columns.

Once the relation shown in Figure 3.34 is implemented as a part of a relational database, it can be populated with data, as shown in Figure 3.35.

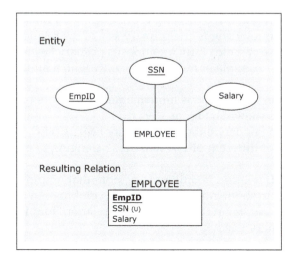

FIGURE 3.34 Entity with candidate keys mapped into a relation.

EMPLOYEE

EmpID	SSN	Salary
1234	111-11-1111	$75,000
2345	222-22-2222	$50,000
3456	333-33-3333	$55,000
1324	444-44-4444	$70,000

FIGURE 3.35 Sample data records for the relation shown in Figure 3.34.

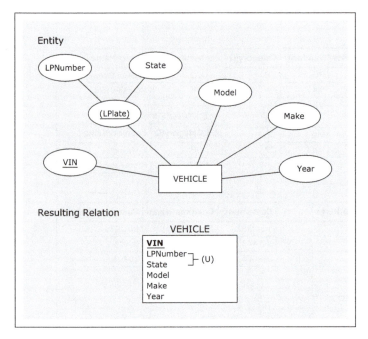

FIGURE 3.36 Entity with regular and composite candidate keys mapped into a relation.

FIGURE 3.37 Sample data records for the relation shown in Figure 3.36.

VEHICLE

VIN	LPNumber	State	Make	Model	Year
11111	X123	IL	Ford	Fiesta	2012
22222	X456	IL	Ford	Escape	2009
33333	X123	MI	Chevrolet	Volt	2012

In cases when the table has both composite and regular (non-composite) candidate keys, choosing a non-composite primary key is usually a preferred choice. Such a case is illustrated by the example in Figure 3.36.

Columns LPNumber (License Plate Number) and State are marked together as components of a composite unique attribute of the relation VEHICLE. Column VIN (Vehicle Identification Number) was chosen as the primary key since it is a non-composite unique attribute.

Once the relation shown in Figure 3.36 is implemented as a part of a relational database, it can be populated with data, as shown in Figure 3.37.

MAPPING ENTITIES WITH MULTIVALUED ATTRIBUTES INTO RELATIONAL DATABASE CONSTRUCTS

As we mentioned in Chapter 2, multivalued attributes are used in cases when instances of an entity can have multiple values for the same attribute. An entity containing the multivalued attribute is mapped without the multivalued attribute. The multivalued attribute is mapped as a separate relation that has a column representing the multivalued attribute and a foreign key column referring to the primary key of the relation resulting from the entity itself. Both of these columns form a composite primary key for the separate relation. Figure 3.38 shows an example of mapping an entity with a multivalued attribute.

Once the relational schema shown in Figure 3.38 is implemented as a relational database, it can be populated with data, as shown in Figure 3.39.

Because of the multivalued attribute PhoneNumber of the entity EMPLOYEE, in the EMPPHONE relation, multiple rows of different phone numbers belonging to the same employee are possible.

Neither column in the EMPPHONE relation is unique (e.g., note that employees *1234*, *3456*, and *1324* share one of their phone numbers) but each combination of EmpID and PhoneNumber is unique. Therefore, in the EMPPHONE relation, EmpID and PhoneNumber form a composite primary key.

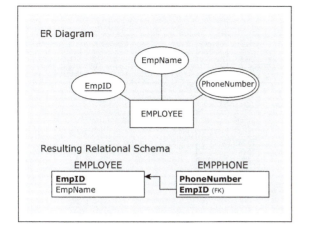

FIGURE 3.38 Entity with a multivalued attribute mapped into a relation.

EMPLOYEE

EmpID	EName
1234	Becky
2345	Molly
3456	Rob
1324	Ted

EMPPHONE

EmpID	PhoneNumber
1234	630-111-4567
1234	630-222-4567
2345	630-333-4567
3456	630-111-4567
3456	630-444-4567
1324	630-111-4567
1324	630-555-4567
1324	630-666-4567

FIGURE 3.39 Sample data records for the relational database shown in Figure 3.38.

MAPPING ENTITIES WITH DERIVED ATTRIBUTES INTO RELATIONS

Recall from Chapter 2 that a derived attribute is an attribute whose value is not permanently stored in a database. Instead, the value of a derived attribute is calculated from the stored values of other attributes and/or additional available data, such as current date. Derived attributes are not mapped as a part of the relational schema, as illustrated by Figure 3.40.

Once the relation shown in Figure 3.40 is implemented as a part of a relational database, it can be populated with data, as shown in Figure 3.41.

Even though derived attributes are not part of the relational schema, they can be implemented as a part of the application based on the created relational database. For example, a front-end application based on the database that contains the STORE relation shown in Figure 3.41 includes an additional calculated column YearsInBusiness that uses a formula extracting the number of years from the expression ((Current Date) – (OpeningDate)). This is illustrated by Figure 3.42, which shows how a user would see this relation in the summer of 2013 in a front-end application.

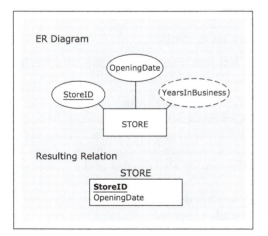

FIGURE 3.40 Entity with a derived attribute mapped into a relation.

STORE (RELATION)

StoreID	OpeningDate
1111	1.1.2000
2222	2.2.2001
3333	3.3.2002
4444	2.2.2001

FIGURE 3.41 Sample data records for the relation shown in Figure 3.40.

STORE

Sid	OpeningDate	YearsInBusiness
1111	1.1.2000	13
2222	2.2.2001	12
3333	3.3.2002	11
4444	2.2.2001	12

FIGURE 3.42 The relation shown in Figure 3.41 as presented to a user in a front-end application.

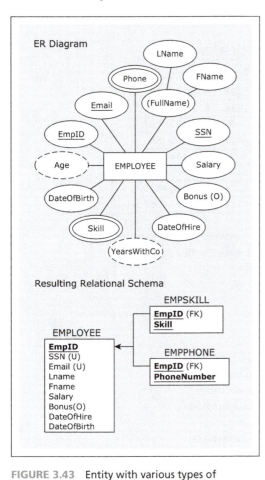

FIGURE 3.43 Entity with various types of attributes mapped into a relation.

EMPLOYEE

EmpID	SSN	Email	FName	LName	Salary	Bonus	DateOfHire	DateOfBirth
1234	111-11-1111	bk@compx.com	Becky	Kaiser	$75,000		1.1.2002	11.12.1970
2345	222-22-2222	mn@compx.com	Molly	Neps	$50,000	$10,000	2.2.2002	9.8.1973
3456	333-33-3333	rd@compx.com	Rob	Duzs	$55,000	$4,000	3.4.2003	11.11.1976
1324	444-44-4444	ti@compx.com	Ted	Lovett	$70,000		9.8.2004	5.6.1971

EMPPHONE

EmpID	PhoneNumber
1234	630-111-4567
1234	630-222-4567
2345	630-333-4567
3456	630-111-4567
3456	630-444-4567
1324	630-111-4567
1324	630-555-4567
1324	630-666-4567

EMPSKILL

EmpID	Skill
1234	CPA
1234	CFP
2345	CPA
3456	CPA
3456	CFP
3456	CPP
1324	CFP

FIGURE 3.44   Sample data records for the relational database shown in Figure 3.43.

EXAMPLE: MAPPING AN ENTITY CONTAINING VARIOUS TYPES OF ATTRIBUTES INTO A RELATIONAL SCHEMA

To summarize the rules for mapping various types of attributes, Figure 3.43 shows a relational schema resulting from mapping the entity EMPLOYEE (shown in Figure 2.25 in the previous chapter, repeated here for convenience).

Once the relational schema shown in Figure 3.43 is implemented as a relational database, it can be populated with data, as shown in Figure 3.44.

MAPPING UNARY RELATIONSHIPS

Unary relationships in ER diagrams are mapped into a relational schema in the same way as binary relationships, using a foreign key in cases of 1:M and 1:1 relationships, and using a new relation with two foreign keys in the case of an M:N relationship. Here we describe and illustrate the mapping of 1:M, M:N, and 1:1 unary relationships.

Mapping 1:M Unary Relationships

The following is the rule for mapping 1:M unary relationships.

*The relation mapped from an entity involved in a 1:M unary relationship contains a **foreign key** that **corresponds to its own primary key**.*

Figure 3.45 illustrates the mapping of a 1:M unary relationship.

Note that the foreign key column ReferredBy has a name that is different from the corresponding primary key column ClientID, which is a legal practice as already mentioned in this chapter. In fact, in this case, renaming is necessary since no two columns in the same relation can have the same name. Renaming also illustrates the role of the foreign key in the table.

Also note that, because of the optional participation on the 1 side of the Refers relationship, the foreign key ReferredBy is optional.

Once the relation shown in Figure 3.45 is implemented as part of the relational database, it can be populated with data, as shown in Figure 3.46.

Note that in Figure 3.46 we have a client (*C111*) that is not referred by anyone, and two clients (*C333* and *C444*) that do not refer anyone. This is possible because the relationship Refers in Figure 3.45 is optional on both sides.

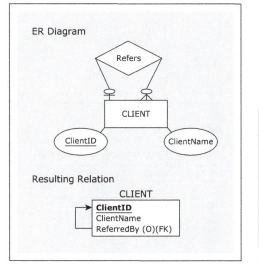

FIGURE 3.45   Mapping a 1:M unary relationship.

CLIENT

ClientID	ClientName	ReferredBy
C111	Mark	
C222	Mike	C111
C333	Lilly	C111
C444	Jane	C222

FIGURE 3.46   Sample data records for the relation shown in Figure 3.45.

Mapping M:N Unary Relationships

The following is the rule for mapping M:N unary relationships.

In addition to the relation representing the entity involved in a unary M:N relationship, **another relation** *is created to* **represent the M:N relationship itself.** *This new relation has* **two foreign keys,** *both of them corresponding to the primary key of the relation representing the entity involved in the unary M:N relationship. Each of the* **foreign keys is used as a part of the composite primary key** *of the new relation.*

Figure 3.47 illustrates the mapping of an M:N unary relationship.

Both of the foreign keys are renamed in order to illustrate their roles in the relation ADVISING. Once the relational schema shown in Figure 3.47 is implemented as a relational database, it can be populated with data, as shown in Figure 3.48.

Because the relationship Advises in Figure 3.47 is optional on both ends, in the relation EMPLOYEE we can have employees who are not advisors (*1324, Ted*), and we can also have employees who are not advisees (*1234, Becky*).

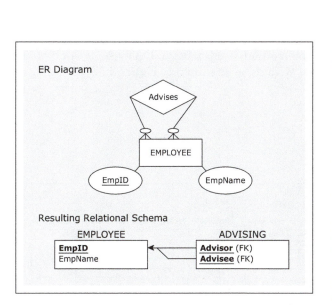

FIGURE 3.47   Mapping an M:N unary relationship.

EMPLOYEE

EmpID	EmpName
1234	Becky
2345	Molly
3456	Rob
1324	Ted

ADVISING

Advisor	Advisee
1234	2345
1234	3456
2345	1324
3456	1324
1234	1324

FIGURE 3.48   Sample data records for the relational schema shown in Figure 3.47.

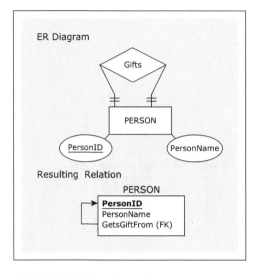

FIGURE 3.49 Mapping a 1:1 unary relationship.

PERSON

PersonID	PersonName	GetsGiftFrom
P111	Rose	P333
P222	Violet	P111
P333	James	P444
P444	Lena	P222

FIGURE 3.50 Sample data records for the relation shown in Figure 3.49.

Mapping 1:1 Unary Relationships

1:1 unary relationships are mapped in the same way as 1:M unary relationships, as illustrated by the example shown in Figure 3.49. This example depicts a gift-giving event (Secret Santa) where each person gives a gift to exactly one person, and each person receives a gift from exactly one person.

Once the relation shown in Figure 3.49 is implemented as a part of a relational database, it can be populated with data, as shown in Figure 3.50.

Note that because the Gifts relationship has mandatory participation on both sides, each person gives a gift and each person receives a gift, as illustrated by the records in table PERSON in Figure 3.50.

MAPPING MULTIPLE RELATIONSHIPS BETWEEN THE SAME ENTITIES

As we noted in Chapter 2, it is not unusual for the same entities in an ER diagram to be related via more than one relationship. Figure 3.51 shows an example of mapping multiple relationships between the same entities.

Note that the relation PACKAGE has two foreign keys, both of which refer to the primary key in the relation EMPLOYEE. Both of the foreign keys are renamed in order to illustrate their roles in the relation EMPLOYEE.

Once the relational schema shown in Figure 3.51 is implemented as a relational database, it can be populated with data, as shown in Figure 3.52.

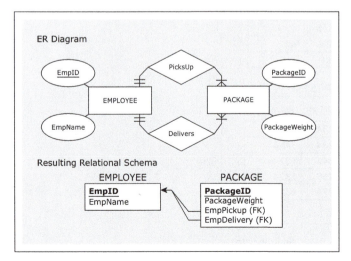

FIGURE 3.51 Mapping multiple relationships between the same entities.

EMPLOYEE

EmpID	EmpName
1234	Becky
2345	Molly
3456	Rob
1324	Ted

PACKAGE

PackageID	PackageWeight	EmpPickup	EmpDelivery
P111	5	1234	2345
P222	12	1234	1324
P333	3	2345	1234
P444	10	3456	1234
P555	7	1324	3456

FIGURE 3.52 Sample data records for the relational schema shown in Figure 3.51.

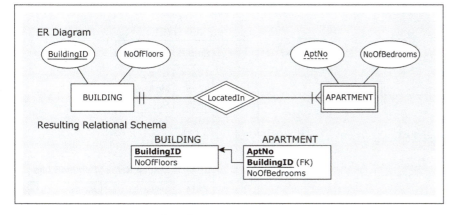

FIGURE 3.53   Mapping a weak entity.

MAPPING WEAK ENTITIES

Weak entities are mapped in a similar way as regular entities with one small addition. The resulting relation has a composite primary key that is composed of the partial identifier *and* the foreign key corresponding to the primary key of the owner entity. Figure 3.53 illustrates the mapping of a weak entity.

Once the relational schema shown in Figure 3.53 is implemented as a relational database, it can be populated with data, as shown in Figure 3.54.

As shown in Figure 3.54, one owner entity instance can be associated with multiple weak entity instances, as long as each of them has a different partial key value. For example, in the relation APARTMENT in Figure 3.54, Building *A* has three apartments, and they each have a different apartment number. The combination of the partial key AptNo and the BuildingID is the primary key for the relation APARTMENT.

Weak entities can have multiple owners. In that case, the relation that results from mapping the weak entity will have a composite primary key composed of the partial identifier and the foreign keys corresponding to the primary keys of all owner entities. Figure 3.55 illustrates the mapping of a weak entity with two owners.

Note that the relation COMPLETION has two foreign keys from the two relations that result from the two owner entities of the weak entity COMPLETION. Those two keys, combined with the partial identifier Semester, form a composite key of the relation COMPLETION.

Once the relational schema shown in Figure 3.55 is implemented as a relational database, it can be populated with data, as shown in Figure 3.56.

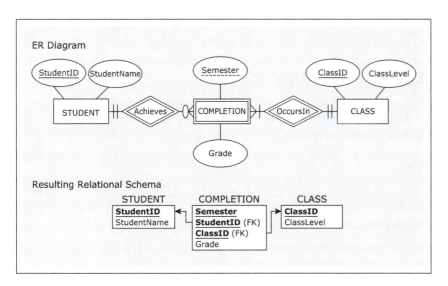

FIGURE 3.55   Mapping a weak entity with two owners.

BUILDING

BuildingID	NoOfFloors
A	3
B	2
C	2

APARTMENT

BuildingID	AptNo	NoOfBedrooms
A	101	4
A	201	4
A	301	5
B	101	2
B	201	2
C	101	3
C	102	3
C	201	4

FIGURE 3.54   Sample data records for the relational schema shown in Figure 3.53.

STUDENT

StudentID	StudentName
1111	Robin
2222	Pat
3333	Jami

CLASS

ClassID	ClassLevel
IS101	Freshman
IS241	Sophomore
IS247	Sophomore

COMPLETION

StudentID	ClassID	Semester	Grade
1111	IS101	Spring10	D
1111	IS101	Spring11	D
1111	IS101	Spring12	A
1111	IS241	Fall12	B
2222	IS101	Fall12	A
2222	IS241	Fall12	C
2222	IS247	Spring13	B
3333	IS101	Fall12	A

FIGURE 3.56   Sample data records for the relational schema shown in Figure 3.55.

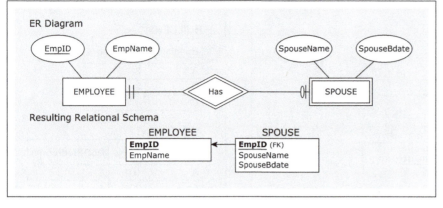

FIGURE 3.57 Mapping a weak entity with no partial identifier.

EMPLOYEE

EmpID	EmpName
1234	Becky
2345	Molly
3456	Rob
1324	Ted

SPOUSE

EmpID	SpouseName	SpouseBdate
1234	Steve	Jan 18
3456	Luchy	Jun 21
1324	Tina	Feb 11

FIGURE 3.58 Sample data records for the relational schema shown in Figure 3.57.

Recall from Chapter 2 that this example depicts a scenario where students can take the same class multiple times until they receive a minimum passing grade of C. So, for example, the student *1111* took the *IS101* class three times. The first two times he received a grade of *D*, and then in his third attempt he received a grade of *A*.

In cases when an identifying relationship is a 1:1 relationship, a weak entity has no partial identifier. In such cases, the primary key of the relation mapped from the owner entity becomes the primary key of the relation mapped from the weak entity as well. Figure 3.57 illustrates the mapping of a weak entity with a 1:1 identifying relationship.

Since the entity SPOUSE has no partial identifier, in the relation SPOUSE the foreign key also serves as its primary key, instead of being combined with the partial key into a composite primary key.

Once the relational schema shown in Figure 3.57 is implemented as a relational database, it can be populated with data, as shown in Figure 3.58.

EXAMPLE: MAPPING ANOTHER ER DIAGRAM INTO A RELATIONAL SCHEMA

To recap the ERD-to-Relational Schema mapping rules introduced in this chapter, Figure 3.59 shows a relational schema resulting from mapping the HAFH Realty Company Property Management Database ER diagram (shown in Figure 2.38 in the previous chapter, repeated here for convenience).

The ER diagram has six entities and two M:N relationships. One of the entities has a multivalued attribute. Consequently, the relational schema has nine relations, one for each of the entities, two for the M:N relationships, and one for the multivalued attribute.

Once the relational schema shown in Figure 3.59 is implemented as a relational database, it can be populated with data, as shown in Figure 3.60.

RELATIONAL DATABASE CONSTRAINTS

As stated earlier, a constraint specifies a rule that a relational database has to satisfy in order to be valid. Relational database rules fit into one of the two categories: **implicit constraints** and **user-defined constraints**.

Implicit Constraints

The implicit relational database model rules that a relational database has to satisfy in order to be valid are known as implicit constraints. The following is a list of the relational database rules that fit into the category of implicit constraints.

- *Each relation in a relational schema must have a different name.*
- *Each relation must satisfy the following conditions:*
  - *each column must have a different name*
  - *each row must be unique*

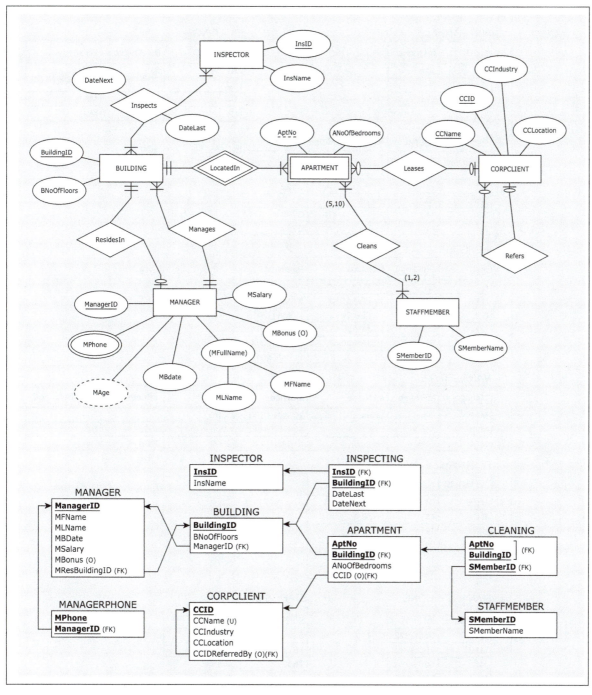

FIGURE 3.59   Another example of mapping an ER diagram into a relational schema: HAFH Realty

- *in each row, each value in each column must be single valued*
- *all values in each column must be from the same predefined domain (this restriction is also known as **domain constraint**)*
- *the order of columns is irrelevant*
- *the order of rows is irrelevant*
- *Each relation must have a primary key, which is a column (or a set of columns) whose value is unique for each row (this restriction is also known as the **primary key constraint**).*
- *No primary key column can have null values (**entity integrity constraint**).*
- *In each row of a relation containing a foreign key, the value of the foreign key either matches one of the values in the primary key column of the referred relation or the value of the foreign key is null (**referential integrity constraint**).*

INSPECTOR

InsID	InsName
I11	Jane
I22	Niko
I33	Mick

BUILDING

BuildingID	BNoOfFloors	BManagerID
B1	5	M12
B2	6	M23
B3	4	M23
B4	4	M34

APARTMENT

BuildingID	AptNo	ANoOfBedrooms	CCID
B1	41	1	
B1	21	1	C111
B2	11	2	C222
B2	31	2	
B3	11	2	C777
B4	11	2	C777

INSPECTING

InsID	BuildingID	DateLast	DateNext
I11	B1	15-MAY-2012	14-MAY-2013
I11	B2	17-FEB-2013	17-MAY-2013
I22	B2	17-FEB-2013	17-MAY-2013
I22	B3	11-JAN-2013	11-JAN-2014
I33	B3	12-JAN-2013	12-JAN-2014
I33	B4	11-JAN-2013	11-JAN-2014

MANAGER

ManagerID	MFName	MLName	MBDate	MSalary	MBonus	MResBuildingID
M12	Boris	Grant	20-JUN-1980	60000		B1
M23	Austin	Lee	30-OCT-1975	50000	5000	B2
M34	George	Sherman	11-JAN-1976	52000	2000	B4

CLEANING

BuildingID	AptNo	SMemberID
B1	21	5432
B1	41	9876
B2	11	9876
B2	31	5432
B3	11	5432
B4	11	7652

MANAGERPHONE

ManagerID	MPhone
M12	555-2222
M12	555-3232
M23	555-9988
M34	555-9999

STAFFMEMBER

SMemberID	SMemberName
5432	Brian
9876	Boris
7652	Caroline

CORPCLIENT

CCID	CCName	CCIndustry	CCLocation	CCIDReferredBy
C111	BlingNotes	Music	Chicago	
C222	SkyJet	Airline	Oak Park	C111
C777	WindyCT	Music	Chicago	C222
C888	SouthAlps	Sports	Rosemont	C777

FIGURE 3.60 Sample data records for the HAFH Realty Company Property Management Database shown in Figure 3.59.

User–Defined Constraints

In addition to the implicit constraints, designers of a relational database can add other constraints specific to the database that is being developed. Such an added constraint is known as a "user-defined constraint." Here we will show a few examples of user-defined constraints (and in Chapter 6 we will show the mechanisms for enforcing user-defined constraints in implemented databases.)

An example of a user-defined constraint is specifying an optional attribute in the ER diagram and the subsequently mapped relational schema. For example, the designer specified that the attribute Bonus is optional in entity EMPLOYEE and in the relation EMPLOYEE in Figures 3.11 and 3.12, respectively.

Another example of a user-defined constraint is specifying a mandatory foreign key, such as in the example illustrated in Figures 3.15 and 3.16. In this example column, DeptID in the relation EMPLOYEE is mandatory, due to the mandatory participation on the 1 side in the relationship ReportsTo by the entity EMPLOYEE.

The same example shown in Figures 3.15 and 3.16 contains another user-defined constraint, a restriction on the relation DEPARTMENT, in which each row must be referred to by at least one foreign key in the relation EMPLOYEE. This is due to the mandatory participation on the M side by the entity DEPARTMENT in the relationship ReportsTo. Note that the same restriction does not exist in the example shown in Figures 3.19 and 3.20, due to the optional participation on the M side in the relationship ReportsTo by the entity DEPARTMENT.

Other examples of user-defined constraints specifying the exact minimum and maximum cardinality are shown in Figures 3.61 and 3.62.

Once the relational schema shown in Figure 3.61 is implemented as a relational database, it can be populated with data, as shown in Figure 3.62. Notice that the entered records are in compliance with the constraints specifying the minimum and maximum cardinality on both sides of the relationship, since each class has five students and each student is taking two classes. As we mentioned previously, we will show the mechanisms for enforcing such constraints in Chapter 6.

So far, the user-defined constraints we mentioned were specified as part of the ER diagram. Another category of user-defined constraints, called **business rules**, specify restrictions on resulting databases that are not a part of the standard notation for creating ER diagrams. Business rules can be added as notes (e.g., footnotes, comments, special symbols, or other types of notes) accompanying the diagrams or listed in separate documentation.

For example, a business rule specifying that no employee can have a salary under *$50,000* or over *$200,000* can be added as a footnote to an ER diagram, as shown in Figure 3.63.

Once the relation shown in Figure 3.63 is implemented as a part of a relational database, it can be populated with data, as shown in Figure 3.64. The entered records

STUDENT

StudentID	SName
1111	Robin
2222	Pat
3333	Jami
4444	Zach
5555	Louie

CLASS

ClassID	ClassLevel
IS346	Junior
IS401	Senior

ENROLLSIN

StudentID	ClassID
1111	IS346
2222	IS346
3333	IS346
4444	IS346
5555	IS346
1111	IS401
2222	IS401
3333	IS401
4444	IS401
5555	IS401

FIGURE 3.62 Sample data records for the relational database shown in Figure 3.61.

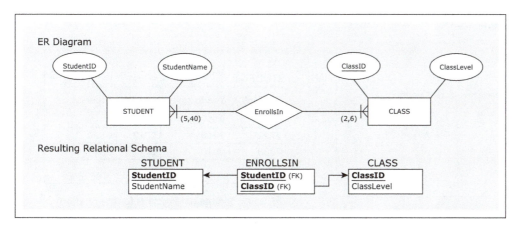

FIGURE 3.61 Specific minimum and maximum cardinalities.

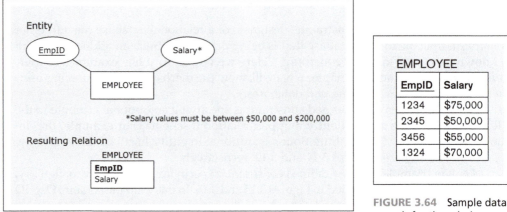

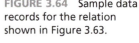

FIGURE 3.63   Business rule for salary amounts.

FIGURE 3.64   Sample data records for the relation shown in Figure 3.63.

are in compliance with the business rule that specifies that no employee can have a salary under *$50,000* or over *$200,000*.

In another example shown in Figure 3.65, a business rule specifies that the year of a student's graduation cannot precede the year of the student's enrollment.

Once the relational schema shown in Figure 3.65 is implemented as a relational database, it can be populated with data, as shown in Figure 3.66. The entered records are in compliance with the business rule that specifies that the year of a student's graduation cannot precede the year of the student's enrollment.

Another example shown in Figure 3.67 includes a business rule specifying that every student organization must have both *male* and *female* students.

Once the relational schema shown in Figure 3.67 is implemented as a relational database, it can be populated with data, as shown in Figure 3.68. The entered records are in compliance with the constraint that every student organization must have both male and female students. A mechanism would verify the compliance of the database with this business rule once the initial data, representing initial memberships in the organizations, is inserted in all three tables.

In Chapter 6, we will discuss the means and methods for enforcing business rules (such as the ones illustrated in examples above) in implemented databases.

This chapter has presented the most fundamental issues related to relational database modeling. The following notes cover several additional issues related to relational database modeling.

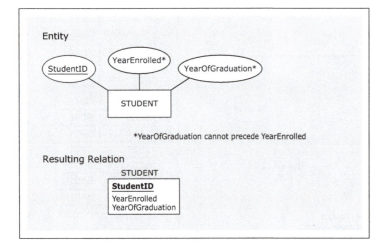

FIGURE 3.65   Business rule for the dates of enrollment and graduation.

STUDENT

StudentID	YearEnrolled	YearOfGraduation
1111	2012	2016
2222	2013	2017
3333	2013	2017

FIGURE 3.66   Sample data records for the relation shown in Figure 3.65.

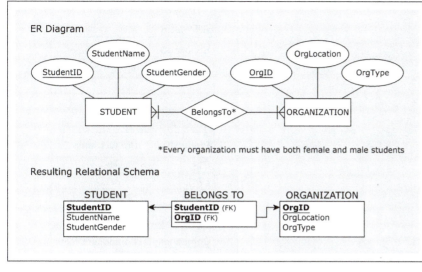

FIGURE 3.67   Business rule for gender of students in an organization.

A Note About Mapping Associative Entities

Recall from Chapter 2 that an associative entity is an ER modeling construct used as an alternative way of depicting M:N relationships. Consequently, associative entities are mapped into relational database constructs in the identical way as M:N relationships. In both cases, an additional relation is created, with two foreign keys pointing to the relations mapped from entities involved in the M:N relationship. These two foreign keys form a composite primary key for the additional relation.

Figure 3.69 illustrates how an M:N relationship and its associative entity version would be mapped in the identical way into a relational schema.

STUDENT

StudentID	StudentName	StudentGender
1111	Robin	M
2222	Pat	M
3333	Jami	F

ORGANIZATION

OrgID	OrgLocation	OrgType
O11	Student Hall	Charity
O41	Damen Hall	Sport
O47	Student Hall	Charity

BELONGSTO

StudentID	OrgID
1111	O11
3333	O11
2222	O11
3333	O41
2222	O41
3333	O47
1111	O47

FIGURE 3.68   Sample data records for the relational database shown in Figure 3.67.

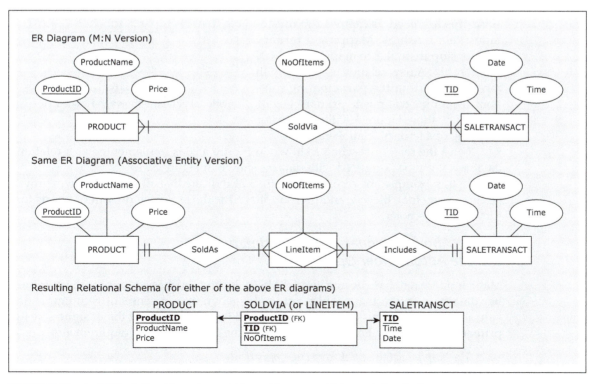

FIGURE 3.69   An M:N relationship and associative entity mapped into a relation in the same way.

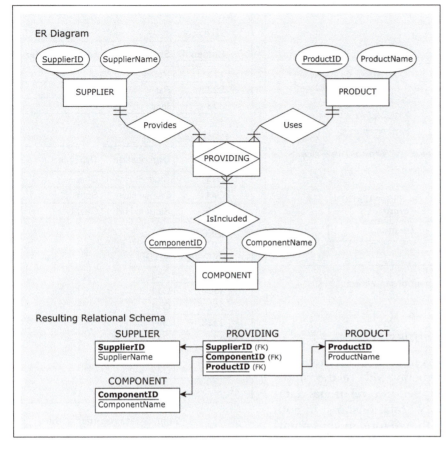

FIGURE 3.70   Mapping a ternary relationship.

SUPPLIER

SupplierID	SupplierName
S1	Acme
S2	Xparts
S3	Compy

PRODUCT

ProductID	ProductName
P1	Bicycle
P2	Tricycle
P3	Scooter

COMPONENT

ComponentID	ComponentName
C1	Wheel
C2	Handle
C3	Seat

PROVIDING

SupplierID	ProductID	ComponentID
S1	P1	C1
S2	P1	C1
S3	P1	C1
S1	P1	C2
S2	P1	C2
S3	P1	C2
S1	P1	C3
S2	P1	C3
S3	P1	C3
S1	P2	C1
S1	P2	C2
S1	P2	C3
S1	P3	C1
S1	P3	C2

FIGURE 3.71   Sample data records for the relational database shown in Figure 3.70.

A Note About Mapping Ternary Relationships

Recall from Chapter 2 that ternary relationships are used as many-to-many-to-many relationships. Mapping a ternary relationship is similar to mapping an M:N relationship. A new relation is created with foreign keys from the participating relations forming a composite primary key of the new relation. Figure 3.70 illustrates the mapping of a ternary relationship.

Once the relational schema shown in Figure 3.70 is implemented as a relational database, it can be populated with data, as shown in Figure 3.71.

In this example, the records in Figure 3.71 indicate that all three suppliers provide all three parts for a bicycle, and that supplier *S1* is the exclusive provider of parts for a tricycle and a scooter.

A Note About Designer–Created Primary Keys and the Autonumber Option

Many modern database design and DBMS tools offer database designers the **autonumber data type** option that enables automatic generation of consecutive numeric data values in a column. This option is mostly used for the creation of the **designer-created primary key** columns. For example, consider the following set of requirements:

- *The hospital database will keep track of patients.*
- *For each patient, the hospital will keep track of his or her unique SSN as well as birthdate and name.*

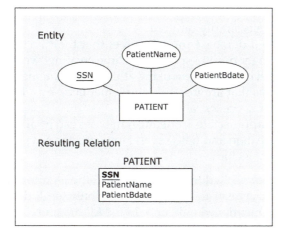

FIGURE 3.72   Entity and the resulting relation PATIENT.

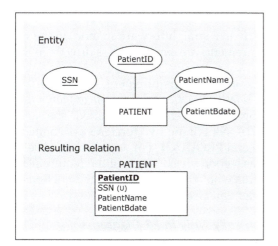

FIGURE 3.73   Entity and the resulting relation PATIENT with a designer-created primary key column added.

PATIENT

PatientID	SSN	PatientName	PatientBdate
1	123-44-4444	Ernest	1/1/1929
2	567-88-8888	Hans	2/2/1931
3	912-33-3333	Sally	4/3/1951

FIGURE 3.74   Sample data records for the relation shown in Figure 3.73.

An entity based on this relationship, and the resulting relation, are shown in Figure 3.72.

The PatientID column was not called for explicitly by the requirements. However, after the discussions with the end users, the designer decided not to use a patient's SSN as the primary key. Instead, the designer decided to create another column PatientID for the relation PATIENT that will serve as a primary key instead of the SSN column, and populate it with the auto-increasing consecutive integer values. First, the requirements were altered as follows:

- *The hospital database will keep track of patients.*
- *For each patient, the hospital will keep track of his or her unique SSN and unique PatientID (which will be a simple integer, where each new patient is assigned the next available consecutive integer), as well as birthdate and name.*

As shown in Figure 3.73, based on the altered requirements, the ER diagram is also altered. As a result, the mapped relation is given an extra column PatientID.

During the implementation of the relation PATIENT, the autonumber data type is chosen for the column PatientID. The data in the relation PATIENT is shown in Figure 3.74. Data in the columns SSN, PatientBdate, and PatientName is entered. The data in the column PatientID is automatically generated by the database system as a result of the autonumber data type for that column.

A Note About Performing Both ER and Relational Modeling

A textbook approach to database modeling calls for the process of requirements collection to be accompanied by the ER modeling and then followed by mapping the ER model into a subsequent relational schema. However, some practitioners prefer to create relational schemas straight from the requirements. In such cases, the ER modeling phase is simply omitted.

Often, experienced database modelers feel that their level of expertise is high enough that they no longer need to spend their time creating two types of diagrams for each database. They feel comfortable looking at the requirements and immediately creating relational schemas that are instantly implementable by a DBMS package, while skipping the ER modeling process all together

Such a shortened approach to modeling databases can be appealing at first glance, as a purported simplification and time-saver. However, we advise against this practice for a number of reasons, including:

- ER modeling is more suited for visualization of the requirements.
- Certain concepts can be visualized graphically only in ER diagrams.
- Every attribute is mentioned only once in the ER diagram.
- An ER model is a better communication and documentation device.

The following discusses each of the reasons listed.

ER Modeling Is More Suited for Visualization of Requirements

All of the requirements are visualized explicitly in a straightforward manner in the ER diagram. On the other hand, some of the requirements are expressed less directly in the relational schema.

Let us take a look at Figure 3.32. For example, the requirement, *Each product is sold via one or more sales transactions and each sales transaction includes one or more products*, is visualized in the ER diagram, depicting the requirement as specified. The same requirement is depicted as a relation SOLDVIA, containing two foreign keys connecting it to the relations SALESTRANSACTION and PRODUCT. For an experienced relational database modeler, this may still work as a good visualization of the requirement above. However, for most business constituents who would need a visual depiction of the requirements, the ER model offers a simpler and clearer option.

Certain Concepts Can Be Visualized Graphically Only in ER Diagrams

Certain concepts that can occur as part of the requirements can be visualized graphically in the ER diagram but not in the relational schema.

Let us take a look at Figure 3.15. The ER diagram captures and visualizes the requirement that *Each department must have at least one employee reporting to it*, while that same requirement is not visualized in the relational schema.

Another example of a concept that can be visualized in an ER diagram, but not in a relational schema, is a composite attribute, as illustrated by Figure 3.6.

Every Attribute Is Mentioned Only Once in the ER Diagram

For grasping which attributes are being represented in the subsequent database, looking at the ER diagram is a simpler method because each attribute is visualized only once.

Let us take a look at Figure 3.59. Attribute BuildingID is an attribute of the entity BULDING. It is shown only once in the ER diagram, as are all other attributes shown in the ER diagram. In the relational schema, attribute BuildingID is shown once in the relation BUILDING and is then repeated four more times as a foreign key in three different relations. An experienced relational database modeler can distinguish between the original attribute and its use as a foreign key. However, a regular business user may be overwhelmed with the task of looking at a relational schema full of foreign keys and recognizing the multiple instances of the same attribute.

The ER Model Is a Better Communication and Documentation Device

For all the reasons listed above, it is easier for all the parties involved in the database design process to communicate using the ER diagram rather than the relational schema. The ER diagram is a better device for explanation, discussion, and verification of the requirements and the resulting database, both during the database development process and later when the implemented database is in use.

Summary

In addition to Table 3.1 shown on the first page of this chapter, Tables 3.2 and 3.3 provide a summary of the basic relational concepts introduced in this chapter.

TABLE 3.2   Summary of Basic Relational Database Constraints

Constraint	Description
Naming a Relation	Each relation in a relational schema must have a different name.
Naming a Column	Within a relation, each column must have a different name.
Row Uniqueness	Within a relation, each row must be unique.
Single-Valued Column Values	Within a relation, in each row, each value in each column must be single valued.
Domain Constraint	Within a relation, all values in each column must be from the same predefined domain.
Order of Columns	Within a relation, the order of columns is irrelevant.
Order of Rows	Within a relation, the order of rows is irrelevant.
Primary Key Constraint	Each relation must have a primary key, which is a column (or a set of columns) whose value is unique for each row.
Entity Integrity Constraint	No primary key column can have null values.
Foreign Key	A foreign key is a column in a relation that refers to a primary key column in another (referred) relation.
Referential Integrity Constraint	In each row of a relation containing a foreign key, the value of the foreign key EITHER matches one of the values in the primary key column of the referred relation OR the value of the foreign key is null (unfilled).

TABLE 3.3   Summary of Basic ER to Relational Schema Mapping Rules

ER Construct	Mapping Rule
Regular Entity	Becomes a relation.
Regular Attribute	Becomes a column in a relation.
Unique Attribute	One unique attribute of the entity becomes a primary key. If there are other unique attributes they are marked as unique (but not as the primary key).
Composite Attribute	Only components of the composite attribute are mapped as columns of a relation (the composite attribute itself is not mapped).
Composite Unique Attribute	Only its components are mapped. The components become a composite primary key only if there are no single unique attributes in the entity. Otherwise, the components are marked as compositely unique (but not as the primary key).
Multivalued Attribute	Becomes a separate relation with a composite primary key. The composite primary key is composed of a column representing the multivalued attribute and the foreign key referring to the primary key of the relation representing the entity that contained the multivalued attribute.
Derived Attribute	Not mapped.
Optional Attribute	Becomes a column, marked as optional.

(Continued)

TABLE 3.3	Summary of Basic ER to Relational Schema Mapping Rules (*Continued*)
ER Construct	**Mapping Rule**
1:M Binary Relationship	The relation mapped from the entity on the M side has a foreign key that corresponds to the primary key of the relation mapped from the 1 side.
M:N Binary Relationship	Becomes a new relation with two foreign keys, corresponding to the primary keys of the two relations representing the two entities involved in the M:N relationship. The two foreign keys form the composite primary key of the new relation representing the M:N relationship. If it exists, an attribute of the relationship becomes a column in the new relation.
1:M Unary Relationship	The relation mapped from an entity involved in the 1:M unary relationship includes a foreign key that corresponds to its own primary key.
M:N Unary Relationship	Becomes a new relation with two foreign keys, both of them corresponding to the primary key of the relation representing the entity involved in the unary M:N relationship. Each of the foreign keys is used as a part of the composite primary key of the new relation.
Associative Entity	Same rule as with mapping an M:N relationship. A new relation is created with foreign keys corresponding to the primary keys of the relations representing the entities involved in the relationships with the associative entity.
Weak Entity	Becomes a new relation with a foreign key corresponding to the primary key of the relation representing the owner entity. The combination of the column mapped from the partial key and the foreign key from the owner becomes a composite primary key (if there is no partial key, the foreign key alone becomes the primary key).
Ternary Relationship	Same rule as with mapping an associative entity.

Key Terms

Attribute (of a relation) 57
Autonumber data type 84
Bridge relation 66
Business rules 81
Column 57
Composite primary key 61
Designer-created primary
    key 84

Domain constraint 79
Entity integrity constraint 62
Field 57
Foreign key 63
Implicit constraints 78
Primary key 59
Primary key constraint 79
Record 57

Referential integrity
    constraint 69
Referential integrity
    constraint lines 69
Relation 57
Relational database 57
Relational database model
    57

Relational DBMS (RDBMS)
    57
Relational schema 57
Relational table 57
Row 57
Table 57
Tuple 57
User-defined constraints 78

Review Questions

Q3.1 Which conditions must hold in order for a table to be a relation?

Q3.2 What is a primary key?

Q3.3 How is a regular entity with regular attributes mapped into a relation?

Q3.4 How is a composite attribute mapped into a relation?

Q3.5 How is a unique composite attribute mapped into a relation?

Q3.6 How is an optional attribute mapped into a relation?

Q3.7 Give a definition of the entity integrity constraint.

Q3.8 What is a foreign key?

Q3.9 How is a 1:M relationship between two entities mapped into a relational schema?

Q3.10 How is an M:N relationship between two entities mapped into a relational schema?

Q3.11 How is a 1:1 relationship between two entities mapped into a relational schema?

Q3.12 Give a definition of the referential integrity constraint.

Q3.13 How are candidate keys mapped into a relation?

Q3.14 How is a multivalued attribute mapped into a relational schema?

Q3.15 How is a derived attribute mapped into a relational schema?

Q3.16 How is a 1:M unary relationship mapped into a relational schema?

Q3.17 How is an M:N unary relationship mapped into a relational schema?

Q3.18 How is a 1:1 unary relationship mapped into a relational schema?

Q3.19 How is a weak entity mapped into a relational schema?

Q3.20 How is a ternary relationship mapped into a relational schema?

Q3.21 List implicit constraints in the relational database model.

Q3.22 What are user-defined constraints?

Q3.23 What are business rules?

Q3.24 What is a designer-created primary key?

Q3.25 What are the main reasons against creating a relational database model without first creating an ER model?

Exercises

E3.1 Create two examples, one of a table that is a relation and one of a table that is not a relation.

E3.2 Create two examples, one of a relation that is in compliance with the entity integrity constraint and one relation that violates the entity integrity constraint.

E3.3 Create two examples, one of a relation that is in compliance with the referential integrity constraint and one relation that violates the referential integrity constraint.

E3.4 Map the entity created in review exercise **E2.1** into a relation.

E3.5 For the ER diagrams created in the following exercises, map the ER diagram into a relational schema and do the following:

E3.5a For exercise **E2.2a**, show several records in each relation and mark those values that indicate mandatory participation on the 1 side and those that indicate optional participation on the M side.

E3.5b For exercise **E2.2b**, show several records in each relation and mark those values that indicate optional participation on the 1 side and those that indicate mandatory participation on the M side.

E3.5c For exercise **E2.2c**, show several records in each relation and mark those values that indicate mandatory participation on the 1 side and those that indicate mandatory participation on the M side.

E3.5d For exercise **E2.2d**, show several records in each relation and mark those values that indicate optional participation on the 1 side and those that indicate optional participation on the M side.

E3.5e For exercise **E2.2e**, show several records in each relation and mark those values that indicate mandatory participation on one side and those that indicate optional participation on the other side.

E3.5f For exercise **E2.2f**, show several records in each relation and mark those values that indicate mandatory participation on one side and those that indicate mandatory participation on the other side.

E3.5g For exercise **E2.2g**, show several records in each relation and mark those values that indicate optional participation on one side and those that indicate optional participation on the other side.

E3.5h For exercise **E2.2h**, show several records in each relation and mark those values that indicate mandatory participation on one side and those that indicate optional participation on the other side

E3.5i For exercise **E2.2i**, show several records in each relation and mark those values that indicate mandatory participation on one side and those that indicate mandatory participation on the other side.

E3.5j For exercise **E2.2j**, show several records in each relation and mark those values that indicate optional participation on one side and those that indicate optional participation on the other side.

E3.6 Map the ER diagram created in exercise **E2.3** into a relation. Show several records in the mapped relation.

E3.7 Map the entity created in exercise **E2.4** into a relation. Show several records in the mapped relation.

E3.8 Map the entity created in exercise **E2.5** into a relation. Show several records in the mapped relation.

E3.9 Map the entity created in exercise **E2.6** into a relation. Show several records in the mapped relation.

E3.10 Map the entity created in exercise **E2.7** into a relational schema. Show several records in each of the mapped relations.

E3.11 Map the entity created in exercise **E2.8** into a relation. Show several records in each of the mapped relation.

E3.12 Map the entity created in exercise **E2.9** into a relation. Show several records in each of the mapped relation.

E3.13 Map the ER diagram created in exercise **E2.10** into a relational schema. Show several records in each of the mapped relations.

E3.14 Map the ER diagram created based on the requirements in exercise **E2.11** into a relational schema. Show several records in each of the mapped relations.

E3.15 Map the ER diagram created based on the requirements in exercise **E2.12** into a relational schema. Show several records in each of the mapped relations.

E3.16 Map the ER diagram created based on the requirements in exercise **E2.13** into a relational schema. Show several records in each of the mapped relations.

E3.17 Create an example of an ER diagram with a business rule. Map the ER diagram and show several records in the resulting relations, indicating compliance with the business rule.

Mini Cases

MC1 Investco Scout

Map the ER diagram for the Investco Scout Funds Database (created in mini case **MC1** in Chapter 2) into a relational schema.

MC2 Funky Bizz

Map the ER diagram for the Funky Bizz Operations Database (created in mini case **MC2** in Chapter 2) into a relational schema.

MC3 Snooty Fashions

Map the ER diagram for the Snooty Fashions Operations Database (created in mini case **MC3** in Chapter 2) into a relational schema.

MC4 Signum Libri

Map the ER diagram for the Signum Libri Operations Database (created in mini case **MC4** in Chapter 2) into a relational schema.

MC5 ExoProtect

Map the ER diagram for the ExoProtect Employees' Computers Database (shown in mini case **MC5**, Figure 2.58 in Chapter 2) into a relational schema.

MC6 Jones Dozers

Map the ER diagram for the Jones Dozers Sales and Rentals Database (shown in mini case **MC6**, Figure 2.59 in Chapter 2) into a relational schema.

MC7 Midtown Memorial

Map the ER diagram for the Midtown Memorial Patients Drug Dispense Database (shown in mini case **MC7**, Figure 2.60 in Chapter 2) into a relational schema.

Chapter 4

Update Operations, Update Anomalies, and Normalization

INTRODUCTION

In the previous chapter, we presented the basic concepts of the relational database model and showed how to properly map an ER diagram into a relational schema. In this chapter, we will focus on examining the operations for *inserting* data into the relations, *modifying* (changing) the existing data in the relations, and *deleting* data from the relations. These three operations are often collectively referred to as **update operations**.

If a relation stores multiple instances of the data referring to the same occurrence (e.g., a table of purchases containing multiple rows with the same customer's address), such instances represent **redundant data**. A less than optimal database design process can result in relations that contain unnecessarily redundant data. The update operations can cause certain anomalies in such relations. In this chapter, we will describe and illustrate these so-called **update anomalies**.

A process called **normalization** is used to improve the design of relational databases that contain redundant data, and are therefore, prone to update anomalies. The result of the normalization process is the elimination of unnecessarily redundant data from relational databases and, in so doing, the elimination of the possibility of update anomalies. In this chapter, we will describe the normalization process in detail.

UPDATE OPERATIONS

The user of a relation can either retrieve the data from a relation or update the data in the relation. The data retrieval operation is also often referred to as a **read operation**, because it is used for reading the data from the relations. Update operations, which are also often referred to as **write operations**, are used to update the data content in the relations.

There are three ways in which the data content in a relation can be updated: entering new data in the relation, removing data from the relation, and changing the existing data in the relation. Hence, there are three update operations for updating the data content in a relation:

- **insert operation**—used for entering new data in the relation
- **delete operation**—used for removing data from the relation
- **modify operation**—used for changing the existing data in the relation

Let us observe examples of each of the three update operations.

Insert Operation Example

Initially, the relation EMPLOYEE in Figure 4.1 has three records. After *inserting* another record, the relation EMPLOYEE has four records.

Before Insert

EMPLOYEE

EmpID	EmpName	Salary
1234	Becky	$75,000
2345	Molly	$50,000
3456	Rob	$55,000

After Insert

Inserting a record

EMPLOYEE

EmpID	EmpName	Salary
1234	Becky	$75,000
2345	Molly	$50,000
3456	Rob	$55,000
1324	Ted	$70,000

FIGURE 4.1 Example of an insert operation.

Delete Operation Example

Initially, the relation EMPLOYEE in Figure 4.2 has three records. After *deleting* a record, the relation EMPLOYEE has two records.

Modify Operation Example

The relation EMPLOYEE in Figure 4.3 has three records. The Salary value in the record referring to the employee *Molly* is changed from *$50,000* to *$60,000*. After this operation the relation EMPLOYEE still has three records, but one of the records is *modified*.

Before Delete

EMPLOYEE

EmpID	EmpName	Salary
1234	Becky	$75,000
2345	Molly	$50,000
3456	Rob	$55,000

Deleting a record

After Delete

EMPLOYEE

EmpID	EmpName	Salary
1234	Becky	$75,000
3456	Rob	$55,000

FIGURE 4.2 Example of a delete operation.

Before Modification

EMPLOYEE

EmpID	EmpName	Salary
1234	Becky	$75,000
2345	Molly	$50,000
3456	Rob	$55,000

Modifying a record

After Modification

EMPLOYEE

EmpID	EmpName	Salary
1234	Becky	$75,000
2345	Molly	$60,000
3456	Rob	$55,000

FIGURE 4.3 Example of a modification operation.

Update Operation Terminology Note

In practice and in the literature, the term "update operation" is often used in two different ways. One usage is "update operation" as a collective term for insert, delete, and modify operations. Another alternative usage is "update operation" as a synonym for the modify operation. Both of these usages are widespread, and it is important to be aware of both. Usually, it is clear from the context of the term usage which of these two designations is used. In this chapter, we use the term "update operation" as a collective term for the insert, delete, and modify operations.[1]

UPDATE ANOMALIES

In relations that contain redundant (unnecessarily repeating) data, each of the three update operations can cause update anomalies. Therefore, there are three types of update anomalies: insertion anomaly, deletion anomaly, and modification anomaly. We will use an example relation AD CAMPAIGN MIX, from the Pressly Ad Agency scenario below, to illustrate each of the three types of update anomalies. Later in this chapter, the same example relation will be used to illustrate functional dependencies and the normalization process.

Example Scenario

The Pressly Ad Agency manages ad campaigns through a variety of campaign modes. Each campaign mode has a mode identifier ModeID (e.g., *1*, *2*, *3*), and it uses one particular media (e.g., *TV*, *Radio*, *Print*) to cover one particular range (e.g., *Local*, *National*). For example, the campaign mode that uses *TV* media covering *Local* range has the ModeID value *1*, the campaign mode that uses *TV* media covering *National* range has the ModeID value *2*, and so on.

Each ad campaign managed by the Pressly Ad Agency has a unique identifier, a unique name, a start date, a duration, and a campaign manager who has a name and a unique identifier. Each ad campaign can use a number of different campaign modes. When an ad campaign uses multiple campaign modes, a percentage of the total ad campaign budget is allocated for each mode. When an ad campaign uses only one campaign mode, 100% of the ad campaign budget is allocated to one mode.

[1]As we will show in Chapter 5, the SQL command UPDATE refers to a command for the modify operation, which is consistent with the other usage of the term "update operation" as a synonym for the modify operation.

Example Relation (Containing Redundant Data)

The Pressly Ad Agency uses a single relation AD CAMPAIGN MIX to store its data. This relation is an example of a relation that contains redundant data and is therefore prone to update anomalies.

Relation AD CAMPAIGN MIX has the following columns:

AdCampaignID	Ad campaign identifier, a unique value for each ad campaign
AdCampaignName	Ad campaign name, a unique name for each ad campaign
StartDate	Beginning date for the ad campaign (more than one ad campaign can start on the same date)
Duration	Duration of the ad campaign in days (more than one ad campaign can have the same duration)
CampaignMgrID	Campaign manager identifier, a unique value for each campaign manager (each ad campaign has only one campaign manager; the same campaign manager can manage multiple campaigns)
CampaignMgrName	Campaign manager name (more than one campaign manager can have the same name)
ModeID	Campaign mode identifier, a unique value for each campaign mode
Media	Media type of a campaign mode (each campaign mode has only one media, but the same media can be used by more than one campaign mode)
Range	Range of a campaign mode (each campaign mode has only one range, but the same range can be used by more than one campaign mode)
BudgetPctg	Budget percentage allocated by a particular ad campaign for a particular campaign mode

Figure 4.4 shows the relation AD CAMPAIGN MIX with its records. One ad campaign can have several modes. Each record in this relation describes one of the modes used in one campaign. Therefore, the attribute that can uniquely distinguish each row in this relation is a composite of a unique attribute of a campaign and of a unique attribute of a mode. Mode itself has only one unique attribute: a unique ModeID. However, each ad campaign has two unique attributes: a unique AdCampaignID and a unique AdCampaignName. A *composite key* AdCampaignID, ModeID is chosen as the *primary key* of this relation. Therefore, a *composite key* AdCampaignName, ModeID is a *candidate key* of this relation that was not chosen to be the primary key.

AD CAMPAIGN MIX

AdCampaignID	AdCampaignName	StartDate	Duration	Campaign MgrID	Campaign MgrName	ModeID	Media	Range	BudgetPctg
111	SummerFun13	6.6.2013	12 days	CM100	Roberta	1	TV	Local	50%
111	SummerFun13	6.6.2013	12 days	CM100	Roberta	2	TV	National	50%
222	SummerZing13	6.8.2013	30 days	CM101	Sue	1	TV	Local	60%
222	SummerZing13	6.8.2013	30 days	CM101	Sue	3	Radio	Local	30%
222	SummerZing13	6.8.2013	30 days	CM101	Sue	5	Print	Local	10%
333	FallBall13	6.9.2013	12 days	CM102	John	3	Radio	Local	80%
333	FallBall13	6.9.2013	12 days	CM102	John	4	Radio	National	20%
444	AutmnStyle13	6.9.2013	5 days	CM103	Nancy	6	Print	National	100%
555	AutmnColors13	6.9.2013	3 days	CM100	Roberta	3	Radio	Local	100%

FIGURE 4.4   Relation AD CAMPAIGN MIX.

AD CAMPAIGN MIX

AdCampaignID	AdCampaignName	StartDate	Duration	Campaign MgrID	Campaign MgrName	ModelID	Media	Range	BudgetPctg
111	SummerFun13	6.6.2013	12 days	CM100	Roberta	1	TV	Local	50%
111	SummerFun13	6.6.2013	12 days	CM100	Roberta	2	TV	National	50%
222	SummerZing13	6.8.2013	30 days	CM101	Sue	1	TV	Local	60%
222	SummerZing13	6.8.2013	30 days	CM101	Sue	3	Radio	Local	30%
222	SummerZing13	6.8.2013	30 days	CM101	Sue	5	Print	Local	10%
333	FallBall13	6.9.2013	12 days	CM102	John	3	Radio	Local	80%
333	FallBall13	6.9.2013	12 days	CM102	John	4	Radio	National	20%
444	AutmnStyle13	6.9.2013	5 days	CM103	Nancy	6	Print	National	100%
555	AutmnColors13	6.9.2013	3 days	CM100	Roberta	3	Radio	Local	100%

The media and range values for campaign mode 1 repeated twice

The name of the campaign manager CM100 repeated three times

The name, start date, and duration of the campaign 222 repeated three times

FIGURE 4.5   **Examples** of redundant data in the relation AD CAMPAIGN MIX.

A **nonkey column** is a column in a relation that is not a primary or a candidate key column. Columns StartDate, Duration, CampaignMgrID, CampaignMgrName, Media, Range, and BudgetPctg are nonkey columns in the AD CAMPAIGN MIX relation.

The design of the AD CAMPAIGN MIX relation causes it to contain redundant data. For example, the name, start date, and duration of campaign *222* is repeated three times, the name of the campaign manager *CM100* is repeated three times, and the media and range values of campaign mode *1* are repeated twice. These examples of redundant data in the AD CAMPAIGN MIX relation are illustrated by Figure 4.5.

Because of the design that allows for the occurrences of redundant data, the AD CAMPAIGN MIX relation can exhibit each of the update anomalies as shown by the following examples illustrated by Figure 4.6.

Insertion Anomaly

An **insertion anomaly** occurs when a user who wants to insert data about one real-world entity is forced to enter data about another real-world entity.

For example, let us assume that the ad agency decided to start using a new campaign mode for future campaigns: *7, Internet, National*. This new mode cannot be entered in the relation AD CAMPAIGN MIX without also entering an actual campaign that uses this mode. However, there is no campaign that is using campaign mode 7 at this time. Since AD CAMPAIGN MIX is the only relation in this database, the data about campaign mode 7 will not exist in the database unless it is inserted into AD CAMPAIGN MIX. Inserting the information in a record in the AD CAMPAIGN MIX relation for campaign mode 7, while leaving the values in the campaign columns empty, would not work. Such an insertion would result in a NULL value for the primary key AdCampaignID, which would violate the entity integrity constraint.

Deletion Anomaly

A **deletion anomaly** occurs when a user who wants to delete data about a real-world entity is forced to delete data about another real-world entity.

For example, let us assume that the ad agency decided to cancel the ad campaign *444*. Deleting the record relating to campaign *444* in the relation AD CAMPAIGN MIX

AD CAMPAIGN MIX

AdCampaignID	AdCampaignName	StartDate	Duration	Campaign MgrID	Campaign MgrName	ModelID	Media	Range	BudgetPctg
111	SummerFun13	6.6.2013	12 days	CM100	Roberta	1	TV	Local	50%
111	SummerFun13	6.6.2013	12 days	CM100	Roberta	2	TV	National	50%
222	SummerZing13	6.8.2013	30 days	CM101	Sue	1	TV	Local	60%
222	SummerZing13	6.8.2013	30 days	CM101	Sue	3	Radio	Local	30%
222	SummerZing13	6.8.2013	30 days	CM101	Sue	5	Print	Local	10%
333	FallBall13	6.9.2013	12 days	CM102	John	3	Radio	Local	80%
333	FallBall13	6.9.2013	12 days	CM102	John	4	Radio	National	20%
444	AutmnStyle13	6.9.2013	5 days	CM103	Nancy	6	Print	National	100%
555	AutmnColors13	6.9.2013	3 days	CM100	Roberta	3	Radio	Local	100%
????	????	????	????	????	????	7	Internet	National	????

Modification Anomaly Example:
To change the duration of the campaign 222 from 30 to 45 days, three records have to be modified

Deletion Anomaly Example:
Cannot delete campaign 444 without also deleting all the data about campaign manager CM103 and campaign mode 6

Insertion Anomaly Example:
Cannot insert new campaign mode 7 without inserting an actual campaign using the new mode 7

FIGURE 4.6   **Examples** of update anomalies in the relation AD CAMPAIGN MIX.

will also delete the campaign mode 6, *Print, National,* because no other campaign is using this mode at this time. Since information about a mode of advertising can only be found in the relation AD CAMPAIGN MIX (because there is no other relation in the database), this deletion will cause information about campaign mode 6 to no longer exist in the database. However, the agency may still want to use campaign mode 6 for future campaigns, so keeping the information about campaign mode 6 in the database may be important.

In addition, note that deleting the record relating to campaign *444* in the relation AD CAMPAIGN MIX will also delete campaign manager *103, Nancy,* because no other campaign is being managed by this campaign manager at this time. Since information about a campaign manager can only be found in the relation AD CAMPAIGN MIX, this deletion will cause information about campaign manager *103* to no longer exist in the database. However, the agency may still want to use campaign manager *103* for managing future campaigns, so keeping the information about campaign manager *103* in the database may be important.

Modification Anomaly

A **modification anomaly** occurs when, in order to modify one value, the same modification has to be made multiple times.

For example, let us assume that the ad agency decided to extend the duration of campaign *222* from *30* days to *45* days. This change has to be made in three different records.[2]

The relations that are susceptible to update anomalies (such as the AD CAMPAIGN MIX relation) can be improved through the process of normalization. Much of the

---

[2]In case a typo is made in one of those modification attempts or one modification was skipped, in addition to having incorrect data in the relation, we would also have multiple versions of duration for this campaign. This would cause a data consistency problem, as discussed in Chapter 6.

CLIENT

ClientID	ClientName	...	...
1001	William	...	...
2001	Matthew	...	...
3001	Lee	...	...
4001	Linda	...	...
5001	William	...	...

FIGURE 4.7   Relation CLIENT.

normalization process is based on understanding the concept of functional dependency. Hence, before we introduce and illustrate the normalization process, we will discuss functional dependencies.

FUNCTIONAL DEPENDENCIES

A **functional dependency** occurs when the value of one (or more) column(s) in each record of a relation uniquely determines the value of another column in that same record of the relation. For example, let us assume that a table containing the information about clients has the columns ClientID and Name as shown in Figure 4.7.

Column ClientID functionally determines column ClientName because a particular ClientID value can be associated with only one ClientName value. On the other hand, column ClientName does not functionally determine column ClientID, because a particular ClientName value can be associated with more than one ClientID. For example, in relation CLIENT, there are two different clients with the name *William*, each of which has a different ClientID.

Functional Dependency Notation

There are several ways to depict a functional dependency. One way is to show a functional dependency as a symbolic written expression as follows:

$$A \rightarrow B$$

The column (or columns) on the left side of the arrow functionally determine the column (or columns) on the right side. For the example, the functional dependency in Figure 4.7 would be depicted as:

ClientID → ClientName

Another way of depicting the functional dependency is graphical, where this same functional dependency is drawn as an arrow on the columns of the table, as shown in Figure 4.8.

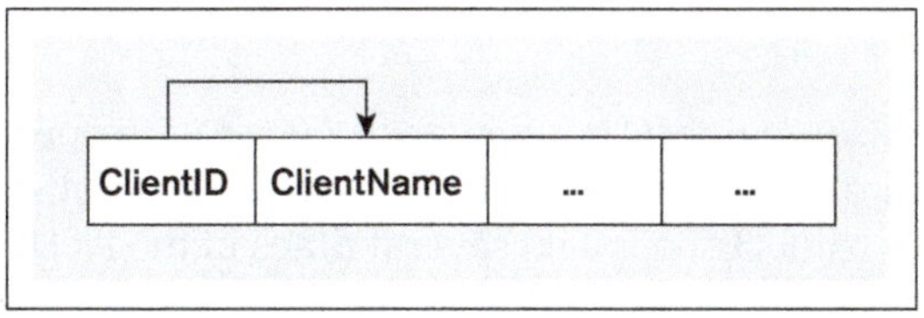

ClientID	ClientName	...	...

FIGURE 4.8   A graphical depiction of a functional dependency.

FUNCTIONAL DEPENDENCIES EXAMPLE

Initially, in the relation AD CAMPAIGN MIX in Figure 4.4 we recognize the following sets of functional dependencies:

Initially recognized sets of functional dependencies in the relation AD CAMPAIGN MIX

(Set 1) CampaignMgrID → CampaignMgrName

(Set 2) ModeID → Media, Range

(Set 3) AdCampaignID → AdCampaignName, StartDate, Duration, CampaignMgrID, CampaignMgrName

(Set 4) AdCampaignName → AdCampaignID, StartDate, Duration, CampaignMgrID, CampaignMgrName

(Set 5) AdCampaignID, ModeID → AdCampaignName, StartDate, Duration, CampaignMgrID, CampaignMgrName, Media, Range, BudgetPctg

(Set 6) AdCampaignName, ModeID → AdCampaignID, StartDate, Duration, CampaignMgrID, CampaignMgrName, Media, Range, BudgetPctg

---

The following is a detailed discussion about these sets of functional dependencies in the relation AD CAMPAIGN MIX.

> **(Set 1)** CampaignMgrID → CampaignMgrName

CampaignMgrID functionally determines CampaignMgrName. Within the records of the AD CAMPAIGN MIX relation, each particular value of CampaignMgrID always appears with the same CampaignMgrName value. For example, CampaignMgrID value *CM100* appears in several records in the AD CAMPAIGN MIX relation, but always with the same CampaignMgrName value *Roberta*. This is true for any CampaignMgrID, as each CampaignMgrID value always appears exclusively with just one CampaignMgrName value. The opposite is not true, since we could eventually hire two different campaign managers with the same name (e.g., we could hire another Roberta), which would, of course, have two different CampaignMgrID values. Therefore, CampaignMgrName does not functionally determine CampaignMgrID, since one CampaignMgrName value is not necessarily associated with just one CampaignMgrID value.

> **(Set 2)** ModeID → Media, Range

Each particular value of ModeID is always associated with just one value of Media and just one value of Range. For example, ModeID value *3* appears several times in the AD CAMPAIGN MIX relation, but it is always associated with the same Media value *Radio* and the same Range value *Local*. On the other hand, individual Media or Range values can be associated with multiple different ModeID values, and therefore, neither the Media nor Range columns determine the ModeID column.

> **(Set 3)** AdCampaignID → AdCampaignName, StartDate, Duration, CampaignMgrID, CampaignMgrName

Each particular value of AdCampaignID is always associated with one value of AdCampaignName, StartDate, Duration, CampaignMgrID, and CampaignMgrName. For example, the AdCampaignID value *333* appears several times in the AD CAMPAIGN MIX relation, but it is always associated with the same StartDate value *6.9.2013*. Every individual AdCampaignID value is always associated exclusively with one StartDate value. The opposite is not true, since two or more different campaigns could start on the same date (e.g., campaigns *333*, *444*, and *555* start on the same date). Therefore StartDate does not functionally determine AdCampaignID, since one StartDate value is not necessarily associated with just one AdCampaignID value. Similar observations could be made about the Duration, CampaignMgrID, and CampaignMgrName columns, since they do not functionally determine AdCampaignID. On the other hand, the AdCampaignName column does determine the AdCampaignID column, as shown in Set 4.

(Set 4) AdCampaignName → AdCampaignID, StartDate, Duration,
CampaignMgrID, CampaignMgrName

Each particular value of AdCampaignName is always associated with one value of AdCampaignID, StartDate, Duration, CampaignMgrID, and CampaignMgrName. For example, the AdCampaignName value *FallBall13* appears several times in the AD CAMPAIGN MIX relation, but it is always associated with the same StartDate value *6.9.2013*. Every individual AdCampaignName value is always associated exclusively with one StartDate value. The opposite is not true, since two or more different campaigns could start on the same date (e.g., campaigns *FallBall13*, *AutmnStyle13*, and *AutmnColors13* start on the same date). Therefore, StartDate does not functionally determine AdCampaignName, since one StartDate value is not necessarily associated with just one AdCampaignName value. Similar observations could be made about Duration, CampaignMgrID, and CampaignMgrName columns, since they do not functionally determine AdCampaignName. On the other hand, AdCampaignID column does determine the AdCampaignName column, as shown in Set 3.

(Set 5) AdCampaignID, ModeID → AdCampaignName, StartDate, Duration,
CampaignMgrID, CampaignMgrName,
Media, Range, BudgetPctg

In any relation, the primary key always functionally determines the rest of the columns in the relation. Therefore, in the relation AD CAMPAIGN MIX, the composite primary key AdCampaignID, ModeID functionally determines all other columns in the AD CAMPAIGN MIX relation. Each particular combined value of AdCampaignID, ModeID is associated with just one value of AdCampaignName, StartDate, Duration, CampaignMgrID, CampaignMgrName, Media, Range, and BudgetPctg.

(Set 6) AdCampaignName, ModeID → AdCampaignID, StartDate, Duration,
CampaignMgrID, CampaignMgrName,
Media, Range, BudgetPctg

In any relation, a candidate key always functionally determines the rest of the columns in the relation. Therefore, in the relation AD CAMPAIGN MIX, the composite candidate key AdCampaignName, ModeID functionally determines all other columns in the AD CAMPAIGN MIX relation. Each particular combined value of AdCampaignName, ModeID is associated with one value of AdCampaignID, StartDate, Duration, CampaignMgrID, CampaignMgrName, Media, Range, and BudgetPctg.

STREAMLINING FUNCTIONAL DEPENDENCIES

The database normalization process is based on analyzing functional dependencies that exist within each relation in the database. Certain functional dependencies are not relevant in the process of normalization, and therefore, we can choose to depict only those functional dependencies that are necessary for undertaking the normalization process. This simplifies the normalization process by reducing the number of functional dependency lines that need to be considered.

For example, so-called **trivial functional dependencies** occur when an attribute (or a set of attributes) functionally determines itself (e.g., A → A; or A, B → A, B) or its subset (e.g., A, B → A). Trivial functional dependencies are not depicted in the set of identified functional dependencies. The depiction of trivial functional dependencies would constitute an unnecessary expansion and complication of the set of functional dependencies under consideration. For example, including trivial functional dependency

> CampaignMgrID, CampaignMgrName → CampaignMgrName

in the sets of identified functional dependencies in the example above would simply mean adding unnecessary clutter.

In addition to the trivial functional dependencies, there are other types of functional dependencies that can be omitted from the graphical depiction without losing the information needed for the normalization process. In particular, **augmented functional dependencies** and **equivalent functional dependencies**, described below, can be pruned from the depicted functional dependencies in order to simplify the normalization process.

Augmented Functional Dependencies

Assume that *Joe is heavier than Sue* is a true statement. In that case, *Joe carrying a sack of potatoes is heavier than Sue* is also a true, but at the same time an unnecessarily augmented statement, given the original statement. A similar concept applies to augmented functional dependencies.

Suppose the following functional dependency exists in a relation:

> A → B

In that case, the functional dependency that contains an existing functional dependency, such as the following:

> A, C → B

is an augmented functional dependency.

For legibility and simplicity reasons, augmented functional dependencies are usually *not depicted*. Therefore, Set 5 would actually be depicted as:

> **(Set 5)** AdCampaignID, ModelID → BudgetPctg

because all other functional dependencies in that set are redundant functional dependencies.

In particular, because of the functional dependency (from Set 3):

> AdCampaignID → AdCampaignName, StartDate, Duration, CampaignMgrID, CampaignMgrName

the functional dependency:

> AdCampaignID, ModelID → AdCampaignName, StartDate, Duration, CampaignMgrID, CampaignMgrName

is augmented, and hence omitted from Set 5.

Also, because of the functional dependency (from Set 2):

> ModelID → Media, Range

the functional dependency:

> AdCampaignID, ModelID → Media, Range

is augmented, and hence omitted from Set 5.

Equivalent Functional Dependencies

Consider a simple scenario, where *British secret service fictional officer James Bond is also known as Agent 007* is a true statement. In that case, the following two statements *James Bond is the most famous British secret service fictional officer* and *Agent 007 is the most famous British secret service fictional officer* are two equivalent statements. A similar concept applies to equivalent functional dependencies.

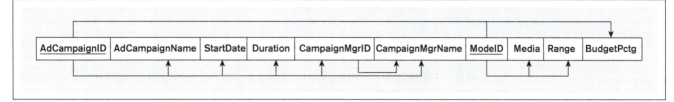

FIGURE 4.9   Functional dependencies in the relation AD CAMPAIGN MIX.

Suppose the following functional dependencies exist in a relation:

$A \rightarrow B$
$B \rightarrow A$

In that case, everything that A determines, B will also determine (and vice versa). Therefore, $A \rightarrow B$ and $B \rightarrow A$ are equivalent functional dependencies. In addition:

$A \rightarrow B, X$
$B \rightarrow A, X$

are equivalent functional dependencies, and

$Y, A \rightarrow B, X$
$Y, B \rightarrow A, X$

are also equivalent functional dependencies.

For legibility and simplicity reasons, when we have multiple sets of equivalent functional dependencies, we can choose to depict only one of them. Because the functional dependency:

AdCampaignID $\rightarrow$ AdCampaignName

and the functional dependency:

AdCampaignName $\rightarrow$ AdCampaignID

are equivalent, Set 3 and Set 4 are equivalent sets and Set 5 and Set 6 are also equivalent sets. Therefore, Set 4 can be omitted from depiction because it is equivalent to Set 3, and Set 6 can be omitted from depiction because it is equivalent to Set 5.

The following is the streamlined list of functional dependencies that would actually be depicted for the AD CAMPAIGN MIX relation.

Streamlined sets of functional dependencies in the relation AD CAMPAIGN MIX

(Set 1) CampaignMgrID $\rightarrow$ CampaignMgrName

(Set 2) ModelID $\rightarrow$ Media, Range

(Set 3) AdCampaignID $\rightarrow$ AdCampaignName, StartDate, Duration, CampaignMgrID, CampaignMgrName

(Set 5) AdCampaignID, ModelID $\rightarrow$ BudgetPctg

Set 5: Reduced by omitting the augmented functional dependencies containing Set 2 and Set 3
Set 4: Omitted, as it is equivalent to Set 3
Set 6: Omitted, as it is equivalent to Set 5

This streamlined set of functional dependencies is also shown in Figure 4.9.

TYPES OF FUNCTIONAL DEPENDENCIES

The functional dependencies that are used as a basis for the typical normalization process can be classified in one of the three categories: **partial functional dependency, full key functional dependency,** and **transitive functional dependency.** The following are descriptions and illustrative examples for each of these three categories of functional dependencies.[3]

Partial Functional Dependency

Partial functional dependency occurs when a column of a relation is functionally dependent on a component of a composite primary key.

Only composite primary keys have separate components; single-column primary keys do not have separate components. Hence, partial functional dependency can occur only in cases when a relation has a composite primary key.

In Figure 4.9, the functional dependencies

AdCampaignID → AdCampaignName, StartDate, Duration, CampaignMgrID,
CampaignMgrName
ModeID → Media, Range

are partial functional dependencies. AdCampaignID is a component of the primary key AdCampaignID, ModeID, and therefore, a dependency where AdCampaignID functionally determines other columns in the relation is a partial functional dependency. Likewise, ModeID is also a component of the primary key AdCampaignID, ModeID, and therefore, a dependency where ModeID functionally determines other columns in the relation is a partial functional dependency.

Full Key Functional Dependency

Full key functional dependency occurs when a primary key functionally determines the column of a relation and no separate component of the primary key partially determines the same column.

If a relation has a single component (non-composite) primary key, the primary key fully functionally determines all the other columns of a relation. However, if a relation has a composite key, and portions of the key partially determine columns of a relation, then the primary key does not fully functionally determine the partially determined columns. In Figure 4.9, the functional dependency

AdCampaignID, ModeID → BudgetPctg

is a full key functional dependency. The columns AdCampaignID and ModeID form the primary key and together functionally determine column BudgetPctg. Neither component of the primary key partially determines column BudgetPctg.

Transitive Functional Dependency

Transitive functional dependency occurs when nonkey columns functionally determine other nonkey columns of a relation.

In Figure 4.9, the functional dependency

CampaignMgrID → CampaignMgrName

is a transitive functional dependency. CampaignMgrID is a nonkey column and CampaignMgrName is a nonkey column as well. Therefore, CampaignMgrID functionally determining CampaignMgrName is a transitive functional dependency.

Figure 4.10 indicates full key dependencies, partial dependencies, and transitive dependencies in the relation AD CAMPAIGN MIX.

ANOTHER FUNCTIONAL DEPENDENCIES EXAMPLE

Identifying partial functional dependencies, full key functional dependencies and transitive functional dependencies is critical for undertaking the typical normalization process. To recap these concepts, let us consider another relation and its functional dependencies.

---

[3]In this chapter, we give simplified definitions of partial and full key functional dependency, sufficient for clear understanding of the typical normalization process. Appendix B gives more elaborate definitions, which are theoretically more complete, but not essential for most real-world scenarios.

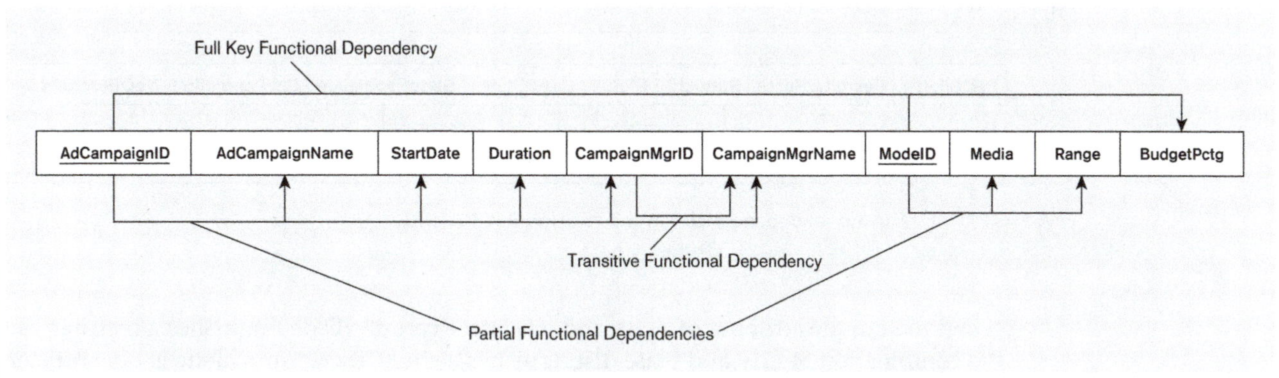

FIGURE 4.10   Functional dependencies in the relation AD CAMPAIGN MIX (types indicated).

Central Plane University uses a single relation RECRUITING to store its data. For each recruiter in the Central Plane University, relation RECRUITING lists the number of recruited students from a particular city. It also lists the population of cities and states from where the Central Plane University recruits students. Relation RECRUITING has the following columns:

RecruiterID	Recruiter's identifier, a unique value for each recruiter
RecruiterName	Recruiter's name
StatusID	Recruiter's status identifier (each recruiter has only one status)
StatusName	Recruiter's status description
City	Name of a city from where the recruiter recruits (A recruiter can recruit from multiple cities and the same city can have more than one recruiter recruiting from it. There can be more than one city with the same name, but within one state each city has a different name.)
State	State where the city is located
StatePopulation	Population of the state
CityPopulation	Population of the city
NoOfRecruits	Number of recruits a particular recruiter recruited from a particular city

Figure 4.11 shows the relation RECRUITING with its records. The primary key of this relation is the composite key RecruiterID, City, State. Each record in this relation describes one recruiter's tally of recruited students in one city. Therefore, the attribute that can uniquely distinguish each row is a composite of the unique attribute of a recruiter

RECRUITING

RecruiterID	RecruiterName	StatusID	Status	City	State	StatePopulation	CityPopulation	NoOfRecruits
R1	Katy	IF	Internal Full Time	Portland	ME	1,350,000	70,000	11
R1	Katy	IF	Internal Full Time	Grand Rapids	MI	9,900,000	190,000	20
R2	Abra	IP	Internal Part Time	Rockford	IL	12,900,000	340,000	17
R3	Jana	CN	Contractor	Spokane	WA	6,800,000	210,000	8
R3	Jana	CN	Contractor	Portland	OR	3,900,000	600,000	30
R3	Jana	CN	Contractor	Eugene	OR	3,900,000	360,000	20
R4	Maria	IF	Internal Full Time	Rockford	IL	12,900,000	340,000	14
R4	Maria	IF	Internal Full Time	Grand Rapids	MN	5,400,000	11,000	9
R5	Dan	CN	Contractor	Grand Rapids	MI	9,900,000	190,000	33

FIGURE 4.11   Relation RECRUITING.

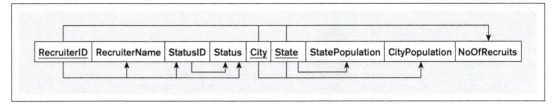

FIGURE 4.12   Functional dependencies in the relation RECRUITING.

and the unique attribute of a city and its state. RecruiterID distinguishes a recruiter, and a combination of City and State distinguishes a city (City column alone is not sufficient, since there can be cities with the same name in different states, as shown in Figure 4.11).

Relation RECRUITING has the following functional dependencies:

RecruiterID → RecruiterName, StatusID, Status
StatusID → Status
State → StatePopulation
City, State → CityPopulation
RecruiterID, City, State → NoOfRecruits

The functional dependencies in the RECRUITING relation are also shown in Figure 4.12.

RecruiterID → RecruiterName, StatusID, Status

Is a partial functional dependency because the component RecruiterID of the primary key RecruiterID, City, State, functionally determines the columns RecruiterName, StatusID, and Status.

StatusID → Status

Is a transitive functional dependency because the nonkey column StatusID determines the nonkey column Status.

City, State → CityPopulation

Is a partial functional dependency because a component City, State of the primary key RecruiterID, City, State functionally determines the column CityPopulation.

State → StatePopulation

Is a partial functional dependency because a component State of the primary key RecruiterID, City, State functionally determines a column StatePopulation.

RecruiterID, City, State → NoOfRecruits

Is a full key functional dependency because the primary key RecruiterID, City, State determines the column NoOfRecruits.

NORMALIZATION

As we mentioned in the introduction, normalization is a process that is used to improve the design of database tables. This process is based on so-called **normal forms**. Each normal form contains a set of particular conditions that a table has to satisfy. There are several normal forms, most fundamental of which are **first normal form (1NF)**, **second normal form (2NF)**, and **third normal form (3NF)**. From a lower to a higher normal form, their conditions are increasingly stricter.

The normalization process involves examining each table and verifying if it satisfies a particular normal form. If a table satisfies a particular normal form, then the next step is to verify if that relation satisfies the next higher normal form. If a table does not satisfy a particular normal form, actions are taken to convert the table into a set of tables that do satisfy the particular normal form.

Normalizing to first normal form is done on non-relational tables in order to convert them to relational tables. Normalizing to subsequent normal forms (e.g., second normal form, third normal form) improves the design of relational tables that contain redundant information and alleviates the problem of update anomalies.

To illustrate first normal form, we will use the non-relational table VET CLINIC CLIENTS introduced below. To illustrate the second and third normal forms we will use the relational table AD CAMPAIGN MIX introduced earlier in this chapter.

First Normal Form (1NF)

1NF states that each value in each column of a table must be a single value from the domain of the column.

1NF

A table is in 1NF if each row is unique and no column in any row contains multiple values from the column's domain.

Recall from Chapter 3 that two of the conditions that have to hold for each relation state the following:

- *Within one table, each row must be unique.*
- *Within each row, each value in each column must be single valued. Multiple values of the content represented by the column are not allowed in any rows of the table.*

Therefore, every relational table is, by definition, in 1NF. Consequently, normalizing to 1NF is not a part of the normalization process of relational databases. Normalizing to 1NF is done only when a non-relational table is being converted to a relation.

The example in Figure 4.13 shows a non-relational table VET CLINIC CLIENT. Each client can have multiple pets. In the table shown in Figure 4.13, records can have multiple values in columns PetNo, PetName, and PetType. Columns PetNo, PetName and PetType are related, since they all refer to the same real-world concept of a pet. Therefore, columns PetNo, PetName, and PetType constitute a group of **related multivalued columns.**[4]

Note that in Figure 4.13, columns PetNo, PetName, and PetType have one single value in the record for the customer *Lisa*, but they have multiple values for other customers. In particular, they have three values in the record for the customer *Lydia* and two values in the record for the customer *Jane*.

Normalizing to 1NF converts the non-relational table into a relation (or a set of relations) by eliminating the possibility of multiple values in the same column of a record.

One way to normalize a non-relational table into 1NF, and thereby convert it into a relation, is to create a separate record for each occurrence of related multivalued columns, as illustrated by Figure 4.14.

As shown in Figure 4.14, the values of the columns ClientID and ClientName that occurred only once in the original non-relational table for each record are repeated as many times as multiple related pet-column values occurred for that record. For example, in Figure 4.14, the values *222, Lydia* were repeated three times because client

VET CLINIC CLIENT

ClientID	ClientName	PetNo	PetName	PetType
111	Lisa	1	Tofu	Dog
222	Lydia	1	Fluffy	Dog
		2	JoJo	Bird
		3	Ziggy	Snake
333	Jane	1	Fluffy	Cat
		2	Cleo	Cat

FIGURE 4.13 Non-relational table (not in 1NF).

---

[4]A group of related multivalued columns is also known as a "repeating group."

VET CLINIC CLIENT

ClientID	ClientName	PetNo	PetName	PetType
111	Lisa	1	Tofu	Dog
222	Lydia	1	Fluffy	Dog
222	Lydia	2	JoJo	Bird
222	Lydia	3	Ziggy	Snake
333	Jane	1	Fluffy	Cat
333	Jane	2	Cleo	Cat

FIGURE 4.14   Normalizing the table in Figure 4.13 to 1NF by increasing the number of records.

Lydia has three pets, while the values *333, Jane* were repeated two times because client *Jane* has two pets. Note that the primary key of the relation normalized to 1NF in this way is a composite key composed of the primary key of the original non-relational table and a nonkey column (or columns) that has a unique value within the related multivalued columns. The nonkey column(s) combined with the original primary key have a unique value for each record. In Figure 4.14, the primary key is composed of the column ClientID, which is the original primary key, and the nonkey column PetNo. The combination ClientID, PetNo uniquely identifies each record in the table shown in Figure 4.14.

Another way to normalize a non-relational table into 1NF is to create a new separate table for each group of related multivalued columns. As shown in Figure 4.15, the new separate table PET captures the group of related pet columns PetNo, PetName, and PetType that had multiple values per record in the original table. The new separate table contains the primary key of the original table (ClientID), which serves both as the foreign key in the new table and as part of the primary key of the new table. The other part of the primary key (PetNo) in the new table is the column (or set of columns) that, combined with the foreign key, has a unique value for each record. Figure 4.15 illustrates the result of this process applied to the table in Figure 4.13.

Note that a newly created table PET containing the group of related multivalued pet columns includes a separate record for each occurrence of related multivalued columns, just as it was done in the case depicted in Figure 4.14. In order to normalize a table to 1NF, a separate record for each occurrence of related multivalued columns is created.

We will now consider an expanded example with multiple groups of multivalued related columns. The table in Figure 4.16 has two groups of related multivalued columns. One group of related multivalued columns includes pet columns PetNo, PetName, and PetType, and the other group of related multivalued columns includes household member columns HHMember, Name, and Relation.

In cases when a table has multiple groups of related multivalued columns, normalizing to 1NF is done by creating separate tables for each group of related multivalued columns. This is illustrated by Figure 4.17. Note that in Figure 4.17, the composite primary key

VET CLINIC CLIENT

ClientID	ClientName
111	Lisa
222	Lydia
333	Jane

PET

ClientID	PetNo	PetName	PetType
111	1	Tofu	Dog
222	1	Fluffy	Dog
222	2	JoJo	Bird
222	3	Ziggy	Snake
333	1	Fluffy	Cat
333	2	Cleo	Cat

FIGURE 4.15   Normalizing the table in Figure 4.13 to 1NF by creating a new, separate table.

VET CLINIC CLIENT

ClientID	ClientName	PetNo	PetName	PetType	HHMember	Name	Relation
111	Lisa	1	Tofu	Dog	1	Joe	Husband
					2	Sally	Daughter
					3	Clyde	Son
222	Lydia	1	Fluffy	Dog	1	Bill	Husband
		2	JoJo	Bird	2	Lilly	Daughter
		3	Ziggy	Snake			
333	Jane	1	Fluffy	Cat	1	Jill	Sister
		2	Cleo	Cat			

FIGURE 4.16   Non-relational table (not in 1NF) with two groups of related multivalued columns.

VET CLINIC CLIENT

ClientID	ClientName
111	Lisa
222	Lydia
333	Jane

PET

ClientID	PetNo	PetName	PetType
111	1	Tofu	Dog
222	1	Fluffy	Dog
222	2	JoJo	Bird
222	3	Ziggy	Snake
333	1	Fluffy	Cat
333	2	Cleo	Cat

HOUSEHOLD MEMBER

ClientID	HHMember	Name	Relation
111	1	Joe	Husband
111	2	Sally	Daughter
111	3	Clyde	Son
222	1	Bill	Husband
222	2	Lilly	Daughter
333	1	Jill	Sister

FIGURE 4.17   Normalizing the table in Figure 4.16 to 1NF.

of each newly created table representing one of the groups of related multivalued columns contains the primary key of the original table. The HOUSEHOLD MEMBER table primary key contains the ClientID (primary key of the original table as well as HHMember. The PET table primary key contains the ClientID (primary key of the original table as well as PetNo.

It is important to keep in mind that normalizing to 1NF is not a part of the normalization process of relations in a relational database because, as we stated earlier, each relation in a relational database is already in 1NF. Normalizing to 1NF is done only when a non-relational table is being converted in a relation. The normalization process of relational database tables starts with the second normal form (2NF).

Second Normal Form (2NF)

For a relational table, the process of normalization starts by examining if a relational table is in 2NF.

2NF

*A table is in 2NF if it is in 1NF and if it **does not contain partial functional dependencies.***

Recall that a partial dependency occurs when a portion of a composite key functionally determines a column of a relation. If a relation has a single-column primary key, then there is no possibility of partial functional dependencies in such a relation. Such a relation is automatically in 2NF and it does not have to be normalized to 2NF. However, relations that have a composite primary key may contain partial functional dependencies. If a relation with a composite primary key has partial dependencies, then it is not in 2NF, and it has to be normalized it to 2NF.

Normalization of a relation to 2NF creates additional relations for each set of partial dependencies in a relation. The primary key of the additional relation is the portion of the primary key that functionally determines the columns in the original relation. The columns that were partially determined in the original relation are now part of the additional table. The original table still remains after the process of normalizing to 2NF, but it no longer contains the partially dependent columns.

We will demonstrate normalizing to 2NF by using the relation AD CAMPAIGN MIX. Consider the functional dependencies shown in Figure 4.10 (on page 103). The partial dependencies in the relation AD CAMPAIGN MIX are:

> AdCampaignID → AdCampaignName, StartDate, Duration, CampaignMgrID,
>   CampaignMgrName
> ModelD → Media, Range

The result of normalizing the AD CAMPAIGN MIX relation to 2NF is shown in Figure 4.18. The partial dependencies in the AD CAMPAIGN MIX relation are eliminated. The resulting modified relation AD CAMPAIGN MIX contains the full functional dependency:

> AdCampaignID, ModelD → BudgetPctg

For each set of partial dependencies, a separate table is created.
A new relation AD CAMPAIGN contains the former partial dependency:

> AdCampaignID → AdCampaignName, StartDate, Duration, CampaignMgrID,
>   CampaignMgrName

A new relation MODE contains the former partial dependency:

> ModelD → Media, Range

The modified relation AD CAMPAIGN MIX no longer contains the columns that were functionally dependent on portions of the primary key (i.e., that were partially dependent).

Third Normal Form (3NF)

For a relational table that is in 2NF, the process of normalization continues by examining if a relational table is in 3NF.

3NF

*A table is in 3NF if it is in 2NF and if it **does not contain transitive functional dependencies**.*

Recall that a transitive dependency occurs when a nonkey column determines another nonkey column of a relation. If a relation has transitive dependencies, then it is not in 3NF, and it has to be normalized it to 3NF.

Normalization of a relation to 3NF creates additional relations for each set of transitive dependencies in a relation. The primary key of the additional relation is the nonkey column (or columns) that functionally determined the nonkey columns in the original relation. The nonkey columns that were transitively determined in the original

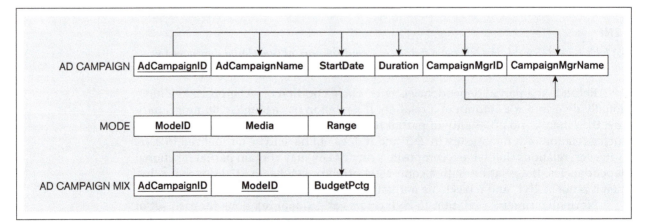

FIGURE 4.18   Pressly Ad Agency example—normalizing to 2NF.

relation are now part of the additional table. The original table still remains after normalizing to 3NF, but it no longer contains the transitively dependent columns.

We will demonstrate normalizing to 3NF by using the AD CAMPAIGN MIX example. Consider the functional dependencies shown in Figure 4.18. Relations AD CAMPAIGN MIX and MODE do not have any transitive dependencies, and they are already in 3NF. However, the relation AD CAMPAIGN has the following transitive dependency:

> CampaignMgrID → CampaignMgrName

so it is not in 3NF. The result of normalizing the AD CAMPAIGN relation to 3NF is shown in Figure 4.19. The transitive dependency in the AD CAMPAIGN relation is eliminated, and a separate relation CAMPAIGN MANAGER is created, containing the former transitive dependency.

The modified relation AD CAMPAIGN no longer contains the nonkey columns that were functionally dependent on portions of other nonkey columns (i.e., that were transitively dependent).

Figure 4.20 shows the data records of the 3NF relations shown in Figure 4.19. Compare the records in Figure 4.20 with the records in Figure 4.4 (on page 94). Notice that both figures show the same data. In Figure 4.4, the data is stored in one non-normalized relation that is prone to update anomalies. That same data is shown in Figure 4.20 in four normalized tables that are not prone to update anomalies.

Notice that in the process of normalizing a relation to 2NF and 3NF, we start with one relation and end up with multiple relations connected through their referential integrity constraints in a relational schema. The four relations shown in Figures 4.19 and 4.20 are the result of normalizing the relation AD CAMPAIGN MIX (from Figure 4.4 to 3NF. Figure 4.21 shows the relational schema depicting referential integrity constraint lines connecting the normalized relations.

Other Normal Forms

In the majority of real-world business problems, normalizing to 3NF by removing partial and transitive functional dependencies as illustrated in this chapter is sufficient to eliminate unnecessary redundancies and the threat of update anomalies. Higher normal forms beyond 3NF based on other types of functional dependencies (beyond full key, partial, and transitive functional dependencies) have mostly theoretical value, and they are presented in Appendix B.

Eliminating Redundancy and Resolving Update Anomalies

As we mentioned earlier in this chapter, in relations that contain redundant data, the update operations can cause update anomalies. We will use the Pressly Ad Agency example to illustrate how normalization eliminates redundancy and resolves update anomalies.

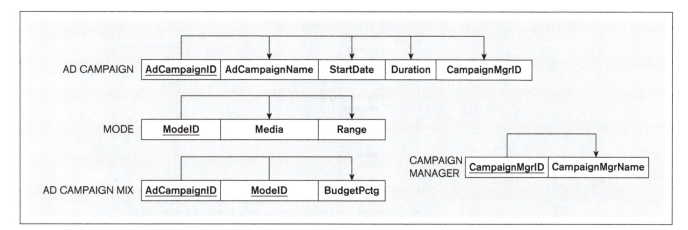

FIGURE 4.19 Pressly Ad Agency example—normalizing to 3NF.

AD CAMPAIGN

AdCampaignID	AdCampaignName	StartDate	Duration	CampaignMgrID
111	SummerFun13	6.6.2013	12 days	CM100
222	SummerZing13	6.8.2013	30 days	CM101
333	FallBall13	6.9.2013	12 days	CM102
444	AutmnStyle13	6.9.2013	5 days	CM103
555	AutmnColors13	6.9.2013	3 days	CM100

CAMPAIGN MANAGER

CampaignMgrID	CampaignMgrName
CM100	Roberta
CM101	Sue
CM102	John
CM103	Nancy

MODE

ModeID	Media	Range
1	TV	Local
2	TV	National
3	Radio	Local
4	Radio	National
5	Print	Local
6	Print	National

AD CAMPAIGN MIX

AdCampaignID	ModeID	BudgetPctg
111	1	50%
111	2	50%
222	1	60%
222	3	30%
222	5	10%
333	3	80%
333	4	20%
444	6	100%
555	3	100%

FIGURE 4.20 Pressly Ad Agency example—normalized relations with data.

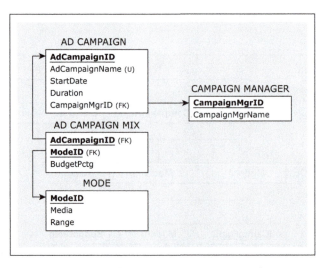

FIGURE 4.21 Pressly Ad Agency example—relational schema of 3NF relations.

Observe the records shown in Figure 4.20. The name, start date, and duration of each campaign is listed only once. The name of each campaign manager is listed only once. The media and range value for each of the campaign modes are also listed only once. The only values that repeat multiple times and refer to the same occurrence are the foreign key values, such as value *CM100* appearing twice in the CampaignMgrID column in relation AD CAMPAIGN, or value *222* appearing three times in the AdCampaignID column in relation AD CAMPAIGN MIX. Multiple appearances of foreign key values in the 3NF set of relational tables represent **necessary redundancy**, which is essential for connecting the tables.

The following examples, shown in Figure 4.22, provide an illustration of how the normalization process resolves update anomalies.

To illustrate how normalization resolves an insertion anomaly issue, consider the following example. Suppose the ad agency decides to start using another campaign mode for future campaigns with ModeID: *7*, Media: *Internet*, and Range: *National*. This new mode cannot be entered in Figure 4.4 in the relation AD CAMPAIGN MIX without also entering an actual campaign that uses this mode. On the other hand, in Figure 4.22,

AD CAMPAIGN

AdCampaignID	AdCampaignName	StartDate	Duration	CampaignMgrID
111	SummerFun13	6.6.2013	12 days	CM100
222	SummerZing13	6.8.2013	45 days	CM101
333	FallBall13	6.9.2013	12 days	CM102
555	AutmnColors13	6.9.2013	3 days	CM100

Modification Anomaly Resolved :
Only one record modified

CAMPAIGN MANAGER

CampaignMgrID	CampaignMgrName
CM100	Roberta
CM101	Sue
CM102	John
CM103	Nancy

MODE

ModeID	Media	Range
1	TV	Local
2	TV	National
3	Radio	Local
4	Radio	National
5	Print	Local
6	Print	National
7	Internet	National

Deletion Anomaly Resolved :
Campaign 444 deleted, but
all the data about the campaign
manager CM103 and the campaign
mode 6 remain in the database

Insertion Anomaly Resolved :
New campaign mode 7 inserted
without inserting an actual campaign
using the new mode 7

AD CAMPAIGN MIX

AdCampaignID	ModeID	BudgetPctg
111	1	50%
111	2	50%
222	1	60%
222	3	30%
222	5	10%
333	3	80%
333	4	20%
555	3	100%

FIGURE 4.22 Pressly Ad Agency example—normalized relations with data; update anomalies resolved.

the new campaign mode *7, Internet, National* was easily entered in the relation MODE without having to enter any other information.

To illustrate how normalization resolves a deletion anomaly issue, consider the following example. If the ad agency decides to cancel ad campaign *444*, deleting the record relating to campaign *444* in the relation AD CAMPAIGN MIX in Figure 4.4 will also delete campaign mode *6, Print, National* (because no other campaign is using this mode at this time) and campaign manager *103, Nancy* (because no other campaign is managed by her at this time). On the other hand, in the same scenario in Figure 4.22, the record relating to campaign *444* was deleted from the relation AD CAMPAIGN (and also from the relation AD CAMPAIGN MIX, but the record for campaign mode *6, Internet, National* remains in the relation MODE, and the record for campaign manager *103, Nancy* remains in the relation CAMPAIGN MANAGER.

To illustrate how normalization resolves a modification anomaly issue, consider the following example. If the ad agency decided to extend the duration of the campaign 222 from *30* days to *45* days, this change would have to be made in three different records in the relation AD CAMPAIGN MIX in Figure 4.4. On the other hand, for the same scenario, in Figure 4.22, change is only needed in one record related to campaign *222* in the relation AD CAMPAIGN.

ANOTHER NORMALIZATION EXAMPLE

To recap the introduced concepts, we will illustrate normalization to 2NF and 3NF of the relation RECRUITING shown in Figure 4.11 (on page 103.

Consider the functional dependencies shown in Figure 4.12 (on page 104). The partial dependencies in the relation RECRUITING are

RecruiterID → RecruiterName, StatusID, Status
City, State → CityPopulation
State → StatePopulation

The result of normalizing the RECRUITING relation to 2NF is shown in Figure 4.23. The partial dependencies in the relation are eliminated. For each set of partial dependencies, a separate table is created.

Consider the functional dependencies shown in Figure 4.23. Relations CITY, STATE, and RECRUITING do not have any transitive dependencies and are already in 3NF. However, the relation RECRUITER has the following transitive dependency:

StatusID → Status

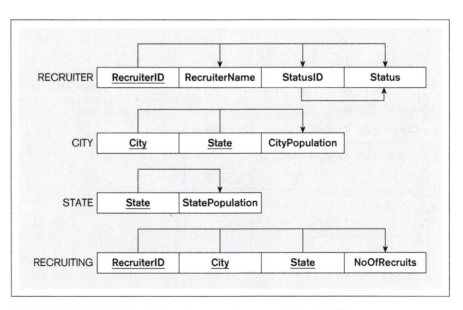

FIGURE 4.23 Central Plane University example—normalizing to 2NF.

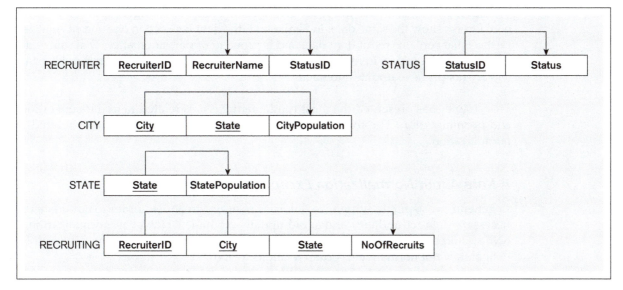

FIGURE 4.24   Central Plane University example—normalizing to 3NF.

so it has to be normalized to 3NF. The result of normalizing the RECRUITER relation to 3NF is shown in Figure 4.24. The transitive dependency in the RECRUITER relation is eliminated, and a separate table STATUS is created, containing the former transitive dependency.

Figure 4.25 shows the records in the 3NF relations shown in Figure 4.24.

RECRUITER

RecruiterID	RecruiterName	StatusID
R1	Katy	IF
R2	Abra	IP
R3	Jana	CN
R4	Maria	IF
R5	Dan	CN

STATUS

StatusID	Status
CN	Contractor
IF	Internal Full Time
IP	Internal Part Time

CITY

City	State	CityPopulation
Portland	ME	70,000
Grand Rapids	MI	190,000
Rockford	IL	340,000
Spokane	WA	210,000
Portland	OR	600,000
Eugene	OR	360,000
Grand Rapids	MN	11,000

STATE

State	StatePopulation
ME	1,350,000
MI	9,900,000
IL	12,900,000
WA	6,800,000
OR	3,900,000
MN	5,400,000

RECRUITING

RecruiterID	City	State	NoOfRecruits
R1	Portland	ME	11
R1	Grand Rapids	MI	20
R2	Rockford	IL	17
R3	Spokane	WA	8
R3	Portland	OR	30
R3	Eugene	OR	20
R4	Rockford	IL	14
R4	Grand Rapids	MN	9
R5	Grand Rapids	MI	33

FIGURE 4.25   RECRUITING example—normalized relations with data.

Compare the records in Figure 4.25 with the records in Figure 4.11. Notice that both figures show the same data. In Figure 4.11, the data is stored in one non-normalized relation that contains redundant data and is prone to update anomalies. That same data is shown in Figure 4.25 in five normalized relations that do not contain redundant data and are not prone to update anomalies.

This chapter has presented the most fundamental issues related to update operations and normalization. The following notes cover several additional issues related to normalization.

A Note About Normalization Exceptions

In general, we aspire to normalize database relations to 3NF in order to eliminate unnecessary data redundancy and avoid update anomalies. However, normalization to 3NF should be done judiciously and pragmatically, which may in some cases call for deliberately not normalizing certain relations to 3NF.

Consider the relation SALES AGENT, shown in Figure 4.26.

The functional dependencies in the relation SALES AGENT are shown in Figure 4.27. The relation SALES AGENT is in 2NF but not in 3NF due to the transitive dependency:

ZipCode → City, State

We can certainly normalize this relation to 3NF, as shown in Figure 4.28. However, we may also decide to leave the relation in SALES AGENT as is. The decision should be made on evaluating whether the payoff of not having the City and State columns in the table SALES AGENT is worth creating a separate relation ZIPCODE-CITY, and thereby increasing the complexity of the relational schema by adding another table and referential integrity constraint to it. For example, if sales agents within the same zip code are rare, the benefits of normalization to 3NF would be marginal. In such a case, we may decide that the redundancy caused by keeping the State and City columns in the original relation is acceptable and would leave the original relation as is. As another

SALES AGENT

SAgentID	SAgentName	City	State	ZipCode
SA1	Rose	Glen Ellyn	IL	60137
SA2	Sidney	Chicago	IL	60611
SA3	James	Chicago	IL	60610
SA4	Violet	Wheaton	IL	60187
SA5	Nicole	Kenosha	WI	53140
SA6	Justin	Milwaukee	WI	53201

FIGURE 4.26 SALES AGENT example.

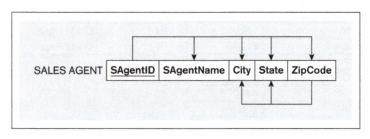

FIGURE 4.27 Functional dependencies in the SALES AGENT example

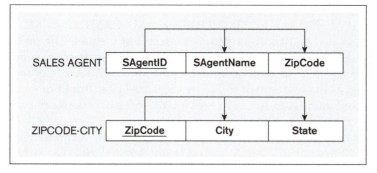

FIGURE 4.28   SALES AGENT example in 3NF.

example, consider a company that has a limit of two sales agents per state. In such a case, the possible redundancy in the original relation is even smaller, and there is even less incentive to normalize it.

Of course, these examples do not mean that normalization is always an optional process. The guideline is to normalize the relational databases to 3NF, while allowing for the possibility of making an exception with certain relations for clear and legitimate reasons.

A Note About Denormalization: Normalization versus Performance

As we demonstrated, during the normalization process, larger relations with columns that contain redundant data are decomposed into smaller relations. One of the implications of this process is that the data that resided in fewer relations prior to normalization is spread out across more relations. This has an effect on the performance of data retrievals. We will demonstrate this effect with the following example.

Compare the relation in Figure 4.4 (on page 94) with the relations in Figure 4.20 (on page 110). Relations in Figure 4.20 represent a normalized version of the relation in Figure 4.4. Let us assume one of the most frequent retrievals in Pressly Ad Agency is:

> *For each mode of a particular campaign, retrieve the following columns: AdCampaignID, AdCampaignName, CampaignMgrID, CampaignMgrName, ModeID, Media, Range, and BudgetPctg.*

The result of this retrieval is shown in shown in Figure 4.29.

Retrieving this information for the table shown in Figure 4.4 simply involves selecting eight columns from the table AD CAMPAIGN MIX. On the other hand,

RETRIEVED DATA

AdCampaignID	AdCampaignName	Campaign MgrID	Campaign MgrName	ModeID	Media	Range	BudgetPctg
111	SummerFun13	CM100	Roberta	1	TV	Local	50%
111	SummerFun13	CM100	Roberta	2	TV	National	50%
222	SummerZing13	CM101	Sue	1	TV	Local	60%
222	SummerZing13	CM101	Sue	3	Radio	Local	30%
222	SummerZing13	CM101	Sue	5	Print	Local	10%
333	FallBall13	CM102	John	3	Radio	Local	80%
333	FallBall13	CM102	John	4	Radio	National	20%
444	AutmnStyle13	CM103	Nancy	6	Print	National	100%
555	AutmnColors13	CM100	Roberta	3	Radio	Local	100%

FIGURE 4.29   Pressly Ad Agency example—a retrieval of data.

retrieving that same information from Figure 4.20 involves joining[5] relations AD CAM-PAIGN, CAMPAIGN MANAGER, MODE, and AD CAMPAIGN MIX and then selecting the requested eight columns from the result of the join. The process of joining relations and then retrieving the data from the result of such a join is more time-consuming than retrieving the data from one non-normalized table. Consequently, some retrievals (such as the one shown in Figure 4.29) are faster from non-normalized than from normalized databases. In such cases a trade-off exists between reducing redundancy vs. faster retrieval (performance).

Denormalization refers to reversing the effect of normalization by joining normalized relations into a relation that is not normalized. Denormalization can be used in dealing with the normalization vs. performance issue. For example, a normalized master version of the relational database (e.g., Figure 4.20) can be kept as a place where all insertions, modifications, and deletions on the data are done in order to avoid update anomalies. At the same time, a physical denormalized copy of the database (e.g., Figure 4.4) can be periodically created from the master version and stored so that it can be used for quicker retrievals. That way, all updates would be done on the master copy that is not prone to update anomalies. Retrievals of the data that are faster on the denormalized relations could be done on the denormalized copy for better performance. Such setup can be convenient, for example, in settings where there are few updates to the data but there are many reads of the data. The denormalized copy can be recreated as often as needed by user's requirements for the most recent data.[6]

Denormalization is not a default process that is to be undertaken in all circumstances. Instead, denormalization should be used judiciously, after analyzing its costs and benefits.

A Note About ER Modeling versus Normalization

As we stated in Chapters 2 and 3, ER modeling followed by mapping into a relational schema is one of the most common database design methods. When faced with a non-normalized table, such as the one in Figure 4.4, instead of identifying functional dependencies and going through normalization to 2NF and 3NF, a designer can analyze the table and create an ER diagram based on it. That ER diagram can then be mapped into a relational schema.

Let us take another look at the relation in Figure 4.4. A database designer analyzing this table (looking at the columns, examining the data records in this table, and talking to the users of this table) would be able to create the following requirements:

The database for the Pressly Ad Agency should capture data about the following:

- *For each **ad campaign**: an AdCampaignID (unique), AdCampaignName (unique), a start date, and a duration of the campaign*
- *For each **ad campaign manager:** a CampaignMgrID (unique) and CampaignMgrName*
- *For each **ad campaign mode**: a ModeID (unique), Media, and Range*
- *Each ad campaign is managed by exactly one campaign manager.*
  Each campaign manager manages at least one ad campaign, but can manage more than one.
- *Each ad campaign uses at least one campaign mode, but can use more than one.*
  An ad campaign mode can be used by multiple campaigns, but it does not have to be used by any.
- *Every time an ad campaign uses a campaign mode, we keep track of the budget percentage used by that ad campaign for that mode.*

Based on these requirements an ER diagram, shown in Figure 4.30, would be created. The result of mapping the ER diagram from Figure 4.30 into a relational schema is shown in Figure 4.31.

---

[5]The join operation will be elaborated on in Chapter 5.
[6]The denormalization approach is used, for example, in data warehouses (covered in Chapters 7, 8, and 9) and materialized views (covered in Chapter 10).

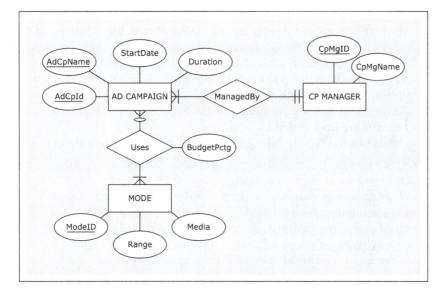

FIGURE 4.30   ER diagram of the Pressly Ad Agency example.

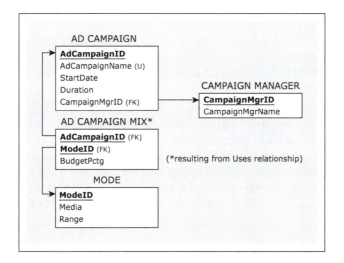

FIGURE 4.31   ER diagram of the Pressly Ad Agency example mapped into a relational schema.

Note that the relational schema in Figure 4.31 is exactly the same as the relational schema in Figure 4.21 (on page 110 that was the result of normalizing the relation AD CAMPAIGN MIX to 3NF.

When the ER modeling technique is used properly, the result is a relational schema with relational tables that are well designed and sufficiently normalized to 3NF. For example, if you examine the relations in the relational schemas in Figures 3.32 (on page 70) or 3.59 (on page 79) in Chapter 3, you will notice that all relations in those schemas are in 3NF.

Normalization, as an explicit process, is not a necessary part of a properly undertaken database design project. Normalization of relational databases to 3NF is done when we are faced with relations that were not properly designed and have to be improved. Such scenarios are not rare, and therefore it is important to be familiar with the process of normalization.

A Note About Designer–Added Entities (Tables) and Keys for Streamlining Database Content

In some cases, even if a relation is in 3NF, additional opportunities for streamlining database content may still exist. The following is a brief discussion of using **designer-added entities (tables)** and **designer-added keys** for such a purpose.

Consider the relation MODE in Figure 4.20. This relation is in 3NF. Each record refers to a different campaign mode. As we stated above, the relation MODE could have resulted from mapping the ER diagram shown in Figure 4.30 to its corresponding relations. A database designer, after discussions with the end users, could decide to replace the repetition of textual values describing media and range for each campaign mode in relation MODE with shorter numeric values. In that case, the database designer would augment the requirements for the ER diagram in Figure 4.30 as follows (new requirements are underlined):

The database for the Pressly Ad Agency should capture the data about the following:

- *For each **ad campaign**: an AdCampaignID (unique), AdCampaignName (unique), a start date, and a duration of the campaign*
- *For each **ad campaign manager**: a CampaignMgrID (unique) and CampaignMgrName*
- *For each **ad campaign mode**: a ModeID (unique)*
- *For each **ad campaign media**: a MediaID (unique) and Media*
- *For each **ad campaign range**: a RangeID (unique) and Range*
- *Each ad campaign is managed by exactly one campaign manager.*
  Each campaign manager manages at least one ad campaign, but can manage more than one.
- *Each ad campaign uses at least one campaign mode, but can use more than one.*
  An ad campaign mode can be used by multiple campaigns, but it does not have to be used by any.
- *Every time an ad campaign uses a campaign mode we keep track of the budget percentage used by that ad campaign for that mode.*
- *Each ad campaign mode includes one media. Each campaign media is included in one or more campaign modes.*
- *Each ad campaign mode covers one range. Each campaign range is covered by one or more campaign modes.*

Based on the newly augmented requirements, the ER diagram will be augmented by adding two designer-added entities as shown in Figure 4.32, and thereby creating two designer-added tables in the ad agency database, as shown in Figure 4.33.

Designer-added keys MediaID and RangeID will serve as primary keys of the MEDIA and RANGE designer-added tables, respectively.

Figure 4.34 shows the records in the augmented AD CAMPAIGN MIX database. Values *TV*, *Radio*, and *Print* are now listed only once in the MEDIA table, while the

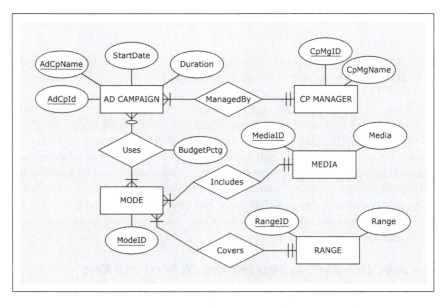

FIGURE 4.32 Augmented ER diagram of the Pressly Ad Agency example.

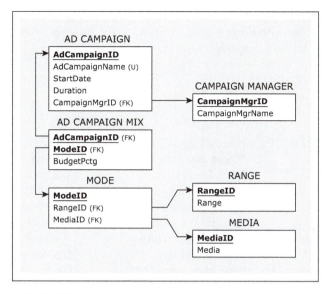

FIGURE 4.33 Augmented ER diagram of the Pressly Ad Agency example mapped into a relational schema.

foreign keys referring to those values are repeated multiple times in the MODE table. Also, textual values *Local* and *National* are now listed only once in the RANGE table, while the foreign keys referring to those values are repeated multiple times in the MODE table.

AD CAMPAIGN

AdCampaignID	AdCampaignName	StartDate	Duration	CampaignMgrID
111	SummerFun13	6.6.2013	12 days	CM100
222	SummerZing13	6.8.2013	30 days	CM101
333	FallBall13	6.9.2013	12 days	CM102
444	AutmnStyle13	6.9.2013	5 days	CM103
555	AutmnColors13	6.9.2013	3 days	CM100

CAMPAIGN MANAGER

CampaignMgrID	CampaignMgrName
CM100	Roberta
CM101	Sue
CM102	John
CM103	Nancy

RANGE

RangeID	Range
L	Local
N	National

MEDIA

MediaID	Media
T	TV
R	Radio
P	Print

AD CAMPAIGN MIX

AdCampaignID	ModeID	BudgetPctg
111	1	50%
111	2	50%
222	1	60%
222	3	30%
222	5	10%
333	3	80%
333	4	20%
444	6	100%
555	3	100%

MODE

ModeID	MediaID	RangeID
1	T	L
2	T	N
3	R	L
4	R	N
5	P	L
6	P	N

FIGURE 4.34 Pressly Ad Agency example—relations from Figure 4.33 populated with data.

Just as was the case with denormalization, augmenting databases with designer-added keys and tables should not be done summarily, but with care and after analyzing pros and cons for each augmentation.

Key Terms

Augmented functional dependencies *100*
Delete operation *91*
Deletion anomaly *95*
Denormalization *116*
Designer-added entities (tables) *117*
Designer-added keys *117*
Equivalent functional dependencies *100*

First normal form (1NF) *104*
Full key functional dependency *101*
Functional dependency *97*
Insert operation *91*
Insertion anomaly *95*
Modification anomaly *96*
Modify operation *91*
Necessary redundancy *111*
Nonkey column *95*

Normal forms *104*
Normalization *91*
Partial functional dependency *101*
Read operation *91*
Redundant data *91*
Related multivalued columns *105*
Second normal form (2NF) *104*

Third normal form (3NF) *104*
Transitive functional dependency *101*
Trivial functional dependencies *99*
Update anomalies *91*
Update operations *91*
Write operations *91*

Review Questions

Q4.1   What are the three update operations?
Q4.2   What is redundant data?
Q4.3   How does an insertion anomaly occur?
Q4.4   How does a deletion anomaly occur?
Q4.5   How does a modification anomaly occur?
Q4.6   What is a functional dependency?
Q4.7   What is a partial functional dependency?
Q4.8   What is a full key functional dependency?

Q4.9   What is a transitive functional dependency?
Q4.10 Give the definition of 1NF.
Q4.11 Give the definition of 2NF.
Q4.12 Give the definition of 3NF.
Q4.13 What is denormalization and what is its purpose?
Q4.14 What is the purpose of designer-added entities, tables, and keys?

Exercises

E4.1   Create an example of a relation (containing several records) that is prone to update anomalies.
E4.2   Using the relation created in exercise **E4.1**, describe an example that illustrates the insertion anomaly.

E4.3   Using the relation created in exercise **E4.1**, describe an example that illustrates the deletion anomaly.
E4.4   Using the relation created in exercise **E4.1**, describe an example that illustrates the modification anomaly.

E4.5 Consider the following relation with sample data.

AIRPORT KLX TABLE

Date	AirlineID	AirlineName	TerminalID	NumberOfGates	NumberOfDepartingFlights
11-Dec	UA	United	A	20	34
11-Dec	NW	Northwest	A	20	17
11-Dec	AA	American	A	20	11
11-Dec	DL	Delta	B	15	20
11-Dec	JB	Jet Blue	B	15	6
12-Dec	UA	United	A	20	29
12-Dec	DL	Delta	B	15	20
12-Dec	SWA	Southwest	C	15	17

- *The AIRPORT KLX Table captures the data about daily departing flights at the KLX Airport.*
- *Each airline operating at KLX airport has a unique Airline ID and an Airline Name.*
- *Each terminal at KLX airport has a unique Terminal ID and a fixed Number of Gates.*
- *Each airline is permanently assigned to one (and only one) terminal at the KLX Airport.*
- *Each terminal at KLX Airport can have multiple airlines assigned to it.*
- *Each day (Date), this table records the Number of Departing Flights at KLX Airport for each airline.*

E4.5a Using the AIRPORT KLX Table, describe an example that illustrates the insertion anomaly.

E4.5b Using the AIRPORT KLX Table, describe an example that illustrates the deletion anomaly.

E4.5c Using the AIRPORT KLX Table, describe an example that illustrates the modification anomaly.

E4.5d Depict full key functional dependencies, partial functional dependencies (if any), and transitive functional dependencies (if any) in the AIRPORT KLX Table.

E4.5e Show the result of normalizing the AIRPORT KLX Table to 2NF.

E4.5f Show the result of normalizing the AIRPORT KLX Table to 3NF.

E4.5g Using the set of tables resulting from **E4.5f**, describe how the anomalies shown in **E4.5a**, **E4.5b**, and **E4.5c** are eliminated.

E4.6 Consider the following relation with sample data.

DEPARTMENT OF TRANSPORTATION (DOT) PROJECT TABLE

ProjectID	ProjectName	CountyID	CountyName	ProjectManagerID	ProjectManagerName	ProjectMilesWithinCounty
1	Road X	1	Wilson	M1	Bob	10.00
1	Road X	2	Ottawa	M1	Bob	17.00
1	Road X	3	Davis	M1	Bob	12.00
2	Road Y	3	Davis	M2	Sue	23.00
3	Bridge A	1	Wilson	M3	Lee	0.50
3	Bridge A	2	Ottawa	M3	Lee	0.30
4	Tunnel Q	2	Ottawa	M1	Bob	2.00
5	Road W	4	Pony	M4	Bob	23.00

- *The DEPARTMENT OF TRANSPORTATION (DOT) Project Table captures the data about projects and their length (in miles).*
- *Each project has a unique Project ID and Project Name.*
- *Each county has a unique County ID and County Name.*
- *Each project manager has a unique Project Manager ID and Project Manager Name.*

- *Each project has one project manager.*
- *A project manager can manage several projects.*
- *A project can span across several counties.*
- *This table records the length of the project in a county in the ProjectMilesWithinCounty column.*

E4.6a Using the DOT PROJECT Table, describe an example that illustrates the insertion anomaly.

E4.6b Using the DOT PROJECT Table, describe an example that illustrates the deletion anomaly.

E4.6c Using the DOT PROJECT Table, describe an example that illustrates the modification anomaly.

E4.6d Depict full key functional dependencies, partial functional dependencies (if any), and transitive functional dependencies (if any) in the DOT PROJECT Table.

E4.6e Show the result of normalizing the DOT PROJECT Table to 2NF.

E4.6f Show the result of normalizing the DOT PROJECT Table to 3NF.

E4.6g Using the set of tables resulting from **E4.6f**, describe how the anomalies shown in **E4.6a**, **E4.6b**, and **E4.6c** are eliminated.

E4.7 Consider the following relation with sample data.

SHIPMENTS TABLE

ShipmentID	ShipmentDate	TruckID	TruckType	ProductID	ProductType	Quantity
111	1-Jan	T-111	Semi-Trailer	A	Tire	180
111	1-Jan	T-111	Semi-Trailer	B	Battery	120
222	2-Jan	T-222	Van Truck	C	SparkPlug	10,000
333	3-Jan	T-333	Semi-Trailer	D	Wipers	5,000
333	3-Jan	T-333	Semi-Trailer	A	Tire	200
444	3-Jan	T-222	Van Truck	C	SparkPlug	25,000
555	3-Jan	T-111	Semi-Trailer	B	Battery	180

- *The SHIPMENTS Table for a car part company captures the data about car shipments.*
- *Each shipment has a unique Shipment ID and a Shipment Date.*
- *Each shipment is shipped on one truck.*
- *Each truck has a unique Truck ID, and a Truck Type.*
- *Each shipment can ship multiple products.*
- *Each product has a unique Product ID and a Product Type.*
- *Each quantity of a product shipped in a shipment is recorded in a table in the column Quantity.*

E4.7a Depict full key functional dependencies, partial functional dependencies (if any), and transitive functional dependencies (if any) in the SHIPMENTS Table.

E4.7b Show the result of normalizing the SHIPMENTS Table to 2NF.

E4.7c Show the result of normalizing the SHIPMENTS Table to 3NF.

E4.8 Consider the following relation with sample data.

LANGUAGE SCHOOL TABLE

CourseID	CourseLanguage	CourseLevel	ClientID	ClientName	Attendance	FinalScore
10	German	Basic	C111	Mr. Smith	100%	80%
11	German	Intermediate	C222	Ms. Jones	90%	90%
12	German	Advanced	C333	Mr. Vance	95%	100%
10	German	Basic	C444	Ms. Clark	100%	100%
11	German	Intermediate	C555	Ms. Wong	90%	95%
12	German	Advanced	C666	Ms. Hess	95%	98%
20	Japanese	Basic	C111	Mr. Smith	100%	100%
21	Japanese	Intermediate	C222	Ms. Jones	95%	100%

- *The LANGUAGE SCHOOL Table keeps track of clients completing language classes.*
- *Each course has a unique Course ID and a Course Language and Course Level.*
- *Each client has a unique Client ID and a Client Name.*
- *Each course can be completed by multiple clients.*
- *Each client can complete multiple courses.*
- *When a client completes a course, his or her attendance and final score in the class are recorded.*

E4.8a Depict full key functional dependencies, partial functional dependencies (if any), and transitive functional dependencies (if any) in the LANGUAGE SCHOOL Table.

E4.8b Show the result of normalizing the LANGUAGE SCHOOL Table to 2NF.

E4.8c Show the result of normalizing the LANGUAGE SCHOOL Table to 3NF.

E4.9 Consider the following relation with sample data.

HEALTH CENTER TABLE

DocID	DocName	PatientID	PatientName	InsuranceCoID	InsuranceCoName	NextAppointmentDate
1	Dr. Joe	111	Max	11	ACME Insurance	1-Dec
1	Dr. Joe	222	Mia	11	ACME Insurance	2-Dec
1	Dr. Joe	333	Pam	12	Purple Star	3-Dec
2	Dr. Sue	333	Pam	12	Purple Star	7-Dec
3	Dr. Kim	555	Lee	13	Tower Block	2-Dec
3	Dr. Kim	111	Max	11	ACME Insurance	3-Dec
4	Dr. Joe	666	Alen	14	All Protect	9-Dec

- *The HEALTH CENTER Table captures the data about patients' appointments with doctors.*
- *Each patient has a unique Patient ID and a Patient Name.*
- *Each doctor has a unique Doc ID and a Doc Name.*
- *Each patient has one insurance company.*
- *Each insurance company has a unique Insurance Co ID and Insurance Co Name.*
- *Each appointment is scheduled between one patient and one doctor.*
- *Each patient can have many appointments scheduled (but only one appointment scheduled with one particular doctor).*

E4.9a Depict full key functional dependencies, partial functional dependencies (if any), and transitive functional dependencies (if any) in the HEALTH CENTER Table.

E4.9b Show the result of normalizing the HEALTH CENTER Table to 2NF.

E4.9c Show the result of normalizing the HEALTH CENTER Table to 3NF.

E4.10 Consider the following relation with sample data.

SURGERY SCHEDULE TABLE

PatientID	PatientName	SurgeonID	SurgeonName	NurseID	NurseName	SurgeryDate	SurgeryType	NurseRole
111	Joe	AAA	Dr. Adams	N1	Mike	1-Jan	Knee Surgery	1st Assistant
111	Joe	AAA	Dr. Adams	N2	Sue	1-Jan	Knee Surgery	2nd Assistant
111	Joe	AAA	Dr. Adams	N2	Sue	2-Jan	Ankle Surgery	1st Assistant
111	Joe	BBB	Dr. Brown	N2	Sue	3-Jan	Elbow Surgery	1st Assistant
222	Pat	CCC	Dr. Crown	N3	Tina	1-Jan	Knee Surgery	1st Assistant
333	Bob	AAA	Dr. Adams	N4	Lee	1-Jan	Hip Surgery	1st Assistant
333	Bob	AAA	Dr. Adams	N3	Tina	1-Jan	Hip Surgery	2nd Assistant
333	Bob	DDD	Dr. Adams	N5	Sue	2-Jan	Shoulder Surgery	1st Assistant
444	Pat	BBB	Dr. Brown	N6	Pam	1-Jan	Hip Surgery	1st Assistant

- *The SURGERY SCHEDULE Table captures the data about scheduled surgeries.*
- *Each patient has a unique Patient ID and a Patient Name.*
- *Each surgeon has a unique Surgeon ID and a Surgeon Name.*
- *Each nurse has a unique Nurse ID and a Nurse Name.*
- *Each scheduled surgery is of one particular type.*
- *Each patient can have multiple surgeries scheduled, but only one surgery per day.*
- *During one surgery, one surgeon works on one patient assisted by one or more nurses.*
- *During each surgery, each nurse has one particular role.*
- *A nurse does not have to have the same role in each surgery that she or he participates in.*
- *Surgeons and nurses can participate in more than one surgery per day.*

E4.10a Depict full key functional dependencies, partial functional dependencies (if any), and transitive functional dependencies (if any) in the SURGERY SCHEDULE Table.

E4.10b Show the result of normalizing the SURGERY SCHEDULE Table to 2NF.

E4.10c Show the result of normalizing the SURGERY SCHEDULE Table to 3NF.

E4.11 Consider the following relation with sample data.

STUDENT INTERNSHIP TABLE

StudentID	StudentName	EmployerID	EmployerName	PositionID	PositionDescription
111	Joe	A	Axel Alarm	1	Sales Intern
222	Mike	A	Axel Alarm	2	IT Help Desk Intern
333	Sue	B	Banex Inc	2	Sales Intern
444	Pat	B	Banex Inc	1	Front Desk Intern
555	Bob	B	Banex Inc	1	Front Desk Intern
666	Joe	C	Calypso Corp	1	Marketing Specialist Intern

- The STUDENT INTERNSHIP Table captures the data about student internships.
- Each student has a unique Student ID and a Student Name.
- Each employer has a unique Employer ID and an Employer Name.
- Within each employer, there are positions available.
- Each position has a unique Position ID within an employer (two positions from two different employers can have the same Position ID) and a Position Description.
- Each student can work for only one employer and can hold only one position within that employer.

- More than one student can work in the same position at the same employer.

E4.11a Depict full key functional dependencies, partial functional dependencies (if any), and transitive functional dependencies (if any) in the STUDENT INTERNSHIP Table.

E4.11b Show the result of normalizing the STUDENT INTERNSHIP Table to 2NF.

E4.11c Show the result of normalizing the STUDENT INTERNSHIP Table to 3NF.

E4.12 Consider the following relation with sample data.

MOVIE ACTORS TABLE

MovieID	MovieName	ActorID	ActorName	ActorAssistantID	ActorAssistantName	ActorMovieSalary
M100	Silent Code	A11	Paloma Luna	AA01	Julie J.	$1,200,000
M100	Silent Code	A22	Logan Jones	AA01	Julie J.	$1,300,000
M100	Silent Code	A33	Esmeralda Po	AA02	Bob B.	$1,200,001
M100	Silent Code	A44	C.C. Rooney	AA02	Bob B.	$500,000
M200	Winter Promises	A11	Paloma Luna	AA03	Lisa L.	$1,000,000
M200	Winter Promises	A33	C.C. Rooney	AA01	Julie J.	$900,000
M200	Winter Promises	A55	Max Smith	AA02	Bob B.	$300,000

- The MOVIE ACTORS Table captures the data about actors appearing in movies.
- Each movie has a unique Movie ID and a Movie Name.
- Each actor has a unique Actor ID and an Actor Name.
- Each actor's assistant has a unique Actor Assistant ID and an Actor Assistant Name.
- Each movie has multiple actors appearing in it. Each actor can appear in multiple movies.

- For each movie engagement, an actor receives a salary for appearing in a movie.
- Each movie hires multiple actor's assistants.
- Each actor in a movie is assigned one actor's assistant. One actor's assistant can be assigned to multiple actors in the same movie.
- An actor's assistant can provide assistance to actor(s) in multiple movies.

E4.12a Depict full key functional dependencies, partial functional dependencies (if any), and transitive functional dependencies (if any) in the MOVIE ACTORS Table.

E4.12b Show the result of normalizing the MOVIE ACTORS Table to 2NF.

E4.12c Show the result of normalizing the MOVIE ACTORS Table to 3NF.

E4.13 Consider the following table with sample data.

BANK ACCOUNTS TABLE

AccountID	AccountType	CurrentBalance	AccountHolderID	AccountHolderName
A111	Checking	$1,000.00	C111 C222	Joe Smith Sue Smith
A222	Checking	$2,000.00	C333	Mary Moore
A333	Money Market	$15,000.00	C444 C555 C666	Pat Clark Lisa Clark Timmy Clark
A444	Savings	$3,000.00	C111 C222	Joe Smith Sue Smith

E4.13a Normalize the BANK ACCOUNTS Table to 1NF by increasing the number of records in the existing table.

E4.13b Normalize the BANK ACCOUNTS Table to 1NF by creating a new separate table in addition to the existing table.

Chapter 5

SQL

INTRODUCTION

In this chapter, we will provide coverage of **Structured Query Language (SQL)** and its functionalities. SQL can be used for more than just querying a database. It can also be used to create the database; add, modify, and delete database structures; and insert, delete, and modify records in the database. We will demonstrate the SQL commands and functionalities for creating and using databases by using illustrative examples.

SQL is used by virtually every modern relational DBMS software. One of the reasons for the success and ubiquity of relational databases is that SQL functions as a standard query language that can be used (with minor dialectical variations) with the majority of relational DBMS software tools. For example, SQL is used by Oracle, MySQL, Microsoft SQL Server, PostgreSQL, Teradata, IBM DB2, and many others.

With SQL being a standardized language, the learning curve for switching from one relational DBMS to another is short. The ability to write queries for data retrieval and other SQL statements is not dependent on a single vendor, but upon the user's knowledge of this universal language.

Even though there is an **SQL standard** (discussed at the end of the chapter), different RDBMS tools may use slightly different versions of the language. Throughout this chapter, we will present the basic SQL commands that are common for most contemporary RDBMS packages.

SQL COMMANDS OVERVIEW

SQL is a comprehensive database language with commands covering multiple functionalities. Based on their functionality, SQL commands can be divided into the following categories:

> **Data Definition Language (DDL)**
>
> **Data Manipulation Language (DML)**
>
> **Data Control Language (DCL)**
>
> **Transaction Control Language (TCL)**

We will first give a brief overview of the purpose of different categories of SQL commands. We will then introduce examples of the individual SQL commands.

Data Definition Language (DDL)

DDL statements are used to *create and modify the structure of the database*. Recall that the structure of a relational database is represented by a relational schema depicting the database relations and their referential integrity constraints. The purpose of the DDL is to enable the implementation of the relational schema (and additional structures, such as indexes and other constraints) as an actual relational database. Examples of the DDL SQL commands are:

```
CREATE
ALTER
DROP
```

Each of these SQL commands for creating and modifying the database structure will be explained and illustrated with examples.

Data Manipulation Language (DML)

DML statements are used to manipulate the data within the database. DML statements include the commands for *inserting, modifying, deleting,* and *retrieval* of the data in the database.

Once a relational schema is implemented as an actual relational database, the data will be inserted into it. During the life span of the database, additional data can be inserted and the data can also be modified and/or deleted. DML includes the following commands for insertion, modification, and deletion of the data records:

```
INSERT INTO
UPDATE
DELETE
```

These SQL commands for inserting, modifying, and deleting the data in the relational database will be explained and illustrated with examples.

DML statements also include the following command for data retrieval:

```
SELECT
```

Data retrieval, also known as a **query**, is the most commonly performed operation on data in databases. Consequently, the SELECT command is the most frequently used SQL command. The SELECT statement can be accompanied by a number of other SQL keywords. The SELECT command and the accompanying SQL keywords will be explained and illustrated with examples.

Data Control Language (DCL) and Transaction Control Language (TCL)

DCL and TCL statements are used in various processes related to database maintenance and administrative use. DCL commands facilitate the process of data access control, while TCL is used to manage database transactions. (We will discuss the DCL and TCL commands in Chapter 10, which provides an overview of database administration.)

SQL DATA TYPES

When relations are created using SQL commands, each column of each relation has a specified data type. The following lists some of the most commonly used **SQL data types**:

CHAR (n)	fixed length n-character string
VARCHAR (n)	variable length character string with a maximum size of n characters
INT	integer
NUMERIC (x, y)	number with x digits, y of which are after the decimal point
DATE	date values (year, month, day)

BRIEF SQL SYNTAX NOTES

Before we illustrate individual SQL commands with examples, a few short notes about SQL syntax:

- A semicolon—;—following the end of an SQL statement indicates the end of the SQL command. In a list of multiple SQL statements, the semicolon indicates where each SQL statement ends.
- SQL keywords—as well as the table and column names used in the SQL commands—are not case-sensitive. We could use upper- or lowercase letters for

the statement (i.e., "SELECT" is the same as "select" or "SeLeCt"). In this book, for readability, we use uppercase letters for SQL keywords and lowercase letters for table and column names (this is one of a number of possible appearance notations that could have been chosen).

- An SQL statement can be written as one long sentence in one line of text. However, for legibility reasons, SQL statements are usually broken down into multiple lines of text.

The SQL examples in this chapter can be executed as written in most modern RDBMS packages.[1] Occurrences when a command listed in this chapter has an alternative syntax are noted at the end of the chapter.

CREATE TABLE

The SQL command **CREATE TABLE** is used for creating and connecting relational tables. To illustrate the utilization of CREATE TABLE commands, we will use the example of the ZAGI Retail Company Sales Department Database shown in Figure 3.32 in Chapter 3, repeated here as Figure 5.1a for convenience.

The SQL code shown in Figure 5.1b uses CREATE TABLE statements to create the tables depicted by the relational schema for the ZAGI Retail Company Sales Department Database, shown in Figure 5.1a.

In the syntax of the CREATE TABLE command, an open parenthesis is placed after the CREATE TABLE <tablename> part of the statement. This is followed by column expressions that specify the column names, data type of the column, and possible column constraints. An example of such a constraint is the NOT NULL constraint, specifying that the column is not optional. Each of the column expressions is separated by a comma.

The expressions specifying column details are followed by the expressions that specify the table constraints, such as primary keys and foreign keys. The CREATE TABLE statement ends with a closing parenthesis.

Observe the CREATE TABLE statements in Figure 5.1b. The first CREATE TABLE statement creates the relation VENDOR, which has two columns: VendorID and VendorName. For each column, a data type is specified. Both columns have a NOT NULL designation, because neither one is an optional column (an optional column would not have a NOT NULL designation). The expressions specifying the details of the columns are followed by the expression specifying which column (or columns) is the primary key. For the VENDOR table, the VendorID column is the primary key. To see an example of a CREATE TABLE statement specifying a composite primary key, observe the CREATE TABLE command for the SOLDVIA relation. This CREATE TABLE statement specifies a composite primary key composed of two columns, ProductID and TID, for the SOLDVIA relation.

If a table has a foreign key, the CREATE TABLE statement specifies the referential integrity constraint by listing the foreign key column and the table to which the foreign key refers. For example, the CREATE TABLE statement for the relation PRODUCT specifies two referential integrity constraints for two foreign keys: VendorID and CategoryID. The expression

```
FOREIGN KEY (vendorid) REFERENCES vendor(vendorid),
```

specifies that the foreign key column VendorID in the relation PRODUCT refers to the primary key column VendorID of the relation VENDOR. In some RDBMS packages, this expression can also be abbreviated as follows:

```
FOREIGN KEY (vendorid) REFERENCES vendor,
```

The abbreviated version of the expression specifies that the foreign key column VendorID in the relation PRODUCT refers to the primary key of the relation VENDOR without explicitly stating the name of the primary key column in the VENDOR relation.

The CREATE TABLE statements in Figure 5.1b are ordered so that the relations that have foreign keys are created *after* the relations referenced by the foreign keys. For

---

[1]SQL statements presented in this chapter can be executed in the consecutive order as they appear, resulting in a created, populated, and queried database. The scripts containing all the SQL statements in this chapter for six popular DBMS packages (Oracle, MySQL, Microsoft SQL Server, PostgreSQL, Teradata, and IBM DB2) are available at *dbtextbook.com*.

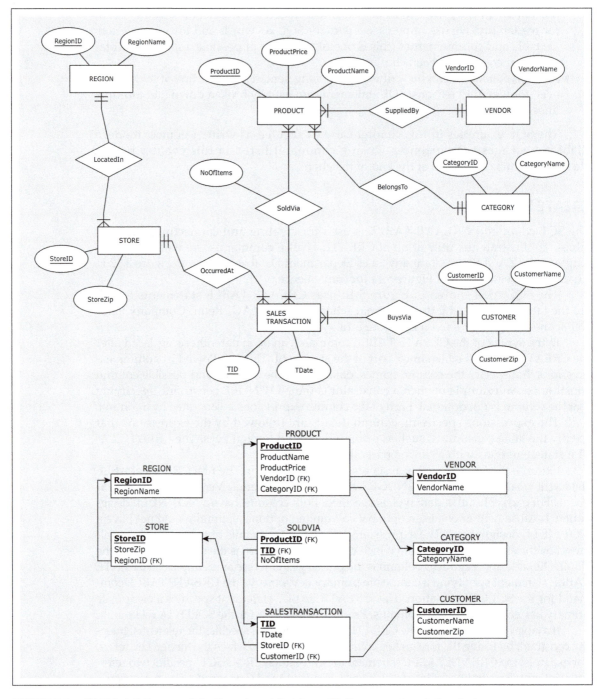

FIGURE 5.1a   ZAGI Retail Company Sales Department Database: ER diagram and a relational schema.

example, we had to create the relations VENDOR and CATEGORY before we could create the relation PRODUCT, because foreign keys in the relation PRODUCT refer to the primary keys of the relations VENDOR and CATEGORY.

In practice, CREATE TABLE statements are often not directly written by the database developers. In many cases, instead of manually writing the CREATE TABLE statements, developers use so-called CASE (computer-aided software engineering) tools, which are capable of issuing the CREATE STATEMENTS automatically, on behalf of the developer. For example, a developer could be using a CASE tool to create a relational schema, such as the one shown in Figure 5.1a, and to specify the data types (and other constraints, such as NOT NULL) for the columns. Once the column details for each relation are specified, the developer could then activate a functionality (e.g., by clicking on the appropriate button in the CASE tool) for automatic creation of the CREATE TABLE statements. This would automatically generate the CREATE TABLE statements shown in Figure 5.1b.

```
CREATE TABLE vendor
(       vendorid              CHAR(2)                    NOT NULL,
        vendorname            VARCHAR(25)                NOT NULL,
        PRIMARY KEY (vendorid) );

CREATE TABLE category
(       categoryid            CHAR(2)                    NOT NULL,
        categoryname          VARCHAR(25)                NOT NULL,
        PRIMARY KEY (categoryid) );

CREATE TABLE product
(       productid             CHAR(3)                    NOT NULL,
        productname           VARCHAR(25)                NOT NULL,
        productprice          NUMERIC(7,2)               NOT NULL,
        vendorid              CHAR(2)                    NOT NULL,
        categoryid            CHAR(2)                    NOT NULL,
        PRIMARY KEY (productid),
        FOREIGN KEY (vendorid) REFERENCES vendor(vendorid),
        FOREIGN KEY (categoryid) REFERENCES category(categoryid) );

CREATE TABLE region
(       regionid              CHAR(1)                    NOT NULL,
        regionname            VARCHAR(25)                NOT NULL,
        PRIMARY KEY (regionid) );

CREATE TABLE store
(       storeid               VARCHAR(3)                 NOT NULL,
        storezip              CHAR(5)                    NOT NULL,
        regionid              CHAR(1)                    NOT NULL,
        PRIMARY KEY (storeid),
        FOREIGN KEY (regionid) REFERENCES region(regionid) );

CREATE TABLE customer
(       customerid            CHAR(7)                    NOT NULL,
        customername          VARCHAR(15)                NOT NULL,
        customerzip           CHAR(5)                    NOT NULL,
        PRIMARY KEY (customerid) );

CREATE TABLE salestransaction
(       tid                   VARCHAR(8)                 NOT NULL,
        customerid            CHAR(7)                    NOT NULL,
        storeid               VARCHAR(3)                 NOT NULL,
        tdate                 DATE                       NOT NULL,
        PRIMARY KEY (tid),
        FOREIGN KEY (customerid) REFERENCES customer(customerid),
        FOREIGN KEY (storeid) REFERENCES store(storeid) );

CREATE TABLE soldvia
(       productid             CHAR(3)                    NOT NULL,
        tid                   VARCHAR(8)                 NOT NULL,
        noofitems             INT                        NOT NULL,
        PRIMARY KEY (productid, tid),
        FOREIGN KEY (productid) REFERENCES product(productid),
        FOREIGN KEY (tid) REFERENCES salestransaction(tid) );
```

FIGURE 5.1b CREATE TABLE statements for the ZAGI Retail Company Sales Department Database.

DROP TABLE

The **DROP TABLE** command is used to remove a table from the database. For example, if we wanted to remove the table SOLDVIA, we would issue the following statement:

```
DROP TABLE soldvia;
```

Note that if we wanted to remove each of the tables from the ZAGI Retail Company Sales Department Database, one by one, we would have to pay attention to the order of the DROP TABLE statements. The referential integrity constraint prevents deletion of a primary key that has existing foreign keys referring to it. Therefore, we would have to drop the tables that have the foreign keys before we could drop the tables to which the foreign keys refer.

For example, the following order of DROP TABLES is not valid:

DROP TABLE sequence ZAGI database—INVALID:

```
DROP TABLE region;
DROP TABLE store;
DROP TABLE salestransaction;
DROP TABLE product;
DROP TABLE vendor;
DROP TABLE category;
DROP TABLE customer;
DROP TABLE soldvia;
```

This sequence of DROP TABLE statements is invalid (i.e., some of the statements will not be executed) because it attempts to drop relations to which other existing relations are referring. We cannot drop the relation REGION while the relation STORE refers to it. We would first have to drop the relation STORE before we can drop the relation REGION.

The following order of DROP TABLES is valid:

DROP TABLE sequence ZAGI database—VALID:

```
DROP TABLE soldvia;
DROP TABLE salestransaction;
DROP TABLE store;
DROP TABLE product;
DROP TABLE vendor;
DROP TABLE region;
DROP TABLE category;
DROP TABLE customer;
```

In this sequence of DROP TABLE statements, no table is dropped before a table with a foreign key referring to it is dropped. If we execute this sequence of DROP TABLE statements, every table in the ZAGI Retail Company Sales Department Database will be dropped. In that case, the ZAGI Retail Company Sales Department can be re-created by executing again all the statements listed in Figure 5.1b.

INSERT INTO

The **INSERT INTO** statement is used to populate the created relations with data. To illustrate the utilization of INSERT INTO commands, we will populate the ZAGI Retail Company Sales Department Database with the records shown in Figure 3.33 in Chapter 3, repeated here as Figure 5.1c for convenience.

Figure 5.1d shows the INSERT INTO statements that populate the ZAGI Retail Company Sales Department Database.

The INSERT INTO <tablename> part of the statement is followed by the keyword VALUES and then an open parenthesis, after which the values to be inserted are listed. The command ends with the closed parenthesis. The first INSERT INTO statement in Figure 5.1d inserts in the relation VENDOR a value *PG* in column VendorID and a value *Pacifica Gear* in column VendorName. The order in which columns appeared in the CREATE TABLE statement dictates the order in which values will be listed within the INSERT INTO statement. The CREATE TABLE statement for the relation VENDOR created the VendorID column first, and the VendorName column second. Therefore, each INSERT INTO statement for the VENDOR relation will list the value to be inserted into the column VendorID first, and the value to be inserted into the column VendorName second.

Alternatively, an INSERT INTO statement can have the following form: INSERT INTO <tablename> (<columnname>, <columnname>, . . .) VALUES (value, value, . . .); where the order of values inserted is dictated by the order of columns appearing after the table name in the INSERT INTO statement.

REGION

RegionID	RegionName
C	Chicagoland
T	Tristate

PRODUCT

ProductID	ProductName	ProductPrice	VendorID	CategoryID
1X1	Zzz Bag	$100	PG	CP
2X2	Easy Boot	$70	MK	FW
3X3	Cosy Sock	$15	MK	FW
4X4	Dura Boot	$90	PG	FW
5X5	Tiny Tent	$150	MK	CP
6X6	Biggy Tent	$250	MK	CP

VENDOR

VendorID	VendorName
PG	Pacifica Gear
MK	Mountain King

STORE

StoreID	StoreZip	RegionID
S1	60600	C
S2	60605	C
S3	35400	T

CATEGORY

CategoryID	CategoryName
CP	Camping
FW	Footwear

SALESTRANSACTION

TID	CustomerID	StoreID	TDate
T111	1-2-333	S1	1-Jan-2013
T222	2-3-444	S2	1-Jan-2013
T333	1-2-333	S3	2-Jan-2013
T444	3-4-555	S3	2-Jan-2013
T555	2-3-444	S3	2-Jan-2013

SOLDVIA

ProductID	TID	NoOfItems
1X1	T111	1
2X2	T222	1
3X3	T333	5
1X1	T333	1
4X4	T444	1
2X2	T444	2
4X4	T555	4
5X5	T555	2
6X6	T555	1

CUSTOMER

CustomerID	CustomerName	CustomerZip
1-2-333	Tina	60137
2-3-444	Tony	60611
3-4-555	Pam	35401

FIGURE 5.1c Records in the ZAGI Retail Company Sales Department Database.

For example, the last INSERT INTO command in Figure 5.1d could have been written as follows:

```
INSERT INTO soldvia(noofitems, tid, productid) VALUES (1, 'T555', '6x6');
```

This way of writing the INSERT INTO allows for an order of values in the IN-SERT INTO statement different from the order specified in the CREATE TABLE statement. On the other hand, it also requires specifying the name of each column, which adds to the syntax of the INSERT INTO command. When column names are explicitly written, not all the columns must be specified. We can populate just the columns for which we have the data. However, columns that are not optional must always be populated, no matter what syntax of INSERT INTO is used.

In SQL statements, values for the columns with character data types, such as CHAR or VARCHAR, have to be delimited with quotation marks, while the values of the numeric data types, such as INT or NUMERIC, are not delimited. For example, both values in the INSERT INTO statements for the relation VENDOR in Figure 5.1d are delimited with quotation marks, because both columns of the relation VENDOR have character data types. On the other hand, the third value in the INSERT INTO statements for the relation PRODUCT is not delimited because the third column in the CREATE TABLE statement for the relation PRODUCT is ProductPrice, and its data type is numeric.

In practice, INSERT INTO statements, like the ones shown in Figure 5.1d, are usually not directly written by the end users in charge of data entry. A common practice is that front-end applications, such as the forms discussed in Chapter 6, issue these statements on behalf of the end users who are performing the data entry using these front-end applications. INSERT INTO statements can also be issued by applications used for loading large amounts of data from outside sources into a relation.

Observe Figure 5.1d and note that tables that do not have foreign keys are populated first. Tables that do have foreign keys cannot have their foreign key columns populated before the values of the primary key columns to which they are referring are populated. Referential integrity constraints require that primary key values that are referred to by a foreign key are entered before the foreign key values can be entered.

```
INSERT INTO vendor    VALUES ('PG','Pacifica Gear');
INSERT INTO vendor    VALUES ('MK','Mountain King');

INSERT INTO category VALUES ('CP','Camping');
INSERT INTO category VALUES ('FW','Footwear');

INSERT INTO product   VALUES ('1X1','Zzz Bag',100,'PG','CP');
INSERT INTO product   VALUES ('2X2','Easy Boot',70,'MK','FW');
INSERT INTO product   VALUES ('3X3','Cosy Sock',15,'MK','FW');
INSERT INTO product   VALUES ('4X4','Dura Boot',90,'PG','FW');
INSERT INTO product   VALUES ('5X5','Tiny Tent',150,'MK','CP');
INSERT INTO product   VALUES ('6X6','Biggy Tent',250,'MK','CP');

INSERT INTO region    VALUES ('C','Chicagoland');
INSERT INTO region    VALUES ('T','Tristate');

INSERT INTO store     VALUES ('S1','60600','C');
INSERT INTO store     VALUES ('S2','60605','C');
INSERT INTO store     VALUES ('S3','35400','T');

INSERT INTO customer VALUES ('1-2-333','Tina','60137');
INSERT INTO customer VALUES ('2-3-444','Tony','60611');
INSERT INTO customer VALUES ('3-4-555','Pam','35401');

INSERT INTO salestransaction VALUES ('T111','1-2-333','S1','01/Jan/2013');
INSERT INTO salestransaction VALUES ('T222','2-3-444','S2','01/Jan/2013');
INSERT INTO salestransaction VALUES ('T333','1-2-333','S3','02/Jan/2013');
INSERT INTO salestransaction VALUES ('T444','3-4-555','S3','02/Jan/2013');
INSERT INTO salestransaction VALUES ('T555','2-3-444','S3','02/Jan/2013');

INSERT INTO soldvia   VALUES ('1X1','T111',1);
INSERT INTO soldvia   VALUES ('2X2','T222',1);
INSERT INTO soldvia   VALUES ('3X3','T333',5);
INSERT INTO soldvia   VALUES ('1X1','T333',1);
INSERT INTO soldvia   VALUES ('4X4','T444',1);
INSERT INTO soldvia   VALUES ('2X2','T444',2);
INSERT INTO soldvia   VALUES ('4X4','T555',4);
INSERT INTO soldvia   VALUES ('5X5','T555',2);
INSERT INTO soldvia   VALUES ('6X6','T555',1);
```

FIGURE 5.1d   INSERT INTO statements for the ZAGI Retail Company Sales Department Database.

SELECT

The most commonly issued SQL statement is the **SELECT** statement, used for the retrieval of data from the database relations. The result of a SELECT statement is a table listing the records requested by the SELECT statement. In its simple form, a SELECT statement is structured as follows:

```
SELECT       <columns>
FROM         <table>
```

In the SELECT clause, the keyword SELECT is followed by the list of columns that will be retrieved, separated by commas. A FROM clause is always preceded by a SELECT clause. In the FROM clause, the keyword FROM is followed by the name of the relation (or relations) from which the data will be retrieved. Query 1 is an example of the simplest form of the SELECT statement:

> *Query 1 text:*   *Retrieve the entire contents of the relation PRODUCT.*

> *Query 1:*   SELECT   productid, productname, productprice, vendorid, categoryid
> FROM   product;

The result of Query 1 is shown in Figure 5.2.

ProductID	ProductName	ProductPrice	VendorID	CategoryID
1X1	Zzz Bag	100	PG	CP
2X2	Easy Boot	70	MK	FW
3X3	Cosy Sock	15	MK	FW
4X4	Dura Boot	90	PG	FW
5X5	Tiny Tent	150	MK	CP
6X6	Biggy Tent	250	MK	CP

FIGURE 5.2   Result of Query 1 and Query 1a.

ProductName	ProductID	VendorID	CategoryID	ProductPrice
Zzz Bag	1X1	PG	CP	100
Easy Boot	2X2	MK	FW	70
Cosy Sock	3X3	MK	FW	15
Dura Boot	4X4	PG	FW	90
Tiny Tent	5X5	MK	CP	150
Biggy Tent	6X6	MK	CP	250

FIGURE 5.2a   Result of Query 2.

Query 1 retrieves the entire contents of the relation PRODUCT.
The same result would have been achieved with Query 1a:

Query 1a: SELECT   *
                FROM   product;

The meaning of the * symbol after the SELECT keyword is "all columns." Listing each column by name or using the * symbol achieves the same result. Therefore, it is shorter and simpler to use the * symbol when we want to show all columns of the relation. The only exception to this guideline is the scenario in which we want to show all columns, but in a different order from the order of columns used in the CREATE TABLE statement. Query 2 illustrates such a case.

Query 2 text: *Retrieve the entire contents of the relation PRODUCT and show the columns in the following order: ProductName, ProductID, VendorID, CategoryID, ProductPrice.*

Query 2:   SELECT   productname, productid, vendorid, categoryid,
                               productprice
               FROM   product;

The result of Query 2 is shown in Figure 5.2a.

Query 3 illustrates a case when the SELECT clause is used to reduce the number of table columns that will be shown in the result of a query.

Query 3 text: *For the relation PRODUCT, show the columns ProductID and ProductPrice.*

Query 3:   SELECT   productid, productprice
               FROM   product;

The result of Query 3 is shown in Figure 5.3.

ProductID	ProductPrice
1X1	100
2X2	70
3X3	15
4X4	90
5X5	150
6X6	250

FIGURE 5.3   Result of Query 3.

ProductID	ProductPrice	ProductPrice*1.1
1X1	100	110
2X2	70	77
3X3	15	16.5
4X4	90	99
5X5	150	165
6X6	250	275

FIGURE 5.3a Result of Query 3a.

In addition to displaying columns, the SELECT clause can be used to display derived attributes (calculated columns) represented as expressions. A SELECT statement can be structured as follows:

```
SELECT      <columns, expressions>
FROM        <table>
```

Query 3a illustrates such a case.

Query 3a text: *For the relation PRODUCT, show the columns ProductID and ProductPrice and a column showing ProductPrice increased by 10%.*

Query 3a:
```
SELECT      productid, productprice, productprice * 1.1
FROM        product;
```

The result of Query 3a is shown in Figure 5.3a.

The SELECT FROM statement can contain other optional keywords, such as WHERE, GROUP BY, HAVING, and ORDER BY, appearing in this order:

```
SELECT      <columns, expressions>
FROM        <tables>
WHERE       <row selection condition>
GROUP BY    <grouping columns>
HAVING      <group selection condition>
ORDER BY    <sorting columns, expressions>
```

We will illustrate the use of these keywords in examples below.

WHERE

The SELECT statement can include the **WHERE** condition, which determines which rows should be retrieved and consequently which rows should not be retrieved. Query 4 shows a simple example of a SELECT query with the WHERE condition.

Query 4 text: *Retrieve the product id, product name, vendor id, and product price for each product whose price is above $100.*

Query 4:
```
SELECT      productid, productname, vendorid, productprice
FROM        product
WHERE       productprice > 100;
```

The result of Query 4 is shown in Figure 5.4.

The rows with ProductPrice value above $100 are retrieved, and the rows whose ProductPrice value is not above $100 are not retrieved.

The logical condition determining which records to retrieve can use one of the following logical comparison operators:

```
=    Equal to
<    Less than
>    Greater than
<=   Less than or equal to
>=   Greater than or equal to
!=   Not equal to
<>   Not equal to (alternative notation)
```

ProductID	ProductName	VendorID	ProductPrice
5X5	Tiny Tent	MK	150
6X6	Biggy Tent	MK	250

FIGURE 5.4   Result of Query 4.

ProductID	ProductName	VendorID	ProductPrice
2X2	Easy Boot	MK	70
3X3	Cosy Sock	MK	15
4X4	Dura Boot	PG	90

FIGURE 5.5   Result of Query 5.

Within one WHERE clause, a multiple comparison expression can be used, connected by the Boolean logical operators AND or OR.

Query 5 shows an example of a multiple comparison expression within one WHERE clause.

Query 5 text: *Retrieve the product id, product name, vendor id, and product price for each product in the FW category whose price is equal to or below $110.*

Query 5:

```
SELECT     productid, productname, vendorid, productprice
FROM       product
WHERE      productprice <= 110 AND
           categoryid = 'FW';
```

The result of Query 5 is shown in Figure 5.5.

Note that when the values of the character data type are used in the query, they have to be delimited with quotation marks (e.g., 'FW'), just as was the case in the INSERT INTO statement.

DISTINCT

The **DISTINCT** keyword can be used in conjunction with the SELECT statement. To illustrate its purpose, first consider Query 6.

Query 6 text: *Retrieve the VendorID value for each record in the relation PRODUCT.*

Query 6:

```
SELECT     vendorid
FROM       product;
```

The result of Query 6 is shown in Figure 5.6.

The relation PRODUCT has six records and the result shown in Figure 5.6 lists a VendorID value for each of the records. Note that although the result of a query is displayed as a table, such table does not correspond to the definition of a relational table, since each row in the table is not unique.

If we wanted to show which VendorID values exist in the PRODUCT table, without repeating them multiple times, we would issue Query 7.

Query 7 text: *Show one instance of all the different VendorID values in the relation PRODUCT.*

Query 7:

```
SELECT     DISTINCT vendorid
FROM       product;
```

The result of Query 7 is shown in Figure 5.7.

VendorID
PG
MK
MK
PG
MK
MK

FIGURE 5.6   Result of Query 6.

VendorID
PG
MK

FIGURE 5.7   Result of Query 7.

Using the keyword DISTINCT following the SELECT keyword eliminated the duplicate values from the result of the query.

ORDER BY

If we wanted to sort the results of the query by one or more columns, we would use the **ORDER BY** keyword within the SELECT query. Consider Query 8, requesting that its results are sorted by product price.

> *Query 8 text:*   *Retrieve the product id, product name, category id, and product price for each product in the FW product category, sorted by product price.*

> *Query 8:*
> ```
> SELECT      productid, productname, categoryid, productprice
> FROM        product
> WHERE       categoryid = 'FW'
> ORDER BY    productprice;
> ```

The result of Query 8 is shown in Figure 5.8.

By default, ORDER BY sorts the data in ascending order. If we want to sort in descending order, we can use the keyword DESC as shown in Query 9.

> *Query 9 text:*   *Retrieve the product id, product name, category id, and product price for each product in the FW product category, sorted by product price in descending order.*

> *Query 9:*
> ```
> SELECT      productid, productname, categoryid, productprice
> FROM        product
> WHERE       categoryid = 'FW'
> ORDER BY    productprice DESC;
> ```

The result of Query 9 is shown in Figure 5.9.

The result of a query can be sorted by multiple columns, as illustrated by Query 10.

> *Query 10 text:*   *Retrieve the product id, product name, category id, and product price for each product, sorted by category id and, within the same category id, by product price.*

> *Query 10:*
> ```
> SELECT      productid, productname, categoryid, productprice
> FROM        product
> ORDER BY    categoryid, productprice;
> ```

The result of Query 10 is shown in Figure 5.10. Query 10 sorts the results first by the CategoryID, and then by ProductPrice.

ProductID	ProductName	CategoryID	ProductPrice
3X3	Cosy Sock	FW	15
2X2	Easy Boot	FW	70
4X4	Dura Boot	FW	90

FIGURE 5.8   Result of Query 8.

ProductID	ProductName	CategoryID	ProductPrice
4X4	Dura Boot	FW	90
2X2	Easy Boot	FW	70
3X3	Cosy Sock	FW	15

FIGURE 5.9   Result of Query 9.

ProductID	ProductName	CategoryID	ProductPrice
1X1	Zzz Bag	CP	100
5X5	Tiny Tent	CP	150
6X6	Biggy Tent	CP	250
3X3	Cosy Sock	FW	15
2X2	Easy Boot	FW	70
4X4	Dura Boot	FW	90

FIGURE 5.10   Result of Query 10.

ProductID	ProductName	ProductPrice	VendorID	CategoryID
2X2	Easy Boot	70	MK	FW
4X4	Dura Boot	90	PG	FW

FIGURE 5.11   Result of Query 11.

LIKE

If we wanted to retrieve the records whose values partially match a certain criteria, we would use the **LIKE** keyword in conjunction with the WHERE clause of the SELECT command. Consider Query 11.

Query 11 text: *Retrieve the record for each product whose product name contains the phrase 'Boot'.*

Query 11:
```
SELECT      *
FROM        product
WHERE       productname LIKE '%Boot%';
```

The result of Query 11 is shown in Figure 5.11.

The meaning of the "%" wild card symbol is "any zero or more characters." Therefore, this query will retrieve all records that have the phrase "Boot" in the ProductName column preceded or followed by any string of characters (including no characters). Another available wild card symbol is "_", meaning "exactly one character."

AGGREGATE FUNCTIONS

For calculating and summarizing values in queries, SQL provides the following **aggregate functions**: **COUNT**, **SUM**, **AVG**, **MIN**, and **MAX**. The COUNT function counts the number of records in the result of the query, while the SUM, AVG, MIN, and MAX functions calculate sum, average, minimum, and maximum values, respectively, for the specified set of values in the query. Functions SUM and AVG operate on numeric values only. Functions MIN and MAX operate not only on numeric values, but on date and character values as well.

Consider Query 12.

Query 12 text: *Retrieve the average price of all products.*

Query 12:
```
SELECT      AVG(productprice)
FROM        product;
```

This query will find the average price of all products. The result of Query 12 is shown in Figure 5.12.

Also consider Query 13.

Query 13 text: *Show how many products we offer for sale.*

Query 13:
```
SELECT      COUNT(*)
FROM        product;
```

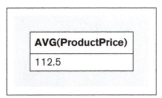

AVG(ProductPrice)
112.5

FIGURE 5.12   Result of Query 12.

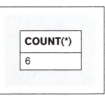

COUNT(*)
6

FIGURE 5.13   Result of Query 13.

COUNT(DISTINCT VendorID)
2

FIGURE 5.14   Result of Query 14.

COUNT(*)	AVG(ProductPrice)	MIN(ProductPrice)	MAX(ProductPrice)
3	166.666667	100	250

FIGURE 5.15   Result of Query 15.

While AVG, SUM, MIN, and MAX functions must use a column name as its argument (e.g., AVG(ProductPrice) in Query 12), the COUNT function can also use the * symbol as the function argument. Query 13 simply counts how many records are in the table PRODUCT. In this query the * symbol in the COUNT(*) function refers to the records. Query 13 calculates the number of records in the table PRODUCT. The result of this query is shown in Figure 5.13.

The result for Query 13 would be the same if we used any of the column names as the argument of the function (e.g., COUNT(ProductID) or COUNT(ProductName)) instead of COUNT(*), because this table has no optional columns and every column has a value for every record. If a table has optional columns containing NULL values, those NULL values are skipped when computing the COUNT. If a column contains NULL values, then using that column for the count will not result in the same value as using COUNT(*).

To count how many distinct vendors we have in the PRODUCT table, we would issue Query 14.

> **Query 14 text:**   *Retrieve the number of vendors that supply our products.*

> **Query 14:**   SELECT   COUNT(DISTINCT vendorid)
>   FROM   product;

The result of Query 14 is shown in Figure 5.14.

It is possible to use more than one aggregate function within one SELECT statement, as illustrated by Query 15.

> **Query 15 text:**   *Retrieve the number of products, average product price, lowest product price, and highest product price in the CP product category.*

> **Query 15:**   SELECT   COUNT(*), AVG(productprice), MIN(productprice),
>   MAX(productprice)
>   FROM   product
>   WHERE   categoryid = 'CP';

The result of Query 15 is shown in Figure 5.15.

GROUP BY

In SQL queries, aggregate functions are often used in conjunction with the **GROUP BY** keyword. This clause enables summarizations across the groups of related data within tables. Consider Query 16.

> **Query 16 text:**   *For each vendor, retrieve the vendor id, number of products supplied by the vendor, and average price of the products supplied by the vendor.*

VendorID	COUNT(*)	AVG(ProductPrice)
PG	2	95
MK	4	121.25

FIGURE 5.16   Result of Query 16.

Query 16:
```
SELECT      vendorid, COUNT(*), AVG(productprice)
FROM        product
GROUP BY    vendorid;
```

The result of Query 16 is shown in Figure 5.16.

As illustrated by Figure 5.16a, Query 16 groups the records in the PRODUCT relation that have the same value in the VendorID column and for each group calculates the number of records in the group and the average product price of the products in the group.

When aggregate functions are used in the SELECT statement, individual columns cannot be a part of the SELECT statement unless a GROUP BY clause is used.

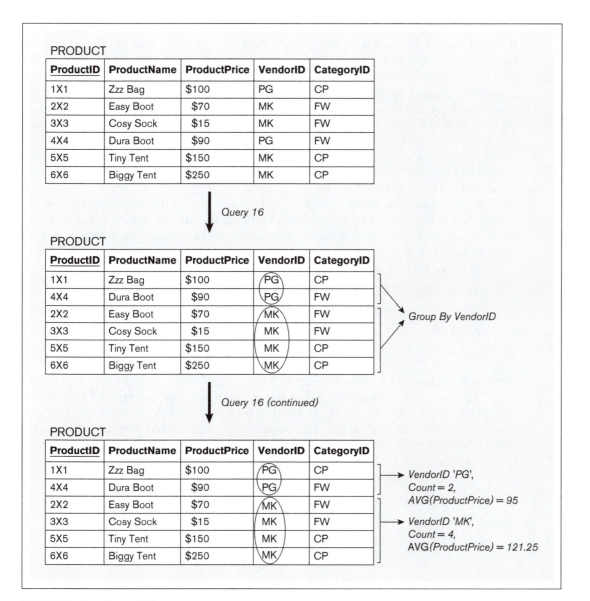

FIGURE 5.16a   Query 16 illustration.

COUNT(*)	AVG(ProductPrice)
2	95
4	121.25

FIGURE 5.17   Result of Query 17.

Observe the following example of an invalid query that attempts to accomplish what is specified in Query 16 text:

Query 16:   SELECT   vendorid, COUNT(*), AVG(productprice)
INVALID   FROM   product; ERROR MESSAGE RETURNED

It is very common for beginners to write an erroneous SQL query for aggregating data within groups. A typical mistake, as shown in Query 16 INVALID, is to list an individual column (VendorID in this case) accompanied by aggregate functions in the SELECT statement without including a GROUP BY statement containing that individual column. This query would not execute. Instead, an error message would be returned. The reason this query is invalid is that aggregate functions (such as COUNT(*), AVG(ProductPrice)) give results across multiple records, and this result cannot be mixed with column values of individual records. Without the GROUP BY statement, COUNT(*) and AVG(ProductPrice) can only be applied to the entire table, resulting in one COUNT and one AVG value. The query cannot combine one COUNT and one AVG value for the entire table with multiple VendorID values of each record. Accordingly, this query needs the GROUP BY VendorID statement at the end in order to be able to execute, as is the case with Query 16. In Query 16, the GROUP BY statement specifies the subsets of the table on which aggregate functions COUNT(*) and AVG (ProductPrice) are to be applied. The number of these subsets corresponds to the number of different VendorID values in the table, and therefore, each VendorID value will have an associated COUNT and AVG value to be displayed with it (as shown in Figure 5.16).

The guideline for using the GROUP BY clause is that the same column (or columns) that is (are) listed after the GROUP BY clause should also be listed after the SELECT clause. The query that does not list in the SELECT clause the columns that are used in the GROUP BY clause will still be executed, and the result will be shown, but often such a result will not be very informative. Consider Query 17.

Query 17 text: *For each vendor, retrieve the number of products supplied by the vendor and the average price of the products supplied by the vendor.*

Query 17:   SELECT   COUNT(*), AVG(productprice)
              FROM   product
              GROUP BY   vendorid;

The result of Query 17 is shown in Figure 5.17.

The correct values are shown, but the end user may not understand to what the displayed values refer. In particular, the end user may not be aware that the first displayed row refers to vendor *PG*, and that the second displayed row refers to vendor *MK*. By adding the VendorID column in the SELECT part of the query (as is done in Query 16), the result of the query becomes more informative.

A query can combine WHERE and GROUP BY clauses. Consider Query 18.

Query 18 text: *For each vendor, retrieve the vendor id and the number of products with a product price of $100 or higher supplied by the vendor.*

Query 18:   SELECT   vendorid, COUNT(*)
              FROM   product
              WHERE   productprice >= 100
              GROUP BY   vendorid;

The result of Query 18 is shown in Figure 5.18.

VendorID	COUNT(*)
PG	1
MK	2

FIGURE 5.18   Result of Query 18.

VendorID	CategoryID	COUNT(*)	AVG(ProductPrice)
MK	CP	2	200
MK	FW	2	42.5
PG	CP	1	100
PG	FW	1	90

FIGURE 5.19   Result of Query 19.

Query 18 groups the records in the PRODUCT relation that have the same value in the VendorID column whose ProductPrice value is $100 or higher. For each such group, the query displays the VendorID value and the number of records in the group.

A GROUP BY clause can group queries by multiple columns. Consider Query 19.

Query 19 text: *Consider the groups of products where each group contains the products that are from the same category supplied by the same vendor. For each such group, retrieve the vendor id, product category id, number of products in the group, and average price of the products in the group.*

Query 19:
```
SELECT      vendorid, categoryid, COUNT(*), AVG(productprice)
FROM        product
GROUP BY    vendorid, categoryid;
```

The result of Query 19 is shown in Figure 5.19.

Query 19 groups the records in the PRODUCT relation that have the same value in the VendorID and CategoryID columns and for each group displays the VendorID value, the CategoryID value, the number of records in the group, and the average price of the products in the group.

To recap and reinforce the GROUP BY concepts, let us consider two more GROUP BY queries on the SOLDVIA relation that contains the data about products sold in each sales transaction.

First, consider Query 20.

Query 20 text: *For each product, retrieve the ProductID value and the total number of product items sold within all sales transactions.*

Query 20:
```
SELECT      productid, SUM(noofitems)
FROM        soldvia
GROUP BY    productid;
```

The result of Query 20 is shown in Figure 5.20.

Now, consider Query 21.

Query 21 text: *For each product, retrieve the ProductID value and the number of sales transactions in which the product was sold.*

ProductID	SUM(NoOfItems)
1X1	2
2X2	3
3X3	5
4X4	5
5X5	2
6X6	1

FIGURE 5.20   Result of Query 20.

ProductID	COUNT(TID)
1X1	2
2X2	2
3X3	1
4X4	2
5X5	1
6X6	1

FIGURE 5.21   Result of Query 21.

Query 21:
```
SELECT      productid, COUNT(*)
FROM        soldvia
GROUP BY    productid;
```

The result of Query 21 is shown in Figure 5.21.

HAVING

The GROUP BY clause can be accompanied by a **HAVING** keyword. A HAVING clause determines which groups will be displayed in the result of a query and, consequently, which groups will not be displayed in the result of the query. A query that contains a HAVING clause must also contain a GROUP BY clause. Observe Query 22.

Query 22 text: *Consider the groups of products where each group contains the products that are from the same category and supplied by the same vendor. For each such group that has more than one product, retrieve the vendor id, product category id, number of products in the group, and average price of the products in the group.*

Query 22:
```
SELECT      vendorid, categoryid, COUNT(*), AVG(productprice)
FROM        product
GROUP BY    vendorid, categoryid
HAVING      COUNT(*) > 1;
```

Query 22 groups the records in the PRODUCT relation that have the same value in the VendorID and CategoryID columns, and for each group that has more than one record, it displays the VendorID value, the CategoryID value, the number of records in the group, and the average price of the products in the group. The result of Query 22 is shown in Figure 5.22.

As illustrated by the Query 22 example, HAVING has the same effect on groups as the WHERE clause has on records. A WHERE condition determines which records from the table will be a part of the result and which will not. A HAVING condition determines which groups will be a part of the result and which will not.

WHERE and HAVING can be contained in the same query, as illustrated by Query 23.

Query 23 text: *Consider the groups of products where each group contains the products that are from the same category, supplied by the same vendor, and whose product price is $50 or higher. For each such*

VendorID	CategoryID	COUNT(*)	AVG(ProductPrice)
MK	CP	2	200
MK	FW	2	42.5

FIGURE 5.22   Result of Query 22.

VendorID	CategoryID	COUNT(*)	AVG(ProductPrice)
MK	CP	2	200

FIGURE 5.23   Result of Query 23.

> *group that has more than one product, retrieve the vendor id, product category id, number of products in the group, and average price of the products.*

Query 23:

```
SELECT      vendorid, categoryid, COUNT(*), AVG(productprice)
FROM        product
WHERE       productprice >= 50
GROUP BY    vendorid, categoryid
HAVING      COUNT(*) > 1;
```

The result of Query 23 is shown in Figure 5.23.

Query 23 identifies all the records in the PRODUCT relation that have a ProductPrice value of $50 or more and then creates groups of these records that have the same value in the VendorID and CategoryID columns. For each such group that has more than one record, it displays the VendorID value, the CategoryID value, the number of records in the group, and the average price of the product in the group.

To recap and reinforce the HAVING concept, let us consider several more GROUP BY queries using a HAVING clause on the SOLDVIA relation.

First, consider Query 24.

Query 24 text: *For each product that has more than three items sold within all sales transactions, retrieve the ProductID value and the total number of product items sold within all sales transactions.*

Query 24:

```
SELECT      productid, SUM(noofitems)
FROM        soldvia
GROUP BY    productid
HAVING      SUM(noofitems) > 3;
```

The result of Query 24 is shown in Figure 5.24.

Now, consider Query 25.

Query 25 text: *For each product that was sold in more than one sales transaction, retrieve the ProductID value and the number of sales transactions in which the product was sold.*

Query 25:

```
SELECT      productid, COUNT(*)
FROM        soldvia
GROUP BY    productid
HAVING      COUNT(*) > 1;
```

The result of Query 25 is shown in Figure 5.25.

ProductID	SUM(NoOfItems)
3X3	5
4X4	5

FIGURE 5.24   Result of Query 24.

ProductID	COUNT(TID)
1X1	2
2X2	2
4X4	2

FIGURE 5.25   Result of Query 25.

The following two queries show the slightly changed versions of the previous two queries to illustrate that the group selection condition in the HAVING clause can contain aggregate functions that were not used in the SELECT clause within the same query.

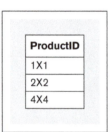

ProductID
3X3
4X4

FIGURE 5.26   Result of Query 26.

Query 26 text: *For each product that has more than three items sold within all sales transactions, retrieve the ProductID value.*

Query 26:

```
SELECT      productid
FROM        soldvia
GROUP BY    productid
HAVING      SUM(noofitems) > 3;
```

The result of Query 26 is shown in Figure 5.26.

In Query 26, the SUM(noofitems) in the HAVING part was not used in the SELECT part within the same query. The same point is demonstrated by Query 27, where the HAVING part contains the aggregate function COUNT(tid) that was not used by the SELECT clause.

ProductID
1X1
2X2
4X4

FIGURE 5.27   Result of Query 27.

Query 27 text: *For each product that was sold in more than one sales transaction, retrieve the ProductID value.*

Query 27:

```
SELECT      productid
FROM        soldvia
GROUP BY    productid
HAVING      COUNT(*) > 1;
```

The result of Query 27 is shown in Figure 5.27.

NESTED QUERIES

In some cases, a query may contain another query (or queries). A query that is used within another query is called a **nested query**. A nested query is also referred to as an **inner query**, whereas the query that uses the nested query is referred to as an **outer query**.

For example, consider a query to retrieve the ProductID, ProductName, and ProductPrice of all products whose price is less than the average price of all products. As shown in Query 28, the WHERE condition refers to the average product price, and the average product price is the result of another query. In this case, the SELECT query starting in the first line of Query 28 is the outer query, and the SELECT query in the parentheses is the nested query (or inner query).

Query 28 text: *For each product whose product price is below the average price of all products, retrieve the product id, product name, and product price.*

Query 28:

```
SELECT      productid, productname, productprice
FROM        product
WHERE       productprice < (SELECT AVG(productprice)
                            FROM product);
```

The result of Query 28 is shown in Figure 5.28.

A common beginner's error is to try to write Query 28 as follows:

Query 28:
INVALID

```
SELECT      productid, productname, productprice
FROM        product
WHERE       productprice < AVG (productprice);
                          ERROR MESSAGE RETURNED
```

ProductID	ProductName	ProductPrice
1X1	Zzz Bag	100
2X2	Easy Boot	70
3X3	Cosy Sock	15
4X4	Dura Boot	90

FIGURE 5.28   Result of Query 28.

Aggregate functions can appear syntactically *only* within the SELECT clause and/ or the HAVING part of the statement. Specifying an aggregate function after the SELECT keyword and before the FROM keyword indicates that the aggregate function is to be performed over all the records in the relation (if there is no GROUP BY clause in the command) or over the groups of records (if there is a GROUP BY clause in the command). If a GROUP BY clause was used in the query, aggregate functions can also be used in the HAVING group selection condition. Other than using aggregate functions within the SELECT or HAVING part of the statement, there is no other valid use for the aggregate function in an SQL query. Consequently, Query 28 INVALID above will not execute. Function AVG(ProductPrice) must be applied to the table, but in Query 28 INVALID, no table is specified for AVG(ProductPrice).

IN

The **IN** keyword is used in SQL for comparison of a value with a set of values. Consider Query 29.

Query 29 text: *For each product that has more than three items sold within all sales transactions, retrieve the product id, product name, and product price.*

Query 29:
```
SELECT      productid, productname, productprice
FROM        product
WHERE       productid IN
            (SELECT     productid
            FROM        soldvia
            GROUP BY    productid
            HAVING      SUM(noofitems) > 3);
```

The result of Query 29 is shown in Figure 5.29.

This query illustrates how the IN keyword is used for a comparison with the set of values resulting from a nested query. In Query 29, the nested query (inner query), which is identical to Query 26, returns the set of ProductID values of products that have more than three items sold. The outer query then uses the set to identify which product's ids match one of the values in the set. In other words, it tests to see if a product id is a member of the set. For those products that are members of the set, it displays the ProductName and ProductPrice.

Query 30 is another example of a nested query using the IN statement.

Query 30 text: *For each product whose items were sold in more than one sales transaction, retrieve the product id, product name and product price.*

ProductID	ProductName	ProductPrice
3X3	Cosy Sock	15
4X4	Dura Boot	90

FIGURE 5.29   Result of Query 29.

ProductID	ProductName	ProductPrice
1X1	Zzz Bag	100
4X4	Dura Boot	90
2X2	Easy Boot	70

FIGURE 5.30 Result of Query 30.

Query 30:

```
SELECT      productid, productname, productprice
FROM        product
WHERE       productid IN
            (SELECT     productid
             FROM       soldvia
             GROUP BY   productid
             HAVING     COUNT(tid) > 1);
```

The result of Query 30 is shown in Figure 5.30.

In Query 30, the nested query (inner query), which is identical to Query 27, returns the set of ProductID values of products that were sold in more than one transaction. The outer query then uses the set to identify which product's ids match one of the values in the set. For those products, it displays the ProductName and ProductPrice.

JOIN

All the queries we have discussed so far query one single table. Now we will describe how multiple tables can be queried at the same time. The **JOIN** operation is used in SQL to facilitate the querying of multiple tables. Query 31 illustrates usage of a JOIN operation.

Query 31 text: *For each product, retrieve the product id, name of the product, name of the vendor of the product, and price of the product.*

Query 31:

```
SELECT      productid, productname, vendorname, productprice
FROM        product, vendor
WHERE       product.vendorid = vendor.vendorid;
```

The result of Query 31 is shown in Figure 5.31.

Query 31 retrieves the product identifier, name of the product, name of the vendor of the product, and price of the product for each product. ProductID, ProductName, and ProductPrice are columns in the relation PRODUCT. However, VendorName is a column in another relation: VENDOR. Therefore, in order to retrieve the requested information, we have to query two tables. The expression following the WHERE keyword is the JOIN condition, which explains how the two tables are to be connected.

ProductID	ProductName	VendorName	ProductPrice
1X1	Zzz Bag	Pacifica Gear	100
4X4	Dura Boot	Pacifica Gear	90
2X2	Easy Boot	Mountain King	70
3X3	Cosy Sock	Mountain King	15
5X5	Tiny Tent	Mountain King	150
6X6	Biggy Tent	Mountain King	250

FIGURE 5.31 Result of Query 31.

Note that in the JOIN condition, column VendorID from the PRODUCT relation and column VendorID from the VENDOR relation are qualified with the relation name and a dot preceding the column name. This is necessary because both columns have the same name, so they have to be distinguished by the names of their relations as well.

It is very important to note the significance of the JOIN condition of the statement in Query 31:

```
WHERE        product.vendorid = vendor.vendorid;
```

To understand the meaning and importance of this part of the query, consider Query 32, which also retrieves data from two tables but does not include the JOIN condition:

Query 32: SELECT   productid, productname, vendorname, productprice
           FROM   product, vendor;

The result of Query 32 is shown in Figure 5.32.

Because it does not have a JOIN condition Query 32 does not display a single record for each product. Instead, it returns a Cartesian product, combining each record from one relation with every record from the other relation. Each record in the PRODUCT table is combined with every record in the VENDOR table, even though they have different VendorIDs. The number of rows in the result of Query 32 is 12, because relation PRODUCT has six records and relation VENDOR has two records (6 X 2 = 12).

The next two examples illustrate how the JOIN operation works. First, consider Query 33. This query is an expanded version of Query 32. It shows all columns of the Cartesian product of relations PRODUCT and VENDOR.

Query 33: SELECT   *
           FROM   product, vendor;

The result of Query 33 is shown in Figure 5.33.

Now, consider Query 34, which adds the join condition to Query 33:

Query 34: SELECT   *
           FROM   product, vendor
           WHERE   product.vendorid = vendor.vendorid;

Figure 5.34a shows how the result of Query 34 is generated.

The SELECT and FROM clauses of the query statement create a Cartesian product (PRODUCT X VENDOR). Then, as shown in Figure 5.34a, the JOIN

ProductID	ProductName	VendorName	ProductPrice
1X1	Zzz Bag	Pacifica Gear	100
2X2	Easy Boot	Pacifica Gear	70
3X3	Cosy Sock	Pacifica Gear	15
4X4	Dura Boot	Pacifica Gear	90
5X5	Tiny Tent	Pacifica Gear	150
6X6	Biggy Tent	Pacifica Gear	250
1X1	Zzz Bag	Mountain King	100
2X2	Easy Boot	Mountain King	70
3X3	Cosy Sock	Mountain King	15
4X4	Dura Boot	Mountain King	90
5X5	Tiny Tent	Mountain King	150
6X6	Biggy Tent	Mountain King	250

FIGURE 5.32   Result of Query 32.

	From relation PRODUCT				From relation VENDOR	
ProductID	**ProductName**	**ProductPrice**	**VendorID**	**CategoryID**	**VendorID**	**VendorName**
1X1	Zzz Bag	100	PG	CP	PG	Pacifica Gear
2X2	Easy Boot	70	MK	FW	PG	Pacifica Gear
3X3	Cosy Sock	15	MK	FW	PG	Pacifica Gear
4X4	Dura Boot	90	PG	FW	PG	Pacifica Gear
5X5	Tiny Tent	150	MK	CP	PG	Pacifica Gear
6X6	Biggy Tent	250	MK	CP	PG	Pacifica Gear
1X1	Zzz Bag	100	PG	CP	MK	Mountain King
2X2	Easy Boot	70	MK	FW	MK	Mountain King
3X3	Cosy Sock	15	MK	FW	MK	Mountain King
4X4	Dura Boot	90	PG	FW	MK	Mountain King
5X5	Tiny Tent	150	MK	CP	MK	Mountain King
6X6	Biggy Tent	250	MK	CP	MK	Mountain King

FIGURE 5.33   Result of Query 33.

condition of the query statement (the WHERE clause) identifies the rows where the value of the VendorID column retrieved from the PRODUCT relation matches the value of the VendorID column retrieved from the VENDOR relation. Figure 5.34b shows the result of Query 34 once the appropriate rows that satisfy the JOIN condition are displayed.

To change Query 34 into Query 31, all we have to do is to replace the * symbol following the SELECT keyword with the list of columns to be displayed: ProductID, ProductName, VendorName, ProductPrice.

	From relation PRODUCT				From relation VENDOR	
ProductID	**ProductName**	**ProductPrice**	**VendorID**	**CategoryID**	**VendorID**	**VendorName**
1X1	Zzz Bag	100	PG	CP	PG	Pacifica Gear
2X2	Easy Boot	70	MK	FW	PG	Pacifica Gear
3X3	Cosy Sock	15	MK	FW	PG	Pacifica Gear
4X4	Dura Boot	90	PG	FW	PG	Pacifica Gear
5X5	Tiny Tent	150	MK	CP	PG	Pacifica Gear
6X6	Biggy Tent	250	MK	CP	PG	Pacifica Gear
1X1	Zzz Bag	100	PG	CP	MK	Mountain King
2X2	Easy Boot	70	MK	FW	MK	Mountain King
3X3	Cosy Sock	15	MK	FW	MK	Mountain King
4X4	Dura Boot	90	PG	FW	MK	Mountain King
5X5	Tiny Tent	150	MK	CP	MK	Mountain King
6X6	Biggy Tent	250	MK	CP	MK	Mountain King

product.vendorid = vendor.vendorid

FIGURE 5.34a   Formation of the result of Query 34.

ProductID	ProductName	ProductPrice	VendorID	CategoryID	VendorID	VendorName
1X1	Zzz Bag	100	PG	CP	PG	Pacifica Gear
4X4	Dura Boot	90	PG	FW	PG	Pacifica Gear
2X2	Easy Boot	70	MK	FW	MK	Mountain King
3X3	Cosy Sock	15	MK	FW	MK	Mountain King
5X5	Tiny Tent	150	MK	CP	MK	Mountain King
6X6	Biggy Tent	250	MK	CP	MK	Mountain King

FIGURE 5.34b   Result of Query 34.

ALIAS

In the FROM part of the query, each relation can be given an **alias**, an alternative (and usually shorter) name. An alias can be used anywhere within a query instead of the full relation name.

An alias can be one or more characters long. The first character must be textual, and the rest of the characters can be alphanumeric.

An alias has no effect on the execution of the query itself, but improves the legibility of the queries for the users or developers who may eventually have to read them. If we precede each column name with an alias of the relation that contains that column, it will be obvious from which table each column name comes from. By using aliases, we do not have to write the actual table name in front of each column. Instead, we can use a shorter alias version, reducing the amount of text in the statement.

For example, Query 31 could have been written slightly differently, by using aliases, as illustrated by Query 31a.

Query 31a:
```
SELECT    p.productid, p.productname, v.vendorname, p.productprice
FROM      product p, vendor v
WHERE     p.vendorid = v.vendorid;
```

Query 31a will execute exactly the same as Query 31 and give exactly the same resulting set of rows. The changes are purely for appearance (legibility) reasons. In the FROM part of the statement, the name of the relation PRODUCT is followed by the alias p. In the same fashion, relation VENDOR is given the alias v. These aliases are used elsewhere in the query statement to qualify each column with the alias referring to the relation where the column is from.

Aliases can also be used to rename the columns in the table resulting from the query, as illustrated by Query 31b.

Query 31b:
```
SELECT    p.productid pid, p.productname pname,
          v.vendorname vname, p.productprice pprice
FROM      product p, vendor v
WHERE     p.vendorid = v.vendorid;
```

Query 31b will also execute exactly the same as Query 31 and give exactly the same resulting set of rows. The only difference is that the column names in the result will now use the alias names instead of the original column names, as shown in Figure 5.31b.

PID	PName	VName	PPrice
1X1	Zzz Bag	Pacifica Gear	100
2X2	Easy Boot	Mountain King	70
3X3	Cosy Sock	Mountain King	15
4X4	Dura Boot	Pacifica Gear	90
5X5	Tiny Tent	Mountain King	150
6X6	Biggy Tent	Mountain King	250

FIGURE 5.31b   Result of Query 31b.

Columns used in the WHERE clause must be listed using their proper names (not aliases). The same rule applies to columns listed in the GROUP BY clause and to columns in the HAVING clause. Table name aliases have no such limitations and could be used everywhere within a SELECT statement.

Alias statements can also include the SQL keyword AS, as illustrated by Query 31c.[2]

Query 31c:
```
SELECT    p.productid AS pid, p.productname AS pname,
          v.vendorname AS vname, p.productprice AS pprice
FROM      product p, vendor v
WHERE     p.vendorid = v.vendorid;
```

Query 31c will execute exactly the same as Query 31b and produce the exact same results.

JOINING MULTIPLE RELATIONS

One query can contain multiple JOIN conditions, joining multiple relations. Consider Query 35.

Query 35 text: *For each line item of a sales transaction, retrieve the transaction identifier, date of the transaction, name of the product that was sold, quantity sold, and amount charged, sorted by tid.*

Query 35:
```
SELECT    t.tid, t.tdate, p.productname,
          sv.noofitems AS quantity,
          (sv.noofitems * p.productprice) AS amount
FROM      product p, salestransaction t, soldvia sv
WHERE     sv.productid = p.productid AND
          sv.tid = t.tid
ORDER BY  t.tid;
```

For every line item of a sale transaction Query 35 retrieves the transaction identifier, date of the transaction, name of the product that was sold, quantity sold, and amount charged. Columns TID and TDate are retrieved from the SALESTRANSACTION relation. Column ProductName is retrieved from the PRODUCT relation. Column NoOfItems is retrieved from the SOLDVIA relation and renamed in the result as Quantity. Amount is derived as the product of the NoOfItems column from the SOLDVIA relation and the ProductPrice column from the PRODUCT relation.

Query 35 has two JOIN conditions connected with the AND operator in the WHERE clause: one for joining the SOLDVIA relation with the PRODUCT relation, and another one for joining the SOLDVIA relation with the SALESTRANSACTION relation. The result of Query 35 is shown in Figure 5.35.

TID	TDate	ProductName	Quantity	Amount
T111	01-JAN-13	Zzz Bag	1	100
T222	01-JAN-13	Easy Boot	1	70
T333	02-JAN-13	Zzz Bag	1	100
T333	02-JAN-13	Cosy Sock	5	75
T444	02-JAN-13	Dura Boot	1	90
T444	02-JAN-13	Easy Boot	2	140
T555	02-JAN-13	Biggy Tent	1	250
T555	02-JAN-13	Dura Boot	4	360
T555	02-JAN-13	Tiny Tent	2	300

FIGURE 5.35   Result of Query 35.

---

[2] See the SQL Syntax Difference Note 3 on page 170 of this chapter for alternative syntax for specifying aliases in different RDBMS packages.

So far, we have demonstrated the SQL commands for the creation and removal of relations, insertion of data into the relations, and retrieval of data from the relations. Next, we will demonstrate how SQL can be used to change the structure of relations (using the ALTER TABLE command), modify data in the relations (using the UPDATE command), and delete data from the relations (using the DELETE command).

ALTER TABLE

The ALTER TABLE command is used in cases when we want to change the structure of the relation, once the relation is already created. For example, if we wanted to add an optional column VendorPhoneNumber to the relation VENDOR, we would issue the following **ALTER TABLE** statement:

Alter Statement 1:   `ALTER TABLE vendor ADD`
`(      vendorphonenumber      CHAR(12));`

This statement[3] will add another column to the relation VENDOR. The values of this column are initially NULL for each record in the relation VENDOR.

The ALTER TABLE statement can be used to drop a column as well. For example, if we wanted to eliminate the column VendorPhoneNumber from the relation VENDOR, we would issue the following ALTER TABLE statement:

Alter Statement 2:   `ALTER TABLE vendor DROP`
`(      vendorphonenumber);`

As we will demonstrate later in this chapter, in addition to adding and dropping columns, the ALTER TABLE command can be used for making other changes to the structure of a relation.

UPDATE

The UPDATE command in SQL is used for modifying the data stored in database relations. Let us insert another product into the relation PRODUCT by issuing the following INSERT INTO statement:

Insert Statement 1:   `INSERT INTO product VALUES ('7x7','Airy Sock',1000,'MK','FW');`

The newly inserted product actually costs $10, but a typo was made within the INSERT INTO statement, and the stated price in the PRODUCT relation for this product is $1,000. To modify the price for this product, we would use the **UPDATE** statement as follows:

Update Statement 1:   `UPDATE      product`
`SET      productprice = 10`
`WHERE      productid = '7x7';`

In the UPDATE statement, the keyword UPDATE is followed by the name of the table where the records will be updated. The SET clause specifies which column (or columns) will be updated and to what value. The WHERE part identifies which record (or records) will be updated.

Let us add another column to the PRODUCT relation by issuing the following ALTER TABLE statement:

Alter Statement 3:   `ALTER TABLE product ADD`
`(discount      NUMERIC(2,2));`

Initially, the value of the newly added column Discount is NULL for every row in the PRODUCT relation. Assume that we want to assign a discount of 20 percent for every product. In that case, we would issue the following UPDATE statement:

Update Statement 2:   `UPDATE      product`
`SET      discount = 0.2;`

---

[3] See the SQL Syntax Difference Note 4 on page 171 of this chapter for alternative ALTER TABLE syntax in different RDBMS packages.

The absence of the WHERE clause in this UPDATE statement will result in the Discount column in every record being set to a value of *0.2*.

Let us now assume that we want to increase the discount for the products supplied by the vendor MK to 30%. The following UPDATE statement would be issued for that purpose:

Update Statement 3:
```
UPDATE     product
SET        discount = 0.3
WHERE      vendorid = 'MK';
```

In the records with the vendor id value of *MK*, the value of the Discount column will now be *0.3*.

If we decide that we no longer want to use the Discount column, we can remove it by issuing another ALTER TABLE statement:

Alter Statement 4:
```
ALTER TABLE product DROP
          (discount);
```

DELETE

The DELETE command in SQL is used for deleting the data stored in database relations. Let us delete the product with the Product ID value *7×7* from the relation PRODUCT by issuing the following **DELETE** statement:

Delete Statement 1:
```
DELETE FROM     product
WHERE           productid = '7×7';
```

In the DELETE statement, the keywords DELETE FROM are followed by the name of the table where the records will be deleted. The WHERE part identifies which record (or records) will be deleted. Note that the DELETE statement can be issued without the WHERE clause and in that case every record in the specified table would be deleted. In such a case, the table still exists, even if all the records in the table have been deleted. This is different from using the DROP TABLE command, which deletes all the records in the table and the table itself.

In practice, similar to INSERT INTO statements, DELETE and UPDATE statements are usually not directly written by the end users in charge of data modifications and deletes. A common practice is that users use front-end applications, such as forms discussed in Chapter 6, to perform these operations. Front-end applications issue the UPDATE and DELETE statements on behalf of the end users who are performing the data modifications and delete operations using the front-end applications.

CREATE VIEW AND DROP VIEW

A **view** is a mechanism in SQL that allows the structure of a query to be saved in the RDBMS. A view, which is also known as a virtual table, is not an actual table and does not have any data physically saved. Every time a view is invoked, it executes a query that retrieves the data from the actual tables. A view can be used in SELECT statements just like any other table from a database. For example, columns of the view can be selected, a view can be joined to other tables or views, data from the view can be grouped, and so on.

Consider the following **CREATE VIEW** statement that creates the view PRODUCTS_MORE_THAN_3_SOLD:

Create View Statement 1:
```
CREATE VIEW     products_more_than_3_sold AS
SELECT          productid, productname, productprice
FROM            product
WHERE           productid IN
                (SELECT     productid
                 FROM       soldvia
                 GROUP BY   productid
                 HAVING     SUM(noofitems) > 3);
```

This statement saves Query 29 as a view that can be used in any query in the FROM part of the SELECT statement. Query 29 can now be executed as:

Query 29a: SELECT   *
               FROM   products_more_than_3_sold;

The result of Query 29a is exactly the same as the result of executing Query 29 itself, shown in Figure 5.29 (on page 147).

The following statement creates the view PRODUCTS_IN_MULTIPLE_TRNSC.

Create View Statement 2:

```
CREATE VIEW     products_in_multiple_trnsc AS
SELECT          productid, productname, productprice
FROM            product
WHERE           productid IN
                (SELECT    productid
                FROM       soldvia
                GROUP BY   productid
                HAVING     COUNT(*) > 1);
```

This view can also be queried as any other regular table, as illustrated by Query 30a.

Query 30a: SELECT   *
               FROM   products_in_multiple_trnsc;

The result of Query 30a is exactly the same as the result of executing Query 30 itself, shown in Figure 5.30 (on page 148).

To remove a view we would use a **DROP VIEW** statement. The following two statements drop the two views created above.

Drop View Statement 1:

```
DROP VIEW products_more_than_3_sold;
```

Drop View Statement 2:

```
DROP VIEW products_in_multiple_trnsc;
```

Of course, if we wanted to recreate these views, we would simply execute Create View Statement 1 and Create View Statement 2 again.

SET OPERATORS: UNION, INTERSECT, EXCEPT (MINUS)

SQL also contains the standard **set operators**: union, intersection, and difference. The SQL set operators are used to combine the results of two or more SELECT statements that are union compatible.

Two sets of columns are union compatible if they contain the same number of columns, and if the data types of the columns in one set match the data types of the columns in the other set. In other words, the first column in one set has a compatible data type with the data type of the first column in the other set, the second column in one set has a compatible data type with the data type of the second column in the other set, and so on.

The set operators can combine results from SELECT statements querying relations, views, or other SELECT queries.

To demonstrate the SQL set operators, we will use the SELECT statements querying views PRODUCTS_MORE_THAN_3_SOLD and PRODUCTS_IN_MULTIPLE_TRNSC (assume that the CREATE VIEW statements from the previous section are executed again). Observe Figures 5.29 and 5.30 showing the results of queries using PRODUCTS_MORE_THAN_3_SOLD and PRODUCTS_IN_MULTIPLE_TRNSC views. Note that these views are union compatible, as they contain the same number of columns with matching data types.

Query 36 illustrates the use of the **UNION** operator.

ProductID	ProductName	ProductPrice
1X1	Zzz Bag	100
2X2	Easy Boot	70
3X3	Cosy Sock	15
4X4	Dura Boot	90

FIGURE 5.36   Result of Query 36.

Query 36 text: *Retrieve the product id, product name, and product price for each product that has more than three items sold within all sales transactions **or** whose items were sold in more than one sales transaction.*

Query 36:
```
SELECT          *
FROM            products_more_than_3_sold
UNION
SELECT          *
FROM            products_in_multiple_trnsc;
```

The result of Query 36 is shown in Figure 5.36.

In Query 36, the first SELECT statement finds the set of products that have more than three items sold within all sales transactions (see Figure 5.29), and the second SELECT statement finds the set of products whose items were sold in more than one sales transaction (see Figure 5.30). The UNION operator combines those two sets and eliminates the duplicates. If a certain product has more than three items sold and also appears in more than one transaction, that product will still be listed only once.

Query 37 illustrates the use of the **INTERSECT** operator.

Query 37 text: *Retrieve the product id, product name, and product price for each product that has more than three items sold within all sales transactions **and** whose items were sold in more than one sales transaction.*

Query 37:
```
SELECT          *
FROM            products_more_than_3_sold
INTERSECT
SELECT          *
FROM            products_in_multiple_trnsc;
```

The result of Query 37 is shown in Figure 5.37.

As in Query 36, in Query 37 the first SELECT statement finds the set of products that have more than three items sold within all sales transactions, and the second SELECT statement finds the set of products whose items were sold in more than one sales transaction. The INTERSECT operator finds the products that appear in both of the sets.

Query 38 illustrates the use of the difference operator **MINUS**, also known as the **EXCEPT** operator in certain RDBMS SQL implementations.[4]

Query 38 text: *Retrieve the product id, product name, and product price for each product that has more than three items sold within all sales transactions but whose items were not sold in more than one sales transaction.*

ProductID	ProductName	ProductPrice
4X4	Dura Boot	90

FIGURE 5.37   Result of Query 37.

---

[4] See the SQL Syntax Difference Note 5 on page 172 of this chapter for alternative syntax for intersect and difference set operators in different RDBMS packages.

ProductID	ProductName	ProductPrice
3X3	Cosy Sock	15

FIGURE 5.38   Result of Query 38.

Query 38:

```
SELECT      *
FROM        products_more_than_3_sold
MINUS
SELECT      *
FROM        products_in_multiple_trnsc;
```

The result of Query 38 is shown in Figure 5.38.

As in the previous two queries, in Query 38, the first SELECT statement finds the set of products that have more than three items sold within all sales transactions, and the second SELECT statement finds the set of products whose items were sold in more than one sales transaction. The MINUS operator finds the products that appear in the first set but not in the second set.

ADDITIONAL SQL EXAMPLES WITH ADDITIONAL SQL COMMANDS

So far in this chapter, we have provided an overview and illustrations of the most commonly used SQL commands and statements by using the ZAGI Retail Company Sales Department Database example. We will use another sample database, the HAFH Realty Company Property Management Database, to reinforce the introduced SQL commands and statements and to introduce a few additional SQL commands. The ER diagram and the relational schema for the HAFH Realty Company Property Management Database are shown in Figure 3.59 in Chapter 3, repeated here as Figure 5.39a for convenience.

CREATE TABLE (ADDITIONAL EXAMPLE)

First, let us observe the set of CREATE TABLE statements that create the relational schema for the HAFH Realty Company Property Management Database shown in Figure 5.39a. The CREATE TABLE statements are shown in Figure 5.39b.

Consider the following remarks about the CREATE TABLE statements shown in Figure 5.39b.

As shown in Figure 5.39a, attributes CCID and CCName in the entity CORPCLIENT are both unique. In the CREATE TABLE statement for the relation CORPCLIENT, we designate the CCID column as the primary key. To indicate that candidate key column CCName is also unique, in the CREATE TABLE statement for the relation CORPCLIENT, we designate CCName as a unique column.

As shown in Figure 5.39a, attributes Bonus in entity MANAGER and CCID in entity APARTMENT are optional. Therefore, columns Bonus in relation MANAGER and CCID in the relation APARTMENT are optional and do not have NOT NULL designation.

As shown in Figure 5.39a, a client can but *does not have to be* referred by another client. Therefore, the CCIDReferredBy foreign key in the relation CORPCLIENT is an optional column, and the CCIDReferredBy column in the relation CORPCLIENT does not have NOT NULL designation.

As shown in Figure 5.39a, two relationships, ResidesIn and Manages, exist between the MANAGER and BUILDING entities. Column MResBuildingID in relation MANAGER is a foreign key referencing relation BUILDING, implementing relationship ResidesIn. Column BManagerID in relation BUILDING is a foreign key

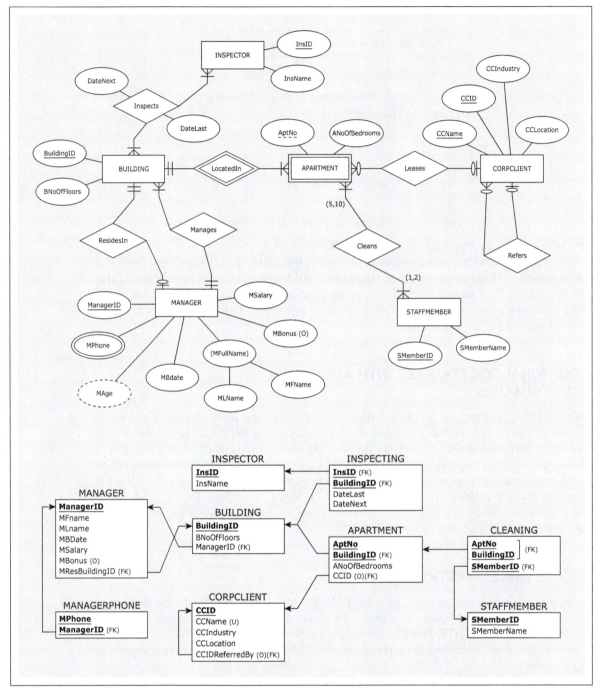

FIGURE 5.39a   HAFH Realty Company Property Management Database: ER diagram and a relational schema.

referencing relation MANAGER, implementing relationship Manages. Yet in the CRE-ATE TABLE statement for the relation MANAGER, the column MResBuildingID is not initially declared as a foreign key column. The MResBuildingID column will eventually be declared a foreign key column referencing the relation BUILDING. However, since relation MANAGER is created before the relation BUILDING, we cannot declare foreign keys referring to the relation BUILDING in the CREATE TABLE statement for the relation MANAGER, because relation BUILDING does not exist.[5] Instead, for the initial creation of the table, the MResBuildingID is not treated as a mandatory column that is

---

[5]Creating relation BUILDING before relation MANAGER would allow declaring the MResBuildingID column in the MANAGER relation as a foreign key, but would also prevent declaring the BManagerID column as a foreign key in relation BUILDING. In other words, one problem would be replaced by another.

```
CREATE TABLE manager
(      managerid                CHAR(4)                      NOT NULL,
       mfname                   VARCHAR(15)                  NOT NULL,
       mlname                   VARCHAR(15)                  NOT NULL,
       mbdate                   DATE                         NOT NULL,
       msalary                  NUMERIC(9,2)                 NOT NULL,
       mbonus                   NUMERIC(9,2),
       mresbuildingid           CHAR(3),
       PRIMARY KEY (managerid) );

CREATE TABLE managerphone
(      managerid                CHAR(4)                      NOT NULL,
       mphone                   CHAR(11)                     NOT NULL,
       PRIMARY KEY (managerid, mphone),
       FOREIGN KEY (managerid) REFERENCES manager(managerid) );

CREATE TABLE building
(      buildingid               CHAR(3)                      NOT NULL,
       bnooffloors              INT                          NOT NULL,
       managerid                CHAR(4)                      NOT NULL,
       PRIMARY KEY (buildingid),
       FOREIGN KEY (bmanagerid) REFERENCES manager(managerid) );

CREATE TABLE inspector
(      insid                    CHAR(3)                      NOT NULL,
       insname                  VARCHAR(15)                  NOT NULL,
       PRIMARY KEY (insid) );

CREATE TABLE inspecting
(      insid                    CHAR(3)                      NOT NULL,
       buildingid               CHAR(3)                      NOT NULL,
       datelast                 DATE                         NOT NULL,
       datenext                 DATE                         NOT NULL,
       PRIMARY KEY (insid, buildingid),
       FOREIGN KEY (insid) REFERENCES inspector(insid),
       FOREIGN KEY (buildingid) REFERENCES building(buildingid) );

CREATE TABLE corpclient
(      ccid                     CHAR(4)                      NOT NULL,
       ccname                   VARCHAR(25)                  NOT NULL,
       ccindustry               VARCHAR(25)                  NOT NULL,
       cclocation               VARCHAR(25)                  NOT NULL,
       ccidreferredby           CHAR(4),
       PRIMARY KEY (ccid),
       UNIQUE (ccname),
       FOREIGN KEY (ccidreferredby) REFERENCES corpclient(ccid) );

CREATE TABLE apartment
(      buildingid               CHAR(3)                      NOT NULL,
       aptno                    CHAR(5)                      NOT NULL,
       anoofbedrooms            INT                          NOT NULL,
       ccid                     CHAR(4),
       PRIMARY KEY (buildingid, aptno),
       FOREIGN KEY (buildingid) REFERENCES building(buildingid),
       FOREIGN KEY (ccid) REFERENCES corpclient(ccid) );

CREATE TABLE staffmember
(      smemberid                CHAR(4)                      NOT NULL,
       smembername              VARCHAR(15)                  NOT NULL,
       PRIMARY KEY (smemberid) );

CREATE TABLE cleaning
(      buildingid               CHAR(3)                      NOT NULL,
       aptno                    CHAR(5)                      NOT NULL,
       smemberid                CHAR(4)                      NOT NULL,
       CONSTRAINT cleaningpk  PRIMARY KEY (buildingid, aptno, smemberid),
       CONSTRAINT cleaningfk1 FOREIGN KEY (buildingid, aptno)
                              REFERENCES apartment(buildingid, aptno),
       CONSTRAINT cleaningfk2 FOREIGN KEY (smemberid)
                              REFERENCES staffmember(smemberid) );
```

FIGURE 5.39b   CREATE TABLE statements for the HAFH Realty Company Property Management Database.

a foreign key but as an optional column that is not a foreign key. Later on, we will demonstrate how the referential integrity constraint is added to an already existing relation.

As shown in Figure 5.39a, relationship Refers is a unary relationship. The CREATE TABLE statement for the CORPCLIENT relation illustrates an implementation of a unary relationship. The foreign key CCIDReferredBy refers to the primary key of the CORPCLIENT relation itself.

To illustrate that constraints (such as declarations of a primary key or foreign key) can have names, the CREATE TABLE statement for the relation CLEANING names its constraints. Naming a constraint is not necessary, but can occasionally be practical. In the constraint management example later in this section, we will illustrate a case in which the practice of naming a constraint is of use.

INSERT INTO (ADDITIONAL EXAMPLE)

Data records for the HAFH Realty Company Property Management Database are shown in Figure 3.60 in Chapter 3, repeated here as Figure 5.39c for convenience.

Let us now observe the INSERT INTO statements in Figure 5.39d, inserting the data records for the HAFH Realty Company Property Management Database.

As we mentioned earlier in this chapter, the order of entering records is important because referential integrity constraints require that the primary key values that are referred to by a foreign key are entered before the foreign key values can be entered. For example, in the CORPCLIENT relation, records are inserted so that a client who is referred by another client is inserted before the referring client.

Also note that we initially do not insert the values in the MResBuildingID in the relation MANAGER. Instead, we leave those columns temporarily empty. The reason, as shown in Figure 5.39a, is that there are two relationships between MANAGER and BUILDING. In one relationship, a MANAGER column refers to the BUILDING, and in another relationship, a BUILDING column refers to the MANAGER. Implementing both of these relationships in a relational schema causes a so-called **circular foreign key dependency**.

We cannot have a constraint in a table referring to a table that is not created yet. Therefore, we chose to initially create only the referential integrity constraints in the BUILDING relation, in which a foreign key column in the BUILDING relation refers to the primary key column in the MANAGER relation. The other referential integrity constraints, in which a foreign key column in the MANAGER relation refers to the primary key column in the BUILDING, are added as described next.

CONSTRAINT MANAGEMENT

Now that the initial data are inserted, we can add the missing referential integrity constraint, in which the foreign key column ResBuildingID in the relation MANAGER refers to the primary key of the relation BUILDING by issuing the following statement:

Alter Statement 5:
```
ALTER TABLE manager
ADD CONSTRAINT fkresidesin
FOREIGN KEY (mresbuildingid) REFERENCES building
                (buildingid);
```

Once the referential integrity constraint FKResidesIn is in place, we can add values to the ResBuildingID column of relation MANAGER by executing the following UPDATE statements:

Update Statement 4:
```
UPDATE    manager
SET       mresbuildingid = 'B1'
WHERE     managerid = 'M12';
```

Update Statement 5:
```
UPDATE    manager
SET       mresbuildingid = 'B2'
WHERE     managerid = 'M23';
```

Update Statement 6:
```
UPDATE    manager
SET       mresbuildingid = 'B4'
WHERE     managerid = 'M34';
```

INSPECTOR

InsID	InsName
I11	Jane
I22	Niko
I33	Mick

BUILDING

BuildingID	BNoOfFloors	BManagerID
B1	5	M12
B2	6	M23
B3	4	M23
B4	4	M34

APARTMENT

BuildingID	AptNo	ANoOfBedrooms	CCID
B1	41	1	
B1	21	1	C111
B2	11	2	C222
B2	31	2	
B3	11	2	C777
B4	11	2	C777

INSPECTING

InsID	BuildingID	DateLast	DateNext
I11	B1	15-MAY-2012	14-MAY-2013
I11	B2	17-FEB-2013	17-MAY-2013
I22	B2	17-FEB-2013	17-MAY-2013
I22	B3	11-JAN-2013	11-JAN-2014
I33	B3	12-JAN-2013	12-JAN-2014
I33	B4	11-JAN-2013	11-JAN-2014

MANAGER

ManagerID	MFName	MLName	MBDate	MSalary	MBonus	MResBuildingID
M12	Boris	Grant	20-JUN-1980	60000		B1
M23	Austin	Lee	30-OCT-1975	50000	5000	B2
M34	George	Sherman	11-JAN-1976	52000	2000	B4

CLEANING

BuildingID	AptNo	SMemberID
B1	21	5432
B1	41	9876
B2	11	9876
B2	31	5432
B3	11	5432
B4	11	7652

MANAGERPHONE

ManagerID	MPhone
M12	555–2222
M12	555–3232
M23	555–9988
M34	555–9999

STAFFMEMBER

SMemberID	SMemberName
5432	Brian
9876	Boris
7652	Caroline

CORPCLIENT

CCID	CCName	CCIndustry	CCLocation	CCIDReferredBy
C111	BlingNotes	Music	Chicago	
C222	SkyJet	Airline	Oak Park	C111
C777	WindyCT	Music	Chicago	C222
C888	SouthAlps	Sports	Rosemont	C777

FIGURE 5.39c Sample data records for the HAFH Realty Company Property Management Database.

```
INSERT INTO manager VALUES ('M12', 'Boris', 'Grant', '20/Jun/1980', 60000, null, null);
INSERT INTO manager VALUES ('M23', 'Austin', 'Lee', '30/Oct/1975', 50000, 5000, null);
INSERT INTO manager VALUES ('M34', 'George', 'Sherman', '11/Jan/1976', 52000, 2000, null);

INSERT INTO managerphone VALUES ('M12','555-2222');
INSERT INTO managerphone VALUES ('M12','555-3232');
INSERT INTO managerphone VALUES ('M23','555-9988');
INSERT INTO managerphone VALUES ('M34','555-9999');

INSERT INTO building VALUES ('B1', '5', 'M12');
INSERT INTO building VALUES ('B2', '6', 'M23');
INSERT INTO building VALUES ('B3', '4', 'M23');
INSERT INTO building VALUES ('B4', '4', 'M34');

INSERT INTO inspector VALUES ('I11', 'Jane');
INSERT INTO inspector VALUES ('I22', 'Niko');
INSERT INTO inspector VALUES ('I33', 'Mick');

INSERT INTO inspecting VALUES ('I11','B1','15/May/2012','14/May/2013');
INSERT INTO inspecting VALUES ('I11','B2','17/Feb/2013','17/May/2013');
INSERT INTO inspecting VALUES ('I22','B2','17/Feb/2013','17/May/2013');
INSERT INTO inspecting VALUES ('I22','B3','11/Jan/2013','11/Jan/2014');
INSERT INTO inspecting VALUES ('I33','B3','12/Jan/2013','12/Jan/2014');
INSERT INTO inspecting VALUES ('I33','B4','11/Jan/2013','11/Jan/2014');

INSERT INTO corpclient VALUES ('C111', 'BlingNotes', 'Music', 'Chicago', null);
INSERT INTO corpclient VALUES ('C222', 'SkyJet', 'Airline', 'Oak Park', 'C111');
INSERT INTO corpclient VALUES ('C777', 'WindyCT', 'Music', 'Chicago', 'C222');
INSERT INTO corpclient VALUES ('C888', 'SouthAlps', 'Sports', 'Rosemont', 'C777');

INSERT INTO apartment VALUES ('B1', '21', 1, 'C111');
INSERT INTO apartment VALUES ('B1', '41', 1, null);
INSERT INTO apartment VALUES ('B2', '11', 2, 'C222');
INSERT INTO apartment VALUES ('B2', '31', 2, null);
INSERT INTO apartment VALUES ('B3', '11', 2, 'C777');
INSERT INTO apartment VALUES ('B4', '11', 2, 'C777');

INSERT INTO staffmember VALUES ('5432', 'Brian');
INSERT INTO staffmember VALUES ('9876', 'Boris');
INSERT INTO staffmember VALUES ('7652', 'Caroline');

INSERT INTO cleaning VALUES ('B1', '21', '5432');
INSERT INTO cleaning VALUES ('B1', '41', '9876');
INSERT INTO cleaning VALUES ('B2', '11', '9876');
INSERT INTO cleaning VALUES ('B2', '31', '5432');
INSERT INTO cleaning VALUES ('B3', '11', '5432');
INSERT INTO cleaning VALUES ('B4', '11', '7652');
```

FIGURE 5.39d   INSERT INTO statements for the records in the HAFH Realty Company Property Management Database.

After executing the UPDATE statements, the records in the MANAGER relation have values in the MResBuildingID column. All the initial data shown in Figure 5.39c are now inserted into the HAFH database.

Now we can fully implement the requirement that the MResBuildingID column is mandatory by issuing the following ALTER TABLE statement:

Alter Statement 6:   ALTER TABLE   manager
                       MODIFY   (mresbuildingid NOT NULL);

All of the future records in the MANGER relation will have to enter a value in the MResBuildingID column that will match the BuildingID value in the BUILDING relation.

Because the FKResidesIn constraint has a name, we have an option, when and if needed, to drop tables MANAGER and BUILDING. Consider first the following sequence of drop table statements:

DROP TABLE sequence HAFH database—First seven tables:

```
DROP TABLE cleaning;
DROP TABLE staffmember;
DROP TABLE apartment;
DROP TABLE corpclient;
DROP TABLE inspecting;
DROP TABLE inspector;
DROP TABLE managerphone;
```

This sequence will drop all the relations other than relations BUILDING and MANAGER. Because BUILDING and MANAGER relations refer to each other, neither this sequence:

DROP TABLE sequence HAFH database—Last two tables (a):

```
DROP TABLE building;
DROP TABLE manager;
```

nor this sequence:

DROP TABLE sequence HAFH database—Last two tables (b):

```
DROP TABLE manager;
DROP TABLE building;
```

can be executed. However, because the FKResidesIn constraint has a name, it can be dropped by the following statement:

Alter Statement 7:   ALTER TABLE manager
                        DROP CONSTRAINT fkresidesin;

that in turn allows us to execute the *DROP TABLE sequence HAFH database—Last two tables (a)*.

Commands for removing the referential integrity constraints in the tables can be used to completely circumvent the issue of *ordering* DROP TABLE statements prior to *executing* DROP TABLE statements. For example, if we removed all the referential constraints in the HAFH database (assuming they were all named), we could execute DROP TABLE statements in any order.

SELECT (ADDITIONAL EXAMPLES)

Below, we will show additional examples of SQL queries, demonstrating additional SQL functionalities and commands. These example queries will query the records from the HAFH database.

JOIN OF A RELATION WITH ITSELF (SELF–JOIN)

When a relation contains a foreign key referring to its own primary key, such a relation can be joined with itself in a query. Such a join is referred to as a **self-JOIN** statement. Consider Query 39.

Query 39 text: *For all corporate clients that were referred by other corporate clients, retrieve the name of the corporate client and the name of the corporate client that referred it.*

Query 39:   SELECT   c.ccname AS client, r.ccname AS recommender
               FROM   corpclient c, corpclient r
               WHERE   r.ccid = c.ccidreferredby;

The result of Query 39 is shown in Figure 5.39.

The query considers the relation CORPCLIENT twice, under two different aliases c and r. The alias c represents the relation CORPCLIENT in the role of a client, and the alias r represents the relation CORPCLIENT in the role of a recommender. These two

Client	Recommender
SkyJet	BlingNotes
WindyCT	SkyJet
SouthAlps	WindyCT

FIGURE 5.39   Result of Query 39.

representations are joined so that the CCIDreferredby value of the client matches the CCIDvalue of the recommender.

Note that in this case, the use of aliases is mandatory since we are referring to the same relation twice. If we did not use the aliases, the query statement would be ambiguous and would not be executed (an error message would be returned).

OUTER JOIN

Recall that the JOIN operation merges the records of the relations where the foreign key of one relation matches the primary key of the other relation. Query 40 shows an example of a JOIN operation on relations APARTMENT and CORPCLIENT.

Query 40:   SELECT   a.buildingid, a.aptno, c.ccname
          FROM   apartment a, corpclient c
          WHERE   a.ccid = c.ccid;

The result of Query 40 is shown in Figure 5.40.

Notice that Apartment *41* in Building *B1* and Apartment *31* in Building *B2* do not appear in the result because their CCIDs do not match the CCID of any corporate client. Similarly, corporate client *South Alps* does not appear in the result because its CCID does not match any CCID of an apartment.

An **OUTER JOIN** statement is a variation of the JOIN[6] operation that supplements the results with the records from one relation that have no match in the other relation. There are three variations of OUTER JOIN: **LEFT OUTER JOIN** statement, **RIGHT OUTER JOIN** statement, and **FULL OUTER JOIN** statement.

For an example of a LEFT OUTER JOIN, consider Query 41.

Query 41:   SELECT   a.buildingid, a.aptno, c.ccname
          FROM   apartment a LEFT OUTER JOIN corpclient c
          ON   a.ccid = c.ccid;

The result of Query 41 is shown in Figure 5.41.

In the LEFT OUTER JOIN statement, all the records from the relation on the left part of the statement (in this case APARTMENT) will be shown in the result, even if they do not have a join condition value that matches a value in the other relation. When a record is being joined this way with a record from the other relation, a NULL value is used when there is no matching record in the other relation. As shown in Figure 5.41,

BuildingID	AptNo	CCName
B1	21	BlingNotes
B2	11	SkyJet
B3	11	WindyCT
B4	11	WindyCT

FIGURE 5.40   Result of Query 40.

---

[6] A regular JOIN is also sometimes referred to as an INNER JOIN, to differentiate it from an OUTER JOIN.

BuildingID	AptNo	CCName
B1	21	BlingNotes
B1	41	
B2	11	SkyJet
B2	31	
B3	11	WindyCT
B4	11	WindyCT

FIGURE 5.41   Result of Query 41.

BuildingID	AptNo	CCName
B1	21	BlingNotes
B2	11	SkyJet
B3	11	WindyCT
B4	11	WindyCT
		SouthAlps

FIGURE 5.42   Result of Query 42.

when the LEFT OUTER JOIN operation is used, Apartment *41* in Building *B1* appears in the result, as does Apartment *31* in Building *B2*, even though they do not have an associated CCName value. Their CCName value is NULL.

For an example of a RIGHT OUTER JOIN, consider Query 42.

Query 42:
```
SELECT    a.buildingid, a.aptno, c.ccname
FROM      apartment a RIGHT OUTER JOIN corpclient c
ON        a.ccid = c.ccid;
```

The result of Query 42 is shown in Figure 5.42.

In the RIGHT OUTER JOIN statement, all the records from the relation on the right part of the statement (in this case CORPCLIENT) will be shown in the result, even if they do not have a match in the relation on the left side of the statement. As shown in Figure 5.42, when the right outer join is used, the Client Name *SouthAlps* appears in the result, even though it does not have associated BuildingID and AptNo values. Instead, NULL values are shown for BuildingID and AptNo.

For an example of a FULL OUTER JOIN, consider Query 43.

Query 43:
```
SELECT    a.buildingid, a.aptno, c.ccname
FROM      apartment a FULL OUTER JOIN corpclient c
ON        a.ccid = c.ccid;
```

The result of Query 43 is shown in Figure 5.43.

BuildingID	AptNo	CCName
B1	21	BlingNotes
B1	41	
B2	11	SkyJet
B2	31	
B3	11	WindyCT
B4	11	WindyCT
		SouthAlps

FIGURE 5.43   Result of Query 43.

MgrID	MgrFname	MgrLname	SmemberID
M12	Boris	Grant	9876

FIGURE 5.44   Result of Query 44.

In the FULL OUTER JOIN statement,[7] all the records from both relations will be shown in the result even if they do not have a match in the other relation.

JOIN WITHOUT USING A PRIMARY KEY/FOREIGN KEY COMBINATION

It is possible to join two tables without joining a foreign key column in one table with a primary key column in another table. A JOIN condition can connect a column from one table with a column from the other table as long as those columns contain the same values. Query 44 shows an example of a JOIN operation joining two columns that are neither primary nor foreign keys.

Query 44 text: *For each manager who has a staff member with the same name as the manager's first name, show the manager's ID, first name, and last name and the ID of the staff members who have the same name as the manager's first name.*

Query 44:
```
SELECT      m.managerid, m.mfname, m.mlname, s.smemberid
FROM        manager m, staffmember s
WHERE       m.mfname = s.smembername;
```

The result of Query 44 is shown in Figure 5.44.

IS NULL

The **IS NULL** comparison is used in queries that contain comparisons with an empty value in a column of a record. Consider Query 45.

Query 45 text: *Retrieve records for all managers who do not have a bonus.*
Query 45:
```
SELECT      *
FROM        manager
WHERE       mbonus IS NULL;
```

The result of Query 45 is shown in Figure 5.45.

EXISTS

In queries where the inner query (nested query) uses columns from the relations listed in the SELECT part of the outer query, the inner query is referred to as a **correlated subquery**. In such cases, the **EXISTS** operator can be used to check if the result of the inner correlated query is empty. Consider Query 46.

ManagerID	MFname	MLname	MDate	MSalary	MBonus	MresBuildingID
M12	Boris	Grant	20-JUN-1980	60000		B1

FIGURE 5.45   Result of Query 45.

---

[7] See the SQL Syntax Difference Note 6 on page 172 of this chapter for alternative syntax for specifying a FULL OUTER JOIN in different RDBMS packages.

BuildingID	BNOofFloors	BManagerID
B1	5	M12
B2	6	M23
B4	4	M34

FIGURE 5.46   Result of Query 46.

Query 46 text: *Retrieve records for all buildings that have managers living in them.*

Query 46:

```
SELECT      *
FROM        building b
WHERE       EXISTS
            (SELECT      *
            FROM        manager m
            WHERE       b.buildingid = m.mresbuildingid);
```

The result of Query 46 is shown in Figure 5.46.

In Query 46, the inner query uses the column BuildingID from the relation BUILDING declared in the outer query. As a result, the inner query is correlated with the outer query. For each building X represented by a record in the BUILDING relation, the EXISTS operator returns the Boolean value TRUE if there is a record in the MANAGER relation for a manager who lives in building X. If there is no record in the MANAGER relation for a manager who lives in building X, the EXISTS operator returns the Boolean value FALSE.

This query is an example of a correlated nested query because the inner query refers to the column BuildingID, which is a column in the BUILDING table in the outer query.

NOT

The **NOT** operator can be used in conjunction with the condition comparison statements returning the Boolean values TRUE or FALSE. Consider Query 47.

Query 47 text: *Retrieve records for all buildings that do not have managers living in them.*

Query 47:

```
SELECT      *
FROM        building b
WHERE       NOT EXISTS
            (SELECT      *
            FROM  manager m
            WHERE b.buildingid = m.mresbuildingid);
```

The result of Query 47 is shown in Figure 5.47.

The SQL keyword NOT can be used in other types of queries using Boolean logic. For example, NOT can be combined with IN to form a NOT IN condition, or with IS NULL to form the IS NOT NULL condition.

BuildingID	BNOofFloors	BManagerID
B3	4	M23

FIGURE 5.47   Result of Query 47.

INSERTING FROM A QUERY

A query retrieving the data from one relation can be used to populate another relation. Consider the following example scenario.

We would like to create a denormalized copy of the CLEANING relation that, in addition to containing the SMemberID column, also contains the SMemberName column. First, we create an empty denormalized relation CLEANINGDENORMALIZED by issuing the following CREATE TABLE statement:

Create Table Statement 1:

```
CREATE TABLE cleaningdenormalized
(       buildingid      CHAR(3)       NOT NULL,
        aptno           CHAR(5)       NOT NULL,
        smemberid       CHAR(4)       NOT NULL,
        smembername     VARCHAR(15)   NOT NULL,
        PRIMARY KEY (buildingid, aptno, smemberid));
```

This new relation can be now populated by issuing the following statement:

Insert Statement 2:

```
INSERT INTO  cleaningdenormalized
SELECT       c.buildingid, c.aptno, s.smemberid, s.smembername
FROM         cleaning c, staffmember s
WHERE        c.smemberid = s.smemberid;
```

By combining the INSERT INTO statement with the SELECT query, we have automated the process of inserting the data in the relation CLEANINGDENORMALIZED.

OTHER SQL FUNCTIONALITIES

The SQL features covered in this chapter provide a basis for understanding typical corporate use of SQL. In addition to what we have presented in this chapter, other SQL functionalities exist. Once you are familiar with the commands presented in this chapter, learning and using other available SQL features, if and when needed, should be a straightforward process.

This chapter has presented the most fundamental issues related to SQL. The following notes cover several additional issues related to SQL.

A Note About Inappropriate Use of Observed Values in SQL

A common beginner's SQL mistake occurs when novice user creates a simplistic query that produces the correct result by inappropriately using observed values. Consider the following request for data retrieval from the ZAGI Retail Company Sales Department Database:

Request A: *For each product that has more than three items sold within all sales transactions, retrieve the product id, product name, and product price.*

Consider the following two SQL queries:

SQL Query A

```
SELECT       productid, productname, productprice
FROM         product
WHERE        productid IN
             (SELECT    productid
              FROM      soldvia
              GROUP BY  productid
              HAVING    SUM(noofitems) > 3);
```

SQL Query B

```
SELECT       productid, productname, productprice
FROM         product
WHERE        productid IN ('3X3','4X4');
```

Due to the fact that products whose ProductID value is '3X3' and '4X4' have more than three items sold within all sales transactions, both queries will produce the same result:

ProductID	ProductName	ProductPrice
3X3	Cosy Sock	15
4X4	Dura Boot	90

However, Query A is an appropriate query for Request A, whereas Query B *is not*.

Query A uses SQL commands to determine which products have more than three items sold within all sales transactions and will produce the correct result even when the values in the database tables are updated.

On the other hand, Query B is based on the observation by the query writer that, at the present time, products whose ProductID value is '3X3' and '4X4' are the products that have more than three items sold within all sales transactions. When that is no longer the case, due to updates to the database (e.g., insertion of new products that have more than three items sold), Query B will produce incorrect results.

As illustrated by this example, SQL queries should not use values directly written in conditions when SQL commands can be used instead to retrieve the needed values for the condition from the database. Note that Query B would have been an appropriate query for the Request B.

Request B: *For products with ProductID value of '3X3' and '4X4,' retrieve the product id, product name, and product price.*

A Note About SQL Standard and SQL Syntax Differences

Developed by IBM in the 1970s, SQL became the standard language for querying data contained in a relational database. By the late 1980s, it was adopted by the American National Standards Institute (ANSI) and the International Organization for Standardization (ISO). The standard itself is broken into many parts. In addition to the language's logical framework and central elements, which we have discussed throughout this chapter, there are several extensions that add further functionalities. These standard extensions include specifications on how SQL is to work with other programming languages, external data, and multimedia in addition to a growing range of other capabilities.

Since its initial adoption, there have been multiple revisions of the ANSI and ISO SQL standard. The latest revision, as were all of its predecessors, is named after the year in which it was adopted, SQL:2011. In general, RDBMS vendors strive to comply with the SQL standard. However, implementations of SQL vary from vendor to vendor, both in how many commands and functionalities prescribed by the standard are implemented and in the extensions of and modifications to the SQL not prescribed by the standard. As a result, SQL scripts (collections of SQL statements) are not always fully transferable from one DBMS to another.

Minor SQL syntax differences exist in SQL implementations in various popular RDBMS packages. To illustrate this issue, we will describe and discuss several *selected* particular SQL syntax differences within several popular RDBMS packages.[8] We limit this discussion to the differences in the SQL code for examples presented in this chapter. This discussion is captured by the SQL syntax difference notes listed below. As demonstrated by these notes, the differences are minor, and a user of SQL in one RDBMS will be able to switch to another RDBMS with very little additional learning effort.

---

[8]Supplementary files to this book (available at *dbtextook.com*) contain the full versions of the entire SQL code for every SQL statement in this chapter for six popular RDBMS packages: Oracle, MySQL, Microsoft SQL Server, PostgreSQL, Teradata, and IBM DB2, each with their own SQL syntax.

SQL Syntax Difference Note 1: DATE and TIME Data Types

Some SQL data types are slightly different syntactically from one RDBMS to another. For example, in addition to the DATE data type used to record date values, many RDBMS packages (such as MySQL, Microsoft SQL Server, PostgreSQL, Teradata, and IBM DB2) also include a TIME data type that can be used to record the time of day values.

However, Oracle does not have a separate data type time. Instead, in Oracle, the data type DATE, in addition to including the date values, can also include the time values. Combining date and time values is implemented by the DATETIME data type in Microsoft SQL Server and MySQL as well.

Besides DATE and TIME data types, other time- and date-related data types exist in most of today's RDBMS packages, such as a TIMESTAMP data type used for recording date and time values with high precision (microseconds or even more precise) and with a possibility of declaring time zones, or an INTERVAL data type used for recording time intervals.

SQL Syntax Difference Note 2: FOREIGN KEY

In many RDBMS packages, a foreign key can be declared without having to explicitly state the name of the primary key column in the relation to which the foreign key refers. For example, the following part of the CREATE TABLE statement is a valid declaration of a foreign key in a number of RDBMS packages (e.g., Oracle, PostgreSQL, Teradata, IBM DB2, and Microsoft SQL Server):

```
FOREIGN KEY (vendorid) REFERENCES vendor,
```

However in some RDBMS packages (such as MySQL), the primary key of the relation to which the foreign key refers to *has to be explicitly stated*, as illustrated by the following:

```
FOREIGN KEY (vendorid) REFERENCES vendor(vendorid),
```

This method of declaring the foreign key will also work in packages that do not mandate (but allow) explicit naming of the primary key in the referred relation (e.g., Oracle and IBM DB2).

SQL Syntax Difference Note 3: Usage of AS Keyword with Aliases

In many RDBMS packages, usage of the AS keyword in alias statements is allowed both for tables and columns. For example, the following query can be written in PostgreSQL, Teradata, MySQL, and Microsoft SQL Server:

```
SELECT      p.productid AS pid, p.productname AS pname,
            v.vendorname AS vname, p.productprice AS pprice
FROM        product AS p, vendor AS v
WHERE       p.vendorid = v.vendorid;
```

However, this statement would not work in Oracle, since Oracle does not allow for use of the AS keyword when specifying the alias of a relation name. In Oracle, the same statement can be written as:

```
SELECT      p.productid AS pid, p.productname AS pname,
            v.vendorname AS vname, p.productprice AS pprice
FROM        product p, vendor v
WHERE       p.vendorid = v.vendorid;
```

or as:

```
SELECT      p.productid pid, p.productname pname,
            v.vendorname vname, p.productprice pprice
FROM        product p, vendor v
WHERE       p.vendorid = v.vendorid;
```

Note that all three of these statements are acceptable for PostgreSQL, Teradata, MySQL, IBM DB2, and Microsoft SQL Server.

SQL Syntax Difference Note 4: ALTER TABLE

In some RDBMS packages (e.g., Oracle, MySQL, and Teradata), the ALTER TABLE statement requires the usage of parentheses when used with the ADD keyword, as shown in the following example:

```
ALTER TABLE vendor ADD
    (    vendorphonenumber    CHAR(11) );
```

However, in other RDBMS packages (e.g., PostgreSQL, IBM DB2, and Microsoft SQL Server), the ALTER TABLE statement does not use parentheses when used with the ADD keyword, and this statement has to be written as follows:

```
ALTER TABLE vendor ADD
        vendorphonenumber    CHAR(11) ;
```

In addition to this discrepancy, in most RDBMS packages, the ALTER TABLE statement does not use parentheses when used with the DROP keyword. The exception to this is Oracle, which does require the use of parentheses. Below are three examples of the same statement in different packages.

The first is not acceptable in Oracle, but is required by PostgreSQL, Teradata, IBM DB2, and MySQL.

```
ALTER TABLE vendor DROP vendorphonenumber;
```

The second is required by Oracle but would not be allowed in the other mentioned packages.

```
ALTER TABLE vendor DROP (vendorphonenumber);
```

The third illustrates yet another discrepancy in regards to the specification of keyword COLUMN that is required by Microsoft SQL Server.

```
ALTER TABLE vendor DROP COLUMN vendorphonenumber;
```

When issuing an ALTER TABLE statement in IBM DB2 to drop a construct within a table (e.g., a column or a constraint), an extra command needs to be issued in order to continue querying the table. This command would be entered after the ALTER TABLE command dropping a construct with a table, as follows:

```
ALTER TABLE vendor DROP vendorphonenumber;
REORG TABLE vendor;
```

Other syntactic differences in the usage of the ALTER TABLE command exist. For example, the following statement can be written in Oracle:

```
ALTER TABLE manager
    MODIFY (mresbuildingid NOT NULL);
```

However, in other RDBMS packages (e.g., PostgreSQL and IBM DB2), the syntax of the same statement is as follows:

```
ALTER TABLE manager
    ALTER mresbuildingid SET NOT NULL;
```

Yet in other RDBMS packages (e.g., MySQL and Microsoft SQL Server), not only does the syntax differ, but each one of a column's attributes (e.g., data type, null/not null specifications) must be included in the alter statement and not just the one to be altered. Thus, the same statement would appear as follows:

MySQL:

```
ALTER TABLE manager
    MODIFY mresbuildingid CHAR(3) NOT NULL;
```

Microsoft SQL Server:

```
ALTER TABLE manager
    ALTER COLUMN mresbuildingid CHAR(3) NOT NULL;
```

SQL Syntax Difference Note 5: Set Operators

While most RDBMS packages implement the union set operator in the same fashion, there are differences in how the intersect and difference set operators are implemented.

For example, the following query performs an intersect operation in Oracle, Teradata, Microsoft SQL Server, IBM DB2, and PostgreSQL:

```
SELECT      *
FROM        products_more_than_3_sold
INTERSECT
SELECT      *
FROM        products_in_multiple_trnsc;
```

MySQL does not implement an explicit intersect operator, so the same query would have to be implemented, for example, as the following query:

```
SELECT DISTINCT       *
FROM                  products_more_than_3_sold
WHERE                 (productid, productname, productprice) IN
                      (SELECT * FROM products_in_multiple_trnsc);
```

As another example, consider the following query, which performs a difference operation in Oracle:

```
SELECT      *
FROM        products_more_than_3_sold
MINUS
SELECT      *
FROM        products_in_multiple_trnsc;
```

The same query would be written in PostgreSLQ and Microsoft SQL Server as:

```
SELECT      *
FROM        products_more_than_3_sold
EXCEPT
SELECT      *
FROM        products_in_multiple_trnsc;
```

Both of the above versions of a query using a difference operation are allowed in Teradata and IBM DB2.

MySQL does not implement an explicit difference operator, so the same query would have to be implemented, for example, as the following query:

```
SELECT      *
FROM        products_more_than_3_sold
WHERE       (productid, productname, productprice) NOT IN
            (SELECT * FROM products_in_multiple_trnsc);
```

SQL Syntax Difference Note 6: FULL OUTER JOIN

Different RDBMS packages differ in the way they implement the FULL OUTER JOIN operator. For example, the following query performs a full outer join in Oracle, PostgreSQL, Teradata, IBM DB2, and Microsoft SQL Server:

```
SELECT      a.buildingid, a.aptno, c.ccname
FROM        apartment a FULL OUTER JOIN corpclient c
ON          a.ccid = c.ccid;
```

Some RDBMS packages do not have an explicit FULL OUTER JOIN operator. Instead, the user must emulate a FULL OUTER JOIN by combining a LEFT OUTER JOIN and RIGHT OUTER JOIN. For example, this same query would be written in MySQL as follows:

```
SELECT      a.buildingid, a.aptno, c.ccname
FROM        apartment a LEFT OUTER JOIN corpclient c
ON          a.ccid = c.ccid;
UNION
SELECT      a.buildingid, a.aptno, c.ccname
FROM        apartment a RIGHT OUTER JOIN corpclient c
ON          a.ccid = c.ccid;
```

SQL Syntax Difference Note 7: Constraint Management

Earlier in this chapter, we illustrated how an integrity constraint can be activated and deactivated in an existing relation by adding it and dropping it. Another way to deal with issues of activating and deactivating integrity constraints during the lifetime of a created database is to use the ENABLE and DISABLE constraint options offered by some RDBMS packages (e.g., Oracle and Microsoft SQL Server).

For example, assume that the first three CREATE TABLE statements from Figure 5.39b were executed and the relation MANAGER was altered with the FKResidesIn constraint added to it. This constraint can be disabled at any time during the lifetime of the HAFH database by issuing the following statements in Oracle and in Microsoft SQL Server respectively:

```
ALTER TABLE manager
DISABLE CONSTRAINT fkresidesin;

ALTER TABLE manager
NOCHECK CONSTRAINT fkresidesin;
```

When needed, the constraint can be reactivated by issuing the following statements in Oracle and in Microsoft SQL Server respectively:

```
ALTER TABLE manager
ENABLE CONSTRAINT fkresidesin;

ALTER TABLE manager
CHECK CONSTRAINT fkresidesin;
```

Just as was the case with the commands for removing the referential integrity constraints in the tables, commands for disabling referential integrity constraints can also be used to circumvent the issue of ordering DROP TABLE statements prior to dropping the tables. For example, if we disabled all the referential constraints in the HAFH database (assuming they were all named), we could execute DROP TABLE statements in any order.

SQL Syntax Difference Note 8: GROUP BY

In standard SQL, when a SELECT command uses the GROUP BY clause, the only column names that can appear after the SELECT keyword (other than the arguments of the aggregate functions) are the column names that also appear after the GROUP BY keyword. For example, the following query on the ZAGI Retail Company Database would be invalid in most RDBMS packages (including PostgreSQL, Oracle, Teradata, IBM DB2, and Microsoft SQL Server), and an error message would be returned:

```
SELECT      vendorid, productname, COUNT(*)
FROM        product
GROUP BY    vendorid; ERROR MESSAGE RETURNED
```

This query is invalid because the ProductName column was not listed after the GROUP BY keyword, but was listed after the SELECT keyword. This violated the rule specifying that the column names that are listed after the SELECT keyword also have to be listed after the GROUP BY keyword.

However, MySQL would allow execution of this query and it would return the following result, which is in essence an incorrect/incomplete result:

VendorID	ProductName	COUNT(*)
MK	Easy Boot	4
PG	Zzz Bag	2

The query correctly lists that there are four products whose VendorID is MK, and two products whose VendorID is PG. However, the query allows listing of the product name (not allowed by the SQL standard) and lists the name of one product in each group, while ignoring the names of other products in the group. The reason why MySQL allows for this departure from the SQL standard is to shorten the writing of certain legal queries.

For example, consider the following query:

```
SELECT      smemberid, smembername, COUNT(*)
FROM        cleaningdenormalized
GROUP BY    smemberid, smembername;
```

producing the following result:

SMemberID	SMemberName	COUNT(*)
7652	Caroline	1
5432	Brian	3
9876	Boris	2

This query could be written in a shorter manner in MySQL as:

```
SELECT      smemberid, smembername, COUNT(*)
FROM        cleaningdenormalized
GROUP BY    smemberid;
```

This query is legal because SMemberName is unique within each group, as is the SMemberID (because each SMemberID is associated with only one SMemberName).

As we just illustrated with the above examples, the nonstandard implementation of GROUP BY in MySQL enables the abbreviation of some legitimate queries, but also permits creation of queries that return ambiguous results.

Key Terms

Aggregate functions *139*
Alias *151*
ALTER TABLE *153*
AVG *139*
Circular foreign key dependency *160*
Correlated subquery *166*
COUNT *139*
CREATE TABLE *129*
CREATE VIEW *154*
Data Control Language (DCL) *127*
Data Definition Language (DDL) *127*

Data Manipulation Language (DML) *127*
DELETE *154*
DISTINCT *137*
DROP TABLE *131*
DROP VIEW *155*
EXCEPT *156*
EXISTS *166*
FULL OUTER JOIN *164*
GROUP BY *140*
HAVING *144*
IN *147*
Inner query *146*
INSERT INTO *132*
INTERSECT *156*

IS NULL *166*
JOIN *148*
LEFT OUTER JOIN *164*
LIKE *139*
MAX *139*
MIN *139*
MINUS *156*
Nested query *146*
NOT *167*
ORDER BY *138*
OUTER JOIN *164*
Outer query *146*
Query *128*
RIGHT OUTER JOIN *164*

SELECT *134*
Self-JOIN *163*
Set operators *155*
SQL data types *128*
SQL standard *127*
Structured Query Language (SQL) *127*
SUM *139*
Transaction Control Language (TCL) *127*
UNION *155*
UPDATE *153*
View *154*
WHERE *136*

Review Questions

Q5.1   What is the purpose of DDL SQL statements?
Q5.2   What is the purpose of DML SQL statements?
Q5.3   What is the purpose of the CREATE TABLE command?
Q5.4   What is the purpose of the DROP TABLE command?
Q5.5   What is the purpose of the INSERT INTO command?
Q5.6   What is the purpose of the SELECT command?

Q5.7   What is the purpose of the WHERE condition?
Q5.8   What is the purpose of the DISTINCT keyword?
Q5.9   What is the purpose of the ORDER BY clause?
Q5.10   What is the purpose of the LIKE keyword?
Q5.11   What aggregate functions are provided by SQL?
Q5.12   What is the purpose of the GROUP BY clause?

Q5.13 What is the purpose of the HAVING clause?

Q5.14 What is a nested query?

Q5.15 What is the purpose of the IN keyword?

Q5.16 What is the purpose of the JOIN condition?

Q5.17 What is the purpose of an alias?

Q5.18 What is the purpose of the ALTER TABLE command?

Q5.19 What is the purpose of the UPDATE command?

Q5.20 What is the purpose of the DELETE command?

Q5.21 What is the purpose of the CREATE VIEW and DROP VIEW commands?

Q5.22 What set operators are available in SQL?

Q5.23 What is the purpose of OUTER JOIN?

Q5.24 What is the purpose of the IS NULL keyword?

Q5.25 What is the purpose of the EXSITS keyword?

Q5.26 What is the purpose of the NOT keyword?

Exercises

E5.1 Write the SQL queries that accomplish the following tasks in the ZAGI Retail Company Sales Department Database:

E5.1a Display the VendorID and VendorName for all vendors.

E5.1b Display the CustomerName and CustomerZip for all customers.

E5.1c Display the ProductID, ProductName, and Product Price for products with a ProductPrice of $100 or higher.

E5.1d Display the ProductID, ProductName, Product-Price, and VendorName for all products. Sort the results by ProductID.

E5.1e Display the ProductID, ProductName, Product-Price, VendorName, and CategoryName for all products. Sort the results by ProductID.

E5.1f Display the ProductID, ProductName, and ProductPrice for products in the category whose CategoryName value is *Camping*. Sort the results by ProductID.

E5.1g Display the TID, CustomerName, and TDate for sales transactions involving a customer buying a product whose ProductName is *Dura Boot*.

E5.1h Display the RegionID, RegionName, and number of stores in the region for all regions.

E5.1i For each product category, display the CategoryID, CategoryName, and average price of a product in the category.

E5.1j For each product category, display the CategoryID and the total number of items purchased in the category.

E5.1k Display the TID and the total number of items (of all products) sold within the transaction for all sales transactions whose total number of items (of all products) sold within the transaction is greater than five.

E5.1l Display the ProductID and ProductName of the cheapest product.

E5.1m Display the ProductID, ProductName, and VendorName for products whose price is below the average price of all products.

E5.1n Display the ProductID for the product that has been sold the most (i.e., that has been sold in the highest quantity.)

E5.1o Rewrite Query 29 using a join statement (no nested queries).

E5.1p Rewrite Query 30 using a join statement (no nested queries).

E5.2 Write the SQL queries that accomplish the following tasks in the HAFH Realty Company Property Management Database:

E5.2a Display the SMemberID and SMemberName for all staff members.

E5.2b Display the CCID, CCName, and CCIndustry for all corporate clients.

E5.2c Display the BuildingID, BNoOfFloors, and the manager's MFName and MLName for all buildings.

E5.2d Display the MFName, MLName, MSalary, MB-date, and number of buildings that the manager manages for all managers with a salary less than *$55,000*.

E5.2e Display the BuildingID and AptNo for all apartments leased by the corporate client *WindyCT*.

E5.2f Display the InsID and InsName for all inspectors that have any inspections scheduled after *1-JAN-2014*. Do not display the same information more than once.

E5.2g Display the SMemberID and SMemberName of staff members cleaning apartments rented by corporate clients whose corporate location is *Chicago*. Do not display the same information more than once.

E5.2h Display the CCName of the client and the CCName of the client who referred him or her, for every client referred by a client in the *Music* industry.

E5.2i Display the BuildingID, AptNo, and ANoOfBedrooms for all apartments that are not leased.

Additional (larger) data sets available at *dbtextbook.com*.

Mini Cases

MC1 Investco Scout

- Write CREATE TABLE statements to create the tables for the Investco Scout Funds Database depicted by the relational schema created in mini case **MC1** in Chapter 3.
- Assume that the following addition is made to the Investco Scout Funds Database requirements listed in mini case **MC1** in Chapter 2:
  Investco Scout will keep track of the CEOFName and CEOL-Name for each investment company (in addition to keeping track

of a unique investment company identifier, a unique investment company name, and names of multiple locations of the investment company for each investment company).

- Change the ER diagram created in mini case **MC1** in Chapter 2 to reflect the new addition to the requirements.
- Change the relational schema created in mini case **MC1** in Chapter 3 to reflect the change in the ER diagram.

- Write ALTER TABLE commands that reflects the change in the relational schema.

- Observe the following information about investment companies and mutual funds , and create INSERT INTO statements that insert the information listed below into the created tables of the Investco Scout Funds Database.

Investment Companies

Company: ACF, Acme Finance	CEO: Mick Dempsey	Locations: Chicago, Denver
Company: TCA, Tara Capital	CEO: Ava Newton	Locations: Houston, New York City
Company: ALB, Albritton	CEO: Lena Dollar	Locations: Atlanta, New York City

Securities (ID, Name, Type)

AE	Abhi Engineering	Stock
BH	Blues Health	Stock
CM	County Municipality	Bond
DU	Downtown Utility	Bond
EM	Emmitt Machines	Stock

Mutual Funds by Investment Company (Inception Date, ID, Name, Mix)

ACF:

1/1/2005	BG	Big Growth	(500 AE Stocks, 300 EM Stocks)
1/1/2006	SG	Steady Growth	(300 AE Stocks, 300 DU Bonds)

TCA:

1/1/2005	LF	Tiger Fund	(1000 EM Stocks, 1000 BH Stocks)
1/1/2006	OF	Owl Fund	(1000 CU Bonds, 1000 DU Bonds)

ALB:

1/1/2005	JU	Jupiter	(2000 EM Stock, 1000 DU Bonds)
1/1/2006	SA	Saturn	(1000 EM Stock, 2000 DU Bonds)

MC2 Funky Bizz

- Write CREATE TABLE statements to create the tables for the Funky Bizz Operations Database depicted by the relational schema created in mini case **MC2** in Chapter 3.
- Use INSERT INTO statements to insert no fewer than 2 and no more than 10 records per table in the Funky Bizz Operations Database.

MC3 Snooty Fashions

- Write CREATE TABLE statements to create the tables for the Snooty Fashions Operations Database depicted by the relational schema created in mini case **MC3** in Chapter 3.
- Use INSERT INTO statements to insert no fewer than 2 and no more than 10 records per table in the Snooty Fashions Operations Database.

MC4 Signum Libri

- Write CREATE TABLE statements to create the tables for Signum Libri Operations Database depicted by the relational schema created in mini case **MC4** in Chapter 3.
- Use INSERT INTO statements to insert no fewer than 2 and no more than 10 records per table in the Signum Libri Operations Database.

MC5 ExoProtect

- Write CREATE TABLE statements to create the tables for ExoProtect Employees' Computers Database depicted by the relational schema created in mini case **MC5** in Chapter 3.
- Use INSERT INTO statements to insert no fewer than 2 and no more than 10 records per table in the ExoProtect Employees' Computers Database.

MC6 Jones Dozers

- Write CREATE TABLE statements to create the tables for Jones Dozers Sales and Rentals Database depicted by the relational schema created in mini case **MC6** in Chapter 3.
- Use INSERT INTO statements to insert no fewer than 2 and no more than 10 records per table in the ExoProtect Employees' Computers Database.

MC7 Midtown Memorial

- Write CREATE TABLE statements to create the tables for Midtown Memorial Patients Drug Dispensal Database depicted by the relational schema created in mini case **MC7** in Chapter 3.
- Use INSERT INTO statements to insert no fewer than 2 and no more than 10 records per table in the Midtown Memorial Patients Drug Dispensal Database.

Data Implementation and Use

INTRODUCTION

The previous chapter described how SQL is used to create and interact with databases. This chapter will deal with additional issues related to the implementation and use of databases. In particular, we will focus on the implementation and use issues that are most relevant from the point of view of business designers and users. (Physical design issues related to hardware and software configurations, such as the physical configuration of the database on hard drives, are beyond the scope of this book.) The topics covered in this chapter include:

- implementing referential integrity constraint options for delete and update[1] operations
- implementing user-defined constraints
- indexing
- database front-end
- data quality issues

REFERENTIAL INTEGRITY CONSTRAINT: DELETE AND UPDATE IMPLEMENTATION OPTIONS

Referential integrity constraints regulate the relationship between a table with a foreign key and a table with a primary key to which the foreign key refers. In Chapter 3, we defined the term as follows:

Referential Integrity Constraint

*In each row of a relation containing a foreign key, the value of the **foreign key EITHER matches** one of the values in the **primary key** column of the referred relation **OR** the value of the **foreign key is null** (empty).*

Consider a simple example shown in Figure 6.1.

In this example, the foreign key DeptID in the relation EMPLOYEE refers to the primary key DeptID in the relation DEPARTMENT.

The example shown in Figure 6.1a illustrates a scenario in which the values in the relations EMPLOYEE and DEPARTMENT are in compliance with the referential

---

[1] As we mentioned in Chapter 4, the term "update" is often used in practice as a synonym for the modify operation (the operation that changes the values within the records of the relation) rather than as a more general term referring to the insert, delete, and modify operations. In this chapter, we will use "update" as a synonym for the modify operation.

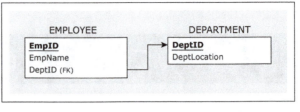

FIGURE 6.1   Two relations and a referential integrity constraint.

integrity constraint, as each value of the foreign key DeptID in the relation EMPLOYEE matches the value of the primary key DeptID in the referred relation DEPARTMENT. The first and third records displayed in the relation EMPLOYEE have the foreign key DeptID value *1*, matching the primary key DeptID value of the first displayed record in the relation DEPARTMENT. The second and fourth records displayed in the relation EMPLOYEE have the foreign key DeptID value *2*, matching the primary key DeptID value of the second displayed record in the relation DEPARTMENT.

A referential integrity constraint has implications for the delete and update (modify) operations on records in relations that are associated via a relationship. Deletions and updates of the records in the relation on the primary key side have an effect on the records in the relation on the foreign key side. On the other hand, deletions and updates of the records in the relation on the foreign key side do not have an effect on the records in the relation on the primary key side. For example, as we will show in this chapter, the deletes and updates of the records in the relation DEPARTMENT can affect the records in the relation EMPLOYEE, while the deletions and updates of the records in relation EMPLOYEE do not affect the records in the relation DEPARTMENT.

Delete Options

Contemporary DBMS packages include several options for implementing referential integrity constraints with regard to delete and update operations. We will illustrate those options by using the example shown in Figure 6.1a.

First, we will discuss various options for implementing referential integrity constraints with regard to the delete operation. These options determine what will take place with the records in the relation containing the foreign key when there is an attempt to delete the primary key value in the referred relation.

DELETE RESTRICT   The **delete restrict** option does not allow a record to be deleted if its primary key value is referred to by a foreign key value.

For example, let us observe the case in which the delete restrict option was enforced in Figure 6.1a on the referential integrity constraint connecting the primary key column DeptID in the relation DEPARTMENT with the foreign key column DeptID

EMPLOYEE

EmpID	EmpName	DeptID
1234	Becky	1
2345	Molly	2
3456	Rob	1
1324	Ted	2

DEPARTMENT

DeptID	DeptLocation
1	Suite A
2	Suite B
3	Suite C

FIGURE 6.1a   A referential integrity constraint—a compliance example.

FIGURE 6.2   A referential integrity constraint—a *delete restrict* option example.

in the relation EMPLOYEE. In this case, the first two records displayed in the relation DEPARTMENT (*1, Suite A*) and (*2, Suite B*) cannot be deleted, but the third record (*3, Suite C*) can be deleted. Any attempt to delete any of the first two records in the relation DEPARTMENT would be prevented by the DBMS, and would be accompanied by the error message to the user that the attempted delete is not permitted. However, the deletion of the third record in the relation DEPARTMENT (*3, Suite C*) would be permitted, because there is no record in the table EMPLOYEE that has the value *3* in the foreign key column DeptID. This is illustrated by Figure 6.2.

DELETE CASCADE   The **delete cascade** option allows a record to be deleted if its primary key value is referred to by a foreign key value. However, all the records whose foreign key value refers to the primary key value of the record that is being deleted will also be deleted. In other words, the delete cascades from the table containing the referred-to primary key to the table with the foreign key.

For example, we consider the case in which the delete cascade option was enforced in Figure 6.1a on the referential integrity constraint connecting the relation DEPARTMENT with the relation EMPLOYEE. Let us assume that the first record displayed in the relation DEPARTMENT (*1, Suite A*) is being deleted. This delete will also automatically cause the deletion of the first and third records displayed in the relation EMPLOYEE (*1234, Becky, 1*) and (*3456, Rob, 1*). The result of this delete operation is shown in Figure 6.3.

FIGURE 6.3   A referential integrity constraint—a *delete cascade* option example.

FIGURE 6.4 A referential integrity constraint—a *delete set-to-null* option example.

Note that if an additional relation has a foreign key value that refers to the EmpID column in the EMPLOYEE table, then the deletion would cascade to that table as well. For example, any row in an additional table with a foreign key that refers to EmpID *1234* or EmpID *3456* would also be deleted.

Also note that the deletion of the record (*3, Suite C*) in the table DEPARTMENT would not cascade to the table EMPLOYEE, because there is no record in the table EMPLOYEE that has the value *3* for its foreign key DeptID.

DELETE SET–TO–NULL   The **delete set-to-null** option allows a record to be deleted if its primary key value is referred to by a foreign key value of a record in another relation. As a consequence, in all of the records where the foreign key value refers to the pri-mary key of the record that is being deleted, the value of the foreign key is set to null.

For example, let us observe the case in which the delete set-to-null option was enforced in Figure 6.1a on the referential integrity constraint connecting the relation DEPARTMENT with the relation EMPLOYEE. Let us assume that the first record displayed in the relation DEPARTMENT (*1, Suite A*) is being deleted. This delete will also automatically cause the deletion of the values in the DeptID column for the first and third records displayed in the relation EMPLOYEE—(*1234, Becky, 1*) and (*3456, Rob, 1*). The result of this delete operation is shown in Figure 6.4.

DELETE SET–TO–DEFAULT   The **delete set-to-default** option allows a record to be deleted if its primary key value is referred to by a foreign key value of a record in another rela-tion. As a result, in all of the records whose foreign key value refers to the primary key of the record that is being deleted, the value of the foreign key is set to a predetermined default value.

As an example, we examine the case in which the delete set-to-default option was enforced in Figure 6.1a on the referential integrity constraint connecting the relation DEPARTMENT with the relation EMPLOYEE. Let us assume that when a department is shut down, and consequently deleted from the relation DEPARTMENT, all the employees of the eliminated department are automatically moved to department *3*. Therefore, the predetermined default value for the foreign key DeptID in the relation EMPLOYEE is set to *3*. The deletion of the first record displayed in the relation DEPARTMENT (*1, Suite A*) will automatically cause the values in the DeptID

Before Delete

EMPLOYEE

EmpID	EmpName	DeptID
1234	Becky	1
2345	Molly	2
3456	Rob	1
1324	Ted	2

DEPARTMENT

DeptID	DeptLocation
1	Suite A
2	Suite B
3	Suite C

Deleting a record

After Delete

EMPLOYEE

EmpID	EmpName	DeptID
1234	Becky	3
2345	Molly	2
3456	Rob	3
1324	Ted	2

DEPARTMENT

DeptID	DeptLocation
2	Suite B
3	Suite C

FIGURE 6.5   A referential integrity constraint—a *delete set-to-default* option example.

column for the first and third records displayed in the relation EMPLOYEE (*1234, Becky, 1*) and (*3456, Rob, 1*) to change to the value of *3*. The result of this delete operation is shown in Figure 6.5.

Note that no matter what delete option (restrict, cascade, set-to-null, set-to-default) is used for the referential integrity constraint, in Figure 6.1a, any record in the table EMPLOYEE can be freely deleted and the deletions in the table EMPLOYEE would not affect the table DEPARTMENT. Records in the table EMPLOYEE can be freely deleted because there is no other relation referencing it (i.e., using its primary key as a foreign key).

Update Options

Next, we will discuss various options for implementing referential integrity constraints with regard to an update operation. These options determine what will take place with the records in the relation containing the foreign key, when there is an attempt to change the primary key value in the referred relation. The update options are equivalent to the delete options described above. As was the case with the delete options, the update options refer to the effect of the updates of the records in the table on the primary key side of the referential integrity constraint and not the records in the table on the foreign key side of the referential integrity constraint.

UPDATE RESTRICT   The **update restrict** option does not allow the primary key value of a record to be changed if its primary key value is referred to by a foreign key value.

For example, consider the case in which the update restrict option was enforced in Figure 6.1a on the referential integrity constraint connecting the relation DEPARTMENT with the relation EMPLOYEE. In that case, the primary key value of the first two records displayed in the relation DEPARTMENT (*1, Suite A*) and (*2, Suite B*) cannot be changed. Any attempt to change the DeptID value of the first two records in the relation DEPARTMENT would be prevented by the DBMS and would result in an error message to the user. However, an update of the primary key value in the record (*3, Suite C*) would be permitted, because there is no record in the table EMPLOYEE that has the value *3* in the foreign key column DeptID. This is illustrated by Figure 6.6.

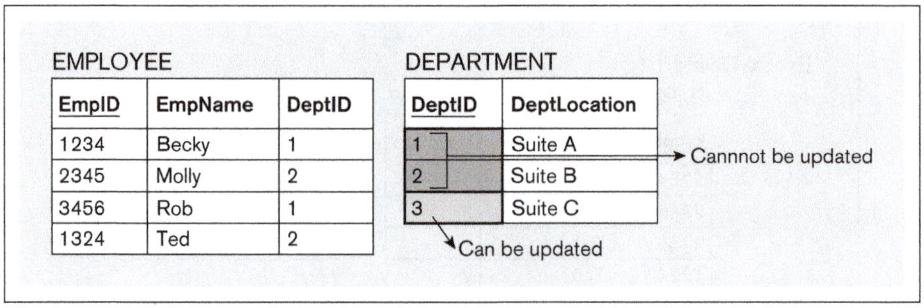

FIGURE 6.6 A referential integrity constraint—an *update restrict* option example.

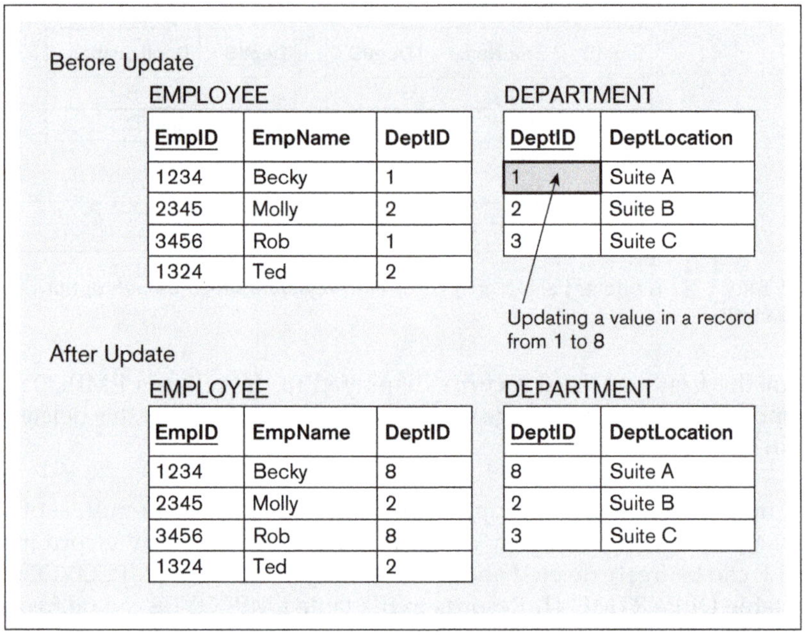

FIGURE 6.7 A referential integrity constraint—an *update cascade* option example.

UPDATE CASCADE The **update cascade** option allows the primary key value of a re-cord to be changed if its primary key value is referred to by a foreign key value. How-ever, all the foreign key values that refer to the primary key being changed are also changed and set to the new value of the primary key. In other words, the update cas-cades from the table that contains the referred-to primary key to the table with the for-eign key.

For example, let us observe the case in which the update cascade option was enforced in Figure 6.1a on the referential integrity constraint connecting the relation DEPARTMENT with the relation EMPLOYEE. Let us assume that the primary key value of the first record displayed in the relation DEPARTMENT (*1, Suite A*) is being changed from the value *1* to the value *8*. This update will also automatically cause the values in the DeptID column for the first and third records displayed in the relation EMPLOYEE (*1234, Becky, 1*) and (*3456, Rob, 1*) to be changed from the value *1* to the value *8*. The result of this update operation is shown in Figure 6.7.

UPDATE SET-TO-NULL The **update set-to-null** option allows a record to be changed if its primary key value is referred to by a foreign key value of a record in another re-lation. As a consequence, in all of the records whose foreign key value refers to the primary key being changed, the value of the foreign key is set to null.

For example, let us observe the case in which the update set-to-null option was enforced in Figure 6.1a on the referential integrity constraint connecting the relation DEPARTMENT with the relation EMPLOYEE. Let us assume that the primary key value of the first record displayed in the relation DEPARTMENT (*1, Suite A*) is being changed

Before Update

EMPLOYEE

EmpID	EmpName	DeptID
1234	Becky	1
2345	Molly	2
3456	Rob	1
1324	Ted	2

DEPARTMENT

DeptID	DeptLocation
1	Suite A
2	Suite B
3	Suite C

Updating a value in a record
from 1 to 8

After Update

EMPLOYEE

EmpID	EmpName	DeptID
1234	Becky	
2345	Molly	2
3456	Rob	
1324	Ted	2

DEPARTMENT

DeptID	DeptLocation
8	Suite A
2	Suite B
3	Suite C

FIGURE 6.8   A referential integrity constraint—an *update set-to-null* option example.

from the value *1* to the value *8*. This update will also automatically cause the deletion of the values in the DeptID column for the first and third records displayed in the relation EMPLOYEE (*1234, Becky, 1*) and (*3456, Rob, 1*). The result of this update operation is shown in Figure 6.8.

UPDATE SET–TO–DEFAULT   The **update set-to-default** option allows a record to be changed if its primary key value is referred to by a foreign key value of a record in another relation. As a consequence, in all of the records whose foreign key value refers to the primary key being changed, the value of the foreign key is set to a pre-determined default value.

For example, let us observe the case in which the update set-to-default option was enforced in Figure 6.1a on the referential integrity constraint connecting the relation

Before Update

EMPLOYEE

EmpID	EmpName	DeptID
1234	Becky	1
2345	Molly	2
3456	Rob	1
1324	Ted	2

DEPARTMENT

DeptID	DeptLocation
1	Suite A
2	Suite B
3	Suite C

Updating a value in a record
from 1 to 8

After Update

EMPLOYEE

EmpID	EmpName	DeptID
1234	Becky	3
2345	Molly	2
3456	Rob	3
1324	Ted	2

DEPARTMENT

DeptID	DeptLocation
8	Suite A
2	Suite B
3	Suite C

FIGURE 6.9   A referential integrity constraint—an *update set-to-default* option example.

DEPARTMENT with the foreign key column DeptID in the relation EMPLOYEE. Let us assume that when a DeptID value of a department number changes, all the employees from that department are automatically moved to the department whose DeptID value is 3. Therefore the predetermined default value for the foreign key DeptID in the relation EMPLOYEE is set to 3. The change of the primary key value in the first record displayed in the relation DEPARTMENT (*1, Suite A*) from *1* to *8* will automatically cause the values in the DeptID column for the first and third records displayed in the relation EMPLOYEE (*1234, Becky, 1* and *3456, Rob, 1*) to change to 3. The result of this update operation is shown in Figure 6.9.

Note that no matter which update option (restrict, cascade, set-to-null, set-to-default was used for the referential integrity constraint, any record in the table EMPLOYEE can be freely updated to any value that does not violate the referential integrity constraint (or other relational database constraints and the updates in the table EMPLOYEE would not affect the table DEPARTMENT. In this case, the values in the DeptID column of the table EMPLOYEE can only be changed to values *1, 2,* or *3.* Any values other than *1, 2,* or *3* would violate the referential integrity constraint.

Implementing Delete and Update Options

The following SQL code contains a statement for implementing the referential integrity constraint between the foreign key DeptID in the table EMPLOYEE and the primary key DeptID in the table DEPARTMENT.

```
CREATE TABLE employee
(       empid              CHAR(4),
        empname            CHAR(20),
        deptid             CHAR(2),
        PRIMARY KEY        (empid),
        FOREIGN KEY        (deptid) REFERENCES department);
```

The default SQL option for both delete and update operations is restrict. In other words, the code above would implement the delete restrict and update restrict options for the referential integrity constraint between the foreign key DeptID in the table EMPLOYEE and the primary key DeptID in the table DEPARTMENT.

However, SQL allows specifying the other delete and update options.[2] First, we will show an example of specifying a delete option that is not restrict. For example, the following SQL code would implement the delete cascade option for the referential integrity constraint between the foreign key DeptID in the table EMPLOYEE and the primary key DeptID in the table DEPARTMENT.

```
CREATE TABLE employee
(       empid              CHAR(4),
        empname            CHAR(20),
        deptid             CHAR(2),
        PRIMARY KEY        (empid),
        FOREIGN KEY        (deptid) REFERENCES department
                                    ON DELETE CASCADE);
```

Next, we will show an example of specifying an update option that is not restrict. The following SQL code would implement the update set-to-null option for the referential integrity constraint between the foreign key DeptID in the table EMPLOYEE and the primary key DeptID in the table DEPARTMENT.

```
CREATE TABLE employee
(       empid              CHAR(4),
        empname            CHAR(20),
        deptid             CHAR(2),
        PRIMARY KEY        (empid),
        FOREIGN KEY        (deptid) REFERENCES department
                                    ON UPDATE SET NULL);
```

---

[2]Not every DBMS has the capability of implementing all the delete and update options mentioned in this chapter. Furthermore, different DBMS packages implement the delete and update options differently. However, the examples we will show here are illustrative, even if the syntax or method for implementing the update and delete options is not exactly the same in every system.

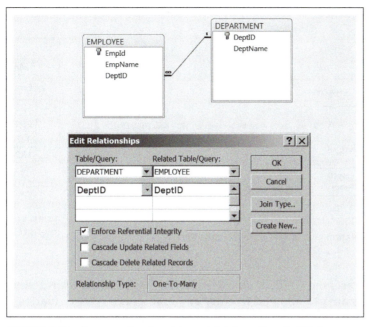

FIGURE 6.10   An example of update and delete options in MS Access.

Finally, we will show an example of specifying the non-restrict delete and update options together. The following SQL code would implement the delete cascade and the update set-to-null options for the referential integrity constraint between the foreign key DeptID in the table EMPLOYEE and the primary key DeptID in the table DEPARTMENT.

```
CREATE TABLE employee
(       empid           CHAR(4),
        empname         CHAR(20),
        deptid          CHAR(2),
        PRIMARY KEY     (empid),
        FOREIGN KEY     (deptid) REFERENCES department
                                 ON DELETE CASCADE
                                 ON UPDATE SET NULL);
```

In addition to the SQL examples above, we also give a quick illustration of how MS Access implements the delete and update options. Figure 6.10 shows a feature in MS Access that enables designers to configure delete and update options. As in SQL-based systems, restrict is a default option for both delete and update operations. However, the user can choose the cascade option for update, delete, or both by clicking on the appropriate boxes shown in Figure 6.10.

IMPLEMENTING USER–DEFINED CONSTRAINTS

In Chapter 3, we defined the term "user-defined constraints" and showed a few examples. As is the case with update and delete options, different DBMS packages implement user-defined constraints differently. Here, we will show one illustrative example of an SQL mechanism for implementing user–defined constraints.

CHECK Clause

One of the methods available for implementing user-defined constraints in SQL is the **CHECK** clause. To illustrate, let us consider the example shown in Figure 6.11.

In this example, a user-defined constraint specifies that the values in the column Salary of the relation EMPLOYEE must be between 50,000 and 200,000.

The following is the SQL CREATE TABLE statement for the relation EMPLOYEE in this example:

```
CREATE TABLE employee
(empid          CHAR(4),
salary          NUMBER(6) CHECK (salary >= 50000 AND salary <= 200000),
PRIMARY KEY     (empid));
```

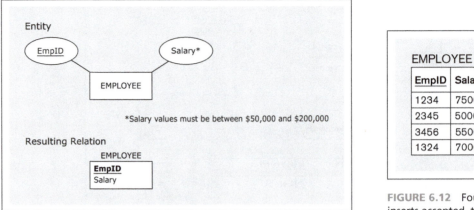

FIGURE 6.11   A relation with a user-defined constraint.

FIGURE 6.12   Four inserts accepted, two inserts rejected.

In this case, the CHECK clause enforces the specified user-defined constraint, and the users are not allowed to enter any employees whose salaries are not in the specified range between 50,000 and 200,000. For example, consider the following six statements:

```
INSERT INTO employee VALUES ('1234', 75000);
INSERT INTO employee VALUES ('2345', 50000);
INSERT INTO employee VALUES ('3456', 55000);
INSERT INTO employee VALUES ('1324', 70000);
INSERT INTO employee VALUES ('9876', 270000);
INSERT INTO employee VALUES ('1010', 30000);
```

The first four statements would be executed, while the last two statements would be rejected because they violate the specified user-defined constraint. The resulting relation EMPLOYEE is shown in Figure 6.12.

As we illustrated, the CHECK clause can be used to specify a constraint on a particular column of a relation. The following example illustrates how the CHECK clause can be used to specify a constraint involving more than one column. Let us consider the example in Figure 6.13.

In this example, a business rule specifies that the year of a student's graduation cannot precede the year of a student's enrollment.

The following is the SQL CREATE TABLE statement for the relation STUDENT:

```
CREATE TABLE student
(studentid        CHAR(4),
yearenrolled      INT,
yearofgraduation INT,
PRIMARY KEY (studentid),
CHECK (yearenrolled <= yearofgraduation));
```

In this case, the CHECK clause enforces the specified user-defined constraint, and the users are not allowed to enter any students whose graduation year precedes the enrollment year. For example, consider the following four statements:

```
INSERT INTO student VALUES ('1111', 2012, 2016);
INSERT INTO student VALUES ('2222', 2013, 2017);
INSERT INTO student VALUES ('3333', 2013, 2017);
INSERT INTO student VALUES ('4444', 2013, 2012);
```

The first three statements would be executed, while the last statement would be rejected because it violates the specified user-defined constraint. The resulting relation STUDENT is shown in Figure 6.14.

Other Mechanisms for Implementing User–Defined Constraints

In addition to the CHECK mechanism, a number of other more complex methods exist for implementing user-defined constraints. Such methods include assertions and

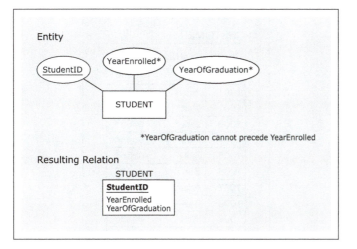

FIGURE 6.13   Another relation with a user-defined constraint.

STUDENT

StudentId	YearEnrolled	YearOfGraduation
1111	2013	2016
2222	2013	2016
3333	2013	2017

FIGURE 6.14   Three inserts accepted, one insert rejected.

triggers (illustrated in the note at the end of this chapter), coding in specialized database programming languages that combine SQL with additional non-SQL statements for processing data from databases (such as PL/SQL), or embedding SQL with code written in regular programming languages (such as C++ or Java). In many cases, the logic of user-defined constraints is not implemented as a part of the database, but as a part of the front-end database application.

For the proper use of the database, it is important that user-defined constraints are implemented fully. As we just mentioned, there are many choices available regarding the method of implementation. From the business use point of view, the enforcement of user-defined constraints is more important than which actual method of implementing the user-defined constraint was chosen. Often, when there is more than one method available, the choice is made based on technical considerations, such as which of the methods provides for the fastest execution.

INDEXING

An **index** is a mechanism for increasing the speed of data search and data retrieval on relations with a large number of records. Most relational DBMS software tools enable the definition of indexes. The following example provides a *conceptual simplified illustration* of the principles on which an index is based.

Figure 6.15 shows a relation CUSTOMER. In reality, a table like this would have a much larger number of records, but for readability reasons, we are showing it with only 13 records. This relation is sorted by the column CustID. Consequently, the remaining columns in this relation, CustName and Zip, are unsorted.

Looking up a particular record based on a value in an unsorted column involves a so-called **linear (sequential) search**. Such a search finds a particular value in a list by checking elements sequentially and one at a time until the searched-for value is found. For example, let us assume that we are looking for the record representing the customer

CUSTOMER

CustID	CustName	Zip
1000	Zach	60111
1001	Ana	60333
1002	Matt	60222
1003	Lara	60555
1004	Pam	60444
1005	Sally	60555
1006	Bob	60333
1007	Adam	60555
1008	Steve	60222
1009	Pam	60333
1010	Ema	60111
1011	Peter	60666
1012	Fiona	60444

FIGURE 6.15   A customer relation.

by the name of *Steve*. Since the CustName column is unsorted, a linear search has to be performed, in which the CustName column value is checked one record at a time, starting with the first record, until the value *Steve* is found. In this case, the CustName in the first eight records would be checked until the record (*1008, Steve, 60222*) is located on the ninth try. This is shown in Figure 6.16.

Looking up a particular record based on a value in a sorted column can be done much more quickly by using a non-linear search. **Binary search** is one example of a non-linear search method that is substantially faster than the linear search. A binary search takes advantage of sorted lists. It divides the sorted list initially in two parts (hence the name *binary)* of the same size by looking up the value in the middle of the list. If the searched-for value is larger than the value in the middle of the list, the top part of the list is eliminated from the search space. Equivalently, if the searched-for value is smaller than the value in the middle of the list, the bottom part of the list is eliminated from the search space. Either way, the search space is reduced by half in one

CUSTOMER

CustID	CustName	Zip	
1000	Zach	60111	→ Step 1 (not Steve)
1001	Ana	60333	→ Step 2 (not Steve)
1002	Matt	60222	→ Step 3 (not Steve)
1003	Lara	60555	→ Step 4 (not Steve)
1004	Pam	60444	→ Step 5 (not Steve)
1005	Sally	60555	→ Step 6 (not Steve)
1006	Bob	60333	→ Step 7 (not Steve)
1007	Adam	60555	→ Step 8 (not Steve)
1008	Steve	60222	→ Step 9 Customer Steve found
1009	Pam	60333	
1010	Ema	60111	
1011	Peter	60666	
1012	Fiona	60444	

FIGURE 6.16   An example of a linear search.

single step. This process of looking up the value in the middle and halving the search space is repeated in the remaining part of the list, until the searched for value is found.

For example, let us assume that we are looking for the record representing the customer with the CustID number *1008*. As shown in Figure 6.17, binary search first looks up a value of the record in the middle of the table, whose CustID value is *1006*. Because *1006* is less than *1008* the search eliminates all the records in the top portion of the table (shown in the blue color) from the search and examines the CustID value of the record in the middle of the remaining part of the table. That value is *1010*. Because *1010* is greater than *1008* the records in the bottom part of the remaining search space (shown in the gray color) are eliminated. The search space is now further reduced. The search continues with again looking up the CustID value of the record in the middle of the remaining search space (shown in the white color). The value in the middle of the remaining search space is *1008*, and the search is completed. The record (*1008, Steve, 6022*) is located.

Note that a binary search requires significantly fewer steps than a linear search. As another example, consider the process of looking up a phone number of a person with a particular last name in a phone book alphabetized by the last name. Since the last name values are sorted, we can apply binary search. We would start by opening a page in the middle of the phone book and then eliminating from consideration the part of the phone book that does not contain the searched-for name. A few additional similar search-space reducing steps are enough to find the entry we were looking for. Let us now suppose that we have a particular phone number in mind and we are looking for a person in the phone book that has that phone number. Since the phone numbers are not sorted, we have to apply linear search. As you can imagine, this linear search is painfully slow and involves a large number of reads of individual phone numbers before finding the person with a particular number we are looking for.

When a relation is sorted by one column, as a consequence, the other columns are unsorted. As we just showed, the search for values on unsorted columns is substantially slower than the search on sorted columns. The idea behind indexing is to enable faster searches even on columns that are not sorted. Figure 6.18 shows an example of an index for the column CustName in the relation CUSTOMER. Within a database system, an index can be implemented as an additional table, with two columns. One column contains the sorted values of the indexed column. The other column contains pointers to the corresponding records in the original table. In this example, the index table CUSTNAME_INDEX has a column that contains sorted CustName values and a column that points to the corresponding record in the CUSTOMER table.

CUSTOMER

CustID	CustName	Zip
1000	Zach	60111
1001	Ana	60333
1002	Matt	60222
1003	Lara	60555
1004	Pam	60444
1005	Sally	60555
1006	Bob	60333
1007	Adam	60555
1008	Steve	60222
1009	Pam	60333
1010	Ema	60111
1011	Peter	60666
1012	Fiona	60444

Step 1 Eliminate records from here, above (since CustID value is lower than 1008)

Step 3 Customer 1008 found

Step 2 Eliminate records from here, below (since CustID value is higher than 1008)

FIGURE 6.17   An example of a binary search.

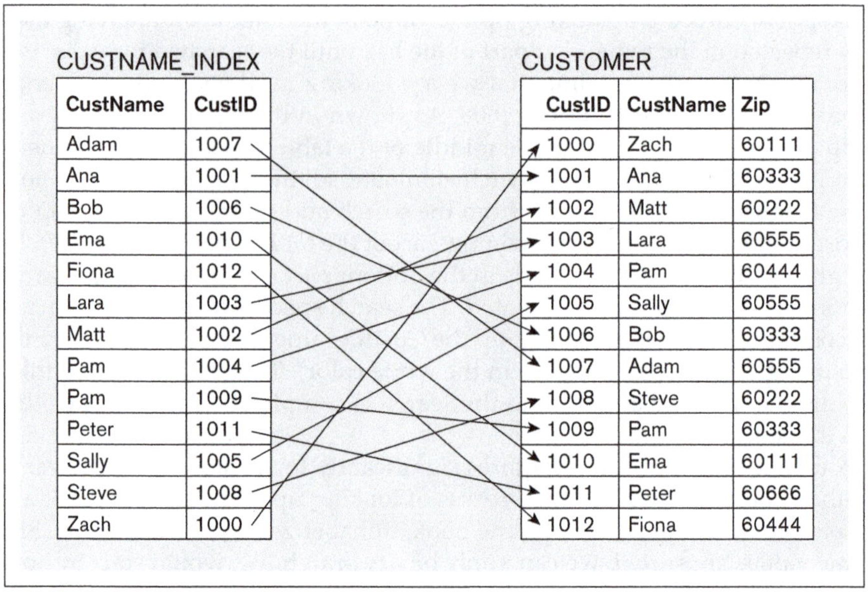

FIGURE 6.18   An example of an index.

Let us now observe how an index increases the search speed. In the example illustrated by Figure 6.16, we illustrated the search for the record whose CustName value is *Steve*. We showed that the linear search required nine steps. In Figure 6.19, we show the binary version of the same search, enabled by the CUSTNAME_INDEX table. Since the CustName column in the index table is sorted, we can apply a binary search when searching for a particular name. In this case, finding the index table record whose CustName is *Steve* took three steps. Once the index record with the CustName value *Steve* was located in the CUSTNAME_INDEX table, its pointer value pointing to the corresponding record in the CUSTOMER table is used to complete the search.

Let us now observe another example illustrating the performance improvement enabled by the use of an index. Let us assume that a user wants to find out how many customers named *Pam* exist in the relation CUSTOMER (note once again that relation CUSTOMER is *not* sorted by the CustName column).

First observe the case illustrated by Figure 6.20, which depicts how such a query would be executed on the relation CUSTOMER (shown in Figure 6.15), without the use of an index.

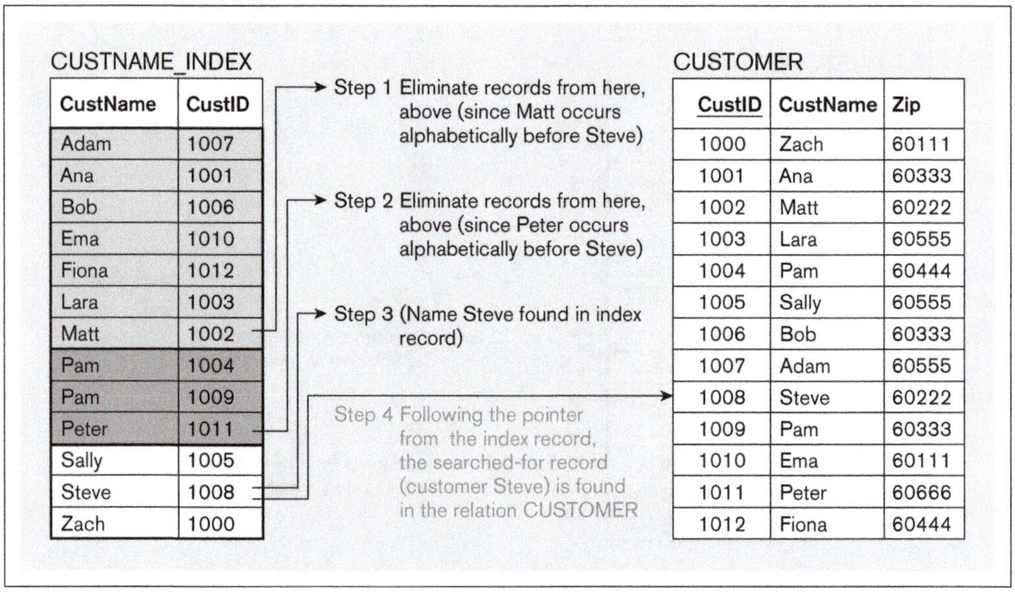

FIGURE 6.19   An example of increased search speed using the index.

CUSTOMER

CustID	CustName	Zip	
1000	Zach	60111	→ Step 1 (not Pam, counter = 0)
1001	Ana	60333	→ Step 2 (not Pam, counter = 0)
1002	Matt	60222	→ Step 3 (not Pam, counter = 0)
1003	Lara	60555	→ Step 4 (not Pam, counter = 0)
1004	Pam	60444	→ Step 5 (Pam, counter = 1)
1005	Sally	60555	→ Step 6 (not Pam, counter = 1)
1006	Bob	60333	→ Step 7 (not Pam, counter = 1)
1007	Adam	60555	→ Step 8 (not Pam, counter = 1)
1008	Steve	60222	→ Step 9 (not Pam, counter = 1)
1009	Pam	60333	→ Step 10 (Pam, counter = 2)
1010	Ema	60111	→ Step 11 (not Pam, counter = 2)
1011	Peter	60666	→ Step 12 (not Pam, counter = 2)
1012	Fiona	60444	→ Step 13 (not Pam, final count = 2)

FIGURE 6.20 Another example of a linear search.

Because the CustName column is not sorted, it has to be searched through linearly by checking each record in the relation Customer. A counter counting how many customers are named *Pam* is initially set to zero. Every time a record is checked, if the CustName value in a record is not *Pam,* the counter's value stays unchanged, and if the CustName value in a record is *Pam,* the counter's value increases by 1. CustName value *Pam* can appear in any record, so every record in the relation has to be checked. Hence, the number of steps in this type of search is equivalent to the number of records. In this case, it took 13 steps to find the result, because the relation has 13 records.

Let us now observe how an index increases the speed of this query. In Figure 6.21, we show a version of the same search using the CUSTNAME_INDEX table shown in Figure 6.19. Since the CustName column in the index table is sorted, we can apply a binary search when searching for a particular name. In this case, finding the index table record whose CustName is *Pam* took three steps. It took several more steps to count

CUSTNAME_INDEX

CustName	CustID
Adam	1007
Ana	1001
Bob	1006
Ema	1010
Fiona	1012
Lara	1003
Matt	1002
Pam	1004
Pam	1010
Peter	1011
Sally	1005
Steve	1008
Zach	1000

→ Step 1 Eliminate records from here, above (since Matt occurs alphabetically before Pam)

→ Step 6 Check the name of the record above (not Pam, final count = 2)

→ Step 3 An instance of the name Pam found (counter = 1)

→ Step 4 Check the name in the record below (not Pam, counter = 1)

→ Step 5 Check the name in the record above (Pam, counter = 2)

→ Step 2 Eliminate records from here, below (since Peter occurs alphabetically after Pam)

FIGURE 6.21 Another example of increased search speed using the index.

all instances of CustName *Pam* and verify that there were no uncounted instances of CustName *Pam*. The number of steps required was smaller than when the index was not used. This advantage in the number of steps becomes much more substantial when the file searched has more records, since every record has to be checked in a linear search method. In an indexed search, only a small portion of records is searched.

The purpose of the examples above was to illustrate how a simple mechanism can improve the speed of search and retrieval. Note that the above examples provide a *simplified explanation of the concept of an index*. In the example above, for the simplicity of illustration, we used the primary key value of the record as the index pointer. In practice, the value of the index pointer can be a physical address of the record on the disk or some other mechanism that relates to the physical location of records. Also, in reality, instead of simply sorting on the indexed column and applying a binary search as shown in the example above, different contemporary DBMS tools implement indexes using different logical and technical approaches, such as clustering indexes, hash indexes, B+ trees, and so on. Such approaches are beyond the scope of this book. For the audience of this book, it is important to know that each of the available approaches has the same mission: to increase the speed of search and retrieval on the columns that are being indexed. No matter what logical and technical approaches are used by the DBMS to implement the index, the main point to be aware of is that when an index is created, it improves the performance of data search and retrieval for end users in a seamless way.

Creating an index for a column of a relation is straightforward and involves writing a CREATE INDEX statement in SQL, such as the following:

```
CREATE INDEX custname_index ON customer(custname);
```

Once this statement is executed, the effect is that the searches and retrievals involving the CustName column in the relation CUSTOMER are faster.

It is important to note that indexing, while improving the speed of search and retrieval, has a cost as well. When indexes are used, additional space for the database is needed, since an extra table is required for each index that is created. Also inserting, deleting, and modifying records in the original table takes more time because it has to be accompanied by adding, modifying, deleting, and/or re-sorting of the index table associated with the original table. Thus, the addition of indexes to the database should be done with both the benefits and cost in mind. Typically, indexes are created for the columns of large tables that are often used in searches and retrievals by many users. If some created index proves to be unnecessary, it can be eliminated by executing an SQL statement DROP INDEX, such as the following:

```
DROP INDEX custname_index
```

This statement drops the index, and the index is no longer used.

DATABASE FRONT-END

In most cases, a portion of intended users (often a majority of the users) of the database lack the time and/or expertise to engage in the direct use of the data in the database. It is not reasonable to expect every person who needs to use the data from the database to write his or her own queries and other statements. Instead, many of the database end users access the database through front-end applications. **Database front-end** applications can have many different components. Here, we will mention some of the most common database front-end components.

A **form** is a database front-end component whose purpose is to enable data input and retrieval for end users in a way that is straightforward and requires no training. It provides an interface into a database relation or query. Figure 6.22 shows a form that provides an interface for data input into the relation CUSTOMER shown in Figure 6.15.

Every time a user enters the values into this form, an SQL statement

```
INSERT INTO customer VALUES (...)
```

is issued on the user's behalf. This is, of course, much more convenient for users than having to manually write an INSERT INTO statement every time a record has to be

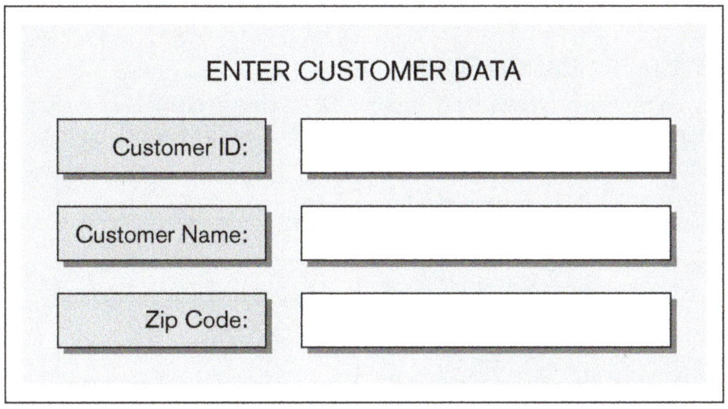

FIGURE 6.22 An example of a form for data input for the relation CUSTOMER.

inserted. The forms can also be used to delete or modify a record. When the end user uses a form to change or delete a record, such as the one shown in Figure 6.23, the corresponding SQL statements (DELETE and UPDATE) are issued on behalf of the end user.

For example, if a user highlights the last record shown in the form in Figure 6.23 and presses the delete key on the keyboard, the following statement will be issued and executed:

```
DELETE FROM customer
WHERE custid = '1012';
```

If a user changes the name of the customer in the first record shown in the form in Figure 6.23 from *Zach* to *Zachary* and presses the enter key on the keyboard, the following statement will be issued and executed:

```
UPDATE customer
SET custname = 'Zachary'
WHERE custid = '1000';
```

Forms can be used for other types of interaction that an end user has with the data in the database. The example in Figure 6.24 shows a form that is used for a search and retrieval.

When data is entered in the Customer Name box and the search button is clicked, an SQL query is issued on the user's behalf. Let us assume the user entered the value

CUSTOMERS

To Delete Records: Highlight the records and press delete on your keyboard
To Change a Record: Change any value in any of the rows and press enter on your keyboard

Customer ID	Customer Name	Zip
1000	Zach	60111
1001	Ana	60333
1002	Matt	60222
1003	Lara	60555
1004	Pam	60444
1005	Sally	60555
1006	Bob	60333
1007	Adam	60555
1008	Steve	60222
1009	Pam	60333
1010	Emma	60111
1011	Peter	60666
1012	Fiona	60444

FIGURE 6.23 An example of a form for data update for the relation CUSTOMER.

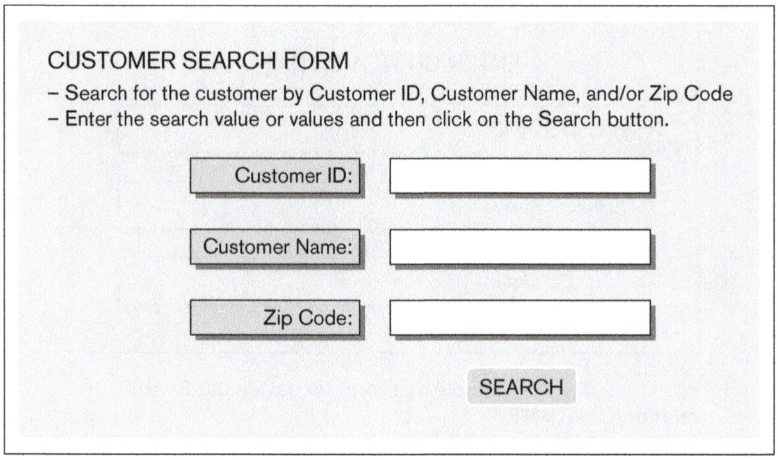

FIGURE 6.24 An example of a form for data search for the relation CUSTOMER.

60555 in the Zip Code box and then pressed the search button. As a consequence, the following query would be issued and executed:

```
SELECT    *
FROM      customer
WHERE     zip = '60555';
```

The result would be returned to the user in a form, such as the one shown in Figure 6.25.

Note that the simple examples shown above give a brief illustration of the basic form features. Database front-end applications can contain complex forms that combine multiple functionalities and retrieve the data from multiple tables.

A **report** is a database front-end component whose purpose is to present the data and calculations on the data from one or more tables from the database in a formatted way. Whereas the purpose of forms is to facilitate the interaction between the end users and the database by enabling users to engage in actions such as update and search, reports are used strictly for the retrieval of data. The data that is retrieved via reports is formatted and arranged in a professional and easy-to-view fashion, to be displayed on the screen or printed as a hard copy.

Figure 6.26 shows a report with all of the records from the relation CUSTOMER grouped and summarized by their zip codes.

As was the case with forms, database front-end applications can contain complex reports. Such reports can combine multiple calculations and retrieve the data from multiple tables.

In addition to forms and reports, database front-end applications can include many other components and functionalities, such as menus, charts, graphs, and maps. The choice of how many different components to use and to what extent is driven by the needs of the end users.

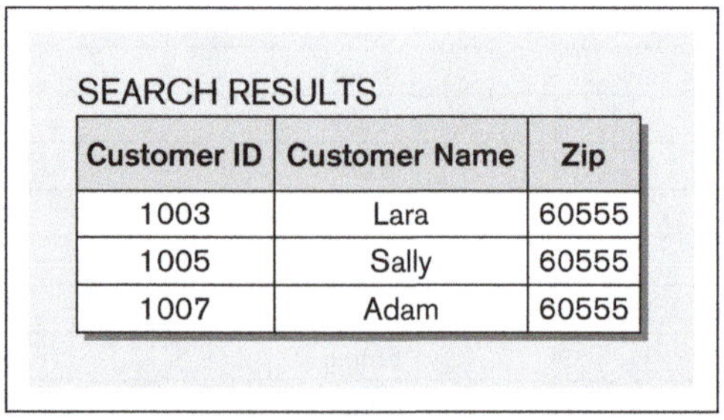
SEARCH RESULTS

Customer ID	Customer Name	Zip
1003	Lara	60555
1005	Sally	60555
1007	Adam	60555

FIGURE 6.25 A form returning the result of the search performed using the form in Figure 6.24.

REPORT: CUSTOMERS IN ZIP CODES

Zip	Customer ID	Customer Name
60111	1000	Zach
	1010	Emma

Total Number of Customers in Zip 60111: 2

60222	1002	Matt
	1008	Steve

Total Number of Customers in Zip 60222: 2

60333	1001	Ana
	1006	Bob
	1009	Pam

Total Number of Customers in Zip 60333: 3

60444	1004	Pam
	1012	Fiona

Total Number of Customers in Zip 60444: 2

60555	1003	Lara
	1005	Sally
	1007	Adam

Total Number of Customers in Zip 60555: 3

60666	1011	Peter

Total Number of Customers in Zip 60666: 1

Total Number of Customers in All Zip Codes: 13

FIGURE 6.26   An example of a report from the Relation CUSTOMER.

A database can have multiple sets of front-end applications for different purposes or groups of end users. These front-end applications can be accessible separately on their own or, as shown in Figure 6.27, via an interface that allows the user to choose an application that he or she needs.

If a user chooses "Customer Management" option for example, an application such as the one shown in Figure 6.28 would appear.

A user can now access a number of different front-end components accessing customer-related data. For example, if a user chooses the "Search for Customers" option, a form such as the one shown in 6.24 would appear. Or, if a user chooses "List All Customers per Zip Code," a report such as the one shown in Figure 6.26 would appear.

A real-world application can contain a number of elaborate forms, reports, and other front-end components organized in a complex fashion, where, for example, selecting a choice on the initial menu leads into another menu with more listed choices.

Most contemporary DBMS packages include features and/or add-on software for creating database front-end interfaces. Also available are third-party software tools specialized for the creation of front-end components that access the data in databases. In addition, front-end components for accessing the data in databases can be created by coding in programming languages.

FIGURE 6.27   An example of an interface to a collection of database front-end applications.

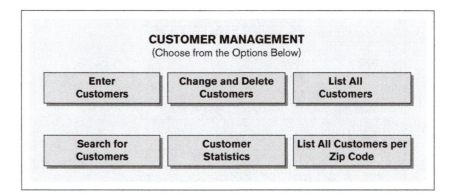

FIGURE 6.28   An example of an interface to a database front-end application.

FIGURE 6.29   A Web page example.

ProductID	ProductName	Price	Picture
1	Rainbow Baby Violet	$16.00	Picture1.gif
2	Rainbow Baby Red	$16.00	Picture2.gif
3	Rainbow Baby Green	$16.00	Picture3.gif
4	Rainbow Baby Light Green	$16.00	Picture4.gif
5	Rainbow Baby Blue	$16.00	Picture5.gif
6	Ikibab Rainbow Baby Blue	$16.00	Picture6.gif
7	Alba Grabbing Rattle	$20.00	Picture7.gif
8	Musical Alba Owl	$22.00	Picture8.gif
9	Ikibab Musical Giraffe	$46.00	Picture9.gif
...	...	...	...
...	...	...	...

FIGURE 6.30 A database relation storing the content of the website in Figure 6.29.

Database front-end interfaces can be Web based, in which case an end user communicates with a database by using a Web browser. Many Web sites are actually interfaces into a database. In such cases, the content of the Web pages is generated from data retrieved from the database. For example, consider a particular page on the Web site of a Web retailer, shown in Figure 6.29.

Figure 6.30 shows a relational table that stores the information about baby toys that is displayed on the Web page. In other words, the central section of the Web page shown in Figure 6.29 is a front-end for the database relation shown in Figure 6.30.

A collection of database relations, such as the one shown in Figure 6.30, provides for a structured and nonredundant way of storing all the data presented on the entire Web site. For example, for a product whose ProductID value is *1*, its Product Name value *Rainbow Baby Violet* may appear on multiple Web pages of the retailer Web site. This name would be stored only once in the database and then be referred to by multiple Web pages. In case the name of this product changes from *Rainbow Baby Violet* to *Rainbow Baby Purple*, this update would have to be done only once. The updated version of the ProductName would replace the old ProductName in the database and, consequently, the updated version would automatically propagate to every Web page that uses this ProductName.

DATA QUALITY ISSUES

In the process of using the data from databases, constant attention should be paid to the issue of **data quality**. The data in a database is considered of high quality if it correctly and nonambiguously reflects the real world it is designed to represent. There are a number of different data properties that define the data quality. The most fundamental data quality characteristics include:

- accuracy
- uniqueness
- completeness
- consistency
- timeliness
- conformity

Accuracy of the data refers to the extent to which data correctly reflects the real-world instances it is supposed to depict. For example, if a customer's name is spelled incorrectly in a database, such an entry has an accuracy data quality problem. Correcting the typo would solve the accuracy data quality problem.

Uniqueness of the data requires each real-world instance to be represented only once in the data collection. The uniqueness data quality problem is sometimes also referred to as **data duplication**. For example, a uniqueness data quality problem would occur if two records in the relation containing the data about customers referred to the exact same customer. Correcting this uniqueness problem would involve first recognizing that two records represent the same customer and then deleting one of those two records or combining the two records into one record.

Completeness of the data refers to the degree to which all the required data is present in the data collection. For example, if a relation containing data about patients has a value for weight that is missing for one of the patients, such an omission indicates the data completeness problem. Every patient has a weight, and the patient record without it is incomplete. On the other hand, a missing value for the insurance policy number of a patient is not necessarily an indication of a completeness data quality problem. If a patient is uninsured, the missing value for the insurance policy number is actually the correct depiction of a real-world situation. However, if a patient is insured, the missing value for an insurance policy number constitutes a completeness data quality problem.

Consistency of the data refers to the extent to which the data properly conforms to and matches up with the other data. For example, an organization may have two different sources of information about the overall company profits. If those two sources list two different figures for company overall profits, those two figures are inconsistent with each other.

Consistency data quality problems in a data set is a consequence of other data quality problems in the data set, such as problems with accuracy or uniqueness. For example, consider a scenario of a police department that has hired 50 male and 50 female police officers. For that reason, the police department has issued 50 sets each of female and male uniforms. Assume that the information, including gender, for all 100 police officers was entered into a table. Also assume that the gender is inaccurately entered in one record in this table as "female" for a male police officer. This particular record has a data accuracy problem. Summarized values based on the correct formula that counts the number of male and female officers in this table will state that we have 49 male and 51 female officers. However, the data about issued uniforms indicate that we have 50 male and 50 female officers. These two sets of numbers are inconsistent. Note that correcting the accuracy error by changing the incorrect value for the inaccurately entered police officer from "female" to "male" automatically addresses the consistency issue. Upon correction of the police officer's gender value, the formulas correctly calculate the number of male and female police officers as 50 and 50. These numbers are consistent with the number of issued uniforms.

Consistency data quality problems can also occur when the correct data appears in the wrong place in the database. For example, a table containing the information about hospital patients could include a record reflecting accurate information (e.g., name, date of birth, gender, etc.) about a person who is an outpatient. This record is accurate insofar as it correctly represents the information about a real patient. However, the existence of this record in the hospital patient table is inaccurate and it would cause an inconsistency with the data about the occupied beds in the hospital. Moving this record from the hospital patient table to the outpatient table would correct this problem.

Timeliness of the data refers to the degree to which the data is aligned with the proper time window in its representation of the real world. Typically, timeliness refers to the "freshness" of the data. If the data is sufficiently current for carrying out the users' tasks at hand, then such data does not have a timeliness problem. On the other hand, if the data is not up-to-date enough for proper use, then such data has a timeliness problem. For example, let us consider a case when a delivery company delivers a cargo shipment but the record about it is not entered into the DELIVERED_CARGO_SHIPMENTS table until three days after the delivery. During this three-day time gap, the DELIVERED_CARGO_SHIPMENTS table had a timeliness data quality problem. Correcting this particular timeliness problem would involve mandating that all data entry persons enter the information about delivered cargo shipments immediately upon delivery.

Conformity of the data refers to the extent to which the data conforms to its specified format. Conformity data quality problems occur when an instance of data does not conform to a preagreed upon format for that data. For example, let us assume that the

To: Albritco Board of Directors
Subject: Strategic Planning Goal Achieved (Confidential)

We are happy to report that the strategic goal of having an equal number of sales and financial managers is achieved as shown below:

MANAGERS HEAD COUNT UNIFORMITY: GOAL ACHIEVED	
Number of Sales Managers:	3
Number of Financial Managers:	3

FIGURE 6.31 A message reporting the head count of the managers in the Albritco company.

dollar amount in a bank transaction has to be stored and presented with the currency symbol $ preceding the amount. If certain bank transactions have dollar amounts formatted with the currency symbol $ following the amount, such records have conformity data quality problems. Correcting this problem would involve formatting every amount in all bank transactions with the currency symbol $ preceding the amount.

To further illustrate accuracy, uniqueness, completeness, consistency, timeliness, and conformity, consider the following example. Let us assume that the Albritco company records the data about its managers. The Albritco company had five managers: two sales managers (*Lilly* and *Carlos*) and three financial managers (*Emma, Robert,* and *Vijay*). It recently hired another sales manager (*Scarlett*). This was done to align the company with its strategic planning goal that specified that the company should have an equal number of sales managers and financial managers. Upon hiring an additional sales manager, the message shown in Figure 6.31 was sent to the board of directors.

The message was composed by the administrator in charge of hiring, who knew that the previous head count of the managers was two sales managers and three financial managers and that the company had just hired another sales manager.

Figure 6.32 shows a database relation where the data about company managers is stored. To facilitate the discussion about data quality factors, the data in this database relation has various data quality problems.

In the first displayed record, the birthdate for manager *Lilly* is missing. Although manager *Lilly* does have a birthdate, it is not entered in the record. Such an omission is an example of a *completeness* problem.

In the second displayed record, the name of the manager *Emma* is misspelled as *Emu*, causing an *accuracy* problem.

FIGURE 6.32 A database relation with data quality issues.

The third and fourth records both refer to the same person. An error occurred during the data entry process and the same person was recorded twice and was given two different ManagerID values. This person was recorded once with his real name and a second time with his nickname. These two records, which refer to the same person, are causing a *uniqueness* problem.

The way the birthdate is recorded for manager *Carlos*, represented by the fifth displayed record, causes a *conformity* problem. All other birthdates are recorded and presented in the following preagreed upon date format: /Month Name/Day as 2 digits/Year as 4 digits/. However, the birthdate for manager *Carlos* is in the /Day as 1 or 2 digits/Month as 1 or 2 digits/Year as 2 digits/ format.

Recently hired manager *Scarlett* is already working for Albritco, but she is not yet recorded in the database relation because the data entry person for this table is on vacation. Until the record about manager *Scarlett* is entered, the data about managers in this relation has a *timeliness* problem.

To illustrate the *consistency* problem, consider the report in Figure 6.33 that is based on the database relation in Figure 6.32.

The calculations in this report are based on the correct mathematical formulas that are properly counting the records with the Title value *Sales Manager* and the records with the Title value *Financial Manager*. The undercounting of sales managers occurs because one of the sales managers (*Scarlett*) is not entered yet due to a timeliness problem in the database relation. The overcounting of financial managers occurs because one of the sales managers (*Robert*) was entered twice as the result of a uniqueness problem in the database relation. These head counts (two sales managers and four financial managers) are inconsistent with the head counts in the table shown in Figure 6.31 (three sales managers and three financial managers).

Data quality problems such as the ones described here can be addressed by both preventive and corrective actions.

Preventive data quality actions that can preclude data quality problems include the following:

- providing data entry personnel with proper training and incentives
- mandating proper data entry practices; for example, mandating prompt entry to avoid timeliness issues
- instituting user-defined constraints and mechanisms; for example, implementing a database user-defined rule that does not allow for an insertion of a date value unless it is in the proper range and implementing a form mechanism (such as input mask) that assures the correct format

Corrective data quality actions that can be undertaken if the data already has data quality problems include the following:

- determining and acknowledging that the data has data quality problems
- using specialized software and standardized lookup databases to identify and correct the specific data quality errors

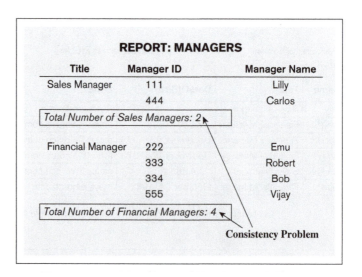

FIGURE 6.33 A report based on the relation in Figure 6.32.

For the scenario depicted in Figure 6.32, the Albritco company could have addressed its data quality problems as follows.

- DateOfBirth could have been declared a mandatory column (e.g., by using a NOT NULL clause in the CREATE TABLE SQL statement), which would prevent the completeness error in the first displayed record.
- Entries in the ManagerName column could have been checked against the database of standard names (e.g., database of 10,000 different first names in common use in the United States), and unusual entries could have been flagged for further verification. Such a procedure would flag the manager listed in this table as *Emu* in the second displayed record for further verification. Such verification would include, for example, researching the other available information about this person, which would establish that her real name is actually *Emma*. This would prompt the correction of the name value in the relation record from *Emu* to *Emma*, addressing the accuracy error.
- The E-mail column could have been declared within the CREATE TABLE statement as a unique column, as it is actually a candidate key. This would prevent the occurrence of the fourth displayed record and leave the third displayed record as the only one referring to the manager in question, thereby preventing the uniqueness error that occurred.
- A form for data entry could have included a mechanism that mandates the entry of birthdates in the /Month Name/Day as 2 digits/Year as 4 digits/ format, preventing the conformity problem in the fifth displayed record.
- Instituting and enforcing an organizational rule mandating that every new manager has to be recorded in the database relation from the moment he or she is hired would have eliminated the timeliness problem that occurred because manager *Scarlett* was not listed in the database relation even though she was already working for the company.
- The consistency problems shown in the report in Figure 6.33 would have been addressed by the above listed actions for correcting uniqueness and timeliness problems in the relation in Figure 6.32. No additional specific action for resolving these particular consistency problems would be required.

Figure 6.34 shows the table from Figure 6.32 with the data quality problems addressed.

Figure 6.35 shows the report based on the table from Figure 6.34. The consistency problems are now eliminated, and the report states that there are three sales managers and three financial managers, which is both correct and consistent with Figure 6.31.

Quality data is essential for the proper use of databases. Consequences of low data quality can be serious, since data of poor quality often leads to flawed decisions. There is no advantage to having a wrong customer count, erroneous information about financial assets, or missing patient-diagnosis data, while the negative effects in such scenarios are virtually guaranteed. Therefore, instituting practices for ensuring data quality is an essential practice in modern business.

This chapter has presented the most fundamental issues related to database implementation and use from the perspective of business designers and users. The following note gives additional information about assertions and triggers.

ManagerID	Name	Title	DateOfBirth	E-mail
111	Lilly	Sales Manager	May 21, 1971	lilly@albritco.com
222	Emma	Financial Manager	June 01, 1966	emma@albritco.com
333	Robert	Financial Manager	December 25, 1973	robert@albritco.com
444	Carlos	Sales Manager	April 13, 1968	carlos@albritco.com
555	Vijay	Financial Manager	October 04, 1981	vijay@albritco.com
666	Scarlett	Sales Manager	July 17, 1984	scarlett@albritco.com

FIGURE 6.34 The database relation from Figure 6.32, with the data quality issues resolved.

REPORT: MANAGERS

Title	Manager ID	Manager Name
Sales Manager	111	Lilly
	444	Carlos
	666	Scarlett

Total Number of Sales Managers: 3

Financial Manager	222	Emma
	333	Robert
	555	Vijay

Total Number of Financial Managers: 3

FIGURE 6.35   A report based on the relation in Figure 6.34.

A Note About Assertions and Triggers

Assertion is one of the mechanisms for specifying user-defined constraints. To illustrate and describe this mechanism, we will use the example shown in Figure 6.36.

In this example, a user-defined constraint states that every professor can advise up to 10 students. The following is the SQL CREATE ASSERTION statement specifying this rule:

```
CREATE ASSERTION profsadvisingupto10students
CHECK (
(SELECT MAX( totaladvised )
FROM (SELECT count(*) AS totaladvised
   FROM student
   GROUP BY advisorid)) < 11);
```

The CHECK statement verifies that the highest number of students advised by any professor is less than 11. The comparison within the CREATE ASSERTION statement would return the value TRUE if there were no advisors who advise more than 10 students. In case there are any professors who do advise more than 10 students, the comparison would return the value FALSE.

Even though CREATE ASSERTION is part of the SQL standard, most RDBMS packages do not implement assertions using CREATE ASSERTION statements (nevertheless, we chose to give an example of a CREATE ASSERTION statement, as it is very illustrative of the process of implementing user-defined constraints). Most RDBMS packages are capable of implementing the functionality of the assertion through different, more complex types of mechanisms, such as triggers.

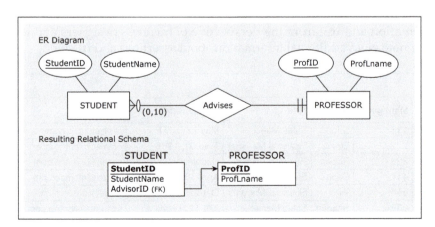

FIGURE 6.36   Each professor can advise up to 10 students.

A **trigger** is a rule that is activated by a deletion of a record, insertion of a record, or a modification (update) of a record in a relation. To illustrate triggers, consider how the assertion ProfsAdvisingUpTo10students could be implemented as the following two triggers (written in MySQL):

```
CREATE TRIGGER studentinserttrigger
      BEFORE INSERT ON student
  FOR EACH ROW
  BEGIN
    DECLARE totaladvised INT DEFAULT 0;
    SELECT COUNT(*) INTO totaladvised
    FROM student
    WHERE advisorid = NEW.advisorid;
    IF (totaladvised >= 10) THEN
       SET NEW.advisorid = NULL;
    END IF;
  END;

CREATE TRIGGER studentupdatetrigger
      BEFORE UPDATE ON student
  FOR EACH ROW
  BEGIN
    DECLARE totaladvised INT DEFAULT 0;
    SELECT COUNT(*) INTO totaladvised
    FROM student
    WHERE advisorid = NEW.advisorid;
    IF (totaladvised >= 10) THEN
      SET NEW.Advisorid = NULL;
    END IF;
  END;
```

The StudentInsertTrigger uses a variable (local to the trigger) TotalAdvised that is initially set to zero. This trigger is executed before each INSERT INTO Student statement is executed. The NEW.AdvisorID refers to the AdvisorID value of the student record being inserted. For example, let us assume that the following INSERT INTO statement is being issued for the relation STUDENT:

```
INSERT INTO student VALUES ('1111', 'Mark', 'P11');
```

The AdvisorID value for the new record being inserted is *P11*, and therefore the NEW.AdvisorID value in this case is *P11*. Before each insert, the SELECT query counts how many records in the STUDENT relation have the same value of AdvisorID as one in the record being inserted (*P11* in this case). This count value is then placed into the TotalAdvised variable. The IF statement in the trigger, following the SELECT query, checks if the count has already reached the value of ten. If it has, the insert would cause the new count to exceed the value of ten. This is not allowed, and the trigger will cause the INSERT INTO statement to be executed as:

```
INSERT INTO student VALUES ('1111', 'Mark', null);
```

thereby leaving the new student without an advisor. However, in that case, since the AdvisorID is a NOT NULL column due to the mandatory participation of the STUDENT entity in the Advises relationship, the entire INSERT INTO statement will be rejected by the RDBMS. However, if the count has not already reached the value of 10, then the insert statement will be executed as originally written:

```
INSERT INTO student VALUES ('1111', 'Mark', 'P11');
```

The StudentUpdateTrigger would work exactly the same as the StudentInsertTrigger, except that it would be triggered by the update (modify) operation, rather than by the insert operation. The StudentDeleteTrigger is not necessary in this case, since we are making sure that the number of advised students does not exceed a certain limit. A delete operation would never increase the number of students advised by any advisor.

Key Terms

Accuracy *197*
Assertion *202*
Binary search *188*
CHECK *185*
Completeness *198*
Conformity *198*
Consistency *198*

Corrective data quality actions *200*
Database front-end *192*
Data duplication *198*
Data quality *197*
Delete cascade *179*
Delete restrict *178*
Delete set-to-default *180*

Delete set-to-null *180*
Form *192*
Index *187*
Linear (sequential) search *187*
Preventive data quality actions *200*
Report *194*
Timeliness *198*

Trigger *203*
Uniqueness *198*
Update cascade *182*
Update restrict *181*
Update set-to-default *183*
Update set-to-null *182*

Review Questions

Q6.1 List options for implementing referential integrity constraints with regard to delete and update operations.

Q6.2 What is the purpose of an index?

Q6.3 What is the purpose of database front-end applications?

Q6.4 What is the purpose of a form?

Q6.5 What is the purpose of a report?

Q6.6 Describe the advantage of a Web site that is an interface with a database.

Q6.7 Define data accuracy.

Q6.8 Define data uniqueness.

Q6.9 Define data completeness.

Q6.10 Define data consistency.

Q6.11 Define data timeliness.

Q6.12 Define data conformity.

Q6.13 Give an example of a preventive data quality action.

Q6.14 Give an example of a corrective data quality action.

Exercises

E6.1 Consider the two tables shown in Figure 6.37. The TerID column in the SALES_REP relation is a foreign key referring to the primary key column TerID in the TERRITORY relation.

  E6.1a If a DBMS enforces a DELETE RESTRICT option on the referential integrity constraint between SALES_REP and TERRITORY, show the records in tables SALES_REP and TERRITORY after a user tries to delete the fourth record (*N, North*) from TERRITORY.

  E6.1b If a DBMS enforces a DELETE RESTRICT option on the referential integrity constraint between SALES_REP and TERRITORY, show the records in tables SALES_REP and TERRITORY after a user tries to delete the second record (*W, West*) from TERRITORY.

  E6.1c If a DBMS enforces a DELETE RESTRICT option on the referential integrity constraint between SALES_REP and TERRITORY, show the records in tables SALES_REP and TERRITORY after a user tries to delete the first record (*1, Joe, E*) from SALES_REP.

  E6.1d If a DBMS enforces a DELETE CASCADE option on the referential integrity constraint between SALES_REP and TERRITORY, show the records in tables SALES_REP and TERRITORY after a user tries to delete the fourth record (*N, North*) from TERRITORY.

  E6.1e If a DBMS enforces a DELETE CASCADE option on the referential integrity constraint between SALES_REP and TERRITORY, show the records in tables SALES_REP and TERRITORY after a

SALES_REP

SRID	SRName	TerID
1	Joe	E
2	Sue	E
3	Meg	C
4	Bob	S
5	Joe	N
6	Pat	N
7	Lee	N
8	Joe	E

TERRITORY

TerID	TerName
E	East
W	West
S	South
N	North
C	Central

FIGURE 6.37 The relations Sales_Rep and Territory.

user tries to delete the second record (*W, West*) from TERRITORY.

E6.1f If a DBMS enforces a DELETE CASCADE option on the referential integrity constraint between SALES_REP and TERRITORY, show the records in tables SALES_REP and TERRITORY after a user tries to delete the first record (*1, Joe, E*) from SALES_REP.

E6.1g If a DBMS enforces a DELETE SET-TO-NULL option on the referential integrity constraint between SALES_REP and TERRITORY, show the records in tables SALES_REP and TERRITORY after a user tries to delete the fourth record (*N, North*) from TERRITORY.

E6.1h If a DBMS enforces a DELETE SET-TO-NULL option on the referential integrity constraint between SALES_REP and TERRITORY, show the records in tables SALES_REP and TERRITORY after a user tries to delete the second record (*W, West*) from TERRITORY.

E6.1i If a DBMS enforces a DELETE SET-TO-NULL option on the referential integrity constraint between SALES_REP and TERRITORY, show the records in tables SALES_REP and TERRITORY after a user tries to delete the first record (*1, Joe, E*) from SALES_REP.

E6.1j If a DBMS enforces a DELETE SET-TO-DEFAULT option on the referential integrity constraint between SALES_REP and TERRITORY, show the records in tables SALES_REP and TERRITORY after a user tries to delete the fourth record (*N, North*) from TERRITORY. Assume that the default value for the DeptID column in the SALES_REP relation is 'E'.

E6.1k If a DBMS enforces a DELETE SET-TO- DEFAULT option on the referential integrity constraint between SALES_REP and TERRITORY, show the records in tables SALES_REP and TERRITORY after a user tries to delete the second record (*W, West*) from TERRITORY. Assume that the default value for the DeptID column in the SALES_REP relation is 'E'.

E6.1l If a DBMS enforces a DELETE SET-TO- DEFAULT option on the referential integrity constraint between SALES_REP and TERRITORY, show the records in tables SALES_REP and TERRITORY after a user tries to delete the first record (*1, Joe, E*) from SALES_REP. Assume that the default value for the DeptID column in the SALES_REP relation is 'E'.

E6.2 Consider the two tables shown in Figure 6.37:

E6.2a If a DBMS enforces an UPDATE RESTRICT option on the referential integrity constraint between SALES_REP and TERRITORY, show the records in tables SALES_REP and TERRITORY after a user tries to change the fourth record (*N, North*) in TERRITORY to (*NO, North*).

E6.2b If a DBMS enforces an UPDATE RESTRICT option on the referential integrity constraint between SALES_REP and TERRITORY, show the records in tables SALES_REP and TERRITORY after a user tries to change the second record (*W, West*) in TERRITORY to (*WE, West*).

E6.2c If a DBMS enforces an UPDATE RESTRICT option on the referential integrity constraint between SALES_REP and TERRITORY, show the records in tables SALES_REP and TERRITORY after a user tries to change the first record (*1, Joe, E*) in SALES_REP to (*1, Joe, C*).

E6.2d If a DBMS enforces an UPDATE CASCADE option on the referential integrity constraint between SALES_REP and TERRITORY, show the records in tables SALES_REP and TERRITORY after a user tries to change the fourth record (*N, North*) in TERRITORY to (*NO, North*).

E6.2e If a DBMS enforces an UPDATE CASCADE option on the referential integrity constraint between SALES_REP and TERRITORY, show the records in tables SALES_REP and TERRITORY after a user tries to change the second record (*W, West*) in TERRITORY to (*WE, West*).

E6.2f If a DBMS enforces an UPDATE CASCADE option on the referential integrity constraint between SALES_REP and TERRITORY, show the records in tables SALES_REP and TERRITORY after a user tries to change the first record (*1, Joe, E*) in SALES_REP to (*1, Joe, C*).

E6.2g If a DBMS enforces an UPDATE SET-TO-NULL option on the referential integrity constraint between SALES_REP and TERRITORY, show the records in tables SALES_REP and TERRITORY after a user tries to change the fourth record (*N, North*) in TERRITORY to (*NO, North*).

E6.2h If a DBMS enforces an UPDATE SET-TO-NULL option on the referential integrity constraint between SALES_REP and TERRITORY, show the records in tables SALES_REP and TERRITORY after a user tries to change the second record (*W, West*) in TERRITORY to (*WE, West*).

E6.2i If a DBMS enforces an UPDATE SET-TO-NULL option on the referential integrity constraint between SALES_REP and TERRITORY, show the records in tables SALES_REP and TERRITORY after a user tries to change the first record (*1, Joe, E*) in SALES_REP to (*1, Joe, C*).

E6.2j If a DBMS enforces an UPDATE SET-TO-DEFAULT option on the referential integrity constraint between SALES_REP and TERRITORY, show the records in tables SALES_REP and TERRITORY after a user tries to change the fourth record (*N, North*) in TERRITORY to (*NO, North*). Assume that the default value for the DeptID column in the SALES_REP relation is 'E'.

E6.2k If a DBMS enforces an UPDATE SET-TO-DEFAULT option on the referential integrity constraint between SALES_REP and TERRITORY, show the records in tables SALES_REP and TERRITORY after a user tries to change the second record (*W, West*) in TERRITORY to (*WE, West*). Assume that the default value for the DeptID column in the SALES_REP relation is 'E'.

TABLE A: INCOMING STUDENTS DEPOSITS

Deposit Date	Deposit Amount
2/12/2013	$1,000
2/12/2013	$1,000
2/13/2013	$1,000
2/13/2013	$1,000
2/14/2013	$1,000
2/14/2013	$1,000
2/15/2013	$1,000
2/15/2013	$1,000
2/16/2013	$1,000
2/16/2013	$1,000
Total No of Students (Deposits)	10
Total Amount of Deposits	$10,000

TABLE B: INCOMING STUDENTS INFORMATION

Student ID	Student Lname	Student Fname	Passport Number	Date of Deposit	Student Home Town	Student Home Country
200602	McCoy	Mark	US2000001	02/12/2013	Detroit	USA
200603	Suzuki	Akiko	JA7000001	02/12/2013	Tokyo	
200604	Jones	Mary	US2000002	02/13/2013	Chicago	USA
200605	Lalime	Patrick	CA3000001	February 13th, 2013	Montreal	Canada
200606	Van Basten	Robin	NE4000001	02/14/2013	Amsterdam	Netherlands
200607	Van Basten	Rob	NE4000001	02/14/2013	Amsterdam	Netherlands
200608	Vrabec	Alen	CR5000001	02/14/2013	Zagreb	Croatia
200609	Popov	Stilian	BU6000001	02/15/2013	Plovdiv	Bulgaria
200610	De Beers	Inge	NE4000002	02/15/2013	Amsterdam	Neverland
Total Number of Incoming Students	9					

FIGURE 6.38   Albus International Academy Tables.

E6.21 If a DBMS enforces an UPDATE SET-TO-DEFAULT option on the referential integrity constraint between SALES_REP and TERRITORY, show the records in tables SALES_REP and TERRITORY after a user tries to change the first record (1, Joe, E) in SALES_REP to (1, Joe, C). Assume that the default value for the DeptID column in the SALES_REP relation is 'E'.

E6.3 Using Figure 6.15, illustrate the steps in a linear search for a customer named Peter.

E6.4 Using Figure 6.15, illustrate the steps in a binary search for the customer 1001.

E6.5 Show the PRODUCT table from Figure 3.33 in Chapter 3 accompanied by a PRODUCTNAME_INDEX table, using the ProductID value as the index pointer.

E6.6 Show the SQL command that will be issued when a user using the form shown in Figure 6.23 changes the zip code of the fifth customer from 60444 to 60999.

E6.7 Show the SQL command that will be issued when a user using the form shown in Figure 6.24 enters the value Pam in the Customer Name box and clicks the Search button. Also, show the result of executing the command.

E6.8 Consider the following scenario.

At Albus International Academy, every incoming student makes a $1,000 deposit. Albus International Academy has 10 incoming students, and each of them has made a deposit. This information is reflected in Table A in Figure 6.38. Table B in Figure 6.38 contains information about the incoming students populated by the data entry person at Albus International Academy. Assume the following:

- Each deposit made by each incoming student is correctly recorded in Table A.
- The spellings of students' last names are correct in Table B.
- The spellings of students' first names (and/or their abbreviations) are correct in Table B.
- All the dates of deposit are correct in Table B. The required format for the date of deposit is MM/DD/YYYY.
- All the passport numbers are correct in Table B.
- The spellings of students' hometowns are correct in Table B.

In Table B in Figure 6.38, identify and classify all instances of data quality problems (i.e., accuracy, uniqueness, completeness, consistency, timeliness, and conformity problems).

Chapter 7

Data Warehousing Concepts

INTRODUCTION

A typical organization maintains and utilizes a number of operational data sources. These operational data sources include the databases and other data repositories that are used to support the organization's day-to-day operations, such as handling cash register transactions, credit card purchases, hotel reservations, or recording student grades.

A data warehouse is created within an organization as a separate data store whose primary purpose is data analysis. Often, the same fact can have both an operational and an analytical purpose. For example, data describing that customer X bought product Y in store Z can be stored in an operational database for business-process support purposes, such as inventory monitoring or financial transaction record keeping. That same fact can also be stored in a data warehouse where, combined with a vast number of similar facts accumulated over a period of time, it serves to reveal important trends, such as sales patterns or customer behavior.

There are two main reasons that compel the creation of a data warehouse as a separate analytical database. The first reason is that the performance of operational day-to-day tasks involving data use can be severely diminished if such tasks have to compete for computing resources with analytical queries. The second reason lies in the fact that, even if performance were not an issue, it is often impossible to structure a database that can be used in a straightforward manner for both operational and analytical purposes (as we will elaborate on in Chapter 8). Therefore, a data warehouse is created as a separate data store, designed for accommodating analytical queries.

In this chapter, we will describe the differences between the analytical and operational information that necessitate the separation of analytical and operational data repositories. We will also describe the main components of a data warehousing system and describe the difference between a data mart and data warehouse. At the end of this chapter, we will outline the main steps in the process of developing a data warehouse.

ANALYTICAL VERSUS OPERATIONAL INFORMATION

As we mentioned in Chapter 1, the information that is collected and used in information systems can be generally used for two purposes: operational and analytical.

Recall that the term **operational information (transactional information)** refers to the information collected and used in support of day-to-day operational needs. Since operational information results from individual transactions, such as an ATM withdrawal or purchase of an airline ticket, operational information is also sometimes referred to as transactional information.

On the other hand, the term **analytical information** refers to the information collected and used for decision support of tasks requiring data analysis. As we noted in Chapter 1, an example of analytical information is information showing a pattern of use of ATM machines (such as what hours of the day have the highest and lowest number of withdrawals) or information revealing sales trends in the airline industry (such as which routes in the United States have the most and fewest sales). It is important to note that analytical information is based on operational information. For example, the analytical information showing a pattern of use of ATM machines at different times of the day is created by combining numerous instances of transactional information resulting from individual ATM withdrawals.

Even though analytical information is based on operational information, there are key differences between the two. The differences between analytical and operational information can be divided into three categories: data makeup differences, technical differences, and functional differences.

Data Makeup Differences

Data makeup differences are differences in the characteristics of the data that comprises the operational and analytical information. Three particular data makeup differences between the operational and analytical data that we describe here are data time-horizon, data level-of-detail, and data time-representation.

DATA TIME-HORIZON DIFFERENCE Operational systems have a *shorter time horizon* of data than analytical systems. For example, in many operational systems, the data time horizon is 60 to 90 days. After that time period, the data is removed from the operational system and (typically) archived.

For example, a telecom company may keep 90 days' worth of data in its operational database, reflecting individual phone calls made by the customers and used by the application serving its customer representatives. The vast majority of customer inquiries concern the last three months of data. So when customers inquire about the charges on their phones made within the past several weeks or months, the information about their phone calls is readily and quickly available to the customer representative using the operational system. If the operational system contained multiple years' worth of individual phone calls, the database application supporting the customer representatives would work much more slowly for typical queries, because the underlying database would be much larger. This would result in an unnecessarily slow response to most of the customer inquiries. That is why an operational system, in this case, would have a data time horizon of 90 days. If a rare request to discuss a phone call from three years ago is made by a customer, the company can accommodate such an unusual request by looking up archived data. Of course, that particular request would be processed slower. However, it is much better to quickly process a large majority of the queries than to significantly slow down a high percentage of the queries for the sake of an occasional atypical inquiry. Most queries that are requested for operational purposes require the data from a relatively short time horizon. Keeping data in the operational system past this time horizon would represent unnecessary clutter, and the operational queries would run slower due to the needlessly large search space.

On the other hand, analytical data repositories typically must be able to provide trend and pattern analysis over years of data. Consequently, analytical databases have a much *longer time horizon* than operational databases. The time horizon for an analytical database often spans years of data. The need for different time horizons of data is one of the main reasons for the physical separation of operational and analytical databases. Operational databases with shorter time horizons serve as sites for the operational use of data, while a separate analytical repository of data with a longer time horizon serves as a site for analytical queries.

DATA LEVEL-OF-DETAIL DIFFERENCE Operational data typically reflects *detailed data*. In other words, the details of every individual transaction are recorded. Such level of detail is also often referred to as *fine detail level*. For example, each phone call is recorded in a telecom company's operational database. Usually the calling number, called number, the time of the call, and the call duration are recorded.

Summarized data, such as the total duration of all of the customer's phone calls this week, can be calculated from the detailed data. Such summarized values are typically not stored in operational databases, because they can usually be calculated almost as quickly as they can be retrieved if they were stored. Also, the summarized data is frequently subject to changes, in which case storing the summarized data becomes pointless. For example, every time the customer makes another phone call, the value of the total duration of weekly calls must change.

Instead of being stored, the summaries are usually implemented in the *operational* databases as *derived* attributes using formulas. Therefore, every time the customer makes another phone call, the total duration of weekly calls is automatically recalculated and updated in the front-end application. On the other hand, *analytical* databases can contain both detailed and summarized data that is *physically stored*. Summarizations, such as a customer's weekly durations of phone calls for all weeks in the past 10 years, are often precomputed and physically stored in analytical databases. Physically storing such summarizations in analytical databases is feasible because these summarizations are not subject to change, due to their historical nature. For example, a summary of weekly durations of phone calls in the previous year is not going to change. If analysts need such summarized information frequently, it makes sense to store the result of such a calculation rather than recalculating it every time it is needed. Recalculations are usually appropriate in operational databases due to the dynamic nature of the data, the relatively small amounts of data stored, and the relatively short time horizon. However, in analytical databases containing huge amounts of data due to long-time horizons, storing summarized data, instead of recalculating it every time it is needed, provides a significant time saver for analytical queries.

DATA TIME–REPRESENTATION DIFFERENCE Operational data typically represents the *current* state of affairs in the real world, while analytical data can represent both the current situation and *snapshots* from the past. For example, a bank customer will have one value in an operational database representing his or her checking account balance. This value will represent the current balance. When the customer makes a withdrawal or a deposit, the checking account balance value will change accordingly, and the old balance will be replaced by the new current balance.

An analytical data repository can contain the client's current balance, but it can also contain values over time, called snapshots, that show, for example, the client's checking account balances at the end of each month for the entire time horizon. These snapshots would be calculated once and then physically stored for the repeated use of the analysts, instead of recalculating the snapshots every time they are needed.

Technical Differences

Technical differences are defined as the differences in the way that operational and analytical data is handled and accessed by the DBMS and applications. In particular, we will describe here the technical differences related to the queried amounts of data and frequency of queries, the update of data, and the redundancy of operational and analytical information.

DIFFERENCE IN QUERIED AMOUNTS OF DATA AND FREQUENCY OF QUERIES Operational queries typically process much *smaller amounts of data* than analytical queries. On the other hand, operational queries are typically *issued much more often* and *by more users* than analytical queries. It is usually possible to configure the system to optimally process frequent queries requiring smaller amounts of data or to optimally process less frequent queries requesting large amounts of data. However, it is usually not possible to technically configure and optimize the system for both of those types of scenarios. This is yet another reason why data warehouses are physically separate data stores.

DATA UPDATE DIFFERENCE Data in operational systems is *regularly updated* by the users. In operational databases, in addition to issuing queries for the retrieval of data, users routinely insert, modify, and delete data. On the other hand, the end users of analytical databases are only able to retrieve data, and *updates* of the data by the end users are *not allowed*.

DATA REDUNDANCY DIFFERENCE As we described in detail in the earlier chapters of this book, *reducing the redundancy* of information is a major goal of operational databases. One of the main reasons for minimizing the redundancy in operational databases is to eliminate the possibility of update anomalies. However, the updating of data by the end users is not allowed in analytical databases, and therefore, there is no particular danger of update anomalies. Hence, *eliminating redundancy is not as critical* in analytical databases as it is in operational databases.

Functional Differences

Functional differences are defined as differences in the rationale for the use of operational and analytical data. Two particular functional differences that we will describe relate to the audience and orientation of operational and analytical data.

DATA AUDIENCE DIFFERENCE Operational data supports day-to-day operations of businesses and organizations and, as such, is *used by all types* of employees, customers, and other users *for various tactical purposes*. For example, a sales clerk uses operational information to charge the appropriate amount to the customer for his or her purchase, or a traveler uses operational information to book a flight to his or her destination. In contrast to the widespread constituency of operational data, analytical data is *used by a more narrow set of users* for *decision-making purposes*. For example, the CEO of a retail chain may use a complex and voluminous set of analytical information to determine which existing stores to close or where to open new stores.

DATA ORIENTATION DIFFERENCE The term "orientation" in the context of the discussion about the operational and analytical information refers to the purpose for which the information is organized. Operational databases are typically created to support an application serving one or more business operations and processes. For example, operational databases, such as a shipping company order-entry database or a dental office appointment management database, serve to facilitate operations by providing a data store for applications supporting those operations. That is why operational databases are referred to as **application-oriented**.

On the other hand, analytical databases are created for the analysis of one or more specific business subject areas, such as sales, returns, cost, or profit. Analytical databases are organized around their subjects of analysis, and that is why they are referred to as **subject-oriented**.

The following example illustrates the difference between the application-oriented and subject-oriented organization of data. This example uses a simple scenario—the Vitality Health Club. This fitness center has regular members who pay a monthly membership fee. The memberships are divided into the two categories—*gold*, with a fee of *$100*, and *basic*, with a fee of *$50*. The members of the *basic* category have access to the entire facility, except for the pool, while members of the *gold* category have ac-cess to the entire facility, including the pool. The Vitality Health Club also allows daily visits from nonmembers. For a *$10* daily fee, a nonmember can use the entire facility, except for the pool, and for a *$15* fee, a nonmember can use the entire facility, including the pool. Figure 7.1 shows an application-oriented data set for the Vitality Health Club, which supports the computer application used by the clerks to handle payments and visits by members and nonmembers.

For simplicity, we only show the first few records in the tables HEALTH CLUB MEMBER and DAILY VISIT FROM NONMEMBERS.

Figure 7.2 shows a subject-oriented data set for the Vitality Health Club, which supports the analysis of the subject revenue.

HEALTH CLUB MEMBER

MemberID	MemberName	MemberGender	MLevelID	DateMembershipPaid
111	Joe	M	A	1/1/2013
222	Sue	F	B	1/1/2013
333	Pam	F	A	1/2/2013
...	...	...	...	...

MEMBERSHIP LEVEL

MLevelID	MLevelType	MLevelFee	MLevelDescription
A	Gold	$100	Includes the Pool Usage
B	Basic	$50	No Pool Usage

DAILY VISIT FROM NONMEMBERS

DVisitTID	DVisitLevelID	DVisitDate	DVisitorGender
11xx22	YP	1/1/2013	M
11xx23	NP	1/2/2013	M
11xx24	YP	1/2/2013	F
...	...	...	...

VISIT LEVEL

DVisitLevelID	DVisitLevelFee	DVisitLevelType
YP	$15	With Pool Usage
NP	$10	Without Pool Usage

FIGURE 7.1   An application-oriented database serving the Vitality Health Club Visits and Payments Application.

The data sets in Figure 7.1 and 7.2 contain the same data, just organized differ-ently. The column RevenueRecordID is added to the table in Figure 7.2 as an auto-increasing (autonumber) integer to provide a primary key for the table, distinguishing one record from another. All the other data in Figure 7.2 is derived from the data in Figure 7.1. For example, record *1000* is a result of joining a part of the first record in table HEALTH CLUB MEMBER with a part of the first record in table MEMBERSHIP LEVEL. The entry *Member* in the column GeneratedBy is derived from the fact that tables HEALTH CLUB MEMBER and MEMBERSHIP LEVEL refer to the Vitality Health Club members. The record *1002* is a result of joining part of the first record in table DAILY VISIT

REVENUE

RevenueRecordID	Date	GeneratedBy	ClientGender	Pool Use Included in Purchase	Amount
1000	1/1/2013	Member	M	Yes	$100
1001	1/1/2013	Member	F	No	$50
1002	1/1/2013	Nonmember	M	Yes	$15
1003	1/2/2013	Member	F	Yes	$100
1004	1/2/2013	Nonmember	M	No	$10
1005	1/2/2013	Nonmember	F	Yes	$15
...				...	...

FIGURE 7.2   A subject-oriented database for the analysis of the subject revenue.

FROM NONMEMBERS with the first record in table VISIT LEVEL. The entry *Nonmember* in the column GeneratedBy is derived from the fact that tables DAILY VISIT FROM NONMEMBERS and VISIT LEVEL refer to nonmembers.

The set in Figure 7.1 is normalized into multiple tables and is well suited for the support of its Vitality Health Club Visits and Payments Application. For example, when a new member signs up, the membership clerk only has to enter one record in the table HEALTH CLUB MEMBER with the appropriate code for the membership (*A* or *B*). This record is then automatically connected to the corresponding record in the table MEMBERSHIP LEVEL. Therefore, the membership clerk can collect the membership fee (*$50* or *$100*) without needing to enter any other information in the database other than the one record in the table HEALTH CLUB MEMBER. This application-oriented database enables efficient functioning of the application it supports.

The set in Figure 7.2 is contained in one singular subject-oriented table organized for the analysis of revenue. Based on what kind of analytically relevant data about revenue was available in the operational database in Figure 7.1, the table in Figure 7.2 contains the columns referring to the revenue amount and the date, type of customer, gender of customer, and the type of use related to the revenue amount. Using this table, the analysis of revenue by the date, type of customer, gender of customer, and the type of use is straightforward and involves querying a single table.

Vitality Health Club could have analyzed its revenue by using the database in Figure 7.1; however, the analysis would not have been as simple and straightforward as with the table in Figure 7.2. To show all revenue, an analyst using the database in Figure 7.1 would first have to join the top two tables, then join the bottom two tables, and then follow it all up by merging the results of the two joins.

In reality, a company like Vitality Health Club could have had other operational database tables depicting additional sources of revenue, such as tables describing purchases in the health club's pro shop or tables describing purchases in the health club's juice-and-protein bar. In such a scenario, a subject-oriented data set that merges all instances of revenue into the table in Figure 7.2 would still provide a straightforward analysis of revenue. On the other hand, analysis by using only operational data sets would, in this case, involve even more steps with complex actions, such as additional joins and joins of joins. Analysts would quickly find themselves spending more time putting the necessary data together (i.e., data preparation) than on the analysis itself.

As we just described, the subject-oriented data set in Figure 7.2 is better suited for the analysis of revenue than the application-oriented data set in Figure 7.1.

Equivalently, the application-oriented data set in Figure 7.1 is well suited for the support of operational applications, while the subject-oriented data set in Figure 7.2 is not appropriate for that purpose.

THE DATA WAREHOUSE DEFINITION

Now that we have examined the differences between the analytical and operational information, we will examine the definition of the most fundamental analytical data repository: the **data warehouse**.

In practice as well as in literature, there are a number of definitions describing the term "data warehouse." These definitions vary slightly from each other, but they are in agreement about the general concepts. Those concepts are captured in the following generic definition.

Data Warehouse

The data warehouse is a structured repository of integrated, subject-oriented, enterprise-wide, historical, and time-variant data. The purpose of the data warehouse is the retrieval of analytical information. A data warehouse can store detailed and/or summarized data.

We will now analyze the basic concepts captured in this definition.

Structured Repository

The data warehouse is a database containing analytically useful information. Any database is a structured repository, with its structure represented in its metadata. Hence, the data warehouse, being a database, is also a structured repository. In other words, the data warehouse is not a disorganized random mass of data.

Integrated

The idea behind a data warehouse is to create a repository of analytical information in the organization. This repository is physically separate from the existing operational databases in the organization. The data warehouse integrates the analytically useful data from those various operational databases. Integration refers to the process of bringing the data from multiple operational databases into a single data warehouse. Of course, in this process, no data is actually removed from the operational sources. Instead, the analytically useful data from various operational databases is copied and brought into the data warehouse.

Subject-Oriented

The term "subject-oriented" refers to the fundamental difference in the purpose of an operational database system and a data warehouse. An operational database system is developed in order to support a specific business operation. On the other hand, a data warehouse is developed to analyze specific business subject areas.

Enterprise-Wide

The data warehouse is a repository of analytically useful information in the organization. The term "enterprise-wide" refers to the fact that the data warehouse provides an organization-wide view of the analytically useful information it contains. For example, if one of the subjects of the data warehouse is cost, then all of the analytically useful data regarding cost within the operational data sources throughout the entire organization will be brought into the data warehouse.

Historical

When compared to operational information, analytical information has a longer time horizon. Given that a data warehouse contains analytical information, its time horizon is longer (usually substantially so) than the time horizon in the operational databases. The term "historical" refers to the larger time horizon in the data warehouse than in the operational databases. For example, many traditional operational databases have a time horizon of 60 to 90 days, where it is quite common for data warehouses to contain multiple years' worth of data.

Time-Variant

The term "time-variant" refers to the fact that a data warehouse contains slices or snapshots of data from different periods of time across its time horizon. With these data slices, the user can create reports for various periods of time within the time horizon. For example, if the subject of analysis is cost and the time horizon is a number of years, we can analyze and compare the cost for the first quarter from a year ago versus the cost for the first quarter from two years ago.

Retrieval of Analytical Information

A data warehouse is developed for the retrieval of analytical information, and it is not meant for direct data entry by the users. The only functionality available to the users of the data warehouse is retrieval. The data in the data warehouse is not subject to modifications, insertions, or deletions by the end users. New data in the data warehouse is periodically loaded from the operational data sources and appended to the existing data, in an automatic fashion. The data that eventually gets older than the required time horizon is automatically purged from the data warehouse (and possibly archived and/or summarized). However, the data in the data warehouse is not subject to changes. That is why the data in the data warehouse is referred to as nonvolatile, static, or read-only.

Detailed and/or Summarized Data

A data warehouse, depending on its purpose, may include detailed data or summary data, or both. The detailed data is also called atomic data or transaction-level data. For example, a table in which each ATM transaction is recorded as a separate record contains detailed data (i.e., atomic or transaction-level data). On the other hand, a table in which a record represents calculations based on multiple instances of transaction-level data contains summarized data at a coarser level of detail. For example, a summarized data record could represent the total amount of money withdrawn in one month from one account via an ATM.

A data warehouse that contains the data at the finest level of detail is the most powerful, because all summaries can be calculated from it and stored if they are to be repeatedly used. However, there are cases when storing all of the analytical data at the transaction-level of detail for large time horizons is cost prohibitive. For example, for some organizations, the financial resources necessary for the specialized hardware and software required to store and process such enormous data sets may be out of reach. Also, in some other cases, organizations may decide that for some subjects of analysis, summarizations are adequate and transaction-level detail data is not necessary. In cases when the company is not able or does not want to have all of its required analytical information at the finest level of detail, the data for some or all (depending on the particular situation) of the subjects of analysis in the data warehouse is kept only at a certain level of summarization.

DATA WAREHOUSE COMPONENTS

Every data warehousing system has three major components at its core: *source systems, extraction-transformation-load (ETL) infrastructure,* and the *data warehouse* itself. Most data warehousing systems also have the *front-end applications* component. In this section, we will briefly illustrate and discuss those components.

Figure 7.3 shows an example scenario in an organization where users use multiple operational data stores for daily operational purposes.

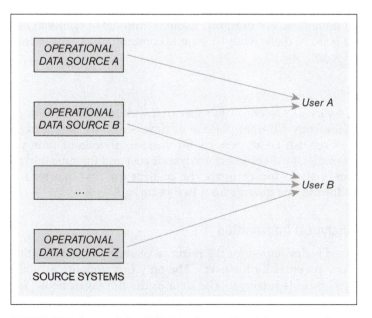

FIGURE 7.3 An example of the use of operational data sources for operational purposes in an organization.

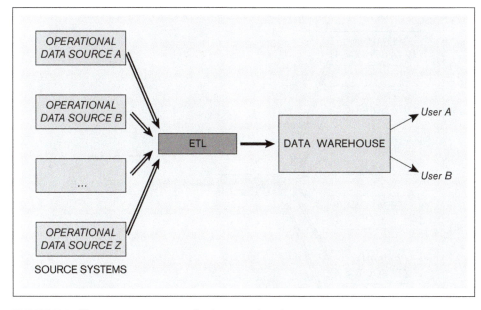

FIGURE 7.4 The core components of a data warehousing system.

However, for analytical purposes, the alternative to rummaging through a series of application-oriented operational data sources, and consequently spending a lot of time on data preparation instead of analysis, is to use a data warehouse, as shown in Figure 7.4.

Source Systems

In the context of data warehousing, **source systems** are operational databases and other operational data repositories (in other words, any sets of data used for operational purposes) that provide analytically useful information for the data warehouse's subjects of analysis. Every operational data store that is used as a source system for the data warehouse has two purposes:

- the original operational purpose
- as a source system for the data warehouse

In its original purpose, the operational data store serves operational users in its operational function. That same operational data store can *also* provide the data for the data warehouse as one of the data warehouse's source systems. It is important to note that both of those functions are done simultaneously. In other words, once it becomes a source system for a data warehouse, an operational data store continues its operational functions in the same way as it did before it was a source system for a data warehouse.

In addition to operational data sources from within the organization, source systems can include external data sources, such as third-party market research data, census data, stock market data, or weather data, to name a few examples. Figure 7.5 illustrates a data warehouse whose source systems include both operational sources from within the organization and external sources.

Data Warehouse

The data warehouse itself is the repository of the analytical data integrated from the source systems. The data warehouse is sometimes referred to as the *target system*, to indicate the fact that it is a destination for the data from the source systems. A typical data warehouse periodically retrieves selected analytically useful data from the operational data sources. In so-called "active" data warehouses, the retrieval of data from operational data sources is continuous.

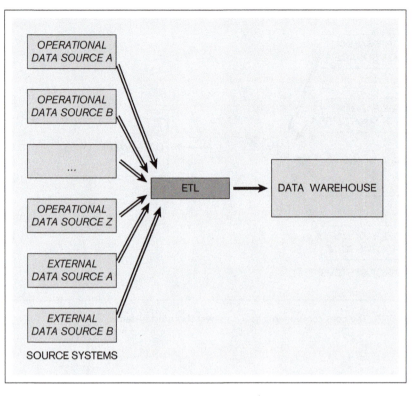

FIGURE 7.5   A data warehouse with internal and external source systems.

ETL

For any data warehouse, the infrastructure that facilitates the retrieval of data from operational databases into the data warehouses is known as an **extraction-transformation-load (ETL)** infrastructure. ETL includes the following tasks:

- extracting analytically useful data from the operational data sources
- transforming such data so that it conforms to the structure of the subject-oriented target data warehouse model while ensuring the quality of the transformed data through processes such as data cleansing or scrubbing
- loading the transformed and quality assured data into the target data warehouse

These three components—source systems, ETL, and data warehouse—form the central part of any data warehousing system.

Data Warehouse Front–End (BI) Applications

Just like operational databases, data warehousing systems usually also have front-end applications that allow straightforward access to their functionalities for users who are engaging in indirect use. This is illustrated by Figure 7.6. Data warehouse front-end applications are also referred to as BI applications.

DATA MARTS

A **data mart** is a data store based on the same principles as a data warehouse, but with a more limited scope. While a data warehouse contains data about multiple subjects of analysis retrieved from operational databases across an entire organization, a data mart is typically smaller, containing data about one subject, and does not necessarily have an enterprise-wide focus. The table in Figure 7.7 summarizes the differences between the terms "data warehouse" and "data mart."

There are two major categories of data marts: independent data marts and dependent data marts.

An **independent data mart** is a stand-alone data mart, created in the same fashion as the data warehouse. It has its own source systems and ETL infrastructure. The

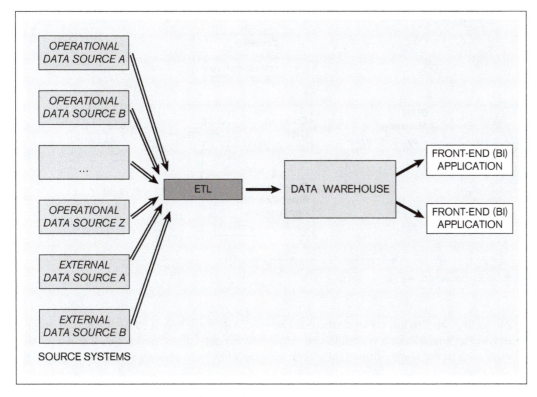

FIGURE 7.6 A data warehouse with front-end applications.

	DATA WAREHOUSE	DATA MART
Subjects	*Multiple*	*Single*
Data Sources	*Many*	*Fewer*
Typical Size	*Very big (routinely terabytes of data and larger)*	*Not as big*
Implementation Time	*Relatively long (months, years)*	*Not as long*
Focus	*Organization-wide*	*Often narrower than organization-wide*

FIGURE 7.7 Data warehouse and data mart properties.

difference between an independent data mart and a data warehouse is in the factors listed in Figure 7.7: a single subject, fewer data sources, smaller size, shorter implementation, and often a narrower focus.

A **dependent data mart** does not have its own source systems. Instead, its data comes from the data warehouse, which explains the term "dependent data mart." Dependent data marts are simply a way to provide users with a subset of the data from the data warehouse, in cases when users or applications do not want, need, or are not allowed to have access to all the data in the entire data warehouse.

In Chapter 8, we discuss how independent and dependent data marts are used in the context of various data warehouse modeling approaches.

STEPS IN DEVELOPMENT OF DATA WAREHOUSES

As was the case with regular database systems, data warehousing systems are developed through various steps that should be taken in a certain order. This is illustrated by Figure 7.8, which depicts the core development activities during the life cycle of a data warehousing (DWH) system.

Once the decision to undertake the data warehousing project is made and the data warehousing project is initiated, the predevelopment activities, such as planning,

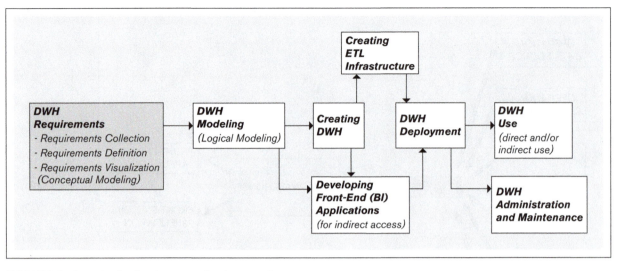

FIGURE 7.8   Steps in the development of a data warehouse.

budgeting, and so on, are undertaken. These activities are followed by the actual process of developing the data warehouse captured in Figure 7.8. Below, we describe and discuss each of the steps of the data warehouse development process shown in Figure 7.8.

Requirements Collection, Definition, and Visualization

The first and most critical step in the development of data warehouses is the **requirements collection, definition, and visualization**. If this step is successful, the remaining steps have a great chance of success. However, if this step is done incorrectly, all of the remaining steps, and consequently the entire project, will be futile. This step is highlighted in Figure 7.8 with a gray background in order to underscore its critical nature.

The results of this step are the end-user requirements specifying the desired capabilities and functionalities of the future data warehouse. These requirements are based on the analytical needs that can be met by the data in the internal data source systems and available external data sources. The requirements collection process aspires to analytically take advantage of all data available for consideration, but it cannot be based on data that is not available or does not exist.

The requirements are collected through interviewing various stakeholders of the data warehouse, including:

- leaders, managers, and other decision makers of the organization to determine and prioritize the subjects of the eventual data warehouse
- technical and business experts of each of the data sources under consideration in order to understand these data sources
- eventual end users of the data warehouse who will be in charge of performing the analytical tasks, to determine the details needed to analyze the chosen subjects

In addition to interviews, additional methods for eliciting requirements from the stakeholders can be used, such as focus groups, questionnaires, surveys, and observations of existing analytical practices to determine what users really do with data and what data they actually use and need.

The collected requirements should be clearly defined and stated in a written document and then visualized as a conceptual data model by using a conceptual data modeling technique, such as ER modeling (covered earlier in Chapter 2) or dimensional modeling (covered later in Chapter 8).

The guidelines and methods for data warehouse requirements collection and definition usually call for an iterative process. A smaller initial set of requirements can be collected, defined, and visualized and then discussed by the data warehouse developers and stakeholders. These discussions can then lead into subsequent iterations of collecting, defining, and visualizing requirements that gradually increase the initial small set of requirements.

Even when a set of requirements is agreed upon within the data warehouse requirements collection, definition, and visualization step, it can still be subject to change initiated by other steps in the data warehouse development process, as illustrated by Figure 7.9.

Instead of trying to collect, define, and visualize all data warehouse requirements in one isolated process and then proceed with all other steps in the development of the data warehouse, the common recommendation is to allow the refining and adding of requirements after each of the steps of the data warehouse development process. This is illustrated by the white dashed lines in Figure 7.9. For example, an initial set of requirements can be collected, defined, and visualized and an initial data warehouse model can be created. The additional requirements can be added in a series of similar iterations. The requirements can also be altered iteratively when other steps, such as the development of front-end applications or actual database use, reveal the need for modifying, augmenting, or reducing the original set of requirements.

Every time the set of requirements is changed, the conceptual model has to be changed accordingly, and the changes in the requirements must propagate, as applicable, through all of the subsequent steps: modeling, creating the data warehouse, creating the ETL infrastructure, creating front-and applications, deployment, use, and administration/maintenance.

No implicit changes of requirements are permitted in any of the data warehouse development steps. For example, during the data warehouse creation process a developer is *not* allowed to create on an ad-hoc basis a new data warehouse construct that is not called for by the requirements. Instead, if it were discovered during the data warehouse creation process that the new construct (such as a new table or a new column in a table) is actually needed and useful, the requirements should be augmented to include the requirement for the new construct. This new requirement should then be reflected accordingly in the modified visualization and the subsequent data warehouse model. Only then should a new data warehouse construct actually be implemented.

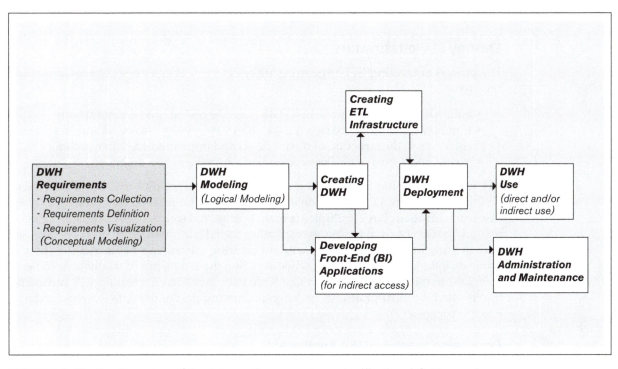

FIGURE 7.9 The iterative nature of the data warehouse requirements collection, definition, and visualization process.

Forming data warehouse requirements is widely recognized as the most important step within the entire data warehouse system development process. The outcome of this step determines the success of the entire data warehousing project. If this step is not done correctly, the data warehouse requirements will not accurately represent the analytical needs of the system's end users. Consequently, the eventual data warehouse will not properly satisfy the analytical needs of its end users.

Data Warehouse Modeling

The first step following requirement collection, definition, and visualization is **data warehouse modeling**. We use the term "data warehouse modeling" to refer to the creation of the data warehouse models that are implementable by the data management software. As we mentioned in Chapter 1, this type of modeling is also known as *logical data modeling* or *implementational data modeling*, as opposed to *conceptual data modeling*, which is simply a visualization of the requirements, independent of the logic on which a particular data management software is based.

Creating the Data Warehouse

Once the data warehouse model is created, the next step is **creating the data warehouse**. This step involves using database management software and implementing the data warehouse model as the actual data warehouse that is initially empty. Typically, data warehouses are modeled as relational databases. For that reason, they are implemented using a relational DBMS. Regular relational DBMS packages, such as Microsoft SQL Server or Oracle, can be used for implementing both operational databases and data warehouses. However, other relational DBMS packages, such as Teradata, that are specialized for processing large amounts of data typically found in data warehouses are also available for implementation of data warehouses.

Creating a data warehouse is a straightforward process that involves data warehouse developers using the functionalities and capabilities of a DBMS to implement the data warehouse model as an actual functioning analytical database.

Creating data marts can be accomplished in the same fashion as creating data warehouses by using relational DBMS packages. In some cases, data marts can also be implemented as so-called "cubes," using a data management technology different from relational DBMS as described in Chapter 9.

Creating ETL Infrastructure

The process of **creating ETL infrastructure** refers to creating necessary procedures and code for:

- automatic extraction of relevant data from the operational data sources
- transformation of the extracted data, so that its quality is assured and its structure conforms to the structure of the modeled and implemented data warehouse
- the seamless load of the transformed data into the data warehouse

ETL infrastructure has to account for and reconcile all of the differences in the metadata and the data between the operational sources and the target data warehouses. In many cases, organizations have multiple separate operational sources with overlapping information. In such cases, the process of creating the ETL infrastructure involves deciding how to bring in such information without creating misleading duplicates (i.e., how to bring in all the useful information while avoiding the uniqueness data quality problem).

Due to the amount of details that have to be considered, creating ETL infrastructure is often the most time- and resource-consuming part of the data warehouse development process.

Developing Front-End (BI) Applications

The process of **developing front-end (BI) applications** refers to designing and creating applications for indirect use by the end users. Front-end applications are included in most data warehousing systems and are often referred to as business intelligence (BI) applications. Data warehouse front-end applications usually contain interfaces, such as forms and reports accessible via a navigation mechanism, such as a menu.

As illustrated by Figure 7.8, the design and creation of data warehouse front-end applications can take place in parallel with data warehouse creation. For example, the look and feel of the front-end applications, as well as the number and functionalities of particular components (e.g., forms and reports), can be determined before the data warehouse is implemented. This can be done based on the data warehouse model and the requirements specifying the capabilities and functionalities of the system needed by the end users. Of course, the actual creation of the front-end application involves connecting it to the implemented data warehouse, which can only be done once the data warehouse is implemented.

Data Warehouse Deployment

After the data warehouse and its associated front-end applications are implemented, the next step is **data warehouse deployment**. This step involves releasing the data warehouse and its front-end applications for use to the end users. Typically, prior to this step, the initial load populating the implemented data warehouse with an initial set of data from the operational data sources via the ETL infrastructure is executed.

Data Warehouse Use

Once the data warehouse is deployed, end users engage in **data warehouse use**. Data warehouse use involves the retrieval of the data contained within the data warehouse. The data warehouse can be used by the end users indirectly via the front-end applications. Data warehouses can also be accessed directly by using the language of the data management software used to host the data warehouse. For example, relational data warehouses can be queried directly by issuing SQL statements. However, a much more common type of direct data warehouse use occurs when end users engage in an ad-hoc analytical querying of data warehouses via the so-called online analytical processing (OLAP) tools, which are also known as business intelligence (BI) tools.[1]

Data Warehouse Administration and Maintenance

To support end users engaging in data warehouse use, various **data warehouse administration and maintenance** activities are undertaken. Similar to operational database administration and maintenance activities, data warehouse administration and maintenance activities include dealing with technical issues, such as providing security for the information contained in the data warehouse, ensuring sufficient hard-drive space for the data warehouse content, or implementing backup and recovery procedures.

THE NEXT VERSION OF THE DATA WAREHOUSE

Typically, a data warehouse in use is followed by another iteration of the data warehouse. The new version of the data warehouse should be created following the same development steps, as shown in Figure 7.10.

As with the initial version of the data warehouse, the development of subsequent versions of the data warehouse will start with the requirements collection, definition, and visualization step. Of course, unlike the initial version, in the subsequent versions, not all requirements will be collected from scratch. Original requirements provide the starting point for additions and alterations. Many of the additions and modifications result from observations by the end users during the use of the previous version indicating the ways in which the data warehouse can be improved or expanded. Other new requirements may stem from changes in the operational data sources or changes in underlying technology. As with any other information system, new subsequent versions are practically inevitable in data warehousing.

---

[1] OLAP/BI Tools are elaborated on in Chapter 9.

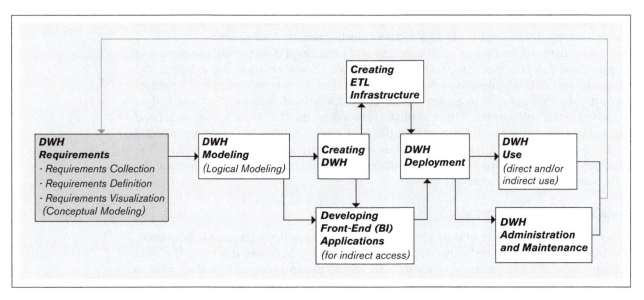

FIGURE 7.10   The development of the next version of the data warehouse.

This chapter provided an overview of the basic data warehousing concepts. Chapters 8 and 9 will give more detail about concepts introduced here. Chapter 8 focuses on data warehouse modeling, and Chapter 9 covers the issues related to the subsequent data warehouse development activities.

Key Terms

Analytical information *207*
Application-oriented *210*
Creating ETL infrastructure *220*
Creating the data warehouse *220*
Data mart *216*
Data warehouse *212*

Data warehouse administration and maintenance *221*
Data warehouse deployment *221*
Data warehouse modeling *220*
Data warehouse use *221*

Dependent data mart *217*
Developing front-end (BI) applications *220*
Extraction-transformation-load (ETL) *216*
Independent data mart *216*

Operational information (transactional information) *207*
Requirements collection, definition, and visualization *218*
Source systems *215*
Subject-oriented *210*

Review Questions

Q7.1   What is the primary purpose of a data warehouse?

Q7.2   Why is a data warehouse created as a separate data store?

Q7.3   Describe the data time-horizon difference between operational and analytical data.

Q7.4   Describe the data level-of-detail difference between operational and analytical data.

Q7.5   Describe the data time-representation difference between operational and analytical data.

Q7.6   Describe the difference in queried amounts of data and frequency of queries between operational and analytical data.

Q7.7   Describe the data update difference between operational and analytical data.

Q7.8   Describe the data redundancy difference between operational and analytical data.

Q7.9   Describe the data audience difference between operational and analytical data.

Q7.10   Describe the data orientation difference between operational and analytical data.

Q7.11   Explain the following parts of the data warehouse definition:

- structured repository
- integrated
- subject oriented
- enterprise-wide
- historical
- time-variant
- developed for the retrieval of analytical information
- may include the data at the fine level of detail or summary data or both

Q7.12 What are the major components of a data warehousing system?

Q7.13 What is a data mart?

Q7.14 What is the difference between a dependent and independent data mart?

Q7.15 What are the steps in the development of data warehouses?

Q7.16 Explain the iterative nature of the warehouse requirements collection, definition, and visualization process.

Q7.17 Briefly describe the process of creating a data warehouse.

Q7.18 Briefly describe the process of creating ETL infrastructure.

Q7.19 Briefly describe the process of developing data warehouse front-end (BI) applications.

Q7.20 What takes place during data warehouse deployment?

Q7.21 What constitutes data warehouse use?

Q7.22 Give examples of data warehouse administration and maintenance activities.

Q7.23 What are the similarities and differences between the development of the initial and subsequent versions of the data warehouse?

Data Warehouse and Data Mart Modeling

INTRODUCTION

Earlier in this book, we gave a detailed overview of the modeling process of operational databases. In Chapter 2, we described the details of ER modeling, a predominant technique for visualizing database requirements used extensively for conceptual modeling of operational databases. In Chapter 3, we gave a detailed overview of relational modeling as the standard method for logical modeling of operational databases. Both these techniques can also be used during the development of data warehouses and data marts. In addition to these two methods, a modeling technique known as dimensional modeling, tailored specifically for analytical database design purposes, is regularly used in practice for modeling data warehouses and data marts.

In the first part of this chapter, we will give a detailed overview of dimensional modeling. In the second part, we will give an overview of the most commonly used data warehouse modeling strategies with respect to how they utilize ER modeling, relational modeling, and dimensional modeling.

DIMENSIONAL MODELING: BASIC CONCEPTS

Dimensional modeling is a data design methodology used for designing subject-oriented analytical databases (i.e., data, warehouses or data marts). Commonly, dimensional modeling is employed as a relational data modeling technique. As a relational modeling technique, dimensional modeling designs relational tables that have primary keys and are connected to each other via foreign keys, while conforming to the standard relational integrity constraints. In addition to using the regular relational concepts (primary keys, foreign keys, integrity constraints, etc.), dimensional modeling distinguishes two types of tables—dimensions and facts:

- **Dimension tables (dimensions)** contain descriptions of the business, organization, or enterprise to which the subject of analysis belongs. Columns in dimension tables contain descriptive information that is often textual (e.g., product brand, product color, customer gender, customer education level), but can also be numeric (e.g., product weight, customer income level). This information provides a basis for analysis of the subject. For example, if the subject of the business analysis is sales, it can be analyzed by product brand, customer gender, customer income level, and so on.
- **Fact tables** contain measures related to the subject of analysis. In addition, fact tables contain foreign keys associating them with dimension tables. The measures in the fact tables are typically numeric and are intended for mathematical

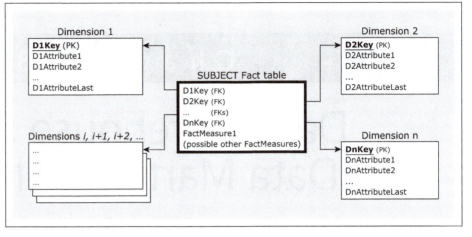

FIGURE 8.1   A dimensional model (star schema).

computation and quantitative analysis. For example, if the subject of the business analysis is sales, one of the measures in the fact table sales could be the sale's dollar amount. The sale amounts can be calculated and recalculated using different mathematical functions across various dimension columns. For example, the total and average sale can be calculated per product brand, customer gender, customer income level, and so on.

The result of relational dimensional modeling is a dimensional relational schema containing facts and dimensions, shown in Figure 8.1. The dimensional schema is often referred to as the **star schema**.

A dimension table contains a primary key and attributes that are used for analysis of the measures in the fact tables. A fact table contains fact-measure attributes and foreign keys that connect the fact table to the dimension tables. In this book, we mark fact tables with a bolded thicker frame to distinguish them from the dimension tables in the figures. The primary key of a fact table is a composite key that combines foreign key columns and/or other columns in the fact table (we will elaborate on this later in this chapter).

Even though any order of columns in a fact table (or in any table, for that matter) is acceptable, for readability reasons, in examples of star schema in this book we will always show measures in the fact table as the last columns in the table.

INITIAL EXAMPLE: DIMENSIONAL MODEL BASED ON A SINGLE SOURCE

The following example illustrates the basic concepts of dimensional modeling. This example uses the same fictional scenario involving the database for the ZAGI Retail Company Sales Department used in Chapters 2 and 3. Figures illustrating the ZAGI Retail Company Sales Department Database and its records are repeated here for convenience.

Figure 8.2 (same as Figure 3.32) shows the ER diagram and the resulting relational schema for the ZAGI Retail Company Sales Department Database.

Figure 8.3 (same as Figure 3.33) shows the records in the relational database for the ZAGI Retail Company Sales Department Database.

Based on its operational database (the ZAGI Retail Company Sales Department Database) shown in Figures 8.2 and 8.3, the ZAGI Retail Company decides to use the dimensional modeling technique to design an analytical database whose subject of analysis is *sales*. The result of this process is the star schema shown in Figure 8.4.

In the star schema, the chosen subject of analysis is represented by a fact table. In this example, the chosen subject of analysis (sales) is represented by the SALES fact table.

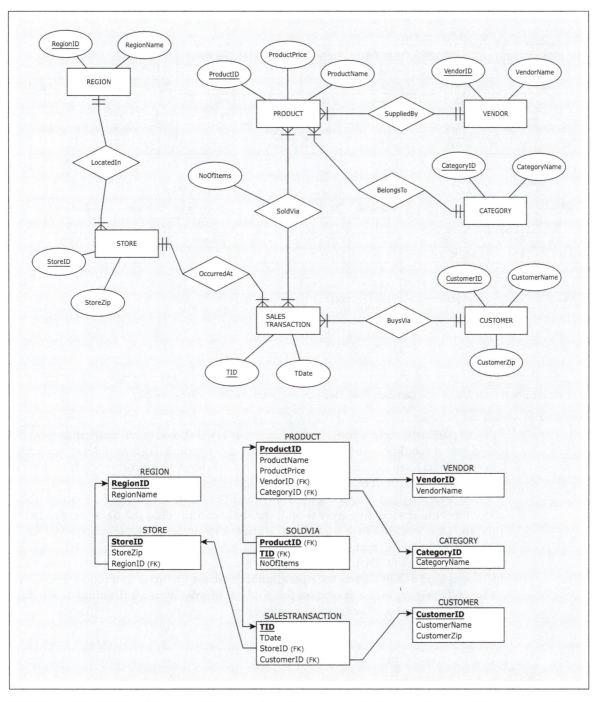

FIGURE 8.2 The ZAGI Retail Company Sales Department Database—an ER diagram and the resulting relational schema.

Designing the star schema involves considering which dimensions to use with the fact table representing the chosen subject. For every dimension under consideration, two questions must be answered:

Question 1: *Can the dimension be useful for the analysis of the chosen subject?*

Question 2: *Can the dimension be created based on the existing data sources?*

In this particular example, the only available data source is the ZAGI Retail Company Sales Department Database shown in Figures 8.2 and 8.3.

The star schema in Figure 8.4 contains four dimensions. The dimensions are named PRODUCT, STORE, CUSTOMER, and CALENDAR. For each of these dimensions, the answer to both Question 1 and Question 2 was *yes*.

REGION

RegionID	RegionName
C	Chicagoland
T	Tristate

STORE

StoreID	StoreZip	RegionID
S1	60600	C
S2	60605	C
S3	35400	T

PRODUCT

ProductID	ProductName	ProductPrice	VendorID	CategoryID
1X1	Zzz Bag	$100	PG	CP
2X2	Easy Boot	$70	MK	FW
3X3	Cosy Sock	$15	MK	FW
4X4	Dura Boot	$90	PG	FW
5X5	Tiny Tent	$150	MK	CP
6X6	Biggy Tent	$250	MK	CP

VENDOR

VendorID	VendorName
PG	Pacifica Gear
MK	Mountain King

CATEGORY

CategoryID	CategoryName
CP	Camping
FW	Footwear

SALESTRANSACTION

TID	CustomerID	StoreID	TDate
T111	1-2-333	S1	1-Jan-2013
T222	2-3-444	S2	1-Jan-2013
T333	1-2-333	S3	2-Jan-2013
T444	3-4-555	S3	2-Jan-2013
T555	2-3-444	S3	2-Jan-2013

SOLDVIA

ProductID	TID	NoOfItems
1X1	T111	1
2X2	T222	1
3X3	T333	5
1X1	T333	1
4X4	T444	1
2X2	T444	2
4X4	T555	4
5X5	T555	2
6X6	T555	1

CUSTOMER

CustomerID	CustomerName	CustomerZip
1-2-333	Tina	60137
2-3-444	Tony	60611
3-4-555	Pam	35401

FIGURE 8.3 Data records for the ZAGI Retail Company Sales Department Database shown in Figure 8.2.

In particular, when considering Question 1, the dimensional modeling team decided that it would be useful to analyze sales per product, customer, store, and date. Therefore, the team decided to *consider creating* the dimensions corresponding to those areas of analysis (product, customer, store, and date).

An examination of Question 2 confirmed that for each of the dimensions under consideration, the existing operational database can provide the data source. Therefore, the team decided to *create* all four dimensions under consideration: PRODUCT, CUSTOMER, STORE, and DATE.

Dimension PRODUCT is the result of joining table PRODUCT with tables VENDOR and CATEGORY from the operational database, in order to include the vendor name and category name. It enables the analysis of sales across individual products as well as across products' vendors and categories.

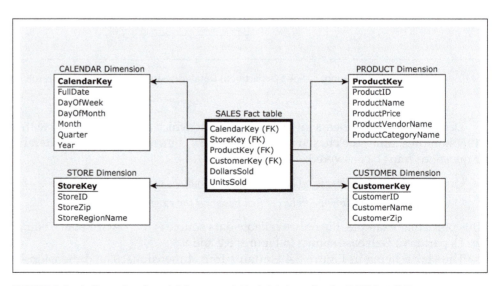

FIGURE 8.4 A dimensional model for an analytical database for the ZAGI Retail Company, whose subject of analysis is sales.

CALENDAR Dimension

CalendarKey	FullDate	DayOf Week	DayOf Month	Month	Qtr	Year
1	1/1/2013	Tuesday	1	January	Q1	2013
2	1/2/2013	Wednesday	2	January	Q1	2013

PRODUCT Dimension

ProductKey	ProductID	Product Name	Product Price	Product Vendor Name	Product Category Name
1	1X1	Zzz Bag	$100	Pacifica Gear	Camping
2	2X2	Easy Boot	$70	Mountain King	Footwear
3	3X3	Cosy Sock	$15	Mountain King	Footwear
4	4X4	Dura Boot	$90	Pacifica Gear	Footwear
5	5X5	Tiny Tent	$150	Mountain King	Camping
6	6X6	Biggy Tent	$250	Mountain King	Camping

STORE Dimension

StoreKey	StoreID	StoreZip	StoreRegionName
1	S1	60600	Chicagoland
2	S2	60605	Chicagoland
3	S3	35400	Tristate

CUSTOMER Dimension

CustomerKey	CustomerID	CustomerName	CustomerZip
1	1-2-333	Tina	60137
2	2-3-444	Tony	60611
3	3-4-555	Pam	35401

SALES Fact table

CalendarKey	StoreKey	ProductKey	CustomerKey	DollarsSold	UnitsSold
1	1	1	1	$100	1
1	2	2	2	$70	1
2	3	3	1	$75	5
2	3	1	1	$100	1
2	3	4	3	$90	1
2	3	2	3	$140	2
2	3	4	2	$360	4
2	3	5	2	$300	2
2	3	6	2	$250	1

FIGURE 8.5   A dimensional model for the analysis of sales in the ZAGI Retail Company populated with the data from the operational data source.

Dimension CUSTOMER is equivalent to the table CUSTOMER from the operational database. It enables the analysis of sales across individual customers as well as across customers' zip codes.

Dimension STORE is the result of joining table STORE with table REGION from the operational database, in order to include the region name. It enables the analysis of sales across individual stores as well as across store regions and zip codes.

Dimension CALENDAR captures the range of the dates found in the TDate (date of sale) column in the SALESTRANSACTION table in the operational database. Date-related analysis is one of the most common types of subject analysis. For example, analyzing sales across months or quarters is a common date-related analysis. Virtually every star schema includes a dimension containing date-related information. In this example, dimension CALENDAR fulfills that role. The structure of the CALENDAR dimension is expanded by breaking down the full date into individual components corresponding to various calendar-related attributes (such as quarter, month, year, and day of the week) that can be useful for analysis.

Figure 8.5 shows the populated tables of the star schema shown in Figure 8.4. All of the data shown in each table in Figure 8.5 was sourced from the data in the operational database source (the ZAGI Retail Company Sales Department Database) shown in Figure 8.3.

Each record in the SALES fact table represents purchases of a particular product by a particular customer in a particular store on a particular day.

In Figure 8.5, the primary key of the SALES fact table is not depicted. Later in this chapter, we will discuss the primary keys of fact tables. This discussion will include the depiction of the primary key of the SALES fact table.

CHARACTERISTICS OF DIMENSIONS AND FACTS AND THE ANALYSIS OF THE INITIAL EXAMPLE

In a typical, properly designed star schema, the number of records (rows) in any of the dimension tables is relatively small when compared to the number of records in a fact table. A typical dimension contains relatively static data, while in a typical fact table, records are added continually, and the table rapidly grows in size. Hence, in a typical dimensionally modeled analytical database, dimension tables have orders of magnitude fewer records than fact tables.

For example, in the case of the ZAGI Retail Company, if the dimensionally modeled analytical database shown in Figures 8.4 and 8.5 were to hold 10 years' worth of data, the dimension CALENDAR would have 3,652 records (365×10 days + 2 days for each leap year, as we are assuming 2 leap years in this particular 10-year period). Assuming that the ZAGI Retail Company has 100 stores and 100,000 customers, and carries 5,000 different items, the dimensions STORE, CUSTOMER, and PRODUCT would have 100, 100,000, and 5,000 records, respectively. Even if we make a very conservative estimate that each store has only 200 unique daily customers purchasing on average only 3 items a day, the fact table will have 219,120,000 records ($200 \times 3 \times 100 \times 3,652$ records), which is orders of magnitude more than the number of records in any of the dimensions.

Typically, in a star schema all dimension tables are given a simple, non-composite system-generated key, also called a **surrogate key**. In Figure 8.4, the dimension CALENDAR has a surrogate key CalendarKey, dimension PRODUCT has a surrogate key ProductKey, dimension STORE has a surrogate key StoreKey, and dimension CUSTOMER has a surrogate key CustomerKey. Values for those keys, as shown in Figure 8.5, are simple autonumber integer values. Surrogate key values have no meaning or purpose except to give each dimension a new column that serves as a primary key within the dimensional model instead of the operational key. For example, instead of using the primary key ProductID from the PRODUCT table in the operational database as the primary key of the PRODUCT dimension, a new surrogate key column ProductKey is created. One of the main reasons for creating a surrogate primary key (e.g., ProductKey), and not using the operational primary key (e.g., ProductID) as a primary key of the dimension, is to enable the handling of so-called slowly changing dimensions. Slowly changing dimensions will be covered later in this chapter.

In the dimensionally modeled database shown in Figures 8.4 and 8.5, the ZAGI Retail Company can now easily create analytical queries, such as:

Query A: *Compare the quantities of sold products on Saturdays in the category Camping provided by the vendor Pacifica Gear within the Tristate region between the 1st and 2nd quarter of the year 2013.*

Such queries in dimensionally modeled databases can be issued by using SQL or by using so-called OLAP/BI tools (covered in Chapter 9).

First consider the following SQL versions of *Query A* using the dimensional (Figures 8.4 and 8.5) database.

SQL Query A - dimensional version (using Figure 8.5):

```
SELECT  SUM(SA.UnitsSold)
,       P.ProductCategoryName
,       P.ProductVendorName
,       C.DayofWeek
,       C.Qtr
FROM
        Calendar C
,       Store    S
,       Product  P
,       Sales    SA
WHERE
        C.CalendarKey        =   SA.CalendarKey
AND     S.StoreKey           =   SA.StoreKey
AND     P.ProductKey         =   SA.ProductKey
AND     P.ProductVendorName  =   'Pacifica Gear'
AND     P.ProductCategoryName =  'Camping'
AND     S.StoreRegionName    =   'Tristate'
AND     C.DayofWeek          =   'Saturday'
AND     C.Year               =   2013
AND     C.Qtr                IN  ( 'Q1', 'Q2' )
```

```
GROUP BY
        P.ProductCategoryName,
        P.ProductVendorName,
        C.DayofWeek,
        C.Qtr;
```

Now consider the following SQL versions of *Query A* using the nondimensional (Figures 8.2 and 8.3) database. Within the following example, we will use the functions to extract the year, quarter, and day of the week from the date.[1]

SQL Query A – nondimensional version (using Figure 8.3):

```
SELECT  SUM( SV.NoOfItems )
,       C.CategoryName
,       V.VendorName
,       EXTRACTWEEKDAY(ST.Date)
,       EXTRACTQUARTER(ST.Date)
FROM
        Region      R
,       Store       S
,       SalesTransaction ST
,       SoldVia     SV
,       Product     P
,       Vendor      V
,       Category    C
WHERE
        R.RegionID      =   S.RegionID
AND     S.StoreID       =   ST.StoreID
AND     ST.Tid          =   SV.Tid
AND     SV.ProductID    =   P.ProductID
AND     P.VendorID      =   V.VendorID
AND     P.CateoryID     =   C.CategoryID
AND     V.VendorName    =   'Pacifica Gear'
AND     C.CategoryName  =   'Camping'
AND     R.RegionName    =   'Tristate'
AND     EXTRACTWEEKDAY(St.Date) =   'Saturday'
AND     EXTRACTYEAR(ST.Date)    =   2013
AND     EXTRACTQUARTER(ST.Date) IN ( 'Q1', 'Q2' )
GROUP BY
        C.CategoryName,
        V.VendorName,
        EXTRACTWEEKDAY(ST.Date),
        EXTRACTQUARTER(ST.Date);
```

Compare the two queries to observe the simplicity advantage for the analyst issuing a query on the dimensional model. Note that *SQL Query A – dimensional version* joins the fact table with three of its dimensions, while *SQL Query A – nondimensional version* joins seven tables and uses functions to extract the year, quarter, and day of the week from the date.

This small example illustrates that, even in a simple case when the dimensional model is based on a small single source, analytical queries on the dimensionally modeled database can be significantly simpler to create than on the equivalent nondimensional database. The convenience of analysis with the dimensionally modeled data is even more evident in cases when data necessary for analysis resides in multiple sources. Situations when analytically useful data is located in multiple separate data systems and stores within an organization are very common. The following example illustrates the usage of dimensional modeling in such situations.

EXPANDED EXAMPLE: DIMENSIONAL MODEL BASED ON MULTIPLE SOURCES

The initial dimensional modeling example illustrated by Figures 8.4 and 8.5 depicts a scenario when an analytical database is based on a single source (a singular operational database: the ZAGI Retail Company Sales Department Database, shown in Figures 8.2 and 8.3).

---

[1] To simplify the example, we use generic EXTRACTYEAR(Date), EXTRACTQUARTER(Date), and EXTRACTWEEKDAY(Date) functions. In reality, the syntax and complexity of SQL functions for extracting year, quarter, and weekday vary from one DBMS to another.

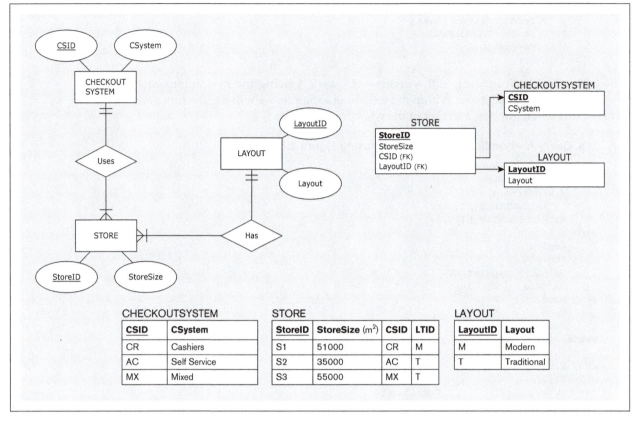

FIGURE 8.6 The ZAGI Retail Company Facilities Department Database ER model, relational model, and populated tables.

More commonly, data warehouses and data marts draw data from multiple sources. The following expansion of the initial example using the scenario of the ZAGI Retail Company adds two additional data sources:

- Within the ZAGI Retail Company, in addition to the Sales Department Database shown in Figures 8.2 and 8.3, the facilities department maintains a database that contains the following information about the physical details of each of the individual stores: Store Size, Store Layout, and Store Checkout System. The ZAGI Retail Company Facilities Department Database is shown in Figure 8.6. ZAGI Retail Company analysts decided that the data about physical details of stores would add a useful aspect of the analysis of sales data and, therefore, the dimensional model was expanded to account for this data as well.
- ZAGI Retail Company analysts decided that demographic data would provide another useful aspect of sales data analysis. The ZAGI Retail Company does not maintain demographic-related data of its customers in any of its operational databases. Instead, the ZAGI Retail Company acquired the demographic-related data table for its customers from a market research company. This acquired external data source Customer Demographic Data Table is shown in Figure 8.7. This external source was used to further expand the dimensional model.

CUSTOMER TABLE

CustomerID	Customer Name	Gender	Marital Status	Education Level	Credit Score
1-2-333	Tina	Female	Single	College	700
2-3-444	Tony	Male	Single	High School	650
3-4-555	Pam	Female	Married	College	623

FIGURE 8.7 A customer demographic data table (external source acquired from a market research company).

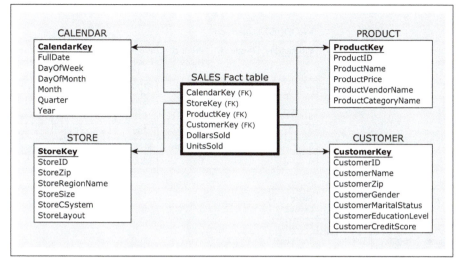

FIGURE 8.8 An expanded dimensional model for the analysis of sales in the ZAGI Retail Company, based on multiple sources.

Figure 8.8 shows an expanded dimensional model that is now based on three different data sources: two internal operational databases (the ZAGI Retail Company Sales Department Database shown in Figures 8.2 and 8.3, and the ZAGI Retail Company Facilities Department Database in Figure 8.6) and one external source (the Customer Demographic Data Table shown in Figure 8.7). Note that the data source ZAGI Retail Company Facilities Department Database enabled the addition of columns StoreSize, StoreCSystem, and StoreLayout to the dimension STORE. Also note that the external data source Customer Demographic Data Table enabled the addition of columns CustomerGender, CustomerMaritalStatus, CustomerEducationLevel, and CustomerCreditScore to the dimension CUSTOMER.

Figure 8.9 shows the populated tables of the dimensional model shown in Figure 8.8.

The ZAGI Retail Company can now ask even more refined analytical questions that consider a larger variety of analysis factors. For example, consider the following question.

Query B: *Compare the quantities of sold products to male customers in Modern stores on Saturdays in the category Camping provided by the vendor Pacifica Gear within the Tristate region between the 1st and 2nd quarter of the year 2013.*

To obtain the answer to the *Query B* from the operational sources, a user would have to issue several queries spanning all three operational sources and then combine the results of those queries to receive the final answer.

Obtaining the answer to *Query B* using the dimensionally modeled database shown in Figure 8.9 is much more straightforward. *SQL Query B – dimensional version* involves a simple extension of *SQL Query A – dimensional version*:

SQL Query B – dimensional version (using Figure 8.9):

```
SELECT  SUM(SA.UnitsSold)
,       P.ProductCategoryName
,       P.ProductVendorName
,       C.DayofWeek
,       C.Qtr
FROM
        Calendar  C
,       Store     S
,       Product   P
,       Customer  CU
,       Sales     SA
WHERE
        C.CalendarKey     = SA.CalendarKey
AND     S.StoreKey        = SA.StoreKey
AND     P.ProductKey      = SA.ProductKey
AND     CU.CustomerKey    = SA.CustomerKey
```

CALENDAR Dimension

CalendarKey	FullDate	DayOf Week	DayOf Month	Month	Qtr	Year
1	1/1/2013	Tuesday	1	January	Q1	2013
2	1/2/2013	Wednesday	2	January	Q1	2013

PRODUCT Dimension

ProductKey	ProductID	Product Name	Product Price	Product Vendor Name	Product Category Name
1	1X1	Zzz Bag	$100	Pacifica Gear	Camping
2	2X2	Easy Boot	$70	Mountain King	Footwear
3	3X3	Cosy Sock	$15	Mountain King	Footwear
4	4X4	Dura Boot	$90	Pacifica Gear	Footwear
5	5X5	Tiny Tent	$150	Mountain King	Camping
6	6X6	Biggy Tent	$250	Mountain King	Camping

STORE Dimension

StoreKey	StoreID	StoreZip	StoreRegion Name	Store Size (m²)	Store CSystem	Store Layout
1	S1	60600	Chicagoland	51000	Cashiers	Modern
2	S2	60605	Chicagoland	35000	Self Service	Traditional
3	S3	35400	Tristate	55000	Mixed	Traditional

CUSTOMER Dimension

CustomerKey	CustomerID	Customer Name	Customer Zip	Customer Gender	Customer MaritalStatus	Customer EducationLevel	Customer CreditScore
1	1-2-333	Tina	60137	Female	Single	College	700
2	2-3-444	Tony	60611	Male	Single	High School	650
3	3-4-555	Pam	35401	Female	Married	College	623

SALES Fact table

CalendarKey	StoreKey	ProductKey	CustomerKey	DollarsSold	UnitsSold
1	1	1	1	$100	1
1	2	2	2	$70	1
2	3	3	1	$75	5
2	3	1	1	$100	1
2	3	4	3	$90	1
2	3	2	3	$140	2
2	3	4	2	$360	4
2	3	5	2	$300	2
2	3	6	2	$250	1

FIGURE 8.9 An expanded dimensional model for the analysis of sales in the ZAGI Retail Company, populated with the data from multiple sources.

```
AND   P.ProductVendorName    =    'Pacifica Gear'
AND   P.ProductCategoryName  =    'Camping'
AND   S.StoreRegionName      =    'Tristate'
AND   C.DayofWeek            =    'Saturday'
AND   C.Year                 =    2013
AND   C.Qtr                  IN   ( 'Q1', 'Q2' )
AND   S.StoreLayout          =    'Modern'
AND   CU.Gender              =    'Male'
GROUP BY
      P.ProductCategoryName,
      P.ProductVendorName,
      C.DayofWeek,
      C.Qtr;
```

A query using dimensionally modeled data, such as Query B above, could be created in an even simpler fashion by utilizing BI/OLAP tools (covered in Chapter 9).

ADDITIONAL POSSIBLE FACT ATTRIBUTES

As we discussed earlier in this chapter, a fact table contains foreign keys connecting it to the dimension tables and the measures related to the subject of analysis. For example, if the subject of the business analysis is sales, typical measures in the fact table

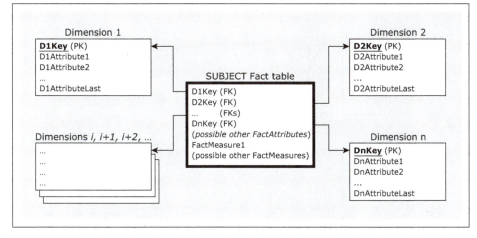

FIGURE 8.10 A dimensional model (star schema) with a fact table containing additional attributes.

sales are the sales' dollar amount and quantity. In addition to the measures related to the subject of analysis, in certain cases, fact tables can contain other attributes that are not measures, as illustrated by Figure 8.10. A row in the SUBJECT fact table (named *possible other FactAttributes*) indicates that the fact table can contain other possible attributes that are not measures.

Two of the most typical additional attributes that can appear in the fact table are the **transaction identifier** and the **transaction time**. We will demonstrate these two additional attributes using the ZAGI Retail Company example.

TRANSACTION IDENTIFIER IN THE FACT TABLE

First, we will demonstrate the transaction identifier concept. Notice that in the ZAGI Retail Company Sales Department Database shown in Figures 8.2 and 8.3, the SALES TRANSACTION relation has a transaction identifier column TID. The TID values do not appear at first glance to have any analytical value. For example, analyzing the sales whose TID ends with an even digit versus the sales whose TID ends with an odd digit is not likely to provide any business insight into sales. However, for certain types of analysis, the TID values *can* provide additional insight. For example, in the case of the ZAGI Retail Company, the TID value can provide information about which products were sold within the same individual transaction. Such information is useful for a variety of analytical tasks. One type of analysis that seeks to establish which products often sell together is commonly referred to as market basket analysis (also known as "association rule mining" or "affinity grouping," covered in Appendix H). Including the TID in the dimensional model would allow business analysts to use this type of analysis.

Once the decision is made to include the TID in the dimensional model, the question remains: Where in the star schema should the TID appear? At first glance, one option is to create a separate TRANSACTION dimension, which would include the TID attribute. However, as we mentioned earlier in this chapter, in a typical properly designed star schema, the number of records (rows) in any of the dimension tables is relatively small when compared to the number of records (rows) in the fact table. If we decided to create a separate TRANSACTION dimension, the number of records in that dimension would be at the same order of magnitude (e.g., millions or billions of records) as the number of records in the SALES fact table and, at the same time, at orders of magnitude higher than the number of records in any other dimension.

A more practical approach is to include the TID as an additional column in the fact table, as shown in Figure 8.11. This simple approach still enables the analysis that considers which products were sold within the same transaction, without the need for creating an additional dimension that would contain an enormous number of records. In practice, the transaction identifier can be represented as sales transaction identifier, order identifier, rental identifier, ticket identifier, bill identifier, and so on. The

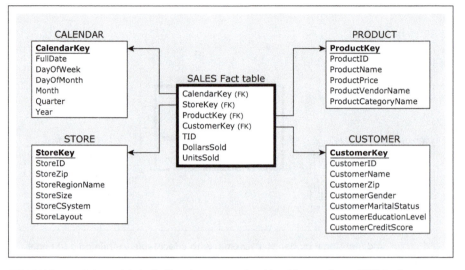

FIGURE 8.11 A fact table including the transaction identifier attribute (TID) in the dimensional model for the analysis of sales in ZAGI Retail.

CALENDAR Dimension

CalendarKey	FullDate	DayOf Week	DayOf Month	Month	Qtr	Year
1	1/1/2013	Tuesday	1	January	Q1	2013
2	1/2/2013	Wednesday	2	January	Q1	2013

PRODUCT Dimension

ProductKey	ProductID	Product Name	Product Price	Product Vendor Name	Product Category Name
1	1X1	Zzz Bag	$100	Pacifica Gear	Camping
2	2X2	Easy Boot	$70	Mountain King	Footwear
3	3X3	Cosy Sock	$15	Mountain King	Footwear
4	4X4	Dura Boot	$90	Pacifica Gear	Footwear
5	5X5	Tiny Tent	$150	Mountain King	Camping
6	6X6	Biggy Tent	$250	Mountain King	Camping

STORE Dimension

StoreKey	StoreID	StoreZip	StoreRegion Name	Store Size (m²)	Store CSystem	Store Layout
1	S1	60600	Chicagoland	51000	Cashiers	Modern
2	S2	60605	Chicagoland	35000	Self Service	Traditional
3	S3	35400	Tristate	55000	Mixed	Traditional

CUSTOMER Dimension

CustomerKey	CustomerID	Customer Name	Customer Zip	Customer Gender	Customer MaritalStatus	Customer EducationLevel	Customer CreditScore
1	1-2-333	Tina	60137	Female	Single	College	700
2	2-3-444	Tony	60611	Male	Single	High School	650
3	3-4-555	Pam	35401	Female	Married	College	623

SALES Fact table

CalendarKey	StoreKey	ProductKey	CustomerKey	TID	DollarsSold	UnitsSold
1	1	1	1	T111	$100	1
1	2	2	2	T222	$70	1
2	3	3	1	T333	$75	5
2	3	1	1	T333	$100	1
2	3	4	3	T444	$90	1
2	3	2	3	T444	$140	2
2	3	4	2	T555	$360	4
2	3	5	2	T555	$300	2
2	3	6	2	T555	$250	1

FIGURE 8.12 Records for the dimensional model shown in Figure 8.11 (TID values included).

approach of including a transaction identifier in the fact table is often referred to in the literature and practice as a **degenerate dimension**, where the term "degenerate" signifies "mathematically simpler than." The term merely indicates that it is simpler to include an event identifier within the fact table than to create a separate dimension for it.

Figure 8.12 shows the records in the dimensions and the fact table in the dimensional model shown in Figure 8.11.

TRANSACTION TIME IN THE FACT TABLE

In order to examine the transaction time concept, we slightly expand the ZAGI Retail Company example. We expand the diagram shown in Figure 8.2 by adding the transaction time (TTime) attribute to the SALES TRANSACTION entity and to the resulting SALESTRANSACTION relation as illustrated by Figure 8.13. All other elements of the ER diagram and the relational schema in Figure 8.13 remain unchanged from Figure 8.2.

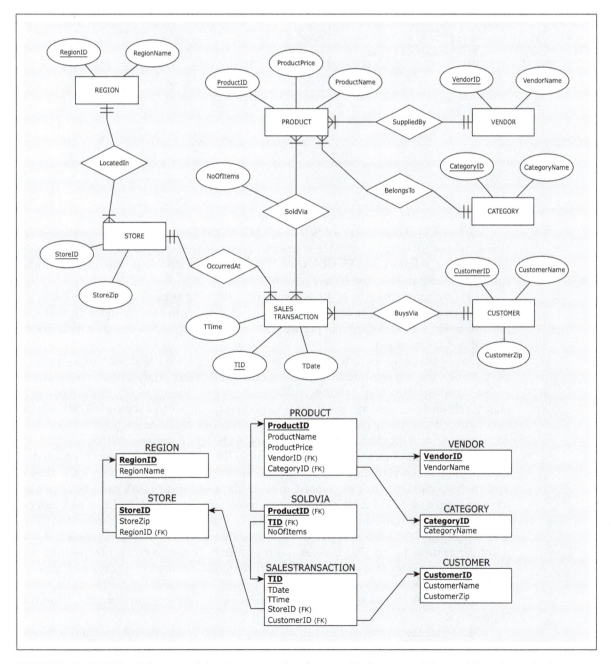

FIGURE 8.13 ZAGI Retail Company Sales Department Database: an ER diagram and the resulting relational schema (TTime attribute added).

REGION

RegionID	RegionName
C	Chicagoland
T	Tristate

STORE

StoreID	StoreZip	RegionID
S1	60600	C
S2	60605	C
S3	35400	T

PRODUCT

ProductID	ProductName	ProductPrice	VendorID	CategoryID
1X1	Zzz Bag	$100	PG	CP
2X2	Easy Boot	$70	MK	FW
3X3	Cosy Sock	$15	MK	FW
4X4	Dura Boot	$90	PG	FW
5X5	Tiny Tent	$150	MK	CP
6X6	Biggy Tent	$250	MK	CP

VENDOR

VendorID	VendorName
PG	Pacifica Gear
MK	Mountain King

CATEGORY

CategoryID	CategoryName
CP	Camping
FW	Footwear

SALESTRANSACTION

TID	CustomerID	StoreID	TDate	TTime
T111	1-2-333	S1	1-Jan-2013	8:23:59 AM
T222	2-3-444	S1	1-Jan-2013	8:24:30 AM
T333	1-2-333	S3	2-Jan-2013	8:15:08 AM
T444	3-4-555	S3	2-Jan-2013	8:20:33 AM
T555	2-3-444	S3	2-Jan-2013	8:30:00 AM

SOLDVIA

ProductID	TID	NoOfItems
1X1	T111	1
2X2	T222	1
3X3	T333	5
1X1	T333	1
4X4	T444	1
2X2	T444	2
4X4	T555	4
5X5	T555	2
6X6	T555	1

CUSTOMER

CustomerID	CustomerName	CustomerZip
1-2-333	Tina	60137
2-3-444	Tony	60611
3-4-555	Pam	35401

FIGURE 8.14 Data records for the ZAGI Retail Company Sales Department Database shown in Figure 8.13 (time values added).

Figure 8.14 shows the records in the ZAGI Retail Company Sales Department Database, whose ER diagram and the relational schema are shown in Figure 8.13. Column TTime in the relation SALESTRANSACTION is populated with the data. All other columns remain unchanged from Figure 8.3.

Let us assume that the business analysts analyzing subject sales in the ZAGI Retail Company would like to incorporate the time of day into their analysis. In that case, the dimensional model shown in Figure 8.11 should be expanded so that it includes the time of day information.

One option is to include the time of day as a separate dimension or as a part of the CALENDAR dimension. In cases when the time of day analysis calls for relatively coarse time segments (e.g., *morning, midday, afternoon, evening, night*), this is a perfectly reasonable and practical approach, as it would result either in a separate TIME dimension with relatively few records (e.g., five records, one each for *morning, midday, afternoon, evening,* and *night* time periods) or in a CALENDAR dimension that is expanded by a relatively small factor (e.g., five records in the calendar dimension for each day, instead of one record in the calendar dimension for each day). However, if the time of day analysis calls for time expressed in seconds, a separate TIME dimension would have 86,400 records (24 × 60 × 60). Alternatively, an expanded CALENDAR dimension would contain millions of records (86,400 × number of days represented). Neither a separate TIME dimension nor the expanded CALENDAR dimension is a very practical approach. Adding time as another attribute to the fact table, as shown in Figure 8.15, represents a simpler approach that still allows for any type of time-of-day related business analysis.

Figure 8.16 shows the populated tables of the dimensional model shown in Figure 8.15.

Note that the concept of including a transaction identifier column and a time of day column in the fact table is applicable to any scenario in which event transactions, such as purchase transactions, orders, rentals, tickets, and bills, provide a basis for a fact table.

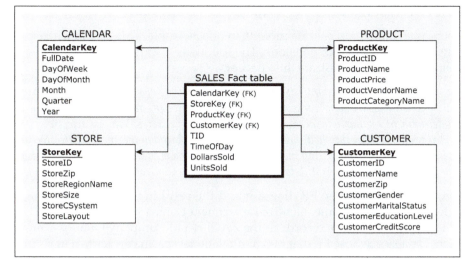

FIGURE 8.15 A fact table including the transaction time attribute (TimeOfDay) in the dimensional model for an analytical database for the analysis of sales in the ZAGI Retail Company.

CALENDAR Dimension

CalendarKey	FullDate	DayOf Week	DayOf Month	Month	Qtr	Year
1	1/1/2013	Tuesday	1	January	Q1	2013
2	1/2/2013	Wednesday	2	January	Q1	2013

PRODUCT Dimension

ProductKey	ProductID	Product Name	Product Price	Product Vendor Name	Product Category Name
1	1X1	Zzz Bag	$100	Pacifica Gear	Camping
2	2X2	Easy Boot	$70	Mountain King	Footwear
3	3X3	Cosy Sock	$15	Mountain King	Footwear
4	4X4	Dura Boot	$90	Pacifica Gear	Footwear
5	5X5	Tiny Tent	$150	Mountain King	Camping
6	6X6	Biggy Tent	$250	Mountain King	Camping

STORE Dimension

StoreKey	StoreID	StoreZip	StoreRegion Name	Store Size (m²)	Store CSystem	Store Layout
1	S1	60600	Chicagoland	51000	Cashiers	Modern
2	S2	60605	Chicagoland	35000	Self Service	Traditional
3	S3	35400	Tristate	55000	Mixed	Traditional

CUSTOMER Dimension

CustomerKey	CustomerID	Customer Name	Customer Zip	Customer Gender	Customer MaritalStatus	Customer EducationLevel	Customer CreditScore
1	1-2-333	Tina	60137	Female	Single	College	700
2	2-3-444	Tony	60611	Male	Single	High School	650
3	3-4-555	Pam	35401	Female	Married	College	623

SALES Fact table

CalendarKey	StoreKey	ProductKey	CustomerKey	TID	TimeOfDay	DollarsSold	UnitsSold
1	1	1	1	T111	8:23:59 AM	$100	1
1	2	2	2	T222	8:24:30 AM	$70	1
2	3	3	1	T333	8:15:08 AM	$75	5
2	3	1	1	T333	8:15:08 AM	$100	1
2	3	4	3	T444	8:20:33 AM	$90	1
2	3	2	3	T444	8:20:33 AM	$140	2
2	3	4	2	T555	8:30:00 AM	$360	4
2	3	5	2	T555	8:30:00 AM	$300	2
2	3	6	2	T555	8:30:00 AM	$250	1

FIGURE 8.16 A fact table populated with data, including the transaction identifier and time of day data.

MULTIPLE FACT TABLES IN A DIMENSIONAL MODEL

A dimensional model can contain more than one fact table. This occurs when multiple subjects of analysis share dimensions. The following example using the ZAGI Retail Company scenario will illustrate this concept.

Within the ZAGI Retail Company, in addition to the tracking of sales by the sales department, the quality control department tracks occurrences of defective products in its stores. The quality control department regularly inspects the shelves in all of the stores. When a defective product is found, it is removed from the shelf. For each instance of a found and removed defective product, the quality control department staff member immediately records the time, date, defect type, and product information in the ZAGI Retail Company Quality Control Department Database.

Figure 8.17 shows the ER diagram and the resulting relational schema of the ZAGI Retail Company Quality Control Department Database.

Figure 8.18 shows the records in the ZAGI Retail Company Quality Control Department Database, whose ER diagram and relational schema are shown in Figure 8.17.

In the ZAGI Retail Company, some of the information in the Quality Control Department Database overlaps with the information in the Sales Department

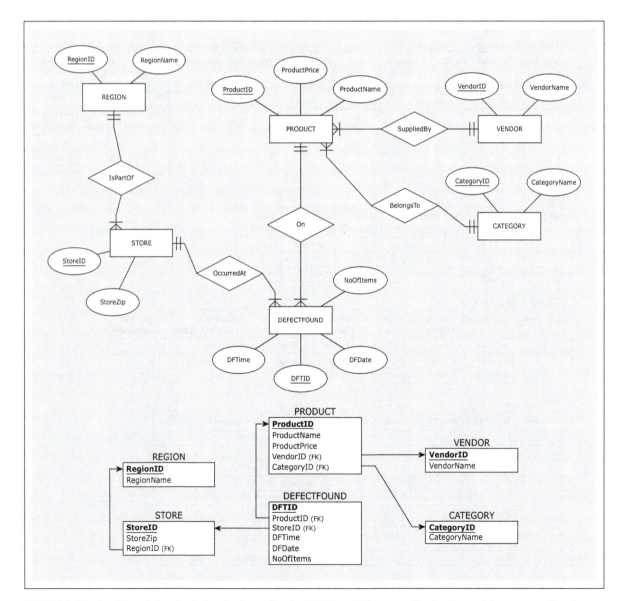

FIGURE 8.17 An ER model and relational schema for the ZAGI Retail Company Quality Control Department Database.

REGION

RegionID	RegionName
C	Chicagoland
T	Tristate

STORE

StoreID	StoreZip	RegionID
S1	60600	C
S2	60605	C
S3	35400	T

PRODUCT

ProductID	ProductName	ProductPrice	VendorID	CategoryID
1X1	Zzz Bag	$100	PG	CP
2X2	Easy Boot	$70	MK	FW
3X3	Cosy Sock	$15	MK	FW
4X4	Dura Boot	$90	PG	FW
5X5	Tiny Tent	$150	MK	CP
6X6	Biggy Tent	$250	MK	CP

DEFECTFOUND

DFTID	ProductID	StoreID	DFTDate	DFTTime	NoOfItems
DFT101	1X1	S1	1-Jan-2013	8:00:00 AM	1
DFT202	2X2	S2	1-Jan-2013	8:30:00 AM	2
DFT303	3X3	S3	2-Jan-2013	8:45:00 AM	6

VENDOR

VendorID	VendorName
PG	Pacifica Gear
MK	Mountain King

CATEGORY

CategoryID	CategoryName
CP	Camping
FW	Footwear

FIGURE 8.18   Data records for the ZAGI Retail Company Quality Control Department Database.

Database shown in Figures 8.13 and 8.14. For example, both databases contain information about the stores and products. As we mentioned in Chapter 7, it is very common for organizations to have separate operational databases with overlapping information.

The ZAGI Retail Company would like to analyze the defects in the same manner as they already analyze sales. The company makes a decision to create a dimensional model that will enable it to analyze the occurrences of defective products found in stores. The dimensions that are needed to analyze defects are already created for the dimensional model for the analysis of sales. Hence, the ZAGI Retail Company data modeling team can simply create another fact table for defects as a part of the already existing dimensional model, as opposed to creating a separate new dimensional model. This is shown in Figure 8.19.

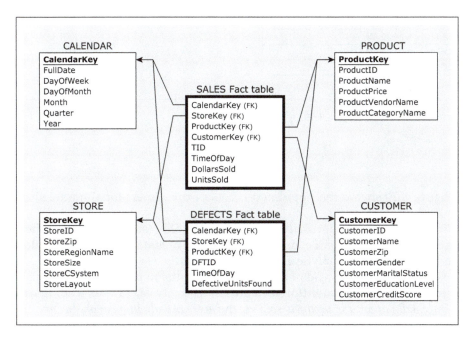

FIGURE 8.19   An expanded dimensional model with two subjects.

CALENDAR Dimension

CalendarKey	FullDate	DayOf Week	DayOf Month	Month	Qtr	Year
1	1/1/2013	Tuesday	1	January	Q1	2013
2	1/2/2013	Wednesday	2	January	Q1	2013

PRODUCT Dimension

ProductKey	ProductID	Product Name	Product Price	Product Vendor Name	Product Category Name
1	1X1	Zzz Bag	$100	Pacifica Gear	Camping
2	2X2	Easy Boot	$70	Mountain King	Footwear
3	3X3	Cosy Sock	$15	Mountain King	Footwear
4	4X4	Dura Boot	$90	Pacifica Gear	Footwear
5	5X5	Tiny Tent	$150	Mountain King	Camping
6	6X6	Biggy Tent	$250	Mountain King	Camping

STORE Dimension

StoreKey	StoreID	StoreZip	StoreRegion Name	Store Size (m^2)	Store CSystem	Store Layout
1	S1	60600	Chicagoland	51000	Cashiers	Modern
2	S2	60605	Chicagoland	35000	Self Service	Traditional
3	S3	35400	Tristate	55000	Mixed	Traditional

CUSTOMER Dimension

CustomerKey	CustomerID	Customer Name	Customer Zip	Customer Gender	Customer MaritalStatus	Customer EducationLevel	Customer CreditScore
1	1-2-333	Tina	60137	Female	Single	College	700
2	2-3-444	Tony	60611	Male	Single	High School	650
3	3-4-555	Pam	35401	Female	Married	College	623

SALES Fact table

CalendarKey	StoreKey	ProductKey	CustomerKey	TID	TimeOfDay	DollarsSold	UnitsSold
1	1	1	1	T111	8:23:59 AM	$100	1
1	2	2	2	T222	8:24:30 AM	$70	1
2	3	3	1	T333	8:15:08 AM	$75	5
2	3	1	1	T333	8:15:08 AM	$100	1
2	3	4	3	T444	8:20:33 AM	$90	1
2	3	2	3	T444	8:20:33 AM	$140	2
2	3	4	2	T555	8:30:00 AM	$360	4
2	3	5	2	T555	8:30:00 AM	$300	2
2	3	6	2	T555	8:30:00 AM	$250	1

DEFECTS Fact table

CalendarKey	StoreKey	ProductKey	DFTID	TimeOfDay	DefectiveUnitsFound
1	1	1	DFT101	8:00:00 AM	1
1	2	2	DFT202	8:30:00 AM	2
2	3	3	DFT303	8:45:00 AM	6

FIGURE 8.20 Records for the dimensional model shown in Figure 8.19.

Figure 8.20 shows the populated tables of the dimensional model shown in Figure 8.19.

A dimensional model with multiple fact tables (such as the one shown in Figure 8.19) is referred to as a **constellation (galaxy) of stars**. This approach allows for quicker development of analytical databases for multiple subjects of analysis, because dimensions are reused instead of duplicated. Also, due to the sharing of dimensions, this approach enables straightforward cross-fact analysis, such as a comparison of the *average daily number of products sold* vs. the *average daily number of defective products found and removed* per store, region, quarter, product category, and so on.

DETAILED VERSUS AGGREGATED FACT TABLES

Fact tables in a dimensional model can contain either **detailed data** or **aggregated data**. In **detailed fact tables**, each record refers to a single fact, while in **aggregated fact tables**, each record summarizes multiple facts. The following example illustrates the difference between the two types of data in fact tables. In order to explain these concepts, we will further expand the set of data in the ZAGI Retail Company Sales Department operational database shown in Figure 8.14. This slightly expanded set is shown in Figure 8.21.

The set in Figure 8.21 is expanded when compared to the set in Figure 8.14 by adding one more record in the SALES TRANSACTION table and two more records in the SOLDVIA table. In this expanded scenario, customer *Tony*, who had already bought two *Tiny Tents* and one *Biggy Tent* in store *S3* at *8:30:00 A.M.*, came back to the same store and made the identical purchase one hour later at *9:30:00 A.M.* This slight expansion of the data set will help us to better illustrate the difference between detailed and aggregated star schemas in the examples below. The set in Figure 8.21 will be used as a data source for the examples below, together with the sets in Figures 8.6 and 8.7.

Detailed Fact Table

Figure 8.22 shows a dimensional model containing a detailed fact table for the subject sales. Figure 8.23 shows the tables in the dimensional model from Figure 8.22 populated with data.

In the ZAGI Retail Company Sales Department Database shown in Figure 8.21, one sales fact is represented by one record in the SOLDVIA table. Because the SALES fact

REGION

RegionID	RegionName
C	Chicagoland
T	Tristate

PRODUCT

ProductID	ProductName	ProductPrice	VendorID	CategoryID
1X1	Zzz Bag	$100	PG	CP
2X2	Easy Boot	$70	MK	FW
3X3	Cosy Sock	$15	MK	FW
4X4	Dura Boot	$90	PG	FW
5X5	Tiny Tent	$150	MK	CP
6X6	Biggy Tent	$250	MK	CP

VENDOR

VendorID	VendorName
PG	Pacifica Gear
MK	Mountain King

STORE

StoreID	StoreZip	RegionID
S1	60600	C
S2	60605	C
S3	35400	T

CATEGORY

CategoryID	CategoryName
CP	Camping
FW	Footwear

SALESTRANSACTION

TID	CustomerID	StoreID	TDate	TTime
T111	1-2-333	S1	1-Jan-2013	8:23:59 AM
T222	2-3-444	S1	1-Jan-2013	8:24:30 AM
T333	1-2-333	S3	2-Jan-2013	8:15:08 AM
T444	3-4-555	S3	2-Jan-2013	8:20:33 AM
T555	2-3-444	S3	2-Jan-2013	8:30:00 AM
T666	2-3-444	S3	2-Jan-2013	9:30:00 AM

SOLDVIA

ProductID	TID	NoOfItems
1X1	T111	1
2X2	T222	1
3X3	T333	5
1X1	T333	1
4X4	T444	1
2X2	T444	2
4X4	T555	4
5X5	T555	2
6X6	T555	1
5X5	T666	2
6X6	T666	1

CUSTOMER

CustomerID	CustomerName	CustomerZip
1-2-333	Tina	60137
2-3-444	Tony	60611
3-4-555	Pam	35401

FIGURE 8.21 Data records for the ZAGI Retail Company Sales Department Database (Figure 8.14 expanded with records added to SALESTRANSACTION and SOLDVIA tables).

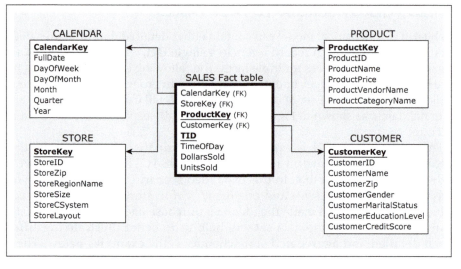

FIGURE 8.22   A dimensional model with a *detailed* fact table.

CALENDAR Dimension

CalendarKey	FullDate	DayOf Week	DayOf Month	Month	Qtr	Year
1	1/1/2013	Tuesday	1	January	Q1	2013
2	1/2/2013	Wednesday	2	January	Q1	2013

PRODUCT Dimension

ProductKey	ProductID	Product Name	Product Price	Product Vendor Name	Product Category Name
1	1X1	Zzz Bag	$100	Pacifica Gear	Camping
2	2X2	Easy Boot	$70	Mountain King	Footwear
3	3X3	Cosy Sock	$15	Mountain King	Footwear
4	4X4	Dura Boot	$90	Pacifica Gear	Footwear
5	5X5	Tiny Tent	$150	Mountain King	Camping
6	6X6	Biggy Tent	$250	Mountain King	Camping

STORE Dimension

StoreKey	StoreID	StoreZip	StoreRegion Name	Store Size (m²)	Store CSystem	Store Layout
1	S1	60600	Chicagoland	51000	Cashiers	Modern
2	S2	60605	Chicagoland	35000	Self Service	Traditional
3	S3	35400	Tristate	55000	Mixed	Traditional

CUSTOMER Dimension

CustomerKey	CustomerID	Customer Name	Customer Zip	Customer Gender	Customer MaritalStatus	Customer EducationLevel	Customer CreditScore
1	1-2-333	Tina	60137	Female	Single	College	700
2	2-3-444	Tony	60611	Male	Single	High School	650
3	3-4-555	Pam	35401	Female	Married	College	623

SALES Fact table

CalendarKey	StoreKey	ProductKey	CustomerKey	TID	TimeOfDay	DollarsSold	UnitsSold
1	1	1	1	T111	8:23:59 AM	$100	1
1	2	2	2	T222	8:24:30 AM	$70	1
2	3	3	1	T333	8:15:08 AM	$75	5
2	3	1	1	T333	8:15:08 AM	$100	1
2	3	4	3	T444	8:20:33 AM	$90	1
2	3	2	3	T444	8:20:33 AM	$140	2
2	3	4	2	T555	8:30:00 AM	$360	4
2	3	5	2	T555	8:30:00 AM	$300	2
2	3	6	2	T555	8:30:00 AM	$250	1
2	3	5	2	T666	9:30:00 AM	$300	2
2	3	6	2	T666	9:30:00 AM	$250	1

FIGURE 8.23   The dimensional model from Figure 8.22 populated with the data.

table in Figure 8.23 is detailed, each record in it refers to one sales fact represented by one record in the SOLDVIA table in Figure 8.21. Hence, both the SALES and SOLDVIA tables have 11 rows. To underscore what is represented by a row in the SALES fact table in Figures 8.22 and 8.23, we explicitly mark its primary key. The primary key is composed of the TID and ProductKey columns, because each record in the fact table refers to a particular line item of a particular sale transaction. TID is not unique in the table because more than one product can be bought in the same transaction. Similarly, ProductKey is not unique because the same product can be associated with more than one transaction. Hence, both TID and ProductKey are needed to form the composite primary key.

Aggregated Fact Table

In contrast, Figure 8.24 shows a dimensional model containing an aggregated fact table for the subject sales. Figure 8.25 shows the tables in the dimensional model from Figure 8.24 populated with data.

To underscore the aggregated nature of the SALES fact table in Figures 8.24 and 8.25, we explicitly mark its primary key. The primary key is composed of the CalendarKey, StoreKey, ProductKey, and CustomerKey columns, because each record in the SALES fact table refers to a summary representing the amount sold in dollars and units on a particular day for a particular product for a particular customer in a particular store.

As noted earlier, the detailed SALES fact table shown in Figure 8.23 has 11 records, which is the same number of records as in the SOLDVIA table shown in Figure 8.21. This is because each record in both tables represents one fact. On the other hand, the SalesPerDPCS table in Figure 8.25 has only nine records, because it is an aggregated fact table. In particular:

- the 8th record in the aggregated SalesPerDPCS fact table in Figure 8.25 summarizes (adds together) the 8th and 10th records from the SALES fact table in Figure 8.23, and consequently the 8th and 10th records from the SOLDVIA table in Figure 8.21
- the 9th record in the aggregated SalesPerDPCS fact table in Figure 8.25 summarizes the 9th and 11th records from the SALES fact table in Figure 8.23 and, consequently, the 9th and 11th records from the SOLDVIA table in Figure 8.21

The aggregation occurs because the TID values are not included in the aggregated SalesPerDPCS fact table in Figure 8.25. The first seven records in the aggregated SalesPerDPCS fact table in Figure 8.25 are summarizations of a single sales fact. Therefore, their values are equivalent to the values in the first seven records in the SALES fact

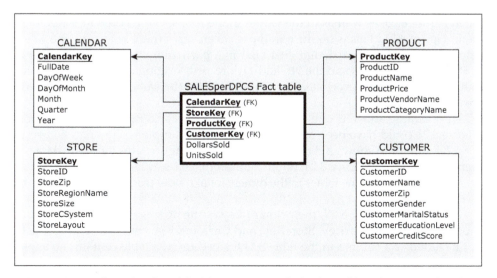

FIGURE 8.24 A dimensional model with an *aggregated* sales fact table: SalesPerDPCS (per day, product, customer, and store).

CALENDAR Dimension

CalendarKey	FullDate	DayOf Week	DayOf Month	Month	Qtr	Year
1	1/1/2013	Tuesday	1	January	Q1	2013
2	1/2/2013	Wednesday	2	January	Q1	2013

PRODUCT Dimension

ProductKey	ProductID	Product Name	Product Price	Product Vendor Name	Product Category Name
1	1X1	Zzz Bag	$100	Pacifica Gear	Camping
2	2X2	Easy Boot	$70	Mountain King	Footwear
3	3X3	Cosy Sock	$15	Mountain King	Footwear
4	4X4	Dura Boot	$90	Pacifica Gear	Footwear
5	5X5	Tiny Tent	$150	Mountain King	Camping
6	6X6	Biggy Tent	$250	Mountain King	Camping

STORE Dimension

StoreKey	StoreID	StoreZip	StoreRegion Name	Store Size (m²)	Store CSystem	Store Layout
1	S1	60600	Chicagoland	51000	Cashiers	Modern
2	S2	60605	Chicagoland	35000	Self Service	Traditional
3	S3	35400	Tristate	55000	Mixed	Traditional

CUSTOMER Dimension

CustomerKey	CustomerID	Customer Name	Customer Zip	Customer Gender	Customer MaritalStatus	Customer EducationLevel	Customer CreditScore
1	1-2-333	Tina	60137	Female	Single	College	700
2	2-3-444	Tony	60611	Male	Single	High School	650
3	3-4-555	Pam	35401	Female	Married	College	623

SALESPerDPCS Fact table

CalendarKey	StoreKey	ProductKey	CustomerKey	DollarsSold	UnitsSold
1	1	1	1	$100	1
1	2	2	2	$70	1
2	3	3	1	$75	5
2	3	1	1	$100	1
2	3	4	3	$90	1
2	3	2	3	$140	2
2	3	4	2	$360	4
2	3	5	2	$600	4
2	3	6	2	$500	2

Amounts from 8th and 10th records in SALES fact table in Figure 8.23 combined (added)

Amounts from 9th and 11th records in SALES fact table in Figure 8.23 combined (added)

FIGURE 8.25   The dimensional model from Figure 8.24 populated with data.

table in Figure 8.23, as well as to the values in the first seven records in the SOLDVIA table in Figure 8.21. This is because in those seven cases there was only one sale of a particular product to a particular customer in a particular store on a particular day. The 8th and 10th records and the 9th and 11th records originate from two transactions in which the same two products were purchased by the same customer in the same store on the same day.

The example above is one of the many ways in which the data from the source in Figure 8.21 could have been aggregated. Another example is shown in Figures 8.26 and 8.27. Figure 8.26 shows a dimensional model that aggregates the same data as the dimensional model in Figure 8.24, but in a different (coarser) fashion.

Figure 8.27 shows the tables in the dimensional model from Figure 8.26 populated with data.

In Figures 8.26 and 8.27, the primary key of the aggregated fact table SALES is composed of the CalendarKey, StoreKey, and CustomerKey columns. The ProductKey is not included as a column in the table SALES, because the table contains an aggregation of data over all products. Each record in the aggregated fact table SALES refers to

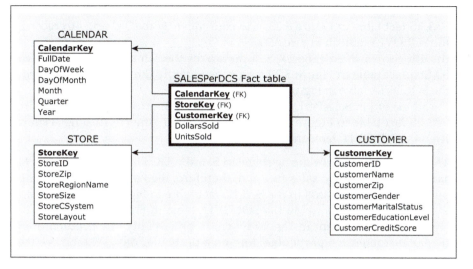

FIGURE 8.26   A dimensional model with an *aggregated* sales fact table: SalesPerDCS (per day, customer, and store).

a summary representing the quantities in dollars and units of all products bought on a particular day in a particular store by a particular customer.

The aggregated fact table, SalesPerDCS in Figure 8.27, has five records. The bottom three records contain the following summarizations:

CALENDAR Dimension

CalendarKey	FullDate	DayOf Week	DayOf Month	Month	Qtr	Year
1	1/1/2013	Tuesday	1	January	Q1	2013
2	1/2/2013	Wednesday	2	January	Q1	2013

STORE Dimension

StoreKey	StoreID	StoreZip	StoreRegion Name	Store Size (m²)	Store CSystem	Store Layout
1	S1	60600	Chicagoland	51000	Cashiers	Modern
2	S2	60605	Chicagoland	35000	Self Service	Traditional
3	S3	35400	Tristate	55000	Mixed	Traditional

CUSTOMER Dimension

CustomerKey	CustomerID	Customer Name	Customer Zip	Customer Gender	Customer MaritalStatus	Customer EducationLevel	Customer CreditScore
1	1-2-333	Tina	60137	Female	Single	College	700
2	2-3-444	Tony	60611	Male	Single	High School	650
3	3-4-555	Pam	35401	Female	Married	College	623

SALESPerDCS Fact table

CalendarKey	StoreKey	CustomerKey	DollarsSold	UnitsSold	
1	1	1	$100	1	
1	2	2	$70	1	*Amounts from 3rd and 4th records in SALES fact table in Figure 8.23 combined (added)*
2	3	1	$175	6	*Amounts from 5th and 6th records in SALES fact table in Figure 8.23 combined (added)*
2	3	3	$230	3	
2	3	2	$1,460	10	*Amounts from 7th through 11th records in SALES fact table in Figure 8.23 combined (added)*

FIGURE 8.27   The dimensional model from Figure 8.26 populated with data.

- the 3rd record in SalesPerDCS summarizes the 3rd and 4th records from the SALES fact table in Figure 8.23, and consequently the 3rd and 4th records from the SOLDVIA table in Figure 8.21
- the 4th record in SalesPerDCS summarizes the 5th and 6th records from the SALES fact table in Figure 8.23, and consequently the 5th and 6th records from the SOLDVIA table in Figure 8.21
- the 5th record in SalesPerDCS summarizes the 7th through 11th records from the SALES fact table in Figure 8.23, and consequently the 7th through 11th records from the SOLDVIA table in Figure 8.21

The first two records in the aggregated SalesPerDCS fact table in Figure 8.27 are summarizations of a single sales fact and, therefore, the values are equivalent to the values in the first two records in the SALES fact table in Figure 8.23 as well as to the values in the first two records in the SOLDVIA table in Figure 8.21. This is because those two records represent instances when there was only one product bought by a particular customer in a particular store on a particular day. When more than one product was bought by a customer in a particular store on a particular day, the records are aggregated in the SalesPerDCS fact table in Figure 8.27.

Detailed versus Aggregated Fact Table

To recap the concept of detailed and aggregated fact tables, we take another look at other fact tables in dimensional models in this chapter and distinguish which ones are detailed and which ones are aggregated.

In the examples illustrated by Figures 8.4 and 8.5, and Figures 8.8 and 8.9, the fact table SALES is an *aggregated* fact table and its primary key is composed of CalendarKey, StoreKey, ProductKey, and CustomerKey columns. The absence of a TID column in the fact table SALES in these examples is an indicator that the fact table is aggregated. In these examples, the fact table SALES has the same number of records as the corresponding SOLDVIA table in Figure 8.3. However, this would no longer be the case if the same customer bought the same product in the same store on the same day in two separate transactions, as illustrated by the example in Figure 8.25.

In the examples illustrated by Figures 8.11 and 8.12, Figures 8.15 and 8.16, and Figures 8.19 and 8.20, the fact table SALES is a *detailed* fact table and its primary key is composed of columns Product Key and TID.

GRANULARITY OF THE FACT TABLE

The **granularity** of the fact table describes what is depicted by one row in the fact table. Detailed fact tables have a fine level of granularity because each record represents a single fact. Aggregated fact tables have a coarser level of granularity than detailed fact tables, as records in aggregated fact tables always represent summarizations of multiple facts.

For example, the SalesPerDPCS fact table in Figures 8.24 and 8.25 has a coarser level of granularity than the SALES fact tables in Figures 8.22 and 8.23 because, as we have shown, records in the SalesPerDPCS fact table summarize records from the SALES fact table in Figures 8.22 and 8.23. The SalesPerDCS fact table in Figures 8.26 and 8.27 has an even coarser level of granularity, because its records summarize records from the SalesPerDPCS fact tables in Figures 8.24 and 8.25. For example, the 3rd record in the SalesPerDCS summarizes the 3rd and 4th records from the SALES fact table in Figure 8.23 and also summarizes the 3rd and 4th records from the SalesPerDPCS fact tables in Figures 8.24 and 8.25.

Due to their compactness, coarser granularity aggregated fact tables are quicker to query than detailed fact tables. However, coarser granularity tables are limited in terms of what information can be retrieved from them. Aggregation is requirement-specific, while a detailed granularity provides unlimited possibility for analysis. In other words, you can always obtain an aggregation from the finest grain, but the reverse is not true.

One way to take advantage of the query performance improvement provided by aggregated fact tables while retaining the power of analysis of detailed fact tables is to have both types of tables coexisting within the same dimensional model, i.e., in the same constellation. For example, the diagrams shown in Figures 8.22, 8.24, and 8.26 could be a part of the same schema, as shown in Figure 8.28.

If a user needs to analyze summarized data about sales per day-product-customer-store or sales per day-customer-store aggregated fact tables SALESPerDPCS and SALESPerDCS which can be queried quickly, are available for that purpose. A user can also perform any other type of sales analysis, albeit more slowly, from the detailed fact table SALES-DETAILED.

Line-Item versus Transaction-Level Detailed Fact Table

Detailed fact tables can represent different types of information, depending on what is depicted by the underlying data sources. The two most common types of detailed fact tables are line-item fact tables and transaction-level fact tables.

In a **line-item detailed fact table**, each row represents *a line item of a particular transaction*. The table SALES shown in Figures 8.22 and 8.23 is a line-item detailed fact table because each row represents a line item of a sale transaction. The finest granularity fact available about the subject sales in the underlying data source (the ZAGI Retail Company Sales Department Database is represented by the single line item of a sales transaction.

In a **transaction-level detailed fact table**, each row represents *a particular transaction*. Consider the example of a ZippyZoom Car Rental Agency, where each rental transaction is performed in one branch and involves one car and one customer. An operational database for ZippyZoom Car Rental Agency would record for each car rental transaction the unique RentalTID and the amount taken in addition to the information about the date of the rental, the car rented, and the customer.

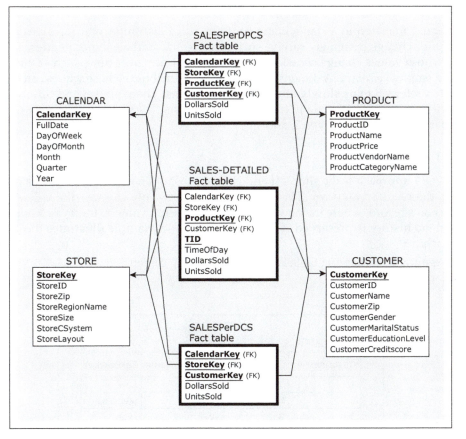

FIGURE 8.28   A constellation of detailed and aggregated facts.

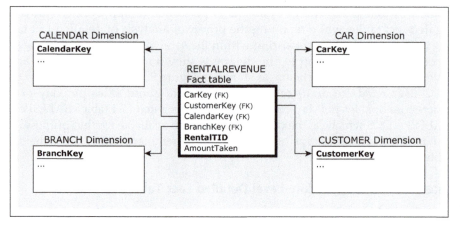

FIGURE 8.29   A dimensional model with a transaction-level fact table.

Based on this operational database, ZippyZoom Car Rental Agency could construct a dimensionally modeled database in order to analyze its rental revenue, as shown in Figure 8.29.

The dimensional model shown in Figure 8.29 includes four dimensions (CALENDAR, CAR, CUSTOMER, and BRANCH) and the fact table RENTALREVENUE. The fact table RENTALREVENUE is a detailed transaction-level fact table. The finest granularity fact available about the subject rental revenue in the underlying data source (the ZippyZoom Car Rental Agency operational database) is represented by the single rental transaction. A rental transaction has no line items, as it includes only one car. Hence, the transaction itself is the lowest level of detail that can be represented in the fact table whose subject is rental revenue.

SLOWLY CHANGING DIMENSIONS AND TIMESTAMPS

A typical dimension in a star schema contains *either* attributes whose values do not change (or change extremely rarely) such as store size and customer gender, *or* attributes whose values change occasionally and sporadically over time, such as customer zip and employee salary. A dimension that contains attributes whose values can change are often referred to as **slowly changing dimensions**. There are several different approaches to dealing with slowly changing dimensions. The most common approaches are referred to as Type 1, Type 2, and Type 3.

Type 1 Approach

The **Type 1 approach** is the simplest and is used most often when a change in a dimension is the result of an error. The Type 1 approach simply changes the value in the dimension's record, where the new value replaces the old value. If the Type 1 approach is used, no history is preserved. The following simple example illustrates the Type 1 approach.

Assume the following table is a slowly changing dimension:

CUSTOMER

CustomerKey	CustomerID	CustomerName	TaxBracket
1	111	Linda	Low
2	222	Susan	Medium
3	333	William	High

Assume that *Susan's* Tax Bracket attribute value has to be changed from *Medium* to *High*. If the Type 1 approach were applied, the result would be the following:

CUSTOMER

CustomerKey	CustomerID	CustomerName	TaxBracket
1	111	Linda	Low
2	222	Susan	High
3	333	William	High

The previous value for the Tax Bracket attribute value in the second row (*Medium*) was simply replaced by the new value (*High*). The Type 1 approach would be appropriate in this scenario if *Susan's* Tax Bracket was *High* from the outset, but was incorrectly recorded as *Medium* and is now corrected.

Type 2 Approach

The **Type 2 approach** is used in cases where history should be preserved. The Type 2 approach creates a new additional dimension record using a new value for the surrogate key every time a value in a dimension record changes. The same example used to illustrate the Type 1 approach will be used to illustrate the Type 2 approach.

Assume the following table is a slowly changing dimension:

CUSTOMER

CustomerKey	CustomerID	CustomerName	TaxBracket
1	111	Linda	Low
2	222	Susan	Medium
3	333	William	High

Assume that *Susan's* Tax Bracket attribute value has to be changed from *Medium* to *High*. If the Type 2 approach is applied, the result would be the following:

CUSTOMER

CustomerKey	CustomerID	CustomerName	TaxBracket
1	111	Linda	Low
2	222	Susan	Medium
3	333	William	High
4	222	Susan	High

A new record containing a new value for *Susan's* Tax Bracket (*High*) is created, while the old record containing *Susan's* previous value for the Tax Bracket attribute

(*Medium*) is retained. The Type 2 approach would be appropriate in this scenario if Susan's TaxBracket at first was indeed *Medium* and then it changed to *High*.

Note the important role of surrogate keys in the Type 2 approach. Due to the multiple occurrences of records with the same operational key value (same CustomerID value in records 2 and 4), it is the surrogate key that is the primary key, while the original operational key is now used to connect the multiple records that refer to the same real world entity. If we wanted to analyze the purchase history of the customer *Susan*, we would look at all sales fact records connected to all dimension records whose CustomerID is *222*. However, if we wanted to look at the purchase patterns of customers in a *High* Tax Bracket, we would combine the sales in the fact table connected to the 3rd record with the sales connected to the 4th record in the dimension Customer. In other words, we would only include purchases made by *Susan* since she entered the *High* tax bracket.

The Type 2 approach is the most commonly used approach for dealing with slowly changing dimensions. It enables straightforward handling of multiple changes of dimension attributes values.

The Type 2 approach is often combined with the use of additional columns in the dimensions, called **timestamps**. Timestamps indicate the time interval for which the values in the record were applicable. Timestamp columns indicating the start and end dates can be added to each column subject to a change of values in the dimension record. Another column entitled **row indicator** can also be added to the entire table. The role of this column is to provide a quick indicator of which records are currently valid. Assuming the Customer table contains the data since the date 1.1.2000, and also assuming that Susan joined the *High* tax bracket on the date 1.1.2008, the following illustrates the use of timestamps and a row indicator by the Type 2 approach:

CUSTOMER

CustomerKey	CustomerID	CustomerName	TaxBracket	Effective StartDate	Effective EndDate	Row Indicator
1	111	Linda	Low	1.1.2000	n/a	Current
2	222	Susan	Medium	1.1.2000	12.31.2007	Not Current
3	333	William	High	1.1.2000	n/a	Current
4	222	Susan	High	1.1.2008	n/a	Current

The columns Effective Start Date and Effective End Date indicate the interval during which the values were valid for each row. The entry 'n/a' (not applicable) indicates that the row values are still currently valid, with no end date yet. In practical implementations, an 'n/a' entry is often recorded as a far future date, such as '12.31.9999', instead of 'n/a', to simplify date related queries. A row indicator is used to quickly distinguish rows containing currently valid data in all columns from the rows with historic data.

Type 3 Approach

The **Type 3 approach** is applicable in cases in which there is a fixed number of changes possible per column of a dimension, or in cases when only a limited history is recorded. The Type 3 approach involves creating a "previous" and "current" column in the dimension table for each column where changes are anticipated.

The same example used to illustrate the Type 1 and Type 2 approaches will be used to illustrate the Type 3 approach.

Assume the following table is a slowly changing dimension:

CUSTOMER

CustomerKey	CustomerID	CustomerName	TaxBracket
1	111	Linda	Low
2	222	Susan	Medium
3	333	William	High

Assume that Susan's Tax Bracket attribute value has to be changed from Medium to High. If the Type 3 approach is applied, the result would be the following:

CUSTOMER

CustomerKey	CustomerID	CustomerName	Previous TaxBracket	Current TaxBracket
1	111	Linda	n/a	Low
2	222	Susan	Medium	High
3	333	William	n/a	High

Two separate columns for the Tax Bracket attribute are created: one for the current value of Tax Bracket and one for the previous value of Tax Bracket. The Type 3 approach would be appropriate in this scenario if customers' tax brackets can change only once, or if only the two latest values for the customers' Tax Bracket attribute are ever needed for analysis in this organization.

The Type 3 approach is also often combined with the use of timestamps. The following illustrates the use of timestamps by the Type 3 approach:

CUSTOMER

CustomerKey	CustomerID	CustomerName	Previous TaxBracket	Previous TaxBracket EffectiveDate	Current TaxBracket	Current TaxBracket EffectiveDate
1	111	Linda	n/a	n/a	Low	1.1.2000
2	222	Susan	Medium	1.1.2000	High	1.1.2008
3	333	William	n/a	n/a	High	1.1.2000

When handling slowly changing dimensions, the most common choices are using Type 1, Type 2, or Type 3 options, or a combination of these approaches, depending on the nature of possible changes within various attributes of the dimension.

ADDITIONAL DIMENSIONAL MODELING ISSUES

We conclude the discussion about dimensional modeling concepts by briefly examining several additional issues related to dimensional modeling.

Snowflake Model

It is very common for a dimension in a star schema to be designed as one not-normalized table containing data that could have been divided between several normalized tables. For example, dimension PRODUCT in Figure 8.24 contains information about products, categories, and vendors, which could be split into three normalized tables: PRODUCT, CATEGORY, and VENDOR. If the dimensions are normalized within the dimensional model, such models are referred to as **snowflake models**. Figure 8.30 shows a snowflake version (i.e., normalized version) of the star-schema model shown in Figure 8.24.

In practice, snowflaking is *usually not used* in dimensional modeling. One reason for not using snowflaking in dimensional modeling is that not-normalized (i.e., not snowflaked) dimensions provide for simpler analysis. A normalized star schema results in a larger number of tables to consider during the analysis, which adds to the complexity of the process. Compare schemas in Figures 8.24 and 8.30. If both schemas were implemented, they would both end up containing the same data. However, an analyst using the schema in Figure 8.24 could perform sales-related analytical tasks using four dimensions, while an analyst using the schema in Figure 8.30 would have to use seven dimensions to perform the same analytical tasks.

Another reason for not snowflaking in dimensional modeling is that normalization is usually not necessary for analytical databases. Recall from Chapter 4 that the primary reason for normalizing operational databases is to avoid update anomalies. Also recall from Chapter 7 that analytical databases, such as data warehouses and data marts, are not subject to update anomalies, since they are "append and read only" databases. Since dimensional modeling is used primarily to design analytical business intelligence databases that cannot be affected by update anomalies, normalization as a prevention of update anomalies is simply not necessary.

Cubes

The relational model is not the only way through which dimensionally modeled databases can be implemented. Another way of implementing dimensionally modeled data is by using so-called cubes. Conceptually, there is no difference in dimensional modeling for relational models or cubes. The conceptual design still involves creating dimensions and facts. The difference is in the physical implementation. Chapter 9 will include

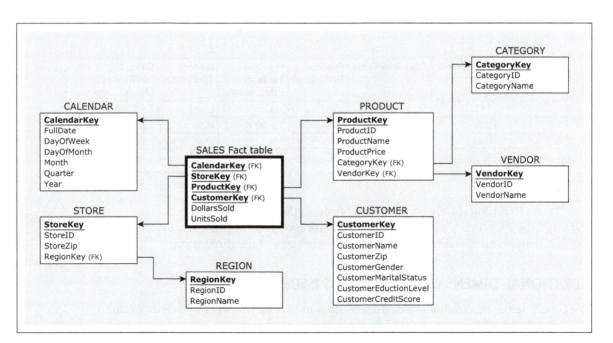

FIGURE 8.30   A snowflaked version of the dimensional model shown in Figure 8.24.

a brief overview of cubes, examining similarities and differences between the relational and cube implementation of the dimensional model, as well as related performance and capacity issues.

DATA WAREHOUSE (DATA MART) MODELING APPROACHES

Contemporary methodologies offer several data modeling options for designing analytical databases, such as data warehouses and data marts. The following are three of the most common data warehouse and data mart modeling approaches:

- normalized data warehouse
- dimensionally modeled data warehouse
- independent data marts

These approaches differ in how they utilize the data modeling techniques we introduced in the earlier chapters in this book. In the remainder of this chapter, we will examine and illustrate the basic concepts of these approaches as well as their differences and similarities.

NORMALIZED DATA WAREHOUSE

One option for modeling data warehouses envisions a data warehouse as an integrated analytical database modeled by using ER modeling and relational modeling, resulting in a normalized relational database schema. The **normalized data warehouse** is populated with the analytically useful data from the operational data sources via the ETL process and serves as a source of data for dimensionally modeled data marts and for any other nondimensional analytically useful data sets. The data warehouse as a normalized integrated analytical database was first proposed by Bill Inmon and, hence, the normalized data warehouse approach is often referred to as the Inmon approach.[2] Figure 8.31 illustrates a normalized data warehouse.

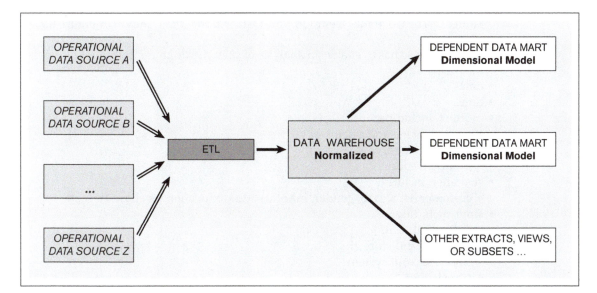

FIGURE 8.31 A normalized data warehouse.

---

[2]See for example, *Building the Data Warehouse,* 4th Edition, W.H. Inmon (Wiley, 2005).

The idea behind this method is to have a central data warehouse modeled as an ER model that is subsequently mapped into a normalized relational database model. The normalized relational database serves as a physical store for the data warehouse. All integration of the underlying operational data sources occurs within a central normalized database schema. Once a data warehouse is completed and populated with the data from the underlying sources via the ETL infrastructure, various analytically useful views, subsets, and extracts are possible based on this fully integrated database. One of the primary types of analytical data sets resulting from the normalized data warehouse is indeed a dimensionally modeled data mart, which can then be queried using OLAP/ BI tools (OLAP/BI tools will be covered in Chapter 9). Such data marts, which result from the larger data warehouse either as views (virtual tables) or as physical extracts, are known as dependent data marts.

Other, nondimensional data sets can also be extracted when they are needed for analysis and decision support. For example, some analyst or some analytical application, such as a data mining tool (data mining is discussed in Appendix G), may require a single large table combining data from various tables of the normalized data warehouse.

AN EXAMPLE OF A NORMALIZED DATA WAREHOUSE

To illustrate how ER modeling and the subsequent mapping into a relational schema can be used to model a normalized data warehouse, we will again use the ZAGI Retail Company scenario.

Let us assume that the ZAGI Retail Company wants to use ER modeling techniques to design a normalized data warehouse for analyzing their sales. The requirements for designing the data warehouse are as follows:

The ZAGI Retail Company wants to create an analytical database to analyze sales.

The three available data sources are:

Source 1: The ZAGI Retail Company Sales Department Database shown in Figures 8.13 and 8.14

Source 2: The ZAGI Retail Company Facilities Department Database shown in Figure 8.6

Source 3: The Customer Demographic Data external table shown in Figure 8.7

The data warehouse has to enable an analysis of sales dollar amounts and quantities by:

- date
- time
- product, including:
  - product name and price
  - product category
  - product vendor
- customer, including:
  - customer name, zip, gender, marital status, education level, credit score
- store, including:
  - individual store
  - store size and store zip
  - store checkout system
  - store layout
  - store region

Figures 8.32 and 8.33 illustrate how a sales analysis data warehouse based on these sources and requirements would be designed if the ER modeling technique were used.

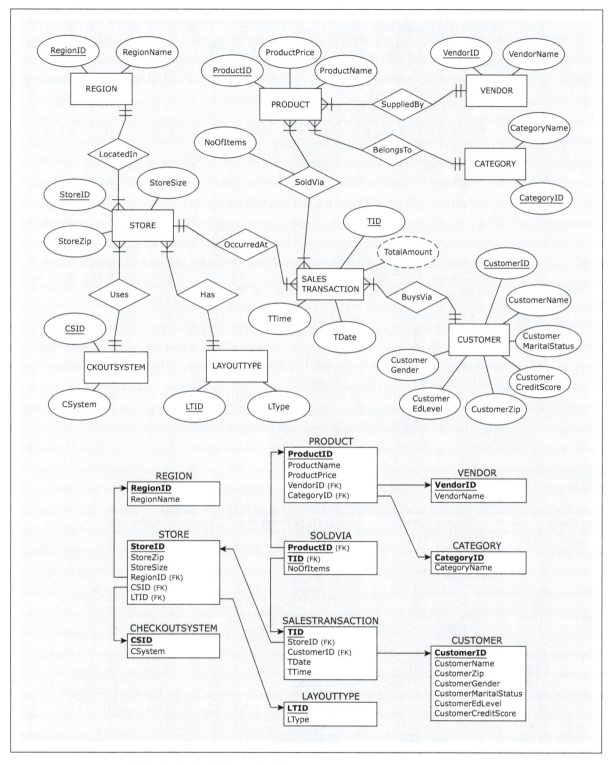

FIGURE 8.32 An ER model and relational schema for the ZAGI Retail Company sales-analysis data warehouse, based on multiple sources.

Figure 8.32 shows the ER model that was developed by merging the ER models from Sources 1 and 2 and adding attributes from Source 3. The ER model captures, as requested by the requirements, the sales dollar amounts and quantities that are the subject of the analysis and all the attributes necessary for the analysis of sales-related data. Figure 8.32 also shows the resulting normalized relational schema mapped from the ER model.

Note the merging of sources that occurred in the ER diagram shown in Figure 8.32. Entity STORE appeared both in Figure 8.13 (Source 1) and in Figure 8.6 (Source 2). Entity CUSTOMER appeared in Figure 8.13 (Source 1) and as a table in Figure 8.7 (Source 3). Entities REGION, PRODUCT, CATEGORY, VENDOR, and SALESTRANSACTION appeared only in Figure 8.13 (Source 1). Entities CKOUTSYSTEM and LAYOUT appeared only in Figure 8.6 (Source 2).

Entity STORE now has three attributes:

- StoreID, which appeared in entity STORE in Figure 8.13 (Source 1) and in the entity STORE in Figure 8.6 (Source 2)
- StoreZip, which only appeared in entity STORE in Figure 8.13 (Source 1)
- StoreSize, which only appeared in entity STORE in Figure 8.6 (Source 2)

Entity CUSTOMER now has seven attributes:

- CustomerID and CustomerName, which appeared in entity CUSTOMER in Figure 8.13 (Source 1) and in the table CUSTOMER in Figure 8.7 (Source 3)
- CustomerZip, which only appeared in entity CUSTOMER in Figure 8.13 (Source 1)
- Gender, MaritalStatus, EdLevel, and CreditScore, which only appeared in the table CUSTOMER in Figure 8.7 (Source 3)

Relationships Uses and Has appeared in Figure 8.6 (Source 2), and relationship LocatedIn, OccurredAt, SoldVia, BuysVia, BelongsTo, and SuppliedBy appeared in Figure 8.13 (Source 1). In essence, the result is an integrated ER diagram that combines the analytically useful (as specified by the requirements) entities, relationships, and attributes from the models of the operational data sources.

Once the relational model shown in Figure 8.32 is implemented in a DBMS, it is then populated with the data from the underlying three sources, via the ETL infrastructure. The result of that process is shown in Figure 8.33.

PRODUCT

ProductID	ProductName	ProductPrice	VendorID	CategoryID
1X1	Zzz Bag	$100	PG	CP
2X2	Easy Boot	$70	MK	FW
3X3	Cosy Sock	$15	MK	FW
4X4	Dura Boot	$90	PG	FW
5X5	Tiny Tent	$150	MK	CP
6X6	Biggy Tent	$250	MK	CP

CATEGORY

CategoryID	CategoryName
CP	Camping
FW	Footwear

VENDOR

VendorID	VendorName
PG	Pacifica Gear
MK	Mountain King

STORE

StoreID	StoreZip	StoreSize (m^2)	RegionID	CSID	LTID
S1	60600	51000	C	CR	M
S2	60605	35000	C	AC	T
S3	35400	55000	T	MX	T

REGION

RegionID	RegionName
C	Chicagoland
T	Tristate

LAYOUTTYPE

LTID	Layout
M	Modern
T	Traditional

CHECKOUTSYSTEM

CSID	CSystem
CR	Cashiers
AC	Self Service
MX	Mixed

SALESTRANSACTION

TID	CustomerID	StoreID	TDate	TTime
T111	1-2-333	S1	1-Jan-2013	8:23:59 AM
T222	2-3-444	S2	1-Jan-2013	8:24:30 AM
T333	1-2-333	S3	2-Jan-2013	8:15:08 AM
T444	3-4-555	S3	2-Jan-2013	8:20:33 AM
T555	2-3-444	S3	2-Jan-2013	8:30:00 AM

SOLDVIA

ProductID	TID	NoOfItems
1X1	T111	1
2X2	T222	1
3X3	T333	5
1X1	T333	1
4X4	T444	1
2X2	T444	2
4X4	T555	4
5X5	T555	2
6X6	T555	1

CUSTOMER

CustomerID	Customer Name	Customer Zip	Customer Gender	Customer Marital Status	Customer Education Level	Customer Credit Score
1-2-333	Tina	60137	Female	Single	College	700
1-2-333	Tony	60611	Male	Single	High School	650
3-4-555	Pam	35401	Female	Married	College	623

FIGURE 8.33 A relational model from Figure 8.32 populated with the data from three underlying sources.

Once a normalized data warehouse (as the one illustrated by Figures 8.32 and 8.33) is created, it serves as an integrated database from which any needed analytical data set can be viewed or extracted.

For example, a dimensionally modeled analytical database, such as the one shown in Figures 8.15 and 8.16 (on page 239) could have been based on the integrated normalized data warehouse, such as the one shown in Figures 8.32 and 8.33, rather than directly on the underlying operational data sources.

DIMENSIONALLY MODELED DATA WAREHOUSE

Another approach views a data warehouse as a collection of dimensionally modeled intertwined data marts (i.e., a constellation of dimensional models) that integrates analytically useful information from the operational data sources. This approach was championed by Ralph Kimball and is often referred to as the Kimball approach.[3] Figure 8.34 illustrates a **dimensionally modeled data warehouse**.

As Figure 8.34 illustrates, this approach is the same as the normalized data warehouse approach when it comes to the utilization of operational data sources and the ETL process. The difference is the technique used for modeling the data warehouse. In this approach, a set of commonly used dimensions known as **conformed dimensions** is designed first. For example, in a retail company, conformed dimensions such as CALENDAR, PRODUCT, STORE can be designed first, as they will be commonly used by subjects of analysis. Fact tables corresponding to the subjects of analysis are then subsequently added. A set of dimensional models is created in which each fact table is connected to multiple dimensions, and some of the dimensions are shared by more than one fact table. In addition to the originally created set of conformed dimensions, other dimensions are included as needed. The result is a data warehouse that is a collection of intertwined dimensionally modeled data marts (i.e., a constellation of stars), such as the one shown in Figure 8.35.

In Figure 8.35, a data warehouse designer could have first created dimensions CALENDAR, CUSTOMER, STORE, and PRODUCT as conformed dimensions, anticipating that they would be useful for multiple subjects represented by fact tables. Then, based on the requirements that called for analysis of two subjects, sales and defects, two fact tables SALES and DEFECTS were created. These fact tables conveniently had

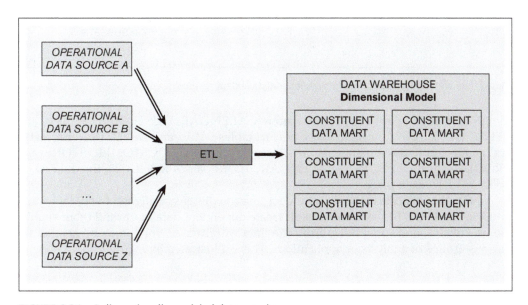

FIGURE 8.34   A dimensionally modeled data warehouse.

[3]See for example, *The Data Warehouse Lifecycle Toolkit*, 2nd Edition, Ralph Kimball et al. (Wiley, 2011).

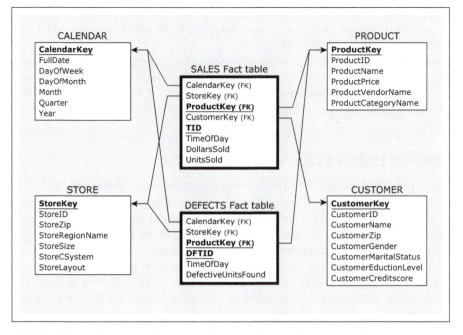

FIGURE 8.35 A dimensionally modeled data warehouse with two constituent data marts.

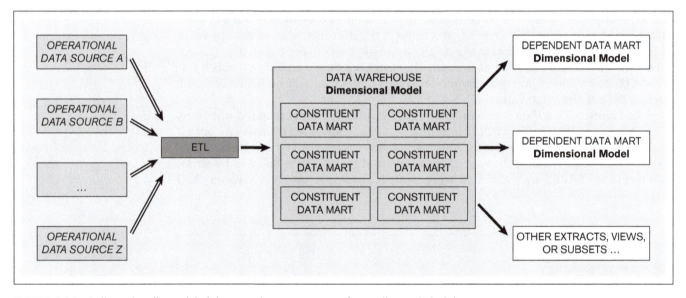

FIGURE 8.36 A dimensionally modeled data warehouse as a source for smaller analytical data sets.

the already-made conformed dimensions CALENDAR, CUSTOMER, STORE, and PRODUCT ready to connect to. Once the fact tables SALES and DEFECTS were created and connected to the dimensions (SALES to CALENDAR, CUSTOMER, STORE, and PRODUCT; and DEFECTS to CALENDAR, STORE, and PRODUCT), the data warehouse model was in place.

Note that in addition to directly querying the dimensionally modeled data warehouse with OLAP/BI tools, we can still create dependent data marts and other smaller views, subsets, and/or extracts from the data warehouse, which may be needed for various groups of analysts or applications. This is illustrated by Figure 8.36.

AN EXAMPLE OF A DIMENSIONALLY MODELED WAREHOUSE

To illustrate how dimensional modeling can be used to model a data warehouse, we will use the same ZAGI Retail Company scenario that we used in the example of the normalized data warehouse.

Let us assume that the ZAGI Retail Company wants to use the dimensional modeling technique to design a data warehouse for analyzing its sales.

The requirements for designing the data warehouse are the same as for the example of the normalized data warehouse earlier in this chapter:

The ZAGI Retail Company wants to create the analytical database to analyze sales.

The three available data sources are:

Source 1: The ZAGI Retail Company Sales Department Database shown in Figures 8.13 and 8.14

Source 2: The ZAGI Retail Company Facilities Department Database shown in Figure 8.6

Source 3: The Customer Demographic Data external table shown in Figure 8.7

The data warehouse has to enable an analysis of sales dollar amounts and quantities by:

- date
- time
- product, including:
  - product name and price
  - product category
  - product vendor
- customer, including:
  - customer name, zip, gender, marital status, education level, credit score
- store, including:
  - individual store
  - store size and store zip
  - store checkout system
  - store layout
  - store region

Figures 8.37 and 8.38 illustrate how a sales analysis data warehouse based on these sources and requirements would be designed if the dimensional modeling technique were used.

In Figure 8.37, the dimensions CALENDAR, STORE, PRODUCT, and CUSTOMER, containing all the necessary attributes for an analysis of sales-related data, as requested by the requirements, would have been created first. These dimensions will connect to the SALES fact table and enable its analysis. If other subjects of analysis are

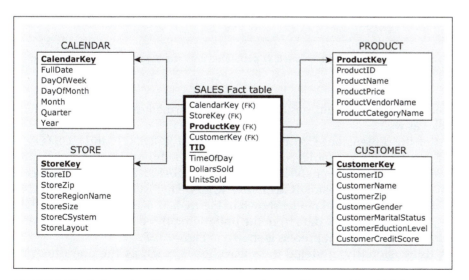

FIGURE 8.37   A dimensionally modeled data warehouse with one subject (*Sales*).

CALENDAR Dimension

CalendarKey	Full Date	DayOf Week	DayOf Month	Month	Qtr	Year
1	1/1/2013	Tuesday	1	January	Q1	2013
2	1/2/2013	Wednesday	2	January	Q1	2013

PRODUCT Dimension

ProductKey	ProductID	Product Name	Product Price	Product Vendor Name	Product Category Name
1	1X1	Zzz Bag	$100	Pacifica Gear	Camping
2	2X2	Easy Boot	$70	Mountain King	Footwear
3	3X3	Cosy Sock	$15	Mountain King	Footwear
4	4X4	Dura Boot	$90	Pacifica Gear	Footwear
5	5X5	Tiny Tent	$150	Mountain King	Camping
6	6X6	Biggy Tent	$250	Mountain King	Camping

STORE Dimension

StoreKey	StoreID	StoreZip	StoreRegion Name	Store Size (m^2)	Store Csystem	Store Layout
1	S1	60600	Chicagoland	51000	Cashiers	Modern
2	S2	60605	Chicagoland	35000	Self Service	Traditional
3	S3	35400	Tristate	55000	Mixed	Traditional

CUSTOMER Dimension

CustomerKey	CustomerID	Customer Name	Customer Zip	Customer Gender	Customer MaritalStatus	Customer EducationLevel	Customer CreditScore
1	1-2-333	Tina	60137	Female	Single	College	700
2	2-3-444	Tony	60611	Male	Single	High School	650
3	3-4-555	Pam	35401	Female	Married	College	623

SALES Fact table

CalendarKey	StoreKey	ProductKey	CustomerKey	TID	TimeOfDay	DollarsSold	UnitsSold
1	1	1	1	T111	8:23:59 AM	$100	1
1	2	2	2	T222	8:24:30 AM	$70	1
2	3	3	1	T333	8:15:08 AM	$75	5
2	3	1	1	T333	8:15:08 AM	$100	1
2	3	4	3	T444	8:20:33 AM	$90	1
2	3	2	3	T444	8:20:33 AM	$140	2
2	3	4	2	T555	8:30:00 AM	$360	4
2	3	5	2	T555	8:30:00 AM	$300	2
2	3	6	2	T555	8:30:00 AM	$250	1

FIGURE 8.38 A dimensional model from Figure 8.37 populated with the data from three underlying sources.

specified later, these dimensions can serve as conformed dimensions for other future fact tables as well.

After the dimensions CALENDAR, STORE, PRODUCT, and CUSTOMER are created, the SALES fact table, containing the sales dollar amounts and quantities that are the subject of the analysis, is created. The SALES fact table is connected via foreign keys to the dimensions CALENDAR, STORE, PRODUCT, and CUSTOMER.

Once the dimensional model shown in Figure 8.37 is implemented in a DBMS, it is then populated with the data from the underlying three sources, via the ETL infrastructure. The result of that process is shown in Figure 8.38.

A dimensionally modeled data warehouse, such as the one illustrated by Figures 8.37 and 8.38, serves as an integrated database from which any needed analytical data set can be viewed or extracted.

INDEPENDENT DATA MARTS

Even though the majority of the discussions about data modeling approaches for data warehouses involve the two above-listed approaches (the normalized and dimensionally modeled data warehouses and their variations), there is a third approach that should also be acknowledged and discussed. This approach involves the creation of so-called independent data marts, as illustrated by Figure 8.39.

In this method, stand-alone data marts are created by various groups within the organization, independent of other stand-alone data marts in the organization. Consequently, multiple ETL systems are created and maintained.

There is a consensus among virtually all members of the data warehousing community about the inappropriateness of using the independent data marts approach as a strategy for designing an enterprise-wide analytical database. There are obvious reasons why independent data marts are considered an inferior strategy. Firstly, this strategy does not result in a data warehouse, but in a collection of unrelated independent data marts. While the independent data marts within one organization may end up as a whole containing all the necessary analytical information, such information is scattered and difficult or even impossible to analyze as one unit. The inability for straightforward analysis across the enterprise is a major weakness of this approach. Another shortcoming of the independent data marts approach is the existence of multiple unrelated ETL infrastructures. ETL, as we mentioned in Chapter 7, is usually the most time- and resource-consuming part of the data warehouse or data mart project. Having multiple unrelated ETL efforts virtually guarantees the unnecessary duplication of similar expensive processes, which of course results in unnecessary waste.

In spite of these obvious disadvantages, a significant number of corporate analytical data stores are developed as a collection of independent data marts. The reason for this seeming paradox lies in the lack of initial enterprise-wide focus when data analysis is concerned.

Simply, a number of departments within an organization take a "go-at-it-alone" approach in developing the data marts for their analytical needs. This is commonly due to the "turf" culture in organizations, where individual departments put more value on their independence than on cross-department collaboration. In those cases, the existence of independent data marts is more of a symptom of the problems with the organization's leadership and culture than a result of deliberately adopting an inferior data warehousing approach.

Moreover, in some cases, the organizational, political or budgetary structure of an organization forces parts of the organization to undertake isolated initiatives. In such scenarios, departments and other constituent groups within organizations

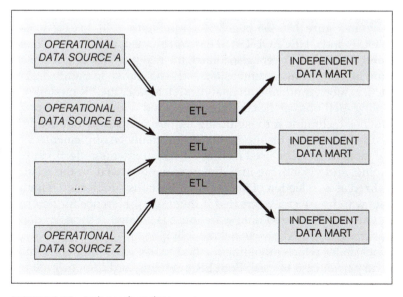

FIGURE 8.39 Independent data marts

contemplating the development of data analysis systems are often presented with the choice of creating independent data marts or doing nothing. Given those two choices, independent data marts certainly represent a better option.

This chapter has presented the most fundamental issues related to data warehouse and data mart design. The following note gives additional information about comparing dimensional modeling and ER modeling as data warehouse/data mart design techniques.

A Note About Comparing Dimensional Modeling and ER Modeling as Data Warehouse/Data Mart Design Techniques

This chapter concludes with a brief discussion comparing ER modeling and dimensional modeling as data warehouse and data mart modeling techniques.

ER modeling is a technique for facilitating the requirements collection process, where all requirements are collected and visualized as the ER model constructs: entities, attributes, and relationships. The ER model provides a clear visualization of the requirements (i.e., conceptual model) for the data warehouse or data mart that is to be created. The ER model of a data warehouse or data mart is subsequently mapped into a relational schema, which is then implemented as a normalized database that hosts the data warehouse or data mart.

Dimensional modeling is a technique that can be used both for visualizing requirements for a data warehouse or data mart (i.e., conceptual modeling), and for creating a data warehouse or data mart model that will be implemented (i.e., logical modeling). When dimensional modeling is used to facilitate the data warehouse or data mart requirements collection process, then the requirements collection involves determining which subjects will be represented as fact tables, and which dimensions and dimension attributes will be used to analyze the chosen subjects. Once the requirements are represented as a dimensional model, the dimensional model can also be directly implemented in a DBMS as the schema for the functioning data warehouse or data mart.

These two methods (ER modeling and dimensional modeling) for modeling data warehouses or data marts are not necessarily as different as they may appear at first glance. The following example illustrates how related the end results of applying the two methods can actually be.

Observe Figure 8.32 (on page 257), which shows the result of modeling a normalized data warehouse using ER modeling. If we join the SOLDVIA and SALESTRANSACT relations into one relation named SALES, add the surrogate keys to the other relations, and add the CALENDAR relation to the schema instead of the Date attribute in the SALES table—the result will be the schema shown in Figure 8.40.

The schema in Figure 8.40 is similar to a snowflaked dimensional schema, such as the one shown in Figure 8.30 (on page 254). If in Figure 8.40 the relations STORE, REGION, LAYOUT, and CHECKOUTSYSTEM were joined, and the relations PRODUCT, VENDOR, and CATEGORY were also joined, the result would be a schema that is similar to the pure non-snowflaked dimensional schema shown in Figure 8.22 and 8.37.

In practice, when modeling an analytical database, the ER modeling and dimensional modeling methods can be combined and used within the same project. In other words, using one technique for visualizing requirements does not preclude using the other technique for creating the model that will actually be implemented. For example, dimensional modeling can be used during the requirements collection process for collecting, refining, and visualizing initial requirements. Based on the resulting requirements visualized as a collection of facts and dimensions, an ER model for a normalized physical data warehouse can be created if there is a preference for a normalized data warehouse. Once a normalized data warehouse is created, a series of dependent data marts can be created using dimensional modeling.

Decisions about which modeling method to use when modeling analytical databases may vary from case to case. Both ER modeling and dimensional modeling approaches offer a viable alternative, and, as we have just discussed, they can both be used within the same project.

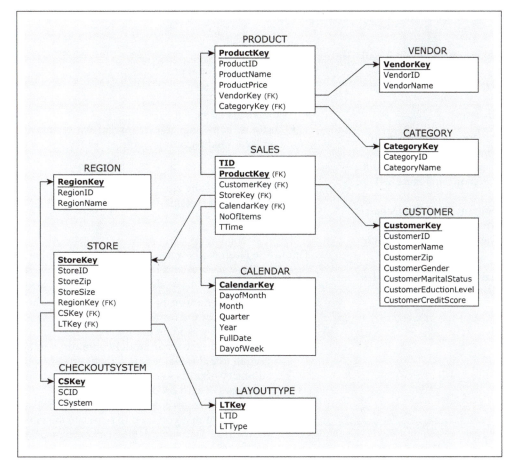

FIGURE 8.40 A modified data warehouse schema.

Key Terms

Aggregated data *243*
Aggregated fact tables *243*
Conformed dimensions *259*
Constellation (galaxy) of
    stars *242*
Degenerate
    dimension *237*
Detailed data *243*
Detailed fact tables *243*

Dimension tables
    (dimensions) *225*
Dimensional modeling *225*
Dimensionally modeled
    data warehouse *259*
Fact tables *225*
Granularity *248*
Line-item detailed fact
    table *249*

Normalized data
    warehouse *255*
Row indicator *252*
Slowly changing
    dimensions *250*
Snowflake models *254*
Star schema *226*
Surrogate key *230*
Timestamps *252*

Transaction identifier
    235
Transaction time *235*
Transaction-level detailed
    fact table *249*
Type 1 approach *250*
Type 2 approach *251*
Type 3 approach *252*

Review Questions

Q8.1 What is the role of dimension tables in the dimensional model?

Q8.2 What is the role of fact tables in the dimensional model?

Q8.3 How does the use of a dimensional model simplify analytical queries?

Q8.4 How is a transaction identifier typically represented in a dimensional model?

Q8.5 How is transaction time typically represented in a dimensional model?

Q8.6 What is a constellation of stars?

Q8.7 What is the difference between a detailed fact table and an aggregated fact table?

Q8.8 What does granularity of the fact table refer to?

Q8.9 What are the most common approaches for handling slowly changing dimensions?

Q8.10 Why is snowflaking usually not used in dimensional modeling?

Q8.11 Describe the components of a normalized data warehouse.

Q8.12 Describe the components of a dimensionally modeled data warehouse.

Q8.13 Describe the independent data marts approach for creating analytical databases.

Exercises

E8.1 Consider the following, slightly modified, ZAGI Retail Company scenario.

The ZAGI Retail Company wants to create an analytical database to analyze *sales*.

The three available data sources are:

Source 1　The ZAGI Retail Company Sales Department Database shown in Figures 8.13 and 8.41 (the schema remains the same as in Figure 8.13 but the data is different, as shown in Figure 8.41 below)

Source 2　The ZAGI Retail Company Facilities Department Database shown in Figure 8.6

Source 3　A Customer Demographic Data external table shown in Figure 8.7

The data warehouse has to enable an analysis of sales dollar amounts and quantities by:

- date, including:
  - full date
  - day of week
  - day of month
  - month
  - quarter
  - year
- time

- product, including:
  - product name and price
  - product category
  - product vendor
- customer, including:
  - customer name, zip, gender, marital status, education level, credit score
- store, including:
  - individual store
  - store size and store zip
  - store checkout system
  - store layout
  - store region

Figure 8.36 illustrates how a sales analysis data warehouse based on these sources and requirements would be designed if the dimensional modeling technique were used.

E8.1a Using the data in Figure 8.41, illustrate how the tables in the dimensional model shown in Figure 8.42 would be populated.

E8.1b Create a dimensional model containing an aggregated fact table, where a fact table shows a summary of units sold and dollars sold for daily purchases of each product in each store.

E8.1c Populate the tables created in **E8.1b** with the data. Use the data that you used to populate the tables shown in the Figure 8.42 as the basis for aggregation.

REGION

RegionID	RegionName
C	Chicagoland
T	Tristate

PRODUCT

ProductID	ProductName	ProductPrice	VendorID	CategoryID
1X1	Zzz Bag	$105	PG	CP
2X2	Easy Boot	$65	MK	FW
3X3	Cosy Sock	$10	MK	FW
4X4	Dura Boot	$95	PG	FW
5X5	Tiny Tent	$140	MK	CP
6X6	Biggy Tent	$240	MK	CP

VENDOR

VendorID	VendorName
PG	Pacifica Gear
MK	Mountain King

STORE

StoreID	StoreZip	RegionID
S1	60600	C
S2	60605	C
S3	35400	T

CATEGORY

CategoryID	CategoryName
CP	Camping
FW	Footwear

SALESTRANSACTION

TID	CustomerID	StoreID	TDate	TTime
T101	3-4-555	S3	1-Jan-2013	8:00:00 AM
T102	1-2-333	S2	2-Jan-2013	8:00:00 AM
T103	2-3-444	S2	2-Jan-2013	8:15:00 AM
T104	1-2-333	S1	2-Jan-2013	8:30:00 AM
T105	2-3-444	S3	3-Jan-2013	8:00:00 AM
T106	3-4-555	S2	3-Jan-2013	8:15:00 AM
T107	1-2-333	S2	3-Jan-2013	8:30:00 AM

SOLDVIA

ProductID	TID	NoOfItems
6X6	T101	1
5X5	T101	2
1X1	T101	1
3X3	T102	3
4X4	T102	1
4X4	T103	1
2X2	T104	1
3X3	T105	4
4X4	T106	1
3X3	T106	5
3X3	T107	3

CUSTOMER

CustomerID	CustomerName	CustomerZip
1-2-333	Tina	60137
2-3-444	Tony	60611
3-4-555	Pam	35401

FIGURE 8.41　Source 1: The ZAGI Retail Company Sales Department Database data set (a different data set).

CALENDAR Dimension

CalendarKey	FullDate	DayOf Week	DayOf Month	Month	Qtr	Year

PRODUCT Dimension

ProductKey	ProductID	Product Name	Product Price	Product Vendor Name	Product Category Name

STORE Dimension

StoreKey	StoreID	StoreZip	StoreRegion Name	Store Size (m²)	Store CSystem	Store Layout

CUSTOMER Dimension

CustomerKey	CustomerID	Customer Name	Customer Zip	Customer Gender	Customer MaritalStatus	Customer EducationLevel	Customer CreditScore

SALES Fact table

CalendarKey	StoreKey	ProductKey	CustomerKey	TID	TimeOfDay	DollarsSold	UnitsSold

FIGURE 8.42

E8.2   Consider the following scenario involving the City Police Department.

The City Police Department wants to create an analytical database to analyze its *ticket revenue*.

The two available data sources, Source 1 and Source 2, are described below.

Source 1   The City Police Department maintains the Ticketed Violations Database, shown in Figure 8.43.

Source 2   The Department of Motor Vehicles (DMV) maintains the Vehicle Registration Table, shown in Figure 8.44.

The data warehouse has to enable an analysis of ticket revenues by:

- date, including:
  - full date
  - day of week
  - day of month
  - month
  - quarter
  - year
- officer, including:
  - officer ID
  - officer name
  - officer rank
- payer of the ticket, including:
  - payer DLN
  - payer name
  - payer gender
  - payer birth year
- vehicle, including:
  - vehicle LPN
  - vehicle make
  - vehicle model
  - vehicle year

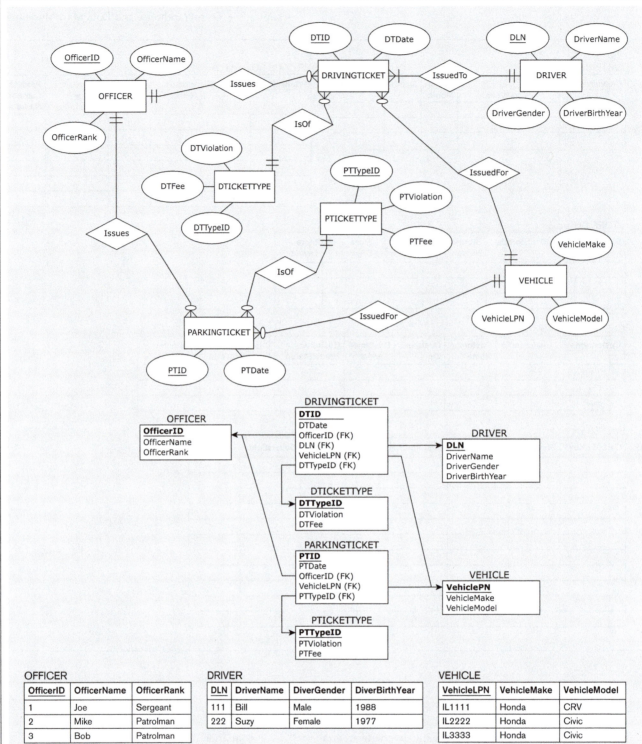

FIGURE 8.43 Source 1: The City Police Department Ticketed Violations Database.

VEHICLE REGISTRATION TABLE

VehicleLPN	VehicleMake	VehicleModel	VehicleYear	OwnerDLN	OwnerName	OwnerGender	OwnerBirthYear
IL1111	Honda	CRV	2007	111	Bill	Male	1988
IL2222	Honda	Civic	2012	222	Suzy	Female	1977
IL3333	Honda	Civic	2005	333	David	Male	1966

FIGURE 8.44   Source 2: The DMV Vehicle Registration Table.

- vehicle owner DLN
- vehicle owner name
- vehicle owner gender
- vehicle owner birth year
- ticket type, including:
  - ticket category (driving or parking)
  - ticket violation
  - ticket fee

Figure 8.45 illustrates how a ticket revenue analysis data warehouse based on these sources and requirements would be designed if dimensional modeling techniques were used.

E8.2a   Using source data from Figures 8.43 and 8.44, illustrate how the empty tables in Figure 8.46 would be populated.

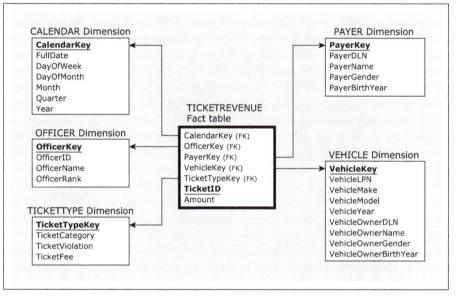

FIGURE 8.45   A dimensionally modeled data warehouse with the subject *ticket revenue.*

CALENDAR Dimension

CalendarKey	FullDate	DayOf Week	DayOf Month	Month	Qtr	Year

PAYER Dimension

PayerKey	PayerDLN	PayerName	Payer Gender	Payer BirthYear

OFFICER Dimension

Officer Key	OfficerID	Officer Name	Officer Rank

VEHICLE Dimension

Vehicle Key	Vehicle LPN	Vehicle Make	Vehicle Model	Vehicle Year	Vehicle OwnerDLN	Vehicle Owner Name	Vehicle Owner Gender	Vehicle Owner BirthYear

TICKETTYPE Dimension

Ticket TypeKey	Ticket Category	Ticket Violation	Ticket Fee

TICKETREVENUE Fact table

CalendarKey	OfficerKey	PayerKey	VehicleKey	Ticket TypeKey	Ticket ID	Amount

FIGURE 8.46

E8.2b   Create a dimensional model containing an aggregated fact table, where a fact table shows a summary of daily revenue amount for each officer.

E8.2c   Populate the tables created in **E8.2b** with the data. Use the data that you used to populate the tables in the Figure 8.46 as a basis for aggregation.

E8.3   Consider the following scenario involving Big Z Inc., an automotive products wholesaler.

Big Z Inc. wants to create the analytical database (data warehouse) to analyze its order quantities.

The two available data sources, Source 1 and Source 2, are described below.

Source 1   The Big Z Inc. Human Resources Department Table, shown in Figure 8.47.

Source 2   The Big Z Inc. Orders Database, shown in Figure 8.48.

The data warehouse has to enable an analysis of order quantities by:

- date, including:
  - full date
  - day of week
  - day of month
  - month
  - quarter
  - year
- time
- product, including:
  - product ID
  - product name
- product type
- product supplier name
- customer, including:
  - customer ID
  - customer name
  - customer type
  - customer zip
- depot, including:
  - depot ID
  - depot size
  - depot zip
- order clerk, including:
  - order clerk id
  - order clerk name
  - order clerk title
  - order clerk education level
  - order clerk year of hire

E8.3a   Based on the sources and requirements listed above, create a dimensional model that will be used for the dimensionally modeled data warehouse for Big Z Inc.

E8.3b   Using data from Figures 8.47 and 8.48, illustrate how the tables in the dimensional model created in **E8.3a** would be populated.

E8.3c   Based on the sources and requirements listed above, create an ER model and a mapped relational model for the normalized data warehouse for Big Z Inc.

E8.3d   Using data from Figures 8.47 and 8.48, illustrate how the tables in the relational model created in **E8.3c** would be populated.

HUMAN RESOURCES DEPARTMENT TABLE (EMPLOYEE DATA)

EmployeeID	Name	Title	EducationLevel	YearOfHire
OC1	Antonio	Order Clerk	High School	2001
OC2	Wesley	Order Clerk	College	2005
OC3	Lilly	Order Clerk	College	2005

FIGURE 8.47   Source 1: The Big Z Inc. Human Resources Department Table.

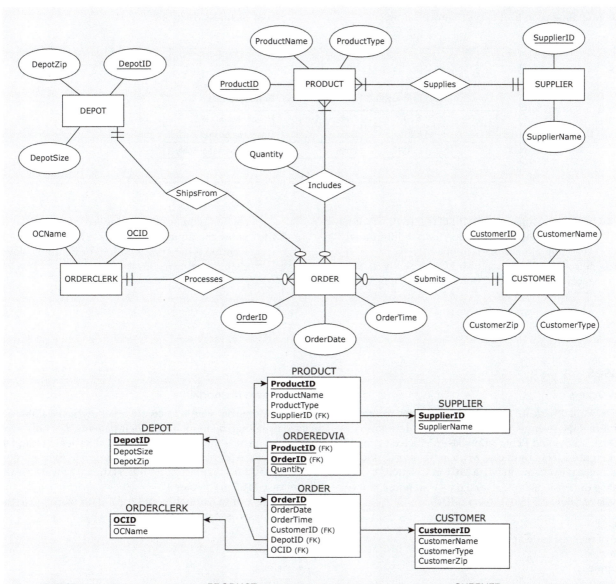

FIGURE 8.48   Source 2: The Big Z Inc. Orders Database.

E8.4. Consider the following scenario involving the slowly changing dimension EMPLOYEE shown below:

Assume Sidney's title changes from Business Analyst to Senior Business Analyst.

EMPLOYEE

EmployeeKey	EmployeeID	EmployeeName	EmployeeTitle
1	E101	Ava	Project Manager
2	E202	Sidney	Business Analyst
3	E303	Lena	Senior Business Analyst

E8.4a Show the dimension EMPLOYEE (with all of its records) if the Type 1 option for handling slowly changing dimensions is applied.

E8.4b Show the dimension EMPLOYEE (with all of its records) if the Type 2 option for handling slowly changing dimensions is applied.

E8.4c Show the dimension EMPLOYEE (with all of its records) if the Type 3 option for handling slowly changing dimensions is applied.

Mini Cases

MC6 Jones Dozers

Jones Dozers wants to create an analytical database to analyze its sales and rentals revenue. The only available data source is the Jones Dozers Sales and Rentals Database (depicted by the ER diagram in Figure 2.59 in mini case **MC6** in Chapter 2, and the relational schema created in mini case **MC6** in Chapter 3).

Create a dimensional model for a data warehouse that enables analysis of sales and rentals revenue by:

- date
- type of revenue (sale or rental)
- customer
- equipment
- sales rep

Each row in the fact table will represent the monetary amount of revenue taken in during one sale or rental transaction.

MC7 Midtown Memorial

Midtown Memorial wants to create an analytical database to analyze drug ingredient intake by their patients. The only available data source is the Midtown Memorial Patients Drug Dispensal Database (depicted by the ER diagram in Figure 2.60 in mini case **MC7** in Chapter 2, and the relational schema created in mini case **MC7** in Chapter 3).

Create a dimensional model for a data warehouse that enables analysis of ingredient intake events by:

- date
- time
- patient
- nurse
- drug
- ingredient

Each row in the fact table will represent the amount (calculated as: quantity × dosage) of one ingredient taken by one patient during one drug intake event.

Data Warehouse Implementation and Use

INTRODUCTION

The previous chapter dealt with the issues related to data warehouse modeling. This chapter focuses on the subsequent steps in the data warehouse development process. In addition to describing and illustrating the data warehouse implementation steps, such as creating a data warehouse, the ETL process, developing data warehouse front-end applications, and data warehouse deployment, we will also discuss how data warehouses are used. The particular aspect of data warehouse use that this chapter focuses on is online analytical processing (OLAP).

The topics here will be illustrated using the modified ZAGI Retail Company example, similar to the example used to illustrate the data warehousing modeling process in Chapter 8. The example is slightly expanded in order to illustrate the topics covered in this chapter.

CREATING A DATA WAREHOUSE

Creating a data warehouse involves using the functionalities of database management software to implement the data warehouse model as a collection of physically created and mutually connected database tables. Most often, data warehouses are modeled as relational databases. Consequently, they are implemented using a relational DBMS.

For example, let us assume that the ZAGI Retail Company already went through the data warehouse modeling stage and created the model for the data warehouse shown in Figure 9.1.

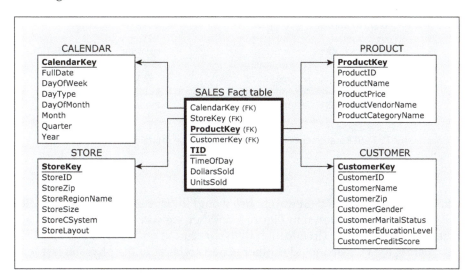

FIGURE 9.1   A data warehouse model.

```
CREATE TABLE calendar
        (       calendarkey                     INT,
                fulldate                        DATE,
                dayofweek                       CHAR(15),
                daytype                         CHAR(20),
                dayofmonth                      INT,
                month                           CHAR(10),
                quarter                         CHAR(2),
                year                            INT,
                PRIMARY KEY                     (calendarkey));

CREATE TABLE store
        (       storekey                        INT,
                storeid                         CHAR(5),
                storezip                        CHAR(5),
                storeregionname                 CHAR(15),
                storesize                       INT,
                storecsystem                    CHAR(15),
                storelayout                     CHAR(15),
                PRIMARY KEY                     (storekey));

CREATE TABLE product
        (       productkey                      INT,
                productid                       CHAR(5),
                productname                     CHAR(25),
                productprice                    NUMBER(7,2),
                productvendorname               CHAR(25),
                productcategoryname             CHAR(25),
                PRIMARY KEY                     (productkey));

CREATE TABLE customer
        (       customerkey                     INT,
                customerid                      CHAR(7),
                customername                    CHAR(15),
                customerzip                     CHAR(5),
                customergender                  CHAR(15),
                customermaritalstatus           CHAR(15),
                customereducationlevel          CHAR(15),
                customercreditscore             INT,
                PRIMARY KEY                     (customerkey));

CREATE TABLE sales
        (       calendarkey                     INT,
                storekey                        INT,
                productkey                      INT,
                customerkey                     INT,
                tid                             CHAR(15),
                timeofday                       TIME,
                dollarssold                     NUMBER(10,2),
                unitssold                       INT,
                PRIMARY KEY                     (productkey, tid),
                FOREIGN KEY (calendarkey)       REFERENCES calendar,
                FOREIGN KEY (storekey)          REFERENCES store,
                FOREIGN KEY (productkey)        REFERENCES product,
                FOREIGN KEY (customerkey)       REFERENCES customer);
```

FIGURE 9.2   CREATE TABLE statements for the data warehouse model shown in Figure 9.1.

In this case, creating a data warehouse would involve executing the five CREATE TABLE SQL statements shown in Figure 9.2. When executed, these statements create the data warehouse tables. (In addition to the execution of the CREATE TABLE statements, creating a database includes other actions related to the physical implementation of the data warehouse, such as indexing). The created data warehouse tables will be populated using the ETL infrastructure.

ETL: EXTRACTION, TRANSFORMATION, LOAD

Once a data warehouse is modeled, the collection of empty data warehouse tables is created using DBMS software, as illustrated above. The next step is to insert data into these tables. A set of processes is used to populate the data warehouse tables with the appropriate relevant data retrieved from the operational databases. This set of processes is known as ETL (extraction, transformation, and load).

We will use the expanded ZAGI Retail Company example to illustrate the ETL processes. The tables shown in Figure 9.1 will be populated with the data from the following three data sources:

Source 1: The ZAGI Retail Company Sales Department Database shown in
Figures 9.3 and 9.4

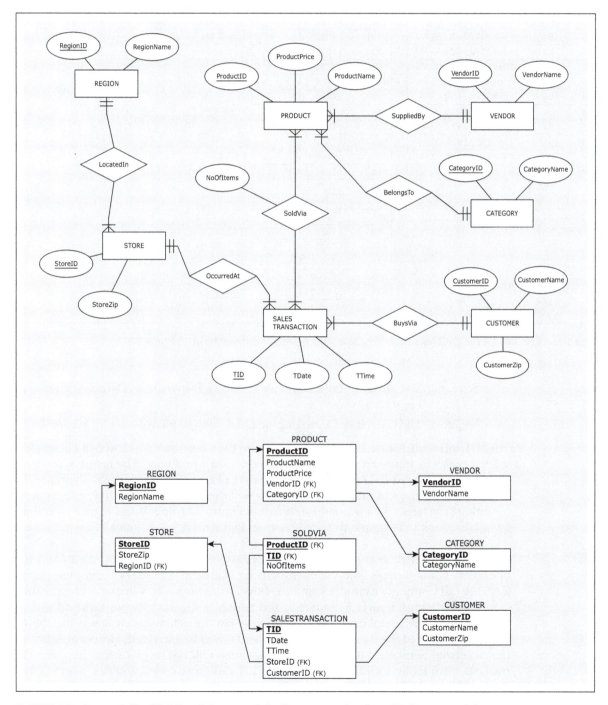

FIGURE 9.3 Source 1: The ZAGI Retail Company Sales Department Database ER diagram and the resulting relational schema.

REGION

RegionID	RegionName
C	Chicagoland
T	Tristate

STORE

StoreID	StoreZip	RegionID
S1	60600	C
S2	60605	C
S3	35400	T

PRODUCT

ProductID	ProductName	ProductPrice	VendorID	CategoryID
1X1	Zzz Bag	$100	PG	CP
2X2	Easy Boot	$70	MK	FW
3X3	Cosy Sock	$15	MK	FW
4X4	Dura Boot	$90	PG	FW
5X5	Tiny Tent	$150	MK	CP
6X6	Biggy Tent	$250	MK	CP

VENDOR

VendorID	VendorName
PG	Pacifica Gear
MK	Mountain King

CATEGORY

CategoryID	CategoryName
CP	Camping
FW	Footwear

SALES TRANSACTION

TID	CustomerID	StoreID	TDate	TTime
T111	1-2-333	S1	1-Jan-2013	8:23:59 AM
T222	2-3-444	S2	1-Jan-2013	8:24:30 AM
T333	1-2-333	S3	2-Jan-2013	8:15:08 AM
T444	3-4-555	S3	2-Jan-2013	8:20:33 AM
T555	2-3-444	S3	2-Jan-2013	8:30:00 AM
T666	2-3-444	S1	3-Jan-2013	8:00:00 AM
T777	3-4-555	S2	3-Jan-2013	8:10:00 AM
T888	1-2-333	S3	4-Jan-2013	8:05:00 AM
T999	2-3-444	S2	4-Jan-2013	9:07:33 AM
T1000	2-3-444	S2	4-Jan-2013	9:07:33 AM

SOLDVIA

ProductID	TID	NoOfItems
1X1	T111	1
2X2	T222	1
3X3	T333	5
1X1	T333	1
4X4	T444	1
2X2	T444	2
4X4	T555	4
5X5	T555	2
6X6	T555	1
1X1	T666	1
2X2	T777	1
3X3	T777	2
1X1	T888	2
1X1	T999	3
3X3	T999	4
4X4	T999	2
1X1	T1000	3
3X3	T1000	4
4X4	T1000	2

CUSTOMER

CustomerID	CustomerName	CustomerZip
1-2-333	Tina	60137
2-3-444	Tony	60611
3-4-555	Pam	35401

FIGURE 9.4 Source 1: Data records for the ZAGI Retail Company Sales Department Database shown in Figure 9.3.

Source 2: The ZAGI Retail Company Facilities Department Database shown in Figure 9.5

Source 3: The Customer Demographic Data external table shown in Figure 9.6

The ETL infrastructure will *extract* the data from the three sources (shown in Figures 9.3, 9.4, 9.5, and 9.6), *transform* it, and *load* it into the data warehouse. The result of this process is the populated data warehouse as shown in Figure 9.7. In order to illustrate each of the three portions of the ETL process, we will describe the ETL activities necessary for linking the target data warehouse shown in Figure 9.1 (model) and Figure 9.7 (populated tables) with the source systems shown in Figures 9.3, 9.4, 9.5, and 9.6.

EXTRACTION Extraction refers to the retrieval of analytically useful data from the operational data sources that will eventually be loaded into the data warehouse. In the ZAGI Retail Company example scenario above, extraction refers to extracting the data from three sources: Source 1, Source 2, and Source 3. The data to be extracted is data that is analytically useful in the data warehouse. For the data warehouse schema shown in Figure 9.1, all of the data from Sources 1 and 3 will be extracted. However, some of the data from Source 2 will be extracted and some will not be extracted. In particular the data from tables CONTRACTOR and BUILTBY in Source 2 will not be extracted. During the modeling stage, it was decided that the data about the contractors who built the stores is not analytically relevant for a target warehouse whose subject of analysis is sales. This decision is reflected in the model shown in Figure 9.1, which does not include table columns for the data regarding the store's building contractors.

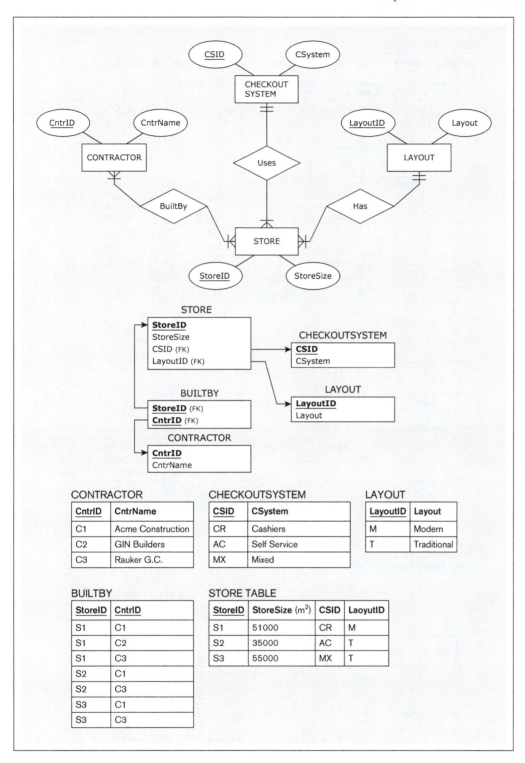

CONTRACTOR

CntrID	CntrName
C1	Acme Construction
C2	GIN Builders
C3	Rauker G.C.

CHECKOUTSYSTEM

CSID	CSystem
CR	Cashiers
AC	Self Service
MX	Mixed

LAYOUT

LayoutID	Layout
M	Modern
T	Traditional

BUILTBY

StoreID	CntrID
S1	C1
S1	C2
S1	C3
S2	C1
S2	C3
S3	C1
S3	C3

STORE TABLE

StoreID	StoreSize (m^2)	CSID	LaoyutID
S1	51000	CR	M
S2	35000	AC	T
S3	55000	MX	T

FIGURE 9.5   Source 2: The ZAGI Retail Company Facilities Department Database.

CUSTOMER TABLE

CustomerID	Customer Name	Gender	Marital Status	Education Level	Credit Score
1-2-333	Tina	Female	Single	College	700
2-3-444	Tony	Male	Single	High School	650
3-4-555	Pammy	Female	Married	College	623

FIGURE 9.6   Source 3: The Customer Demographic Data external table.

CALENDAR Dimension

Calendar Key	FullDate	DayOfWeek	DayType	DayOfMonth	Month	Qtr	Year
1	1/1/2013	Tuesday	Weekend/Holiday	1	January	Q1	2013
2	1/2/2013	Wednesday	Workday	2	January	Q1	2013
3	1/3/2013	Thursday	Workday	3	January	Q1	2013
4	1/4/2013	Friday	Workday	4	January	Q1	2013

PRODUCT Dimension

ProductKey	ProductID	ProductName	ProductPrice	ProductVendor Name	ProductCategory Name
1	1X1	Zzz Bag	$100	Pacifica Gear	Camping
2	2X2	Easy Boot	$70	Mountain King	Footwear
3	3X3	Cosy Sock	$15	Mountain King	Footwear
4	4X4	Dura Boot	$90	Pacifica Gear	Footwear
5	5X5	Tiny Tent	$150	Mountain King	Camping
6	6X6	Biggy Tent	$250	Mountain King	Camping

STORE Dimension

StoreKey	StoreID	StoreZip	StoreRegion Name	Store Size (m²)	Store CSystem	Store Layout
1	S1	60600	Chicagoland	51000	Cashiers	Modern
2	S2	60605	Chicagoland	35000	Self Service	Traditional
3	S3	35400	Tristate	55000	Mixed	Traditional

CUSTOMER Dimension

Customer Key	CustomerID	Customer Name	Customer Zip	Customer Gender	Customer Marital Status	Customer Education Level	Customer Credit Score
1	1-2-333	Tina	60137	Female	Single	College	700
2	2-3-444	Tony	60611	Male	Single	High School	650
3	3-4-555	Pam	35401	Female	Married	College	623

SALES Fact table

CalendarKey	StoreKey	ProductKey	Customer Key	TID	TimeOfDay	Dollars Sold	UnitsSold
1	1	1	1	T111	8:23:59 AM	$100	1
1	2	2	2	T222	8:24:30 AM	$70	1
2	3	3	1	T333	8:15:08 AM	$75	5
2	3	1	1	T333	8:15:08 AM	$100	1
2	3	4	3	T444	8:20:33 AM	$90	1
2	3	2	3	T444	8:20:33 AM	$140	2
2	3	4	2	T555	8:30:00 AM	$360	4
2	3	5	2	T555	8:30:00 AM	$300	2
2	3	6	2	T555	8:30:00 AM	$250	1
3	1	1	2	T666	8:00:00 AM	$100	1
3	2	2	3	T777	8:10:00 AM	$70	1
3	2	3	3	T777	8:10:00 AM	$30	2
4	3	1	1	T888	8:05:00 AM	$200	2
4	2	1	2	T999	9:07:33 AM	$300	3
4	2	3	2	T999	9:07:33 AM	$60	4
4	2	4	2	T999	9:07:33 AM	$180	2

FIGURE 9.7 A data warehouse populated with the data from Sources 1, 2, and 3.

Even if the contractor-related data were somehow deemed relevant for the analysis of sales, it would be difficult to include the contractor-related data in the data warehouse. Note in Figure 9.5 that stores have multiple contractors. Therefore, store building contractor information cannot be represented as an attribute of the dimension STORE. Also keep in mind that the subject of analysis in this data warehouse is sales. It is unclear how a particular contractor's work affects the sales in the stores that the contractor builds. Each store has multiple contractors, and the underlying data source has no information about what percentage of work on the store was done by which contractor. The result is the inability to account for the exact actual effect of a contractor on sales in a store. Therefore, the data from tables CONTRACTOR and BUILTBY is left out of the target data warehouse.

The issue of what to extract is dealt within the requirements and modeling stages. Requirements and modeling stages of the data warehouse include the examination of the available sources. During the creation of the ETL infrastructure, the data model (that already captures the decisions on what data to include from the underlying data sources) provides a blueprint for the extraction procedures. It is possible that in the process of creating the ETL infrastructure, the data warehouse development team may realize that certain ETL actions should be done differently from what is prescribed by the given data model. In such cases, the project will move iteratively back from the creation of ETL infrastructure to the requirement stage, as shown in Figure 7.9 in Chapter 7. Recall that no implicit changes of requirements are permitted in any of the data warehouse development steps, including the step of creating the ETL infrastructure. Any changes in requirements must be documented and reflected in the subsequent visualizations and models.

TRANSFORMATION   Transformation refers to the process of transforming the structure of extracted data in order to fit the structure of the target data warehouse model.

In the case of the ZAGI Retail Company, the transformation process is illustrated by the following steps. The records from the Source 1 CUSTOMER table in Figure 9.4 are merged with the records from the Source 3 CUSTOMER table in Figure 9.6. In other words, data about customers involved in sales transactions is merged with customers' demographic data. The surrogate key is added to each record and data is transformed in such a way to fit the structure of the dimension CUSTOMER in the target data warehouse, as shown in Figure 9.7.

In addition to changing the structure of the extracted data, the transformation part of the ETL process also includes data quality control and, if needed, data quality improvement. Even though it would be ideal if every underlying operational source contained the data of the highest quality, in reality it is quite common that some of the data in the data sources exhibit data quality problems, such as the ones described in Chapter 6. In those cases, the process of transformation has to enable the detection and correction of the low-quality data. This part of the transformation process is often referred to as **data cleansing (scrubbing)**.

Two tables from Source 1 in Figure 9.4 contain records with the uniqueness data quality problem. In particular, the last displayed record in the SALESTRANSACTION table and the last three records in the SOLDVIA table are a result of the uniqueness data quality problem. The data entry process in Source 1 incorrectly recorded the same transaction twice, using two different TID values (*T999* and *T1000*). Both recorded transactions involve the same customer, store, and products and occurred on the same day at the exact same time. The data cleansing action that took place during the transformation process identified this uniqueness data quality problem and solved it by excluding the records with the TID value of *T1000* from the set of extracted data. Consequently, as shown in Figure 9.7, this low-quality data did not end up in the SALES fact table in the data warehouse.

In addition to correcting the data quality problems in the underlying sources, the process of transformation may involve standardizing different versions of the same data present in different data sources. It is very common for organizations to have separate operational databases with overlapping information. For example, in the ZAGI

Retail Company Source 1 and Source 2 databases, both have overlapping information about stores (Store ID and Store Zip). Fortunately, this information is recorded in the exact same fashion in Sources 1 and 2. However, Source 1 and Source 3 contain an instance of overlapping information about customers that is not recorded in the same fashion. In particular, the customer whose ID is *3-4-555* in table CUSTOMER in Source 1 (shown in Figure 9.4) has her name recorded as *Pam*. That same customer in table CUSTOMER in Source 3 (shown in Figure 9.6) has her name recorded as *Pammy*. The transformation process recognizes that these are both variations of the same name belonging to the same person and chooses one of them (in this case, *Pam*) to be used in the dimension CUSTOMER, as shown in Figure 9.7.

LOAD   Load refers to the process of loading the extracted, transformed, and quality assured data into the target data warehouse. The ETL infrastructure facilitates the load as a batch process that inserts the data into the data warehouse tables in an automatic fashion without user involvement. The initial load, which populates initially empty data warehouse tables, is known as the **first load**. The first load can involve large amounts of data, depending on the desired time horizon of the data in the newly initiated data warehouse. Every subsequent load is referred to as a **refresh load**. The **refresh cycle** refers to the frequency with which the data warehouse is reloaded with new data. The refresh cycle is determined in advance, based on the analytical needs of the business users of the data warehouse and the technical feasibility of the system. For example, a data warehouse can be refreshed once every day or once every few hours. In the case of so-called **active data warehouses**, the loads occur in micro batches that happen continuously, ensuring that the data in the data warehouse is updated close to real time (enabling analysis of the latest data).

The data warehouse is loaded for the first time with the data from the sources and sources' archives. The data warehouse is then refreshed according to the chosen refresh cycle, with the new data from the sources.

The ETL processes are facilitated by the ETL infrastructure. Typically, the process of creating the ETL infrastructure includes using specialized ETL software tools and/or writing code. Due to the amount of detail that has to be considered, creating ETL infrastructure is often the most time- and resource-consuming part of the data warehouse development process. Although labor intensive, the properly undertaken process of creating the ETL infrastructure is essentially predetermined by the results of the requirements collection and data warehouse modeling processes that specify the sources and the target.

ONLINE ANALYTICAL PROCESSING (OLAP)

OLAP is an acronym that stands for online analytical processing. The term OLAP was devised as a contrast to another acronym, OLTP, which stands for online transaction processing. Before we explain the term OLAP, we will first briefly clarify the term OLTP.

Online transaction processing (OLTP) refers to the updating (i.e., inserting, modifying, and deleting), querying, and presenting data from databases for operational purposes. In addition to the retrievals of data from operational databases, OLTP encompasses all the everyday update transactions done on the operational database systems, such as a transaction reflecting a withdrawal from a checking account or a transaction creating an airline reservation. An often-used technical term for an operational database is an "OLTP system."

Online analytical processing (OLAP) refers to querying and presenting data from data warehouses and/or data marts for analytical purposes. While OLTP is the term used in conjunction with traditional databases for operational (day-to-day) purposes, the term OLAP relates to the use of the data from data warehouses and data marts. Another difference between OLAP and OLTP is that OLTP systems are capable of *updating, querying, and presenting* data, whereas OLAP tools can only engage in *querying and presenting* data. While OLTP systems routinely perform transactions that insert, modify, and delete data from databases, OLAP tools are *read only*. OLAP tools are used exclusively for the retrieval of data from analytical repositories to be used in the decision-making process. Users of OLAP tools can quickly read and interpret data that is gathered and structured specifically for analysis and subsequently make fact-based decisions.

The terms OLTP and OLAP predate the Internet era. The word "online," used in both of these terms, is not associated with the Internet. Instead, "online" refers to a type of computer processing in which the computer responds immediately (or at least very quickly) to user requests. In today's world, we are accustomed to the fact that computers perform the processing, updating, and retrieving of data instantaneously. However, at the time the term OLTP was created, many computers still used pre-hard-drive devices, such as magnetic tapes and punch-card readers. The word "online" was meant to underscore the immediacy of the results, in which database systems used a direct access type of storage, such as a hard drive, instead of a sequential (slow) access storage device, such as a magnetic tape.

OLAP/BI TOOLS

The data in a data warehouse can be accessed directly by the users via the language of the database management software (e.g., SQL). However, a more common method of direct use of this data is access and analysis via **online analytical processing OLAP tools**. OLAP tools are also known as **business intelligence (BI) tools**. In this book, we will refer to these tools as **OLAP/BI tools** to capture both naming alternatives.

OLAP/BI tools are designed for the analysis of dimensionally modeled data. As we discussed in Chapter 8, regardless of which data warehousing approach is chosen, the data that is accessible by the end user is typically structured as a dimensional model. Therefore, OLAP/BI tools can be used on analytical data stores created with different modeling approaches, as illustrated in Figure 9.8.

OLAP/BI tools allow users to query fact and dimension tables by using simple point-and-click query-building applications. Based on the point-and-click actions by the user of the OLAP/BI tool, the tool writes and executes the code in the language (e.g., SQL) of the database management system that hosts the data warehouse or data mart that is being queried.

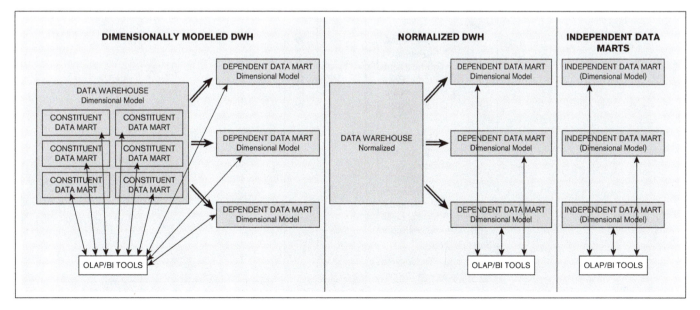

FIGURE 9.8 OLAP/BI tools as an interface to data warehouses modeled using different approaches.

OLAP/BI TOOLS FUNCTIONALITIES

There are numerous OLAP/BI tools (by vendors such as Microstrategy, Cognos-acquired by IBM, Business Objects-acquired by SAP, Hyperion-acquired by Oracle, Microsoft, and others) available in the marketplace today. Here, we give an overview of functionalities that are common for all OLAP/BI tools. The three basic OLAP/BI tool features regularly used by analysts are commonly referred to as:

- slice and dice
- pivot (rotate)
- drill down and drill up

We will use examples related to the ZAGI Retail Company scenario to illustrate these operations. The examples are based on the dimensionally modeled data set shown in Figure 9.7.

Let us assume that an analyst end user from the ZAGI Retail Company wants to use an OLAP/BI tool to analyze the DollarsSold and UnitsSold sales facts across all attributes of all dimensions in Figure 9.7. In that scenario, an OLAP/BI tool interface, such as the one shown in Figure 9.9, would be given to the user. The user

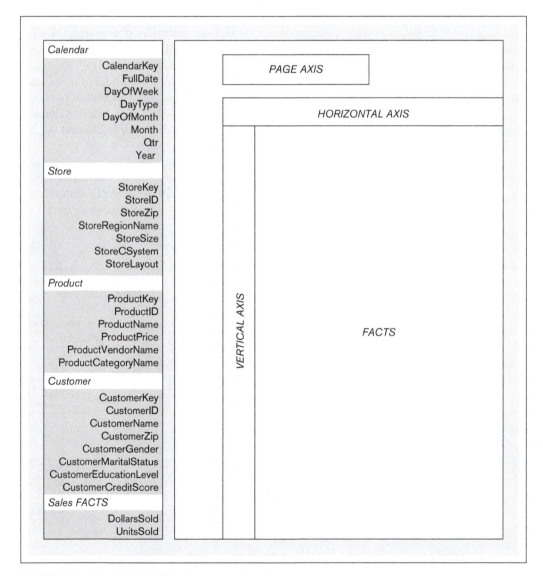

FIGURE 9.9   A typical OLAP/BI tool query construction space.

would specify any of the particular queries analyzing DollarsSold and/or UnitsSold across the dimensions by simply choosing the attributes needed for the query via the drag-and-drop method.

For example, let us assume that an analyst wants to display the results of the following query:

OLAP Query 1: *For each individual store, show separately for male and female shoppers the number of product units sold for each product category.*

Specifying this query in an OLAP/BI tool is straightforward. The user would drag the attributes needed for the query from the part of the graphical interface representing the schema and drop them on the part of the graphical interface representing the query construction space. The typical basic form of the result of a query created with an OLAP/BI tool is a table-shaped report whose rows and columns are captioned with the names of the dimensions' attributes and whose content is data taken from a fact table. This data is summarized in a way that satifies the conditions of a query.

The query construction space in a typical OLAP/BI tool contains the vertical, horizontal, and page axes as well as the area for facts. By dragging a dimension attribute to a vertical axis, the user specifies that results referring to that dimension attribute will be put in rows. By dragging a dimension attribute to a horizontal axis, the user specifies that results referring to that dimension attribute will be put in columns.

Let us observe how such a query construction space is utilized. In the case of OLAP Query 1, the user would drag the attribute StoreID from dimension STORE, the attribute Gender from dimension CUSTOMER, and the attribute Category from dimension PRODUCT to one of the axes. For example, StoreID and Gender can be dragged to the vertical axis, and Category can be dragged to the horizontal axis. Also, the attribute UnitsSold from the SALES fact table would be dragged into the fact area of the query construction space. This is illustrated in Figure 9.10.

Once the query is constructed, as shown in Figure 9.10, and then executed, the results will be shown on screen. Figure 9.11 illustrates how a typical OLAP/BI tool would display the result of OLAP Query 1.

When a query has displayed the results on a computer screen, such as in Figure 9.11, the user has the option to perform any of the three basic OLAP operations: slice and dice, pivot (rotate), and drill down or drill up.

In a typical OLAP/BI tool, slice and dice, pivot, and drill down/drill up functionalities involve a simple combination of point-and-click and drag-and-drop actions. We will now describe and illustrate each of these functionalities.

Slice and Dice

The **slice and dice** operation adds, replaces, or eliminates specified dimension attributes (or particular values of the dimension attributes) from the already displayed result. For example, the user using the OLAP/BI tool can modify OLAP Query 1 so that only the results for stores 1 and 2 are displayed. In other words, the results showing sales in store 3 will be "sliced out" from the original query shown in Figure 9.11. The modified query is specified as follows:

OLAP Query 2: *For stores 1 and 2, show separately for male and female shoppers the number of product units sold for each product category.*

Figure 9.12 shows the result of OLAP Query 2, created by performing a slice and dice operation on the query shown in Figure 9.11.

In addition to eliminating dimension attributes or selected values of dimension attributes, a slice and dice operation can replace or add dimension attributes. This is illustrated in the next example, in which the user modifies the query shown in Figure 9.11 by replacing the ProductCategory attribute from the PRODUCT dimension

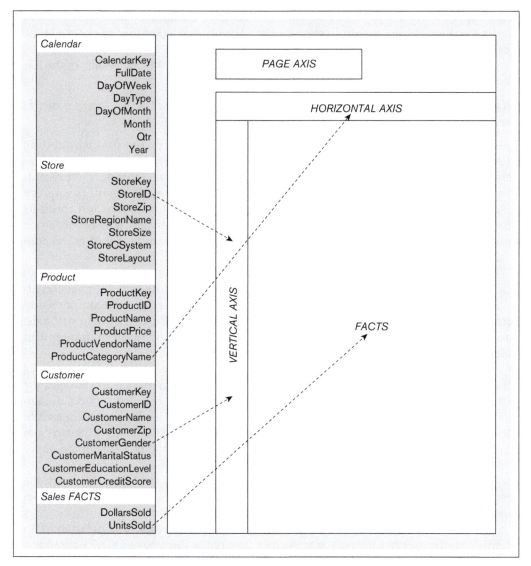

FIGURE 9.10   OLAP/BI tool query construction actions for OLAP Query 1.

with the DayType attribute from the CALENDAR dimension. The wording of the modified query is as follows:

OLAP Query 3: *For each individual store, show separately for male and female shoppers the number of product units sold on workdays and on weekends/holidays.*

		Camping	Footwear
		Sales-Units Sold	
Store 1			
	Female	1	0
	Male	1	0
Store 2			
	Female	0	3
	Male	3	7
Store 3			
	Female	3	8
	Male	3	4

FIGURE 9.11   OLAP Query 1 results.

		Camping	Footwear
		Sales-Units Sold	
Store 1			
	Female	1	0
	Male	1	0
Store 2			
	Female	0	3
	Male	3	7

FIGURE 9.12   The first example of slice and dice: OLAP Query 2 results.

	Sales-Units Sold	
	Weekend/ Holiday	Workday
Store 1		
Female	1	0
Male	0	1
Store 2		
Female	0	3
Male	1	9
Store 3		
Female	0	11
Male	0	7

FIGURE 9.13 The second example of slice and dice: OLAP Query 3 results.

Figure 9.13 shows the result of OLAP Query 3, created by performing another slice and dice operation on the query shown in Figure 9.11.

Pivot (Rotate)

Unlike the slice and dice operation, the **pivot (rotate)** operation does not change the values displayed in the original query, it simply reorganizes them.

The following example of a pivot operation uses the query shown in Figure 9.11 as a starting point and then simply swaps the axes for the ProductCategory attribute and the StoreID attribute. The result of this pivot action is shown in Figure 9.14.

Because the pivot action does not change the values shown to the user, the wording for the queries shown in Figures 9.11 and 9.14 is the same:

OLAP Query 1: For each individual store, show separately for male and female shoppers the number of product units sold for each product category.

In Figure 9.11, ProductCategory was placed on the horizontal axis and CustomerGender was placed on the vertical axis. In Figure 9.14, the pivoting action was performed and ProductCategory was rotated onto the vertical axis, whereas CustomerGender was moved to the horizontal axis.

	Sales-Units Sold	
	Female	Male
Store 1		
Camping	1	1
Footwear	0	0
Store 2		
Camping	0	3
Footwear	3	7
Store 3		
Camping	3	3
Footwear	8	4

FIGURE 9.14 The first example of pivot.

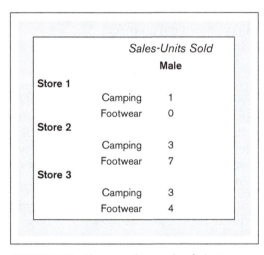

FIGURE 9.15 The second example of pivot: page axis.

		Sales-Units Sold
		Male
Store 1		
	Camping	1
	Footwear	0
Store 2		
	Camping	3
	Footwear	7
Store 3		
	Camping	3
	Footwear	4

FIGURE 9.16 The second example of pivot: page axis (another value).

In addition to the vertical axis and the horizontal axis, most OLAP/BI tools feature the so-called "page axis." This is an additional axis that can be used during the pivot operation. Figure 9.15 illustrates the result of using the query shown in Figure 9.14 and pivoting the CustomerGender attribute from the horizontal axis to the page axis. As shown in Figure 9.15, the page axis allows viewing the table per single value of the attribute placed in the page axis. In this case, the table shows the sales in different stores per product category for *Female* shoppers only.

Users can easily switch from one value of the attribute (*Female,* as shown in Figure 9.15) to another value of the attribute (*Male,* as shown in Figure 9.16) by using a point-and-click menu mechanism that usually accompanies the page axis feature in a typical OLAP/BI tool. As a result, the table in Figure 9.16 shows the sales in different stores per product category for *Male* shoppers only.

Drill Down and Drill Up

The purpose of the **drill down** operation is to make the granularity of the data in the query result *finer*; in the case of **drill up**, it is to make it *coarser*.

The following example uses the Query 1 result shown in Figure 9.11 as a starting point and then drills down in the PRODUCT dimension from ProductCategory to ProductName. The wording of the query is expanded in the following way:

OLAP Query 4: *For each individual store, show separately for male and female shoppers the number of product units sold for each individual product in each product category.*

Figure 9.17 shows the result of OLAP Query 4, created by performing a drill down operation on the query shown in Figure 9.11.

The drill down operation allows users to drill through hierarchies within dimensions. A hierarchy is a set of attributes within a dimension where an attribute is related to one or more attributes at a lower level but only related to one item at a higher level. For example, ProductName and ProductCategory are in a hierarchy because each ProductName belongs to one ProductCategory, while each ProductCategory can have more than one ProductName. For another example of a hierarchy, consider the following attributes in the Store dimension: StoreID, StoreZip, and StoreRegionName. These three attributes form the hierarchy StoreRegionName → StoreZip → StoreID because of the following:

- one StoreID has one StoreZip and one StoreRegionName
- one StoreZip has one StoreRegionName but can have many StoreID values
- one StoreRegionName can have many StoreZip values and subsequently even more StoreID values.

Multiple stores can exist in the same zip code, and multiple zip codes can exist in the same region. Each zip code belongs to one region and each store has one zip code and, therefore, belongs to one region. Thus, sales in the zip codes can be expanded to show sales in individual stores (drill down) or merged into sales within regions (drill up).

Some dimensions can have more than one hierarchy. For example, the STORE dimension has the following hierarchies:

StoreRegionName → StoreZip → StoreID
StoreSize → StoreID
StoreCSystem → StoreID
StoreLayout → StoreID

The hierarchies described above are also known as drill hierarchies. They allow the user to expand a value at one level to show the details below it (drill down), or collapse the details to show only the higher-level values (drill up).

To illustrate the drill up operation, we can simply consider Figure 9.17 as a starting query and then look at Figure 9.11 as the product of a drill up operation from ProductName to ProductCategory.

| | | Camping | | | Footwear | |
		Biggy Tent	Tiny Tent	Zzz Bag	Cosy Sock	Dura Boot	Easy Boot
Store 1							
	Female	0	0	1	0	0	0
	Male	0	0	1	0	0	0
Store 2							
	Female	0	0	0	2	0	1
	Male	0	0	3	4	2	1
Store 3							
	Female	0	0	3	5	1	2
	Male	1	2	0	0	4	0

Sales-Units Sold

FIGURE 9.17 An example of drill down: OLAP Query 4 results.

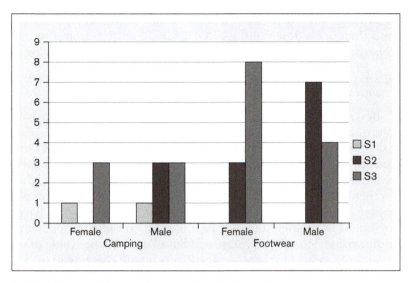

FIGURE 9.18   OLAP Query 1 results, visualized as a chart.

Additional OLAP/BI Tools Functionality Notes

Closer analysis of the above examples reveals that the dimensional model is essential for OLAP. The underlying data must be organized dimensionally, with a fact table in the center connected to a number of dimension tables. If the data were not organized in a dimensional way, the three basic OLAP operations could not be performed effectively or properly.

Along with the ability to perform slice and dice, pivot, and drill down/drill up, many other capabilities are found in various contemporary OLAP tools. In modern OLAP/BI tools, the ability to visualize the answers in a number of graphical ways is a standard feature. For example, any modern OLAP/BI tool is capable of visualizing the answer to Query 1 shown in Figure 9.11 as the chart shown in Figure 9.18.

In addition to the standard operations (pivot, slice and dice, drill up/drill down) and various graphical visualization capabilities, OLAP/BI tools are able to create and examine calculated data; determine comparative or relative differences; conduct exception analysis, trend analysis, forecasting, and regression analysis; and perform a number of other useful analytical functions. However, those functionalities are found in other non-OLAP applications, such as statistical tools or spreadsheet software. What truly distinguishes OLAP/BI tools from other applications is their capability to easily interact with the dimensionally modeled data marts and data warehouses and, consequently, their capability to perform OLAP functions on large amounts of data.

Contemporary spreadsheet software packages include functionalities for performing basic OLAP functions on the limited amount of data they can store. Spreadsheet packages can store significantly less data than the typical amount of data stored in a data warehouse or data mart. However, some spreadsheet tools can be configured to access the data directly from dimensionally modeled data marts and data warehouses hosted by DBMS tools. The spreadsheet tools that can be configured in such a fashion can be effectively considered OLAP/BI tools.

Many existing OLAP/BI tools are Web based, which eliminates the need for installing software at the end user's workstation. Instead, the query construction space, such as the one shown in Figure 9.9, is provided to the end user via a Web browser.

The OLAP/BI tools can be based on several different architectural approaches. At the end of this chapter, we give a brief note outlining the most common OLAP/BI tools architectures.

OLAP/BI TOOLS PURPOSE

OLAP/BI tools can be used for the following two purposes: for *ad-hoc direct analysis* of dimensionally modeled data and for the *creation of front-end applications* for indirect access of dimensionally modeled data.

Ad-hoc direct analysis occurs when a user accesses the data in the data warehouse via an OLAP/BI tool and performs such actions as pivoting, slicing, and drilling. This process is also sometimes referred to as data interrogation, because often the answers to one query lead to new questions. For example, an analyst may create a query using an OLAP/BI tool. The answer to that query may prompt an additional question, which is then answered by pivoting, slicing, or drilling the result of the original query.

In addition to ad-hoc direct analysis, OLAP/BI tools are often used in the process of creating data warehouse front-end applications. The data warehouse front-end application can simply be a collection of the OLAP/BI tool queries created by OLAP/BI tool expert users. Such a collection of queries can be accompanied by a menu structure for navigation and then provided to the users of the data warehouse who do not have the access privilege, expertise, and/or the time to use OLAP/BI tools directly.

DATA WAREHOUSE/DATA MART FRONT–END (BI) APPLICATIONS

In most cases, a portion of the intended users of a data warehouse (often a majority of the users) lack the time and/or expertise to engage in open-ended direct analysis of the data. It is not reasonable to expect everyone who needs to use the data from the data warehouse as a part of their workplace responsibilities to develop their own queries by writing the SQL code or engaging in the ad-hoc use of OLAP/BI tools. Instead, many of the data warehouse and data mart end users access the data through front-end applications. Data warehouse/data mart front-end applications are also commonly referred to as BI applications. Figure 9.19 shows a data warehousing system with front-end applications.

As illustrated front-end applications in a data warehousing system can retrieve data either from the data warehouse itself or from dependent data marts that contain a subset of the data from the data warehouse. Front-end (BI) applications can also retrieve the data from independent data marts when a company stores its analytical data in a collection of independent data marts.

The data warehouse/data mart front-end applications are collections of pre-developed queries organized for simple access, navigation, and use by the end user.

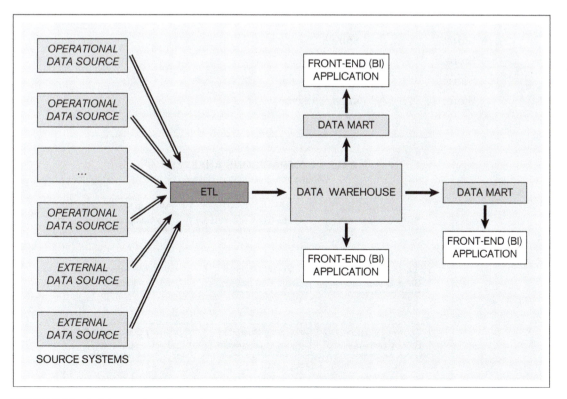

FIGURE 9.19   A data warehousing system with front-end applications.

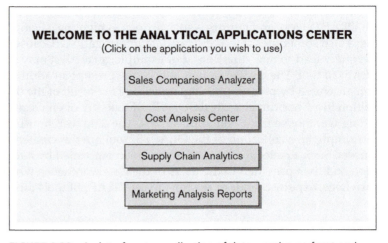

FIGURE 9.20 An interface to a collection of data warehouse front-end applications.

Figure 9.20 shows an example of an interface to a collection of front-end data warehouse applications.

In this example, each of the offered applications contains a set of predeveloped queries retrieving data from the portions of the data warehouse relevant for the given application. For example, choosing the option Sales Comparison Analyzer in Figure 9.20 activates the application shown in Figure 9.21, containing the set of queries retrieving sales comparison data from the data warehouse.

Choosing the Quarterly Store Sales Comparisons option in Figure 9.21 opens up a query presented as an interactive form, such as the one shown in Figure 9.22.

Let us suppose that a user chooses the following parameters in Figure 9.22:

Year 1:	*2012*
Quarter in Year 1:	*Q4*
Year 2:	*2013*
Quarter in Year 2:	*Q3*
Store:	*Store 1*
Store:	*Store 3*
Store:	*Store 7*
Store:	*<none chosen>*
Store:	*<none chosen>*

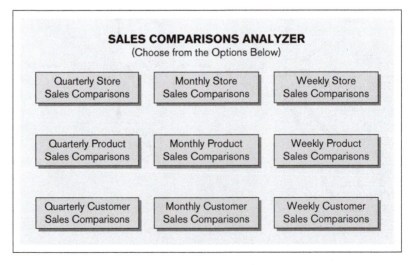

FIGURE 9.21 An interface to a data warehouse front-end application.

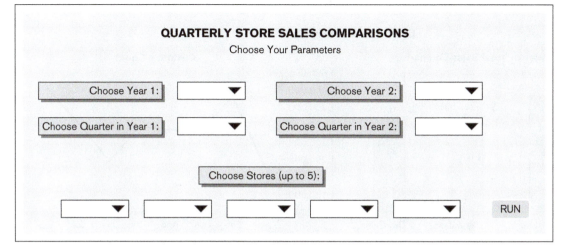

FIGURE 9.22 An interface to a predeveloped data warehouse query.

Once those parameters are chosen in Figure 9.22 and the RUN button is clicked, a report containing the results in a table and graphical chart format is produced, as shown in Figure 9.23.

Developing front-end applications includes creating the set of predeveloped queries and the interfaces to those queries. The process of developing front-end applications can incorporate the use of OLAP/BI tools, other reporting tools, or writing code from scratch. For example, most OLAP/BI tools include functionalities for creating front-end interfaces, such as the ones shown in the examples above. Note that the interface shown in Figure 9.22 accesses the query based on the dimensionally modeled data (modeled as the star schema shown in Figure 9.1). The query on which the interface shown in Figure 9.22 is based could have been created by the OLAP/BI tool shown in Figure 9.9. Using the interface shown in Figure 9.9, a developer would drag attributes Year and Quarter on the horizontal axis, attribute StoreID on the vertical axis, and Sales fact attribute DollarsSold into the Facts space. A query developed in this fashion would then be set up so that the application shown in Figure 9.22, when in use, would slice out all values for Year, Quarter, and StoreID that were not chosen by the user of the application.

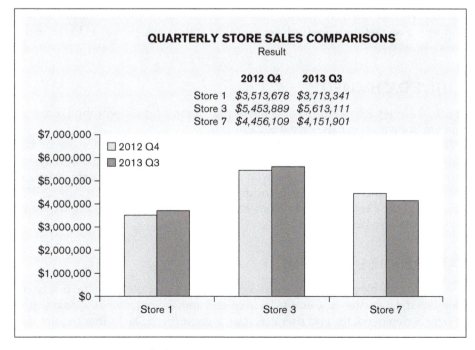

FIGURE 9.23 The results of selecting particular parameter values in Figure 9.22.

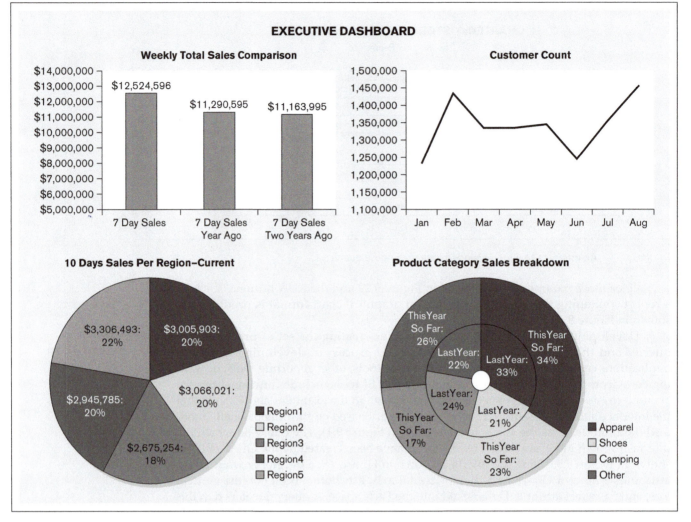

FIGURE 9.24   An executive dashboard.

As is the case with the OLAP/BI tools, access to front-end applications can also be Web based. Web-based front-end applications eliminate the need to install software at the end user's workstation. Instead, access to the interface is provided to the end users via a Web browser.

EXECUTIVE DASHBOARD

Figure 9.24 shows an example of a particular form of data warehouse front-end application known as an executive dashboard.

The **executive dashboard**, as the term suggests, is intended for use by higher-level decision makers within an organization. It contains an organized, easy-to-read display of a number of critically important queries describing the performance of the organization. In general, the use of executive dashboards requires little or no effort or training. As is the case with other front-end data warehouse applications, executive dashboards can also be Web based.

DATA WAREHOUSE DEPLOYMENT

Data warehouse deployment refers to allowing the end user access to the newly created and populated data warehouse and to its front-end applications. Once the data warehousing system is deployed, the end user can start using it for the tasks that require the data from the data warehouse. Typically, the deployment does not occur all at once for the entire population of intended end users. Instead, the deployment process is more gradual.

Like most other information systems, the data warehousing system often goes through a testing phase before it is fully deployed to all of its users. During the so-called **alpha release**, a data warehouse and the associated front-end applications are deployed internally to the members of the development team for initial testing of its functionalities. In the subsequent release (the so-called **beta release**) the data warehousing system is deployed to a selected group of users to test the usability of the system. The feedback from the testing phases may result in making modifications to the system prior to the actual deployment of a functioning data warehousing system. The actual deployment of a functioning data warehousing system is also known as the **production release**.

This chapter has presented the most fundamental issues related to data warehouse implementation and use, from the perspective of business designers and users. The following notes give additional information about database models for OLAP/BI tools and about OLAP/BI architecture options.

A Note About OLAP/BI Tools Database Models

As we stated, OLAP/BI tools are designed for access of dimensionally modeled data. Here, we will give a brief discussion of the two different database models that are used to implement the dimensionally modeled data stores:

- relational database model
- multidimensional database model

Recall that the relational database model is the basis for the contemporary relational DBMS software packages, which are used to implement the majority of today's operational corporate databases. Examples of relational DBMS software include Oracle, MySQL, Microsoft SQL Server, PostgreSQL, IBM DB2, and Teradata.[1] As we explained in Chapter 3, a relational database model is a collection of two-dimensional tables in which each row of the table represents a database record.

The relational model is not the only way through which dimensionally modeled databases can be implemented. Another alternative for implementation of dimensionally modeled data is via the **multidimensional database model**. In this model, a database is a collection of so-called **cubes**. Conceptually, there is no difference in dimensional modeling for relational models or cubes. The conceptual design still involves creating star schemas with dimensions and facts. The difference is in the physical implementation. In order to illustrate the multidimensional database model and contrast it with the relational model, we will use the simple example shown in Figure 9.25.

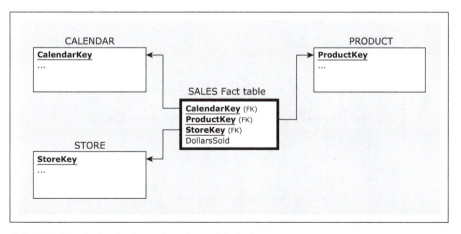

FIGURE 9.25   A simple dimensionally modeled schema.

---

[1]Teradata is an example of a DBMS that was developed specifically to accommodate large data warehouses, whereas the other DBMS mentioned here can be used for hosting operational databases as well as data warehouses.

SALES FACT TABLE

CalendarKey	ProductKey	StoreKey	DollarsSold
1	1	1	$100
1	2	1	$70
1	3	1	$15
.	.	.	.

FIGURE 9.26 The relational implementation of the fact table SALES from Figure 9.25.

The example in Figure 9.25 illustrates a star schema with three dimensions and one fact table. Figure 9.26 shows the relational implementation of the fact table SALES from Figure 9.25. The fact table contains the keys of all dimension tables to which it is connected, and the numeric fact DollarsSold. Each record corresponds to the monetary DollarsSold amount of a specific Product sold in a specific Store on a certain Day.

A multidimensional database model can be visualized as a cube with a number of dimensions. Unlike a geometrical cube, the multidimensional database cube can have more than three dimensions. However, for simplicity's sake, our example has exactly three dimensions.

Figure 9.27 shows the multidimensional implementation of the fact table from Figure 9.25. Each cell in the cube corresponds to the DollarsSold for a specific Product sold in a specific Store on a certain Day. For clarity, only one cell with the amount of $100 is shown, which corresponds to the first record in the fact table SALES in Figure 9.26.

The key difference between the two models is in the method of locating the data. In the relational model, a search has to take place in the fact table in order to locate a record. The speed of the search depends on various issues, such as how the records are sorted or whether the table is indexed. In the multidimensional cube, every record can be looked up directly, eliminating the need for a search. This is because each cell has an address composed of the values of the dimensions' attributes, which can be used for direct access. In order to find data, the dimension values are used to calculate the position and directly access the value in the cell. For example, let us assume that we are performing two retrievals:

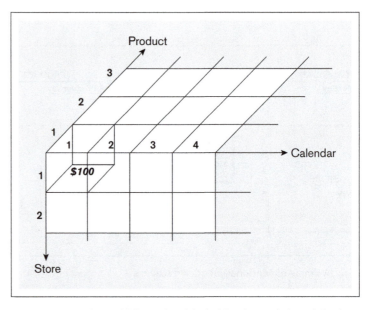

FIGURE 9.27 The multidimensional (cube) implementation of the fact table SALES from Figure 9.26.

- retrieving the DollarsSold value for Store *1*, Product *1*, and Calendar (Day) *1*—depicted as *(1,1,1)* for the purpose of this example
- retrieving the DollarsSold value for Store *1*, Product *3*, and Calendar (Day) *1*—depicted as *(1,3,1)* for the purpose of this example

In the cube, the dimension values *(1,1,1)* directly lead to the sale amount of *$100*, and the dimension values *(1,3,1)* directly lead to the sale amount of *$15*. In other words, searching through other records was not required. On the other hand, in the relational implementation, a search that involves reading and comparing values of other records before reaching the desired record is required. For example, in a fact table implemented as a relational table, such as the one shown in Figure 9.26, the linear search for *(1,3,1)* will involve comparing the searched-for values *(1,3,1)* with values in the table for the first *(1,1,1)* and second *(1,2,1)* record, until we get a match with the third record.

Of course, in real data warehouse data sets, the search space is much bigger. Therefore, the speed of a search is a very critical factor for the performance and usability of a data warehouse. Using direct access enabled by cubes is one way to provide the needed speed of a search. As we mentioned in Chapter 6, the speed of searches in relational tables can be significantly improved by using sorting/indexing in conjunction with different search algorithms.

A Note About OLAP/BI Tools Data Architecture Options

Depending on which database model is used to implement the dimensions and facts, there are several different categories of architectures for OLAP/BI tools. Here, we will describe the three common categories, known as MOLAP, ROLAP, and HOLAP.

MOLAP

A typical **multidimensional online analytical processing (MOLAP)** architecture is shown in Figure 9.28. In the MOLAP the data from the warehouse or from the operational sources is stored in multidimensional cubes. The complexity of the underlying data is hidden from the MOLAP tool user. In other words, users perform common functions in a standard point-and-click way, as shown in Figure 9.10, without having to understand how the cubes are formed and how they differ from relational tables. The query is executed in the MOLAP server, and the resulting data set is sent to the end-user OLAP/BI tool, which presents it to the user in a similar fashion to that shown in Figures 9.11 to 9.18. If an OLAP/BI tool is used as a basis for an end-user application, the queries can be specified as shown in Figure 9.22, and the results can be presented as shown in Figure 9.23.

Generally, a MOLAP server contains a limited amount of data. The main characteristic of MOLAP is that it enables very fast analysis. The way the MOLAP server achieves this goal is through precalculating as many outcomes as possible and storing them in cubes.

It is important to note that while MOLAP cubes perform very well when analyzing aggregated data, they are not appropriate for holding transaction-level detail data.

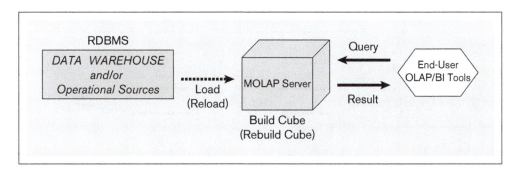

FIGURE 9.28 A typical MOLAP architecture.

As we mentioned earlier in this book, the transaction-level detail data is at the finest granularity where each record corresponds to a single real-world transaction. Cubes are limited in space, and in a typical organization, the sheer amount of transaction-level data would surpass the capacity of a cube. Even if the transaction-level data could somehow fit into the cube, other issues, such as data sparsity, make cubes inappropriate for dealing with nonaggregated data. Most dimension attribute intersections are empty in the case of transaction-level data. For example, if there were no product with a product key of 2 sold in the store with a store key of 2 on the day with calendar key 1, then the cell (2,2,1) would be empty.

MOLAP facilitates very fast execution of queries, as each cell in a cube has a direct address and the answers to common queries are precalculated. The calculation engine can create new information from existing data through formulas and transformations. Preaggregated summary data and precalculated measures enable quick and easy analysis of complex data relationships. Often the query "processing" part boils down to a direct data lookup.

While MOLAP performs very well when it comes to data retrieval, the updating of a cube can be quite slow. Data loading can take hours, and the cube calculation can take even more time. This is because every time new data is available, the cube has to be reloaded and recalculated (rebuilt), as shown in Figure 9.28. However, the speed with which analytical queries can be answered is often a much more important factor than the speed of loading the new data and creating an updated cube.

In typical cases, data is loaded into MOLAP servers from data warehouses hosted on relational DBMS (RDBMS) platforms. However, there are instances in practice when the data is loaded into cubes directly from the operational data sources to satisfy current-data analysis needs. In such cases, the cube itself is a data mart, and there is no data warehouse.

ROLAP

Another important category of OLAP/BI tools is relational OLAP/BI tools, commonly referred to as **relational online analytical processing (ROLAP)** tools. A high-level view of a typical ROLAP architecture is shown in Figure 9.29. The ROLAP tool provides the same common OLAP functionalities described earlier in this chapter. Queries are created in a standard point-and-click way, as shown in Figure 9.10. The ROLAP server translates the queries into SQL statements. The SQL version of the query is sent to the data warehouse hosted on the RDBMS platform. The query is executed in the RDBMS, and the resulting data set is sent to the ROLAP server and then to the end-user OLAP/BI tool, which presents it to the user in a form similar to Figures 9.11 to 9.18. If an OLAP/BI tool is used as the basis for an end-user application, the queries can be specified as shown in Figure 9.22, and the results can be presented as shown in Figure 9.23.

ROLAP architecture imposes no limitations on the size of the database or on the kind of analysis that may be performed. However, due to the fact that results are not precalculated, the performance of queries is not as fast as with MOLAP tools.

The trade-off of MOLAP vs. ROLAP is the trade-off between performance and storage. Queries are executed faster with MOLAP tools, but ROLAP is capable of handling much larger quantities of data, which makes it suitable for processing transaction-level detail data. Also, the continuous advances in the speed of query processing

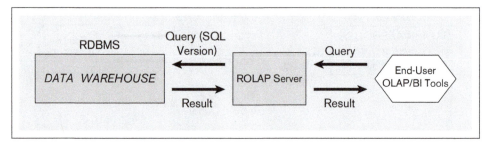

FIGURE 9.29   A typical ROLAP architecture.

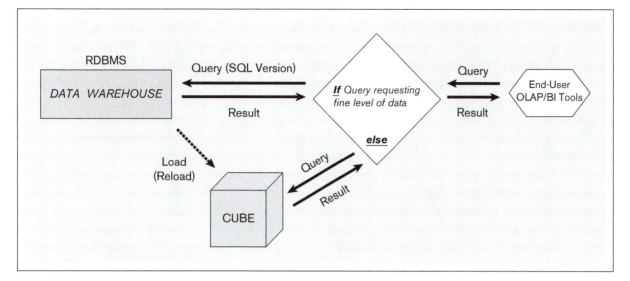

FIGURE 9.30   A typical HOLAP architecture.

with RDBMS software are shrinking the performance gap between MOLAP and RO-LAP tools.

HOLAP

Hybrid online analytical processing (HOLAP) architecture combines MOLAP and ROLAP approaches. The typical HOLAP architecture is shown in Figure 9.30.

HOLAP architecture aspires to take advantage of the strengths of both methods. In a hybrid solution, as shown in Figure 9.30, the relational database can be used to store the detailed transaction-level data, and the multidimensional cube can be used to store summary data. If a query created by the end-user OLAP/BI tool is requesting fine-level detailed data, it is directed to the relational database. On the other hand, if a query is requesting summarized data that is available in the cube, it is directed toward the cube.

Key Terms

Review Questions

Q9.1   How is database management software used in the process of creating a data warehouse?

Q9.2   Briefly describe the extraction process.

Q9.3   Briefly describe the transformation process.

Q9.4   What is the purpose of data cleansing?

Q9.5   Briefly describe the load process.

Q9.6   What is the difference between the first load and a refresh load?

Q9.7   What is the difference between OLAP and OLTP?

Q9.8   What are the three basic OLAP/BI tool features?

Q9.9   What are the two main purposes of OLAP/BI tools?

Q9.10 What is the purpose of data warehouse/data mart front-end applications?

Q9.11 What is an executive dashboard?

Q9.12 Briefly describe the data warehouse deployment process.

Q9.13 What is the difference between the relational and the multidimensional data base model?

Q9.14 Briefly describe MOLAP architecture.

Q9.15 Briefly describe ROLAP architecture.

Q9.16 Briefly describe HOLAP architecture.

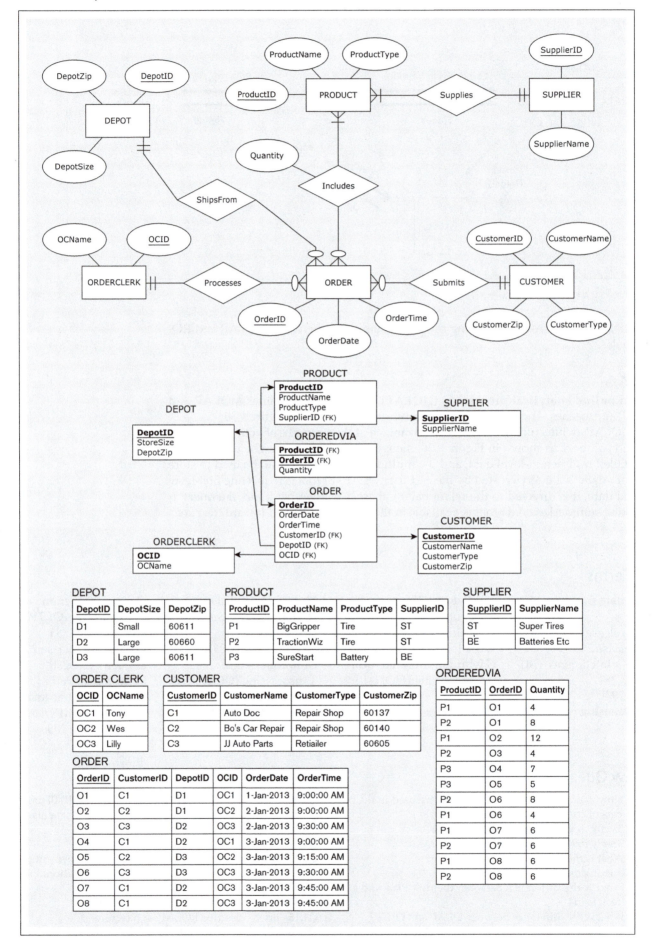

FIGURE 9.31 Source 1: The Big Z Inc. Orders Database.

HUMAN RESOURCES DEPARTMENT TABLE (EMPLOYEE DATA)

EmployeeID	Name	Title	EducationLevel	YearofHIre
OC1	Antonio	Order Clerk	High School	2001
OC2	Wesley	Order Clerk	College	2005
OC3	Lilliana	Order Clerk	College	2005

FIGURE 9.32   Source 2: The Big Z Inc. Human Resources Department Table.

Exercises

E9.1   Consider the following scenario involving Big Z Inc., an automotive products wholesaler.

Big Z Inc. wants to create the analytical database (data warehouse) to analyze its order quantities.

The two available data sources, Source 1 and Source 2, are described below.

Source 1: The Big Z Inc. Orders Database, shown in Figure 9.31.

Source 2: The Big Z Inc. Human Resources Department Table, shown in Figure 9.32.

The data warehouse has to enable an analysis of order quantities by:

- date, including:
  - full date
  - day of week
  - day of month
  - month
  - quarter
  - year
- time
- product, including:
  - product ID
  - product name
  - product type
  - product supplier name
- customer, including:
  - customer ID
  - customer name
  - customer type
  - customer zip
- depot, including:
  - depot id
  - depot size
  - depot zip
- order clerk, including:
  - order clerk id
  - order clerk name

- order clerk title
- order clerk education level
- order clerk year of hire

E9.1a   Based on the sources and requirements listed above, create a dimensional model that will be used for the dimensionally modeled data warehouse for Big Z Inc. (The result for **E9.1a** is the same as the result for **E8.3a**—if you already solved exercise **E8.3a**, you can use that solution as the solution for **E9.1a**.)

E9.1b   Using data from Figures 9.31 and 9.32, illustrate how the tables in the dimensional model created in **E9.1a** would be populated. Make the following assumptions:

- The ETL process chooses the longest version of the name in cases when more than one version of a personal name for the same person is available.
- The ETL process recognizes that the same order was incorrectly recorded twice with two different OrderID values (O7 and O8) in the Big Z Inc. Orders Database.

E9.2   Using OLAP Query 1 shown in Figure 9.11 (based on data from Figure 9.7) as a starting point, give an example that illustrates a pivot operation.

E9.3   Using OLAP Query 1 shown in Figure 9.11 (based on data from Figure 9.7) as a starting point, give an example that illustrates a slice and dice operation.

E9.4   Using OLAP Query 1 shown in Figure 9.11 (based on data from Figure 9.7) as a starting point, give an example that illustrates a drill down operation.

E9.5   Using OLAP Query 1 shown in Figure 9.11 (based on data from Figure 9.7) as a starting point, give an example that illustrates a drill up operation.

More exercises available at *dbtextbook.com*.

PART 3 OTHER TOPICS

Chapter 10

Overview of DBMS Functionalities and Database Administration

INTRODUCTION

The principal mission of this book is to provide coverage of issues related to the design and use of modern operational and analytical databases. This mission is reflected in the content of the previous chapters that focus on the requirements, implementation, and business use of databases.

Comprehensive coverage related to the functioning of database software and hardware, database physical storage details, administration of database systems, and other technical issues is beyond the scope of this book. However, in this chapter we give a concise overview of DBMS components and some of the most essential database administration tasks.

DBMS COMPONENTS

Database management system (DBMS) software is used for the *creation* of databases, the *manipulation* of the data in the databases (i.e., insertion, storage, retrieval, update and deletion), and the *maintenance* of databases. Some DBMS packages also have functionalities for creating front-end applications. Figure 10.1 illustrates the main components of typical DBMS software.

The **data definition component** is used by database designers to create the infrastructure components of the database, such as database tables and referential integrity constraints connecting the created tables. The SQL commands from the DDL (Data Definition Language) category, covered in Chapter 5, are used for this purpose.

```
┌─────────────────────────────────────────┐
│                  DBMS                    │
│  ┌─────────────────────────────────────┐ │
│  │      Data Definition Component      │ │
│  └─────────────────────────────────────┘ │
│  ┌─────────────────────────────────────┐ │
│  │     Data Manipulation Component     │ │
│  └─────────────────────────────────────┘ │
│  ┌─────────────────────────────────────┐ │
│  │  Database Administration Component  │ │
│  └─────────────────────────────────────┘ │
│  ┌─────────────────────────────────────┐ │
│  │   Application Generation Component  │ │
│  └─────────────────────────────────────┘ │
└─────────────────────────────────────────┘
```

FIGURE 10.1 Components of typical DBMS software.

The **data manipulation component** allows the end users to insert, read, update, and delete information in a database. The SQL commands from the DML (Data Manipulation Language) category, covered in Chapter 5, are used for this purpose.

The data manipulation component can be used by end users either directly (direct use) or indirectly via front-end applications (indirect use). In the case of indirect use, the end-user applications communicate with the data manipulation component on the user's behalf. In some DBMS packages, the data manipulation component is primarily intended for use, either directly or indirectly, by one user at a time. Such systems are referred to as a **single-user system** (e.g., MS Access). In professional robust packages, the data manipulation component can be used either directly or indirectly by multiple users at the same time. Such systems are referred to as a **multiuser system** (e.g., Oracle, MySQL, Microsoft SQL Server, PostgreSQL, IBM DB2, and Teradata, to name a few).

The **database administration component** is used to perform the technical, administrative, and maintenance tasks of database systems, such as ensuring security, optimizing performance, and providing backup and recovery. The SQL commands from the DCL (Data Control Language) category and TCL (Transaction Control Language) category, which are typically used during the administrative and other database-related technical processes, are briefly illustrated in this chapter.

The **application development component** provides functionalities to the developers of front-end applications. In some DBMS packages, this component is a part of the DBMS; in other packages, it is available as an add-on.

DATABASE ADMINISTRATION OVERVIEW

Database administration encompasses the activities that are necessary for the proper functioning of a deployed database system. In addition to monitoring and maintaining the database system, data administration activities include security-related tasks, such as data access control, data backup and recovery, and data integrity assurance. Database administration also includes activities related to the performance of the system and to the management of standards and policies for data creation and use.

In the remainder of this chapter, we will briefly illustrate the following principal data administration tasks:

- monitoring and maintaining the database system
- securing the database against unauthorized access
- providing database backup and recovery
- ensuring database integrity
- optimizing database performance
- developing and implementing database policies and standards

MONITORING AND MAINTAINING THE DATABASE SYSTEM

When a database system is launched, its control is turned over *from* the team in charge of database design, implementation, and deployment *to* the database administrators (DBAs). One of the activities that a DBA engages in is monitoring the use and functioning of the database systems.

Regular monitoring helps the DBA recognize instances when maintenance activities are needed. For example, as a result of monitoring activities, a DBA may notice that at the current pace of the end users' data input activities, the database system will run out of hard-drive space within weeks. Based on this observation, the DBA may decide to increase the amount of hard-drive space for the database system.

Another example of monitoring is examining who is using which tables, and how. For instance, a DBA may notice that two tables are very frequently joined in a query by a large percentage of users in order to repeatedly create the same report. Based on this observation, the DBA may suggest that the database development team denormalizes those two tables by merging them into one table. Another approach a DBA may take in this scenario is to create a materialized view of the join of the two tables so users can query the view directly. As we mentioned in Chapter 5, a regular view is not an actual table and does not have any physically saved data. When a user accesses a view, the query that is used to construct the view is executed, and the data is retrieved from the tables used by the query. **View materialization** refers to saving a view as an actual physical table. Such a view is referred to as "materialized view." The idea behind view materialization is to improve the performance of queries on frequently used views. For example, a DBA can set up automatic view materialization by creating a mechanism for saving a view (as an actual table with real records) for each view that was used a certain number of times in queries. Depending on the DBMS and the rate of changes in the original tables, the materialized view can be updated periodically.

Maintenance activities also include managing and upgrading the database software and hardware resources. For example, a DBA is in charge of upgrading the database system to a new version of the DBMS software or moving the database system to a new hardware platform.

Maintenance activities may also include upgrades to the structure of the database. As we stated earlier in the book (see Figure 1.6 and Figure 7.9), database requirements are subject to change initiated by any of the steps in the database development lifecycle, including the use of the database system. In other words, during the lifecycle of a database system, a need may arise to change the database schema. For example, during the use of the database system, it may become apparent that a new relation needs to be added to the database.[1] The decision to add the new relation to the database will rest with the database developers. However, if a decision is made to make such an addition, as the person in charge of the database system, the DBA will be directly involved in this process of incorporating the new table into the existing database.

Data Dictionary

In the process of monitoring and maintaining the functioning database system, as well as during regular use of a database system, access is needed not only to the data stored in the database, but also to the metadata. Access to the metadata of the database is provided through a data dictionary.

A **data dictionary** is a repository of the metadata (data about the data) of the database. The data dictionary, also sometimes called the metadata repository,[2] contains information such as the names of the tables, names and types of columns in them, the primary keys, referential integrity constraints, and so on. The metadata showing the structure of the functioning database system is automatically stored by the DBMS in the data dictionary. The data dictionary created by the DBMS is often referred to as the **catalog**.

Figure 10.2 illustrates an example of the type of information that is stored in the data dictionary.

TableName	ColumnName	DataType	DataLength
Vendor	VendorId	Char	2
Vendor	VendorName	VarChar	25

FIGURE 10.2 Sample entries in a data dictionary.

---

[1]Recall that the proper course of action is to go back to the requirements and perform all the steps shown in Figure 1.6 (for an operational database) or Figure 7.9 (for a data warehouse or data mart) before actually creating the new table.

[2]Somewhat confusingly, the term "repository" is often used in practice to mean "metadata repository," while in other instances, it is used simply to refer to any data store. Here we use the term "metadata repository" to eliminate this ambiguity.

Data dictionary tables allow for quick identification of the metadata for the relations in the database. The entries in the data dictionary in Figure 10.2 indicate that the relation Vendor has a column with the name of VendorID of data type Char(2), and a column with the name of VendorName of data type Varchar(25).

Users can query the data dictionary tables using SQL statements. Data dictionary tables include USER_TABLES, which provides information about all tables accessible to the user; USER_VIEWS, which provides information about all views accessible to the user; and USER_CONSTRAINTS, which lists the constraints to which the user has access. While different DBMS may have different names for such tables, they all provide similar information and serve a similar purpose.

For example, assuming that the ZAGI Retail Company Sales Department database (shown in Figure 3.32 or Figure 5.1a) was created in Oracle, the following SQL query could be issued to show the names and data types of all columns in all relations:

```
SELECT      table_name, column_name, data_type, data_length
FROM        user_tab_columns;
```

In Oracle, the USER_TAB_COLUMNS contains the metadata for columns of the relations. The result of this query is shown in Figure 10.3.

Issuing queries on tables from the data dictionary allows the DBAs and the users to quickly access the information about the structure of the database. If a regular user issues a query on tables from the data dictionary, the result will only contain information about the tables to which the user has access (access control is discussed in the following section).

TableName	ColumnName	DataType	DataLength
Vendor	VendorId	Char	2
Vendor	VendorName	VarChar2	25
Category	CategoryId	Char	2
Category	CategoryName	VarChar2	25
Product	ProductId	Char	3
Product	ProductName	VarChar2	25
Product	ProductPrice	Number	22
Product	VendorId	Char	2
Product	CategoryId	Char	2
Region	RegionId	Char	1
Region	RegionName	VarChar2	25
Store	StoreId	VarChar2	3
Store	StoreZip	Char	5
Store	RegionId	Char	1
Customer	CustomerId	Char	7
Customer	CustomerName	VarChar2	15
Customer	CustomerZip	Char	5
SalesTransaction	TId	VarChar2	8
SalesTransaction	CustomerId	Char	7
SalesTransaction	StoreId	Varchar2	3
SalesTransaction	TDate	Date	7
SoldVia	ProductId	Char	3
SoldVia	TId	VarChar2	8
SoldVia	NoOfItems	Number	22

FIGURE 10.3   Data dictionary entries for the Sales Department ZAGI Retail Company database

SECURING THE DATABASE AGAINST UNAUTHORIZED ACCESS

One of the principal database administration tasks is preventing unauthorized access to data. Preventing unauthorized access to data requires controlling access to the database. In a multiuser database system, access to a database begins with the **authentication** of the user through the use of the user's account identifier and password for a login procedure. Based on the user's identity, an access control strategy is used to determine the components of the database he or she is authorized to access. Depending on their job duties and positions in the company, different users may be allowed to access different portions of the same database. Typically, in contemporary database systems, this is based on the granting and revoking of **access privileges** to users of the database. An access privilege can be assigned on the user account and involves such actions as creating tables or creating views. Privileges can be specific to a particular relation or view. Access privileges include the following actions:

SELECT	performing a select (read) operation
UPDATE	updating records
ALTER	altering the table (e.g., adding a column, dropping a column, etc.)
DELETE	deleting records
INSERT	inserting records

These privileges are typically implemented by maintaining an **authorization matrix** composed of subjects and objects. This matrix is usually provided by the DBMS and available for manipulation by the DBA. The subjects of the matrix are the users of the database, and the basic objects of the matrix are the relations, views, or attributes. An entry in the matrix indicates the particular privilege assigned to a user for a particular object. For example, given the authorization matrix in Figure 10.4, user Bob can read (i.e., perform a SELECT operation on) the VENDOR relation and can read and update the CATEGORY relation, user Alice can read the CATEGORY relation but cannot access the VENDOR relation, and user Lee can perform all operations on the VENDOR and CATEGORY relations.

The user who is the creator of a table is considered the owner of the table and given all privileges on that table. The database administrators and the owners of a table can grant and/or revoke privileges on that table to other users, using the DCL (Data Control Language) SQL statements **GRANT** and **REVOKE**. For example, the SQL statement:

```
GRANT SELECT, UPDATE ON vendor TO alice;
```

grants user Alice the privilege to perform SELECT and UPDATE operations on the VENDOR relation. Similarly, the following statement revokes Alice's privilege.

```
REVOKE UPDATE ON vendor FROM alice;
```

After this statement, Alice will no longer be allowed to update the VENDOR table, although she will still be allowed to perform a select operation on the table.

This type of access control, in which each user is assigned an individual set of privileges for accessing individual database objects, is easy to implement and use in a small multiuser environment. However, it does not scale well as the number of users

User	Relation **VENDOR**	Relation **CATEGORY**	...
Bob	SELECT	SELECT, UPDATE	...
Alice	–	SELECT	...
Lee	ALL	ALL	...
...	...	...	...

FIGURE 10.4 An example of an authorization matrix.

and objects grows. In many cases, it may not be feasible to maintain a matrix of privileges of individual users for a database that is accessed by a large number of users. In such cases, instead of identifying the privileges associated with individual users, a **role-based access control** system can be used. In such a system users are assigned to roles that have predefined privileges. The DBA defines the roles and assigns the permissions to these roles; the DBA then assigns users to the roles. The GRANT statement and REVOKE statement in SQL can be used when implementing role-based access control. For example, in the following sequence of SQL statements:

```
CREATE ROLE accountant;
GRANT SELECT ON payroll TO accountant;
GRANT accountant TO brian;
```

the role Accountant is created with the privilege of performing a SELECT operation on the PAYROLL table. User Brian is assigned to the role of Accountant and is therefore allowed to perform a SELECT on the PAYROLL table.

In a role-based access control system, the permissions associated with roles are stable, while the membership of users in roles can change. Users can change membership from one role to another as their role in an organization changes. Depending on their duties, users can be assigned several database roles. Users that are assigned several roles have all the privileges given to every role to which they are assigned.

When dealing with especially sensitive data, another layer of protection against unauthorized access can be provided through **encryption** of data. Encryption involves changing information using a scrambling algorithm referred to as an **encryption key**, so that the information becomes unreadable. The only users who can read the encrypted information are the ones in possession of the **decryption key**, containing the decryption algorithm that reverts the information back to its original state. With particularly confidential data, database data can be encrypted and only a selected group of users authorized to access such data can be provided with the decryption key.

PROVIDING DATABASE BACKUP AND RECOVERY

Backup and **recovery** mechanisms are needed to ensure that no loss of data occurs. Many companies have stories from the early days of computers in which all customer information was lost due to a computer failure. In today's business database systems, backup and recovery mechanisms are used to ensure the database remains in a consistent state with no data lost.

The data in a database is typically stored on a hard disk drive. When a user issues a request to read or update the data in the database, the data must be loaded from the disk into memory. Any updates (i.e., insertions, deletions, modifications) to the data are written to the copy of the data that is stored in memory before it is ultimately moved to the disk. There is much overhead associated with writing an update to the data file on the disk and, because of that, updates are recorded to the disk in batches. Instead of writing updates to the data file on disk after each update, the update is recorded in a **recovery log**. The recovery log ensures that even if the update performed on the data in memory is somehow lost before it is written to the disk during its batch, the recovery log still has the information about the update. An entry in the recovery log contains information about which data value is updated, the before and after values of the update, and the user requesting the update. Because the before and after values of the update are recorded, the recovery log allows the DBMS to redo any updates as well as undo any updates. After multiple updates are recorded in the recovery log, the updates in the log are then written to the data in the data file.

Periodic backup copies of the database are made through the use of the recovery logs and **checkpoints**. A checkpoint is a part of a recovery log. When a checkpoint is created, all updates recorded in the recovery log—and as a result any updates to data stored in memory—are written to the database in the data file on the disk. After a checkpoint is created, the recovery log is cleared, and the DBMS begins to record any subsequent updates to the database to the recovery log. Checkpoints are created regularly, after a specified amount of time has passed or after a specified amount of data has been written to the recovery log.

In the event of a failure, the DMBS can recover by "rolling back" to the checkpoint state and then using the recovery log to redo the updates that have been recorded in the log since the checkpoint. In other words, the database in the data file on disk is used as the starting point, and the updates recorded in the recovery log are applied to the data.

SQL TCL commands, such as **COMMIT** and **ROLLBACK**, are used in this process. The COMMIT command causes all updates on the database to be recorded on the disk. It is automatically issued during the checkpoints, but can also be manually issued by the user or the DBA. The ROLLBACK command rolls back all the updates since the last COMMIT.

The procedures described above are a common part of the everyday functioning of a typical database system. They provide options for recovering from data update failures caused by power outages, hardware failures, aborted transactions, software failure, and other similar reasons.

In addition to the mechanisms for ensuring recovery from these common data update failures, modern database systems include mechanisms for dealing with complete database destruction caused, for example, by a catastrophic event such as a natural disaster. For that reason, multiple **complete mirrored backup** copies of databases are kept, often at more than one physical location. Such backup copies are continuously updated so that they completely correspond to the original database. In case the original database suffers destruction, a backup copy can be used to replace the original database in the database system.

ENSURING DATABASE INTEGRITY

Ensuring database integrity refers to preventing unauthorized or accidental insertion, modification, or deletion actions that result in invalid, corrupt, or low-quality data in the database. Protecting database integrity is achieved through a combination of multiple methods and procedures related to the security and use of data in database systems.

One of the ways the integrity of data in databases can be compromised is through **unauthorized malicious data updates**. For example, an unethical competitor may attempt to falsely increase prices of products in the database that is used by an online retailer. Access control methods, described earlier in this chapter, protect against such unauthorized updates that would result in the loss of data integrity.

Another way the integrity of data in databases may be threatened is through an **update failure**. For example, a bank database server may crash during an ATM transfer-funds transaction from account A to account B at the moment the money was withdrawn from account A but before it was deposited into account B. Without the backup and recovery mechanism, the bank client would lose his money during this transfer. However, the backup and recovery methods using a recovery log as described earlier, protect against this loss of data (and money, in this case). For example, the transaction can be rolled back so no money is actually withdrawn from account A.

Data integrity can also be endangered by the **accidental misuse** of the database system. For example, a data entry person may, by mistake, enter that a product is supplied by a nonexistent vendor. Implementing constraints, such as referential integrity constraints and user-defined constraints described in Chapter 6, serves to protect the data integrity in such cases. In this example, a referential integrity constraint would not allow assigning a product to a nonexisting vendor. Other methods for protecting data integrity from improper use by end users are the preventative and corrective data quality assurance actions described in Chapter 6.

OPTIMIZING DATABASE PERFORMANCE

Another task in the purview of data administration is the optimization of database performance. Optimizing database performance seeks to minimize the response time for queries that retrieve data from the database. Database administration actions related to optimizing database performance include indexing (discussed in Chapter 6), de-normalization (discussed in Chapter 4), view materialization (discussed earlier in this chapter), and query optimization.

Query optimization involves examining multiple ways of executing the same query and choosing the fastest option. The DBMS has a feature called the **query optimizer** that determines how to execute an SQL statement in an efficient manner. When users issue an SQL statement to query the database, they specify what they want to retrieve from the database, but they do not specify how the retrieval is to be performed. Instead, it is the role of the query optimizer to identify the many possible ways to execute the query, called a query plan, and to choose the query plan that is the best.

In the context of query optimization, the term **query cost** refers to the time length of execution. The cost of processing a query is affected by such factors as the order in which the operations are executed and whether one or more indexes are used. The order in which the operations are performed can affect the efficiency of the query. For example, if a query requires performing a JOIN and SELECT operation on two tables, it is usually more efficient to perform a SELECT operation first. Suppose a JOIN operation involves a table with students of all ages, where only students who are 18 years old are requested in the query. It would be more efficient to first SELECT the students who are 18 years old and then perform the JOIN operation, as opposed to performing a JOIN involving the table of students first and then SELECT the students who are 18 years old.

In order to make query optimization decisions, the query optimizer maintains various relevant pieces of information, such as the number of records in a table, the size of the records, the number of distinct values in a column, and the minimum and maximum values in a column. The query optimizer also maintains similar information about each index. A query developer cannot tell the query optimizer how to process the query, but he or she can give so-called **query hints**. Query hints override the default behavior of the query optimizer. Normally, the query optimizer will pick the best optimization method without hints being specified, and hints are only intended to be used by experienced database administrators for fine-tuning.

DEVELOPING AND IMPLEMENTING DATABASE POLICIES AND STANDARDS

The last data administration task that we will consider in this chapter is developing and implementing **database policies and standards**. A proper business database system has certain policies and standards for the development, use, and administration of the database.

For example, a database system can have naming conventions for naming database constructs, such as the ones described in Chapter 2. These conventions can include rules, such as "each column in a database table must have a prefix that is the first three letters of the database table name", which should be enforced during the initial database design phase and throughout the modifications of the database structure during the lifecycle of the database. The DBA could verify adherence to this policy by checking the name of each new column in a database table to confirm that it starts with first three letters of the name of the database table.

In addition to the policies and standards for database development, a database system can have database use policies and standards. For example, a database system can include a policy that the only vendors that can be entered in the database are members of the American Association of Registered Vendors. That policy could be implemented as a business rule that compares each new entry in the VENDOR relation in the database against a lookup table containing the names of all vendors that are members of the American Association of Registered Vendors and prevents the entry of any records that do not have a match in the lookup table.

A database system can also have policies and standards guiding the database management and administration functions. For example, a database administration policy may require the development of a database administration table that includes particular administration tasks, such as access control or database performance optimization, and the names of data administration personnel in charge of conducting the particular roles within the task. A policy may further require that each task have one primary person with ultimate responsibility for the task.

Database policies and standards may range from policies and standards for implementation of various database objects to policies and standards regulating actions and procedures that are performed on data in databases on a regular basis. Regardless of their scope, a common purpose for all database policies and standards is to reflect and support business processes and business logic.

Key Terms

Access privileges *305*
Accidental misuse *307*
Application development component *302*
Authentication *305*
Authorization matrix *305*
Backup *306*
Catalog *303*
Checkpoints *306*
COMMIT *307*

Complete mirrored backup *307*
Data definition component *301*
Data dictionary *303*
Data manipulation component *302*
Database administration component *302*
Database policies and standards *308*

Decryption key *306*
Encryption *306*
Encryption key *306*
GRANT *305*
Multiuser system *302*
Query cost *308*
Query hints *308*
Query optimization *308*
Query optimizer *308*
Recovery *306*
Recovery log *306*

REVOKE *305*
Role-based access control *306*
ROLLBACK *307*
Single-user system *302*
Unauthorized malicious data updates *307*
Update failure *307*
View materialization *303*

Review Questions

Q10.1 What are the four components of typical DBMS software?

Q10.2 What is the purpose of the DBMS data definition component?

Q10.3 What is the purpose of the DBMS data manipulation component?

Q10.4 What is the purpose of the DBMS data administration component?

Q10.5 What is the purpose of the DBMS application development component?

Q10.6 What activities are encompassed by database administration?

Q10.7 Give several examples of database system maintenance activities.

Q10.8 What is a materialized view?

Q10.9 What is a data dictionary?

Q10.10 List actions on which access privileges can be assigned.

Q10.11 Briefly describe the role-based access control system.

Q10.12 What is the purpose of backup and recovery mechanisms?

Q10.13 Give several examples of compromised database integrity.

Q10.14 What is the goal of optimizing database performance?

Q10.15 Give several examples of database policies and standards.

APPENDIX A
Enhanced ER

The term enhanced ER (EER) modeling refers to an expanded ER notation that depicts additional database modeling concepts beyond standard ER modeling. The most important EER addition to ER modeling is the concept of a **superclass entity** and a **subclass entity**. In this appendix we will illustrate this EER addition to ER modeling in several examples.

SUPERCLASS AND SUBCLASS ENTITIES

The concepts of superclass and subclass entities are used in situations when, in addition to a set of attributes shared by all instances of the entity, certain groups of entity instances have additional attributes applicable only to those groups. The next three examples will illustrate the concept of superclass and subclass entities.

EER Example 1–Disjointed Subclasses, Total Specialization

Consider the following example:

- *For each store, Company X keeps track of a store ID (unique) and zip code.*
- *Within Company X, certain stores are company owned. For such stores, Company X keeps track of their real-estate value.*
- *Within Company X, certain stores are rented. For such stores, Company X keeps track of their annual rent cost.*

Figure A.1 illustrates how this scenario would be modeled using the EER notation. In the figure, entity STORE represents a superclass, while entities COMPANYSTORE and RENTEDSTORE represent the subclasses of the superclass STORE. All instances of a subclass inherit the attributes from its superclass. In this example, all company stores and all rented stores will have a StoreID value and a Zip-Code value. In addition, all company stores will have a RealEstateValue value, while all rented stores will have an AnnualRent value.

In this notation,[1] the relationship between a superclass and its subclasses is marked by a circle to which the subclass and superclass lines are connected. The relationship between a superclass and its subclasses is referred to as an IS-A

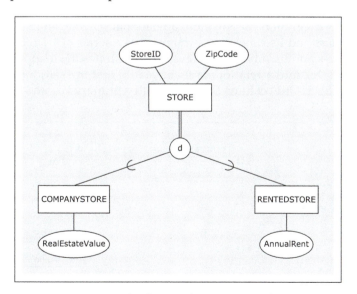

FIGURE A.1 An example of a superclass and subclass for Company X.

---

[1]As we mentioned in Chapter 2, there is no one/single universally adopted standard ER notation. Likewise, there is no single universal EER notation. Depending on which EER notation is used, subclasses and superclasses can be represented differently but always have the same meaning.

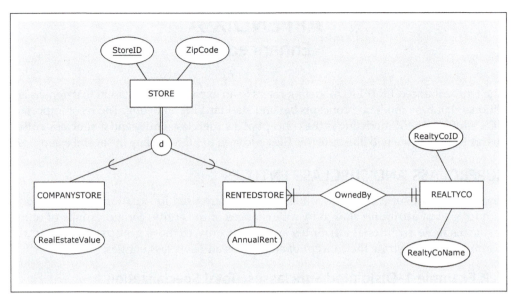

FIGURE A.2 An example of an EER diagram for Company X.

relationship (in this case, indicating that a company store IS-A store and a rented store IS-A store). Subclasses are recognized by the semi-oval attached to the line connected to the subclass. The letter in the circle indicates whether subclasses are disjointed (letter *d*) or overlapping (letter *o*). In this case, subclasses COMPANYS-TORE and RENTEDSTORE are **disjointed subclasses**, which means that an instance of subclass COMPANYSTORE cannot at the same time be an instance of the subclass RENTEDSTORE, and vice versa.

The double line connecting superclass STORE with the circle indicates **total specialization**. In the case of total specialization, every instance of a superclass must also be an instance of its subclass. In this example, total specialization means that there is no store that is neither a company store nor a rented store.

Within an EER diagram, both superclasses and subclasses can be involved in regular relationships with regular entities. This is illustrated by the expanded example shown in Figure A.2, in which subclass RENTEDSTORE is involved in a binary 1:M relationship with a regular entity REALTYCO.

When an EER diagram is mapped into a relational schema, an IS-A relationship between a superclass and its subclasses is mapped as a series of 1:1 relationships between the superclass and its subclasses. Figure A.3 illustrates the mapping of the EER diagram in Figure A.2 into a relational schema. Note that in relations COMPANY-STORE and RENTEDSTORE, column StoreID is both a primary key and a foreign key.

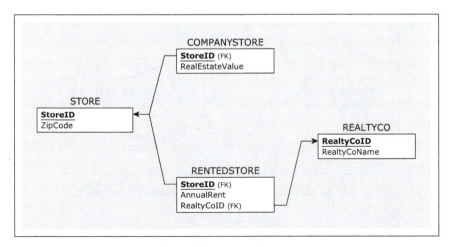

FIGURE A.3 An EER diagram mapped into a relational schema for Company X.

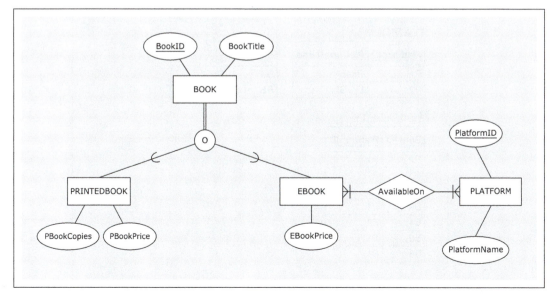

STORE

StoreID	ZipCode
S1	60600
S2	60605
S3	35400
S4	60611
S5	35405
S6	35405

REALTYCO

RealtyCoID	RealtyCoName
R1	Braun CR
R2	Shea Prop

COMPANY STORE

StoreID	RealEstateValue
S1	$9,000,000
S2	$11,000,000
S4	$8,000,000

RENTEDSTORE

StoreID	AnnualRent	RealtyCoID
S3	$450,000	R1
S5	$550,000	R2
S6	$400,000	R1

FIGURE A.4   Sample data for Company X.

Figure A.4 illustrates a data sample in the Company X database resulting from the EER diagram in Figure A.2.

Note that due to total specialization, every store is either a company store or a rented store. Also note that because subclasses are disjointed, no company store is at the same time a rented store, and no rented store is at the same time a company store.

EER Example 2–Overlapping Subclasses, Total Specialization

Consider the following example:

- *For each book, Publisher X keeps track of book ID (unique) and book title.*
- *Within Publisher X, some books are printed books. For each such book, Publisher X keeps track of its number of printed copies (PBookCopies) and its printed copy price (PBookPrice).*
- *Within Publisher X, some books are e-books. For each such book, Publisher X keeps track of its price (EBookPrice).*
- *Each e-book is available on a number of platforms (each platform has a unique platform ID and a platform name). Each platform has number of e-books available on it.*

Figure A.5 illustrates how this scenario would be modeled using EER notation.

FIGURE A.5   An example of an EER diagram for Publisher X.

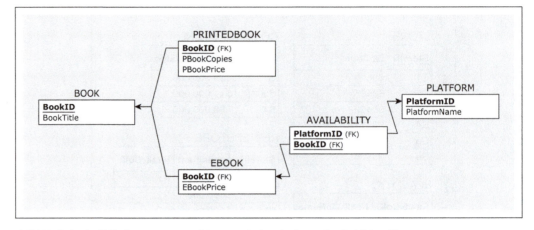

FIGURE A.6   An EER diagram mapped into a relational schema for Publisher X.

The letter *o* in the circle indicates that the subclasses PRINTEDBOOK and EBOOK are **overlapping subclasses**. The instance of subclass PRINTEDBOOK can be at the same time an instance of the subclass EBOOK, and vice versa. In other words, a book can be available at the same time as a printed book and an electronic book.

Total specialization, represented by the double line connecting the superclass BOOK with the circle, states that there is no book that is neither a printed book nor an electronic book.

Figure A.6 illustrates the mapping of the EER diagram in Figure A.5 into a relational schema.

Figure A.7 illustrates a data sample in the Publisher X database resulting from the EER diagram.

BOOK

BookID	BookTitle
B1	Winter Game
B2	Solitude
B3	Code Q
B4	Pam & Sue
B5	Arrival
B6	My Mind

PRINTEDBOOK

BookID	PBookCopies	PBookPrice
B1	10,000	$90
B2	20,000	$70
B4	25,000	$65

EBOOK

BookID	EBookPrice
B2	$60
B3	$110
B4	$55
B5	$55
B6	$70

PLATFORM

PlatformID	PlatformName
P1	Bimble
P2	EyeGlad

AVAILABILITY

BookID	PlatformID
B2	P1
B3	P1
B3	P2
B4	P1
B4	P2
B5	P1
B6	P1

FIGURE A.7   Sample data for Publisher X.

Note that due to total specialization, there is no book that is neither a printed book nor an electronic book. Also note that because the subclasses are overlapping, some books are at the same time printed books and electronic books.

EER Example 3–Disjointed Subclasses, Partial Specialization

Consider the following example:

- *For each employee, Airline X keeps track of employee ID (unique) and employee name.*
- *Certain employees of Airline X are pilots. For each pilot, Airline X keeps track of his or her number of flight hours (NoFHours).*
- *Certain employees of Airline X are mechanics. For each mechanic, Airline X keeps track of his or her mechanic type (MeType).*
- *Certain employees of Airline X are flight attendants. For each flight attendant, Airline X keeps track of his or her flight attendant level (FALevel).*
- *There are other employees in Airline X that are neither pilots, flight attendants, nor mechanics. For such employees, Airline X does not keep any additional data beside the employee ID and employee name.*

Figure A.8 illustrates how this scenario would be modeled using EER notation.

Partial specialization is represented by the single line connecting the superclass EMPLOYEE with the circle. In this case, partial specialization states that some employees are neither pilots, mechanics, nor flight attendants.

The letter *d* in the circle indicates that the subclasses PILOT, MECHANIC, and FLIGHTATTENDANT are disjointed.

Figure A.9 illustrates the mapping of the EER diagram in Figure A.8 into a relational schema.

Figure A.10 illustrates a data sample in the Airline X database resulting from the EER diagram.

Note that due to partial specialization, not every employee is a pilot, mechanic or flight attendant. Some employees (*Luc* and *Stu*) are just generic employees. Also note that because subclasses are disjointed, there are no employees that are both pilots and mechanics, or pilots and flight attendants, or mechanics and flight attendants at the same time.

The superclass and its subclasses can be one of the following four categories:

- disjointed subclasses, total specialization
- overlapping subclasses, total specialization

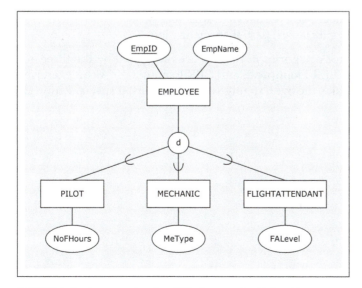

FIGURE A.8   An example of an EER diagram for Airline X.

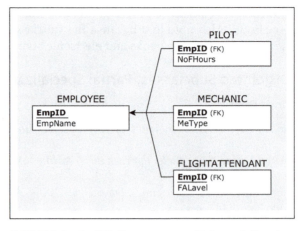

FIGURE A.9 An EER diagram mapped into a relational schema for Airline X.

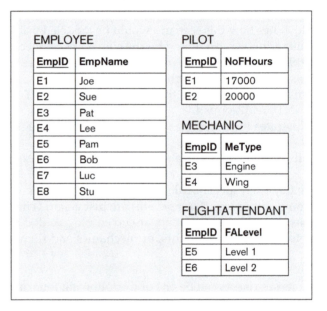

FIGURE A.10 Sample data for Airline X.

- disjointed subclasses, partial specialization
- overlapping subclasses, partial specialization

The first three categories in this list are illustrated by the three above examples (EER Example 1, EER Example 2, and EER Example 3.) As an exercise, create an example that illustrates the overlapping subclasses, partial specialization case.

APPENDIX B
Further Notes on Normalization and Higher Normal Forms

The coverage of functional dependencies and normalization given in Chapter 4 is sufficient for the understanding of the normalization process that occurs in typical corporate and organizational settings. This appendix gives an extended coverage of functional dependencies and normalization.

CANDIDATE KEYS AND FUNCTIONAL DEPENDENCIES

In addition to the primary key, relations can also have one or more additional candidate keys. Consider the example relation CITY shown in Figure B.1. Relation CITY has a primary key CityID and an additional candidate key CityName, State.

Functional dependencies in the relation CITY are shown in Figure B.2. When a relation has other candidate keys in addition to its primary key, the following expanded definition of partial and full functional dependencies apply:

Partial functional dependency occurs when a component of a primary key or any other candidate key on its own functionally determines the nonkey columns of a relation.

Full key functional dependency occurs when a key (primary or any other candidate key) functionally determines a column of a relation while no component of the key partially deter-mines the same column.

Note in Figure B.2 that the relation CITY has a primary key CityID and a composite candidate key CityName, State. The primary key CityID fully functionally determines all the remaining columns in the relation. Candidate key CityName, State also fully functionally determines all the remaining columns in the relation. The column State functionally determines column StatePopulation. This functional dependency is a

CITY

CityID	CityName	State	StatePopulation	CityPopulation
C1	Portland	ME	1,350,000	70,000
C2	Grand Rapids	MI	9,900,000	190,000
C3	Rockford	IL	12,900,000	340,000
C4	Spokane	WA	6,800,000	210,000
C5	Portland	OR	3,900,000	600,000
C6	Eugene	OR	3,900,000	360,000
C7	Grand Rapids	MN	5,400,000	11,000

FIGURE B.1   Relation CITY with a primary key and a candidate key.

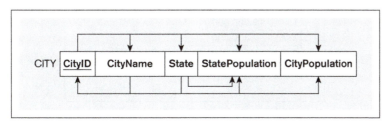

FIGURE B.2   Functional dependencies in the relation CITY.

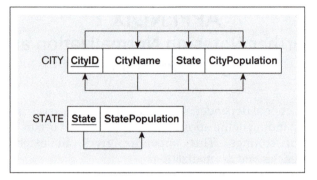

FIGURE B.3   Normalizing relation CITY.

partial functional dependency, because column State is a component of a candidate key CityName, State.

Recall the 2NF definition:

2NF—A table is in 2NF if it is in 1NF and if it does not contain partial functional dependencies.

Relation CITY is not in 2NF because it contains a partial functional dependency. Normalizing relation CITY to 2NF involves eliminating the partial functional dependency by decomposing the relation CITY into two relations, as shown in Figure B.3.

Figure B.4 shows the records in the normalized tables.

Recall the definition of a transitive functional dependency:

Transitive functional dependency occurs when nonkey columns functionally determine other nonkey columns of a relation.

Also recall the 3NF definition:

3NF—A table is in 3NF if it is in 2NF and if it does not contain transitive functional dependencies.

CITY

CityID	CityName	State	CityPopulation
C1	Portland	ME	70,000
C2	Grand Rapids	MI	190,000
C3	Rockford	IL	340,000
C4	Spokane	WA	210,000
C5	Portland	OR	600,000
C6	Eugene	OR	360,000
C7	Grand Rapids	MN	11,000

STATE

State	StatePopulation
ME	1,350,000
MI	9,900,000
IL	12,900,000
WA	6,800,000
OR	3,900,000
MN	5,400,000

FIGURE B.4   Data in the normalized relations for the CITY example.

The existence of the candidate key does not call for augmenting the definition of a transitive dependency, because transitive dependency is defined as a dependency between the nonkey columns.

The relations in Figure B.3 are already in 3NF.

How would the CITY relation in Figure B.2 be normalized if we did not acknowledge CityName, State as a candidate key? In that case the functional dependency:

State → StatePopulation

would be considered a transitive functional dependency. As such it would be eliminated in the process of normalizing to 3NF instead of being eliminated in the process of normalizing to 2NF. The final result of normalization would be exactly the same as in Figure B.3. In other words, relation CITY would end up normalized the same, whether CityName, State was treated as a key or not.

BOYCE–CODD NORMAL FORM (BCNF)

Boyce-Codd normal form (BCNF) is an extension of the third normal form (3NF). The following is a definition of BCNF:

BCNF–A table is in BCNF if it contains no functional dependencies other than full key functional dependencies (where only primary key or other candidate keys fully determine other columns).

In most cases, relations that are in 3NF are also in BCNF. A 3NF relation that has no candidate keys other than the primary key is by definition in BCNF. However, there are cases when relations that have candidate keys in addition to the primary keys may be in 3NF while not being in BCNF. For example, consider the relation TEAMPLAYEROF-THEGAME shown in Figure B.5. The data in this relation records a team's player of the game for each game in which the team played. In this example, the table contains data for a single season, there are no trades of players (players stay with the same team for the entire season), and no two players have the same name (player's names are unique.)

Functional dependencies for the relation TEAMPLAYEROFTHEGAME shown in Figure B.5 are shown in Figure B.6.

TEAMPLAYEROFTHEGAME

GameOfSeason	Team	TeamPlayerOfTheGame
1st	Tigers	Joe Jones
2nd	Tigers	Tim Smith
3rd	Tigers	Joe Jones
1st	Sharks	Scott McHill
2nd	Sharks	Scott McHill
3rd	Sharks	Lee Hicks

FIGURE B.5 Relation TEAMPLAYEROFTHEGAME (in 3NF but not in BCNF).

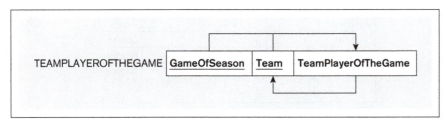

FIGURE B.6 Functional dependencies in relation TEAMPLAYEROFTHEGAME (in 3NF but not in BCNF).

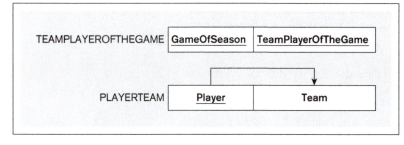

FIGURE B.7 Relation TEAMPLAYEROFTHEGAME normalized to BCNF.

TEAMPLAYEROFTHEGAME

GameOfSeason	TeamPlayerOfTheGame
1st	Joe Jones
2nd	Tim Smith
3rd	Joe Jones
1st	Scott McHill
2nd	Scott McHill
3rd	Lee Hicks

PLAYERTEAM

Player	Team
Joe Jones	Tigers
Tim Smith	Tigers
Scott McHill	Sharks
Lee Hicks	Sharks

FIGURE B.8 Data in the normalized relations for the TEAMPLAYEROFTHEGAME example.

The relation TEAMPLAYEROFTHEGAME is in 3NF because it does not contain any partial or transitive dependencies. However, this relation is not in BCNF because nonkey column TeamPlayerOfTheGame determines the key column Team.

The relation TEAMPLAYEROFTHEGAME is normalized to BCNF by creating two relations as shown in Figure B.7.

Figure B.8 shows the records in the normalized tables.

The issue of normalizing the relation TEAMPLAYEROFTHEGAME to BCNF could have been avoided by choosing a different primary key for the relation. Notice that there are two candidates for the primary key for relation TEAMPLAYEROFTHEGAME shown in Figure B.5:

- GameOfSeason, Team
- GameOfSeason, TeamPlayerOfTheGame

In Figure B.5, GameOfSeason, Team was chosen to be the primary key of the relation TEAMPLAYEROFTHEGAME. Figure B.9 shows the relation TEAMPLAYEROFTHEGAME with the other candidate (GameOfSeason, TeamPlayerOfTheGame) chosen to be its primary key.

Functional dependencies for the relation TEAMPLAYEROFTHEGAME shown in Figure B.9 are shown in Figure B.10.

This version of the relation TEAMPLAYEROFTHEGAME is not in 2NF because it contains a partial dependency. It is normalized to 2NF in a standard way (described in Chapter 4) by creating an additional relation for the partial dependency, as shown in Figure B.11.

TEAMPLAYEROFTHEGAME

GameOfSeason	TeamPlayerOfTheGame	Team
1st	Joe Jones	Tigers
2nd	Tim Smith	Tigers
3rd	Joe Jones	Tigers
1st	Scott McHill	Sharks
2nd	Scott McHill	Sharks
3rd	Lee Hicks	Sharks

FIGURE B.9 Relation TEAMPLAYEROFTHEGAME with an alternate primary key.

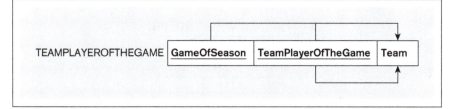

FIGURE B.10 Functional dependencies in relation TEAMPLAYEROFTHEGAME with an alternate primary key.

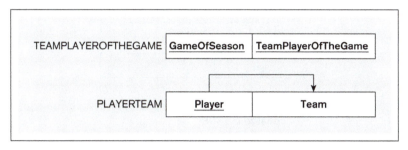

FIGURE B.11 Relation TEAMPLAYEROFTHEGAME with an alternate primary key, normalized to 2NF (and subsequently to 3NF and BCNF).

Note that the relations shown in Figure B.11 are also normalized to 3NF and BCNF. In fact, the relations in Figure B.11 are identical to the relations in Figure B.7. Conversely, the data records for the relations shown in Figure B.11 are the same as the data records shown in Figure B.8.

By choosing a different primary key, the normalization process involved dealing with a partial functional dependency instead of dealing with a functional dependency where a nonkey attribute determines a key column. In other words, by choosing a different primary key, the normalization process consisted of normalizing to 2NF in order to normalize the relation instead of normalizing to BCNF in order to normalize the relation.

Fourth Normal Form (4NF)

Consider the relation ORGANIZATION_STUDENT_CHARITY in Figure B.12.

In this example, organizations have student members and organizations support various charities. The relation ORGANIZATION_STUDENT_CHARITY shows for each organization both its members and the charities the organization supports. Columns StudentID and Charity are both related to the column OrgID, but they are not related to each other. One OrgID value can be associated with multiple StudentID

ORGANIZATION_STUDENT_CHARITY

OrgID	StudentID	Charity
011	1111	Food Pantry
011	1111	Stop Diabetes
011	1111	River Care
022	1111	River Care
022	2222	River Care

FIGURE B.12 Relation ORGANIZATION_STUDENT_CHARITY (not in 4NF).

ORGANIZATION_STUDENT

OrgID	StudentID
011	1111
022	1111
022	2222

ORGANIZATION_CHARITY

OrgID	Charity
011	Food Pantry
011	Stop Diabetes
011	River Care
022	River Care

FIGURE B.13 Relation
ORGANIZATION_STUDENT_CHARITY
normalized to 4NF.

values, and *separately* one OrgID value can be associated with multiple charity values. Formally this is depicted as:

OrgID —↠ StudentID and OrgID —↠ Charity

where the symbol —↠ (double arrow) indicates a **multivalued dependency**. Multivalued dependencies are often referred to as "tuple (row) generating dependencies." For example, because of OrgID —↠ Charity, every time a new student joins an organization, several new rows have to be generated (one for each charity that the organization is associated with). Also, because of OrgID —↠ StudentID, every time a new charity becomes associated with an organization, several new rows have to be generated (one for each student member of the organization).

As we illustrated, multivalued dependencies occur when separate columns of the same relation contain unrelated values (i.e., when the same relation represents separate relationships of cardinality greater than 1). The following is a definition of **fourth normal form (4NF)**:

4NF—A table is in fourth normal form (4NF) if it is in BCNF and does not contain multivalued dependencies.

Consequently, a relation is not in 4NF if it contains multivalued dependencies.

Because of the multivalued dependencies, the relation ORGANIZATION_ STUDENT_CHARITY is not in 4NF. Normalizing to 4NF simply involves creating a separate relation for each of the multivalued dependencies as shown in Figure B.13.

In most cases, in practice, relations that are in 3NF are also already in 4NF. For example, most designers modeling the organization depicted in the example above would immediately create the two relations shown in Figure B.13 that are in 3NF and 4NF. Only a particularly artificial and/or inept effort would result in creating a table shown in Figure B.12 that is in 3NF and then normalizing it to 4NF as shown in Figure B.13.

OTHER NORMAL FORMS

In addition to 4NF, there are other higher normal forms, such as fifth normal form (5NF) and domain key normal form (DKNF). Such normal forms use theoretical concepts that are rarely encountered in practice. Consequently, these concepts are beyond the scope of this book.

APPENDIX C
Enterprise Resource Planning (ERP)

An "integrated information system" refers to a system in which data within one system is shared by multiple functional areas of the organization that is using the system. Examples of functional areas in a corporate organization are marketing, sales, human resources (HR), and so on. Any database that stores data in a nonredundant fashion and is available for use by different functional areas constitutes an integrated information system.

Enterprise resources planning (ERP) system is a term used in industry to describe a *premade*, integrated (multifunctional) corporate information system. ERP systems are designed, created, and sold by ERP vendors (such as SAP, Oracle, or Lawson). A company that purchases and installs an ERP system populates it with its own data.

From a database point of view, an ERP system is a premade database with multiple premade front-end interfaces intended for various groups of users. The idea behind the ERP concept is to create an empty database whose tables and columns are designed to capture the data used by various groups of constituent users of a typical corporation. The ERP database is accompanied by a number of different modules containing front-end applications accessing the tables created for different groups of users. Figure C.1 shows a high-level view of ERP system architecture.

The modules available in a typical ERP system reflect the departmental and organizational structure of a typical corporation. For example, an ERP system may contain the following modules:

- human resources (HR) module
- finance and accounting module
- sales module
- marketing module
- manufacturing module
- other modules

Figure C.2 illustrates an ERP system with a number of available modules.

When a company purchases and installs an ERP system such as the one shown in Figure C.2, they populate the premade tables in the ERP database with their own data pertaining to HR, finance/accounting, sales, marketing, manufacturing, and so on. If certain data pertains to more than one department, it is still stored only once and then accessed by multiple modules. For example, the data about customers is stored once in the central database but may be accessed by multiple modules, such as the sales module, marketing module, or finance and accounting module.

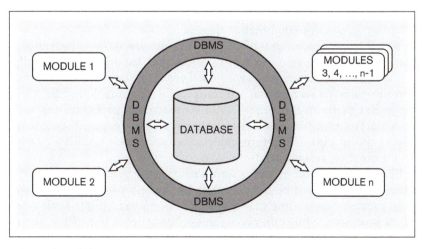

FIGURE C.1   ERP system.

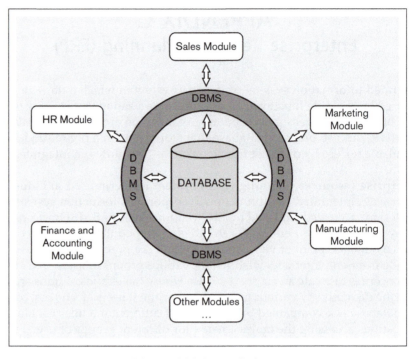

FIGURE C.2 Various modules available in a typical ERP system.

When a company purchases an ERP system, it does not have to buy and install all of the available modules. Instead, an ERP system can be initially configured with one or a few modules, while additional modules can be added later if and when needed.

ERP systems are typically bought by a corporation to facilitate processes that are uniform across industries. For example, an HR module within an ERP system contains the front-end applications that access the columns and tables in the ERP database that accommodate the data used in standard HR processes and procedures, such as recruiting, hiring and payroll. During the process of designing the HR module and the HR portion of the ERP database, the ERP vendor uses the knowledge and experience of HR experts in order to account for and facilitate all typical HR functionalities in a professional manner. Other modules within the ERP system implement other standardized processes and are created in the same fashion.

An ERP system is designed to reflect the best industry practices of the particular business process. In cases where a company has acquired an ERP system, but has a business process that differs somewhat from the way it is implemented by the ERP system, that company has the option to either modify its operations to match the best practice embedded in the ERP system, to make allowable adjustments to the ERP system to match company's practice, or some combination thereof.

Not all business processes within corporations are standardized business processes. Many of the processes in successful companies are original, especially the processes that create or add competitive advantages. The details of such processes are usually closely guarded secrets that are completely unavailable to ERP vendors. Database tables and modules that support nonstandardized processes are not available in ERP systems. For such processes, corporations have to develop their own databases and front-end applications. Therefore, companies cannot rely on ERP systems to fulfill all of their information system needs.

The ERP databases and modules standardize every process in a certain way, and that particular way may not be the way that a company prefers to store and use the data for that process. Some companies use ERP systems to facilitate some or all of their standardized processes, while other companies choose not to use ERP systems at all.

Purchasing and implementing an ERP system may appear to be a simple and straightforward undertaking. However, the deployment time for an ERP system can span a number of months (and even several years), and many ERP projects end in failure. One of the main causes for ERP system implementation failure is the client's lack of upfront detailed examination of the ERP system and comparison with their own business processes. This can result in a poor fit between the capabilities of the ERP system and the needs and practices of the company that purchased it.

It is also important to note that the ERP systems force an organization to adapt to the ERP, not the other way around. The needed adjustments are not always smooth (even when they represent an improvement from existing practices) and can lead to friction and resistance.

APPENDIX D
Data Governance and Master Data Management

DATA GOVERNANCE

Data governance is a broad term describing a set of initiatives within an organization aimed at formally regulating how, when, and by whom the organizational data and metadata are created, stored, updated (inserted, modified, deleted), and archived.

Even though data is one of most important assets (if not the most important) in many organizations, it is often not treated with the same level of organizational rigor as other assets, such as real estate, money, or vehicles, which are more traditionally perceived and appreciated as resources. However, more and more corporations are becoming aware of the importance of a regulated approach toward the data. This awareness usually results in implementing data governance.

The goal of data governance is to establish and enforce proper rules and policies for the treatment of data. By doing so, organizations formally regulate the management of data, similarly to the way they regulate the management of their other important assets, such as financial resources. For example, most corporations have very firm rules about who is allowed to use the company's money, for what purposes, on which occasions, by whose permission, and so on. Data governance institutes similar rules for dealing with corporate data.

An example of data governance is the development and implementation of the database policies and standards described in Chapter 10. Another example of a data governance initiative is creating policies that require the undertaking of the preventive and corrective data quality actions described in Chapter 6. In many cases, data governance initiatives are related to the broader laws and regulations that govern the actions of the organizations. For example, U.S. health-care organizations have to align their data management practices with the Health Insurance Portability and Accountability Act (HIPAA) imposed by the U.S. federal government. Among other provisions, this act has strict privacy rules that regulate the use and disclosure of patients' information. In U.S. health-care organizations, these rules must be implemented in database systems that host patient information as part of their overall data governance framework.

In most organizations the role of a **data steward** encompasses tasks related to data governance. Data stewards are responsible for the proper use of the data in databases. Typical data stewardship activities include:

- the creation and enforcement of policies or standards for appropriate data entry, update, and use
- the creation and implementation of data quality control activities
- the creation, implementation, and maintenance of business metadata (such as business rules and descriptions of tables and columns)
- other activities ensuring compliance with data governance policies

In addition to the role of a data steward, many organizations also establish the role of data custodian. A **data custodian** is responsible for the technical aspects of data management and use, such as protection, transport, and storage of data. In many organizations, there is a significant overlap between the roles of a data steward, data custodian, and/or database administrator (DBA). The distribution of the titles and associated responsibilities vary broadly from organization to organization.

MASTER DATA MANAGEMENT

Master data management (MDM) is one of the most common organizational data governance initiatives. **Master data** in an organization contains an authenticated quality version of the key data that provides a common point of reference for the organization's information systems. Once the master data is in place, operational information systems within the organization align their data with the master data.

For example, the ZAGI Retail Company could maintain the table MASTER-PRODUCT containing information about all products that are sold by the ZAGI Retail Company. All information systems within the ZAGI Retail Company that use product information would have to verify that their product information is consistent with the product information in the MASTERPRODUCT table.

Master data management involves creating and maintaining a collection of quality master data tables and ensuring that the use of master data is embedded across the operational information systems in the organization. It is essential that the master data is of the highest quality. Master data must exhibit all the properties of high-quality data (accuracy, uniqueness, completeness, consistency, timeliness, and conformity) described in Chapter 6.

Not all data in operational information systems is master data. However, the data that corresponds to master data must be aligned with the master data. Consider the example where a store clerk in the ZAGI Retail Company working in a *store* records in the sales management information system that a certain *customer* bought *three* items of a certain *product* at *8:00 A.M.* The quantity (*three*) and time (*8:00 A.M.*) are not related to the master data. However, assuming the existence of the master tables MASTERPRODUCT, MASTERCUSTOMER, and MASTERSTORE, the data about *product*, *customer*, and *store* in the sales information system have to be verified against and aligned with the data in these master tables.

The main benefit of proper master data is that the key information in use throughout the organization is consistent. The concept of master data for operational systems is similar to the concept of conformed dimensions for data warehouses discussed in Chapter 8. Whereas conformed dimensions provide a set of quality reference data for consistent analytical use, master data provides a set of quality reference data for consistent operational use.

There are various architectures used for management of master data. Three main approaches are:

- centralized approach
- registry
- hybrid approach

In a centralized approach, a single central copy of the master data is used by operational information systems. Nonmaster data is still collected and maintained by the operational information systems, but all instances of master data are retrieved from and updated in the central master data copy. The centralized approach is illustrated by Figure D.1.

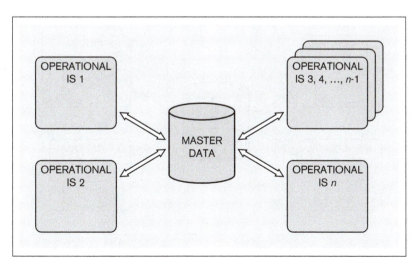

FIGURE D.1 Centralized master data.

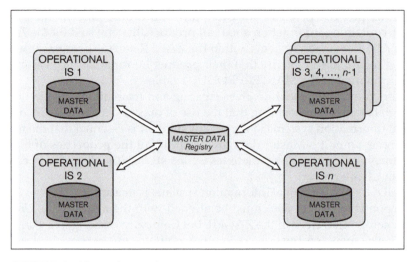

FIGURE D.2   Master data registry.

An opposite approach to centralized master data is keeping all master data at various individual operational information systems. Such dispersed master data is connected via a central master data registry. A **master data registry** contains only a list of keys that is used to connect and coordinate the actual master data that resides in operational systems. The master data registry allows any individual information system to access master data from other information systems in order to align and supplement its own master data. A master data registry is illustrated by Figure D.2.

The hybrid approach to storing master data combines the two approaches described above. There is an actual central master data copy, but individual operational systems may contain their own copies of the master data as well. The central master data copy and master data copies are connected and coordinated via the central master data registry. The hybrid approach is illustrated by Figure D.3.

In some implementations of the hybrid approach, master data can be updated (inserted, deleted, modified) only in the central copy and all the updates are propagated to the copies in the operational systems. Other implementations allow master

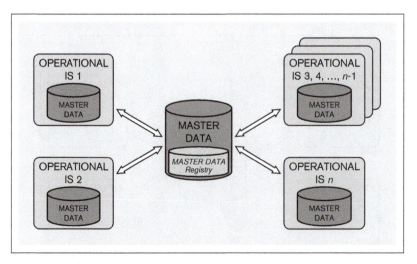

FIGURE D.3   A hybrid MDM approach.

data to be updated in individual operational systems. These changes are propagated to the central copy and then to the other individual systems.

Also, in some implementations the entire set of master data is present in the central copy and in all individual systems, while in other implementations, portions of the master data are present in the individual systems and/or central copy.

APPENDIX E
Object–Oriented Databases

An **object-oriented database (OODB)** system, also called an object database system (ODBS), is a database system that is based on so called object-oriented concepts. This appendix will give a brief overview of such concepts and of how they are used by OODB. Object-oriented concepts were first introduced by object-oriented programming languages. An object-oriented database management system (OODBMS) combines the features of a database system and the object-oriented features originating from object-oriented programming languages.

OODBMS were proposed as a way to address the limitations of existing databases, such as relational databases, and for designing and implementing complex database applications. Some examples of these complex database applications are multimedia databases, geographical information systems (GIS), and databases for computer-aided design and computer-aided manufacturing (CAD/CAM). These databases require storing and manipulating objects, such as images, maps, and video, which are not the data types typically used in the relational model. They do not fit well into the concept of rows and columns in a relational table and require more than the typical relational operations.

OBJECT–ORIENTED CONCEPTS

An **object** in an OODB corresponds to a real world object in the same sense as the entity in ER modeling corresponds to an object in the real world. In addition to **object attributes** (which are equivalent to the attributes of an entity), an object has **object operations** (also called "methods," described later in this appendix) and an **object identifier (OID)** that is typically system generated. Within an object-oriented database (OODB), objects that share the same structure and operations are grouped into a **class**. The objects of a particular class are called **class instances**.

An OID differs from a primary key because an OID value is automatically assigned by the OODB system and is considered to be immutable. On the other hand, in a relational database a primary key is value based (i.e., values are entered in the primary key column in the same way as values of any other column in the relation), and a primary key value can change. OID values are unique across the entire object-oriented database, whereas in a relational database, two primary key values in two separate relations can be identical. Consider an example in Figure E.1.

PRIMARY KEY (Relational Database)

EMPLOYEE

EID	EName
100	Anne
101	Bob
102	Cliff

CUSTOMER

CID	CName
100	Adam
101	Betty
102	Cindy

OID (Object-Oriented Database)

EMPLOYEE

OID	EName
100	Anne
101	Bob
102	Cliff

CUSTOMER

OID	CName
201	Adam
202	Betty
203	Cindy

FIGURE E.1   A comparison of a primary key and OID.

The top part of Figure E.1 shows two relational tables: table EMPLOYEE with primary key column *EID* and column *EName* and table CUSTOMER with primary key column *CID* and column *CName*. The bottom part of Figure E.1 shows two classes of objects, EMPLOYEE and CUSTOMER with attributes *EName* and *CName*, respectively, where every object has its own OID value. In relational tables, the value of a particular primary key can be changed, and despite the primary key value change, the row with the modified primary key value would still represent the same instance (e.g., the row with the changed *EID* value still represents the same employee). However, in an OODB, every object has one and only one OID that cannot be changed. OID values cannot be reused for other objects, even in other classes. That is why all OID values shown in the bottom part of Figure E.1 are unique. Note that OID is not an attribute of an object. The only purpose of the OID is to distinguish each object from all other objects. It carries no other information and is not displayed to the database users, unlike object attributes' values.

As we mentioned, objects that share the same structure and operations are grouped into classes. For example, the HAFH database (used in Chapters 2, 3, and 5) can be expanded to include information about renters who are individuals as well as the renters that are corporate clients. The data objects in the database representing renters of apartments can be grouped into the class INDIVIDUAL and the class CORPORATECLIENT. The classes in an OODB can be organized into a **class hierarchy (specialization hierarchy)**. Figure E.2 illustrates a class hierarchy composed of the classes RENTER, INDIVIDUAL, and CORPORATECLIENT. A specialization hierarchy is described by an "IS-A" relationship. Figure E.2 shows that a CORPORATECLIENT *IS-A* RENTER of an apartment and an INDIVIDUAL *IS-A* RENTER of an apartment.

In Figure E.2, CORPORATECLIENT and INDIVIDUAL are both a **subclass** of the class RENTER, and the class RENTER is the **superclass** of the class CORPORATECLIENT and of the class INDIVIDUAL. Each class in the class hierarchy can have its own attributes. New classes are created from existing classes (e.g., a subclass is created from a superclass), and the attributes of the superclass are inherited by the subclasses. For example, in Figure E.2, the attributes of the RENTER class are *RenterName* and *LeaseDate*. The attributes of the INDIVIDUAL class are *Address*, *Employer*, and *SSN*, along with the attributes *RenterName* and *LeaseDate* that are inherited from the RENTER class. The attributes of the CORPORATE CLIENT class are *CCIndustry* and *CCLocation*, as well as the attributes *RenterName* and *LeaseDate* that are inherited from the RENTER class.

In addition to the traditional built-in data types, e.g., varchar or date, an OODB allows user defined types to be created and used. A **user-defined type (UDT)** has the format:[1]

```
CREATE TYPE type_name AS (<components>)
```

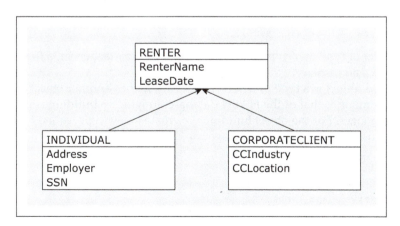

FIGURE E.2   An example of a class hierarchy.

---

[1]The examples in this section utilize a DDL and DML consistent with those of an object-relational database (described at the end of this Appendix) using a UDT that is provided in contemporary SQL extensions.

We will illustrate the UDT concept using the example of RENTER, COR-PORATECLIENT, and INDIVIDUAL classes from Figure E.2. For example, the *renter_type* is constructed of two components, the *rentername* and *leasedate*, of type varchar and date, respectively. The *individual_type* is constructed of three components, the *address* and *employer* of type varchar and *ssn* of type char, while the *corporateclient_type* is constructed of two components, *ccindustry* and *cclocation*, both of type varchar.

The keyword UNDER is used to indicate that the type being defined is a subclass and will inherit the attributes and methods of the specified superclass. In other words, the type being defined is "under" the specified superclass in the class hierarchy.

```
CREATE TYPE renter_type AS
  (rentername   VARCHAR (25),
   leasedate    DATE);

CREATE TYPE individual_type UNDER  renter_type AS
  (address      VARCHAR(25),
   employer     VARCHAR(20),
   ssn          CHAR (9));

CREATE TYPE corporateclient_type UNDER  renter_type AS
  (ccindustry   VARCHAR(25),
   cclocation   VARCHAR(25));
```

The *individual_type* is a subclass of *renter_type* and inherits all of the attributes from *renter_type*. This means an *individual_type* object will have the attributes *rentername*, *leasedate*, *address*, *employer*, and *ssn*. Similarly, *corporateclient_type* is a subclass of *renter_type* and also inherits all of the attributes from *renter_type*. A *corporateclient_type* object will have the attributes *rentername*, *leasedate*, *ccindustry*, and *cclocation*.

Newly created types can be used to define another new type. For example, we can create a *name_type* that is constructed of the three components: *firstname*, *minitial*, and *lastname*.

```
CREATE TYPE name_type AS
  (firstname    VARCHAR(10),
   minitial     CHAR (1),
   lastname     VARCHAR (10));
```

We can then create a new type for the MANAGER class, called *mgr_type*, which contains the attribute *mname* of type *name_type*.

```
CREATE TYPE mgr_type AS
  (managerid    CHAR (4),
   mname        name_type,
   msalary      NUMERIC (9,2));
```

An object of type mgr_type will have the attributes managerid, a firstname, minitial, lastname, and msalary.

A **nested object** is a type of object that occurs within another object. We consider an example similar to that of the HAFH database, in which a building is managed by a particular manager. For the object building we create a new type, called *bldg_type_nest*, which contains the nested object bmanager of *type mgr_type*.

```
CREATE TYPE bldg_type_nest AS
  (buildingid CHAR (3),
   bnooffloors INT,
   bmanager    mgr_type);
```

An object of type *bldg_type_nest* will have the attributes *buildingid* and *bnooffloors* as well as the attributes *managerid*, *mname*, and *msalary*, which are related to the manager of the building. Another example of a nested object is the *mname* in *mgr_type*.

A **reference object** is a type of object that occurs when an object is referenced by another object. To indicate that the object is a reference type, the keyword REF is specified as the type of the object. A reference type is typically implemented as the OID of the object. When the data is inserted into the database, a reference to a particular manager must be specified. We consider the building object again. Instead of defining the *manager* of a *building* as a nested type, we can define it as a reference type. We create a new type, called *bldg_type_ref*, which contains the reference object *bmanager* of type *mgr_type*.

```
CREATE TYPE bldg_type_ref AS
  (buildingid  CHAR (3),
  bnooffloors  INT,
  bmanager     REF mgr_type)
```

The implementation of a nested object differs from a reference object. A nested object contains the actual values of the nested object. This means that the values for *managerid*, *mname*, and *msalary* will be copied and placed into the *bmanager* attribute of the *building* object. This is different from a reference object, in which only the OID is copied and placed into the *bmanager* attribute of the *building* object.

In addition to having its own unique attributes, each class in the class hierarchy can have its own functions implementing methods associated with the objects of the class. This is illustrated by Figure E.3.

When defining types, functions can also be defined in addition to attributes. For example, in the case illustrated by Figure E.3, a function *VerifyLeaseExpiration()*, returning TRUE if the current date occurs less than a year from the *LeaseDate* and returning FALSE if the current date is one year or more from the *LeaseDate*, is defined when creating *renter_type*. A function *CalculateIndDiscount()*, returning the discount value associated with a particular *employer* value, is defined when creating *individual_type*. Similarly, a function *CalculateCorpDiscount()* is defined when creating the *corporateclient_type*. In class hierarchies, both the attributes and the methods of the superclass are inherited by the subclasses. For example, in Figure E.3, the attributes of the RENTER class are *RenterName* and *LeaseDate,* and the method of the RENTER class is *VerifyLeaseExpiration()*. The attributes of the INDIVIDUAL class are *Address, Employer, SSN, RenterName,* and *LeaseDate*, and the methods of the INDIVIDUAL class are *VerifyLeaseExpiration()* and *CalculateIndDiscount()*. The attributes of the CORPORATECLIENT class are *CCIndustry, CCLocation, RenterName,* and *LeaseDate,* and the methods of the CORPORATECLIENT class are *VerifyLeaseExpiration()* and *CalculateCorpDiscount()*.

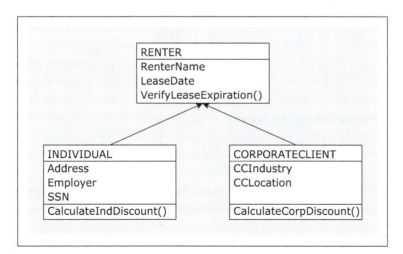

FIGURE E.3 An example of a class hierarchy, expanded with class methods.

OBJECT–ORIENTED QUERIES

When types for the objects in a class are defined, the following create table statements can be used to create objects of the type *mgr_type* and *bldg_type*.

```
CREATE TABLE manager AS mgr_type;
CREATE TABLE building AS bldg_type_nest;
```

Once the corresponding objects (tables) have been created, and the additional commands are issued to insert data instances, the objects are available for data updates and retrievals. The language[2] contains abilities that provide for querying and updating nested and referenced objects.

This is illustrated by the following example that considers manager and building objects similar to those in the HAFH database.

Query X text: *List the building ID and the name of the manager of each building.*

Using the types and tables created above, the query is:

Query X for OODB:

```
SELECT       buildingid, bmanager.firstname,
             bmanager.minitial, bmanager.lastname
FROM         building;
```

In *Query X for OODB*, dot notation is used to qualify the names of attributes in the nested object, with the name of the nested object. For example, the attribute firstname in the nested object bmanager is specified as bmanager.firstname. *Query X for OODB* is called a "path query," because it uses dot notation for traversing nested objects. Notice that the query requires that the building table alone is specified in the FROM clause, while the manager table is not specified.

We compare *Query X for OODB* to the same query in a relational database whose manager table and building table are defined as:

```
CREATE TABLE manager
        (managerid        CHAR (4),
        mfirstname        VARCHAR(10),
        minitial          CHAR (1),
        mlastname         VARCHAR (10))
        msalary           NUMERIC (9,2)
        PRIMARY KEY       (managerid));

CREATE TABLE building
        (buildingid       CHAR (3),
        bnooffloors       INT,
        bmanagerid        CHAR(4)
        PRIMARY KEY       (buildingid),
        FOREIGN KEY       (bmanagerid) REFERENCES
                                manager(managerid) );
```

Using the two tables created above, *Query X for Relational Database* is defined as follows:

Query X for Relational Database:

```
SELECT       buildingid, mfirstname, minitial, mlastname
FROM         manager, building
WHERE        managerid = bmanagerid;
```

Query X for Relational Database requires a join operation between the MANAGER and BUILDING tables, as specified by listing both tables in the FROM clause and the

---

[2]Object Query Language (OQL) is an SQL-like query language designed by the Object Data Management Group (ODMG) in an effort to provide a standardized query language for ODBS. OQL is complex, and no commercial databases have implemented the entire OQL language. However, an SQL-like query language is typically available in an OODB or ORDB.

join condition *managerid = bmanagerid* in the WHERE clause. A path query, as shown in the case of *Query X for OODB*, has eliminated the need for a join operation. As a result, processing a path query can be faster than processing a query that requires a join.

The need for join operations in an OODB is not completely eliminated in every case. Depending on the design of the OODB and the query, joins may still be needed.

OBJECT–RELATIONAL DATABASE

An **object-relational database (ORDB)** is a relational database that contains some object-oriented features. An ORDB management system is considered an extension of a relational database system. An ORDB typically contains the most widely used object-oriented features, such as OIDs, inheritance, arbitrary data types, nested objects, reference objects, and methods. A typical ORDB allows users to create types as objects and to create object tables. ORDBMS are successful in managing media objects and complex data for applications such as geospatial and financial time series data systems. A disadvantage to an ORDB is decreased performance in certain cases, because the object-oriented features are built on top of an existing relational database management system, making it difficult to optimize for performance. An ORDB is convenient for users who are already familiar with relational databases but need the additional features offered by the object-oriented aspects. Most commercially available relational databases provide object-relational features. While commercially available object-oriented databases also exist, they are not as widely used as object-relational databases.

APPENDIX F
Distributed Databases, Parallel Databases, and Cloud Computing

A **distributed database system (DDBS)** is a database system in which the database is distributed among separate computers. A DDBS allows for the sharing of data and offers local database control and autonomy. A distributed database mirrors the organizational structures that are naturally distributed. As an example of a distributed database, consider an enterprise that consists of a headquarters and multiple branches. The enterprise needs to maintain information about the customers of each branch as well as administrative information about its headquarters. With the distributed database shown in Figure F.1, each branch can maintain information in its local database about its customers and may also access customer data from other branches without having to store that information in its local database. In addition, the headquarters of the enterprise can maintain administrative information about all of the branches in its enterprise. Branches may access some of this administrative data from the database at the headquarters location, while other administrative data may be replicated in the database at each branch location.

End users should not be concerned with the distributed nature of the system. In other words, the users should not have to know if the data being accessed is stored locally or remotely at an entirely different geographical location. The property of a DDBS that ensures that the end users can use the distributed database in the same fashion as if it were not distributed (i.e., without knowing the details of the distribution of the data or even if the data is distributed) is called **distribution transparency**.

In a DDBS, the data from the database is distributed among a number of separate computers that do not share any processing or storage devices, and each computer contains its own DBMS. The computers in a DDBS are connected by a network, so they may reside in the same building or be dispersed across different continents. In a **homogeneous DDBS**, all the computers run the same DBMS, while in a **heterogeneous DDBS**, different DBMS can run on different computers (e.g., due to a recent merger between two companies). In a heterogeneous DDBS, for example, one machine in the DDBS can use Oracle, and another can use PostgreSQL as its DBMS.

A distributed database makes certain performance advantages possible. A distributed database allows users of the database to access different parts of the database at the same time without interfering with each other. This is particularly beneficial if most of the queries within the entire DDBS involve local users using local data; for example, if most of the queries on the data in Branch 1 involve local users at the Branch 1 site, and most of the queries on the data in Branch 2 involve local users at the Branch 2 site, and so on. When compared to all queries being processed on one database (as is the

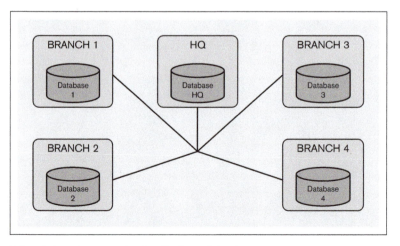

FIGURE F.1 An example of a distributed database system.

case with the nondistributed database), a distributed database composed of databases stored at multiple locations results in fewer queries per computer. This allows for faster processing of the data in cases when most queries are local. In those cases, the data accessed most often is stored locally for each computer, which decreases access time. In addition, a distributed database can provide increased reliability and availability if the data is replicated at more than one location. If there is a problem accessing data from the database at one location, the data can be accessed from another location where the data is replicated.

It is important to note that distributed databases, when compared to nondistributed databases, are more complex. Additional functions are needed to perform tasks, such as keeping track of the location of the data and any replicas, determining which copy of the data to use for a query, and making sure updates are applied to all copies of the data. A distributed directory containing information about all local as well as all remote data in the database has to be maintained. One example of the increased complexity occurs when processing a query across the entire distributed database. In order to process a query, it is necessary to determine the location of the data needed for a query to identify the parts of the query that require local data and the parts of the query that require data from remote locations. When data needed for the query is at a remote location, the part of the query that requires remote data is sent to the appropriate remote location to be run. Once the results of the query from the remote locations are returned, they are combined with the local results.

Database fragmentation is a strategy for distributing the data across different locations in a distributed database. In a distributed database, entire tables can be stored at different locations, or fragments of a table can be stored at different locations. The database can be fragmented horizontally or vertically.

In **horizontal fragmentation**, subsets of the records from a table are stored at different locations in the DDBS. All of the columns in the table are stored at a location, but different subsets of records from the table are stored at different locations. To reconstruct the complete table, all of the fragments must be brought together using the *union* operator. Figure F.2 shows an example of a horizontally fragmented table.

EMPLOYEE (Not Fragmented)

EmpID	EmpName	EmpGender	EmpPhone	EmpBdate
0001	Joe	M	x234	1/11/1985
0002	Sue	F	x345	2/7/1983
0003	Amy	F	x456	8/4/1990
0004	Pat	F	x567	3/8/1971
0005	Mike	M	x678	5/5/1965

EMPLOYEE (Horizontally Fragmented - Location A)

EmpID	EmpName	EmpGender	EmpPhone	EmpBdate
0001	Joe	M	x234	1/11/1985
0002	Sue	F	x345	2/7/1983
0003	Amy	F	x456	8/4/1990

EMPLOYEE (Horizontally Fragmented - Location B)

EmpID	EmpName	EmpGender	EmpPhone	EmpBdate
0001	Joe	M	x234	1/11/1985
0004	Pat	F	x567	3/8/1971
0005	Mike	M	x678	5/5/1965

FIGURE F.2   An example of horizontal fragmentation.

In this example, the following query would create a *union* of two fragments (each containing three records) and thereby reconstruct the complete table (containing five records, as the fragments share the same record for employee *Joe*):

```
SELECT * FROM employee_location_a
UNION
SELECT * FROM employee_location_b;
```

The distribution transparency property of the DDBS would allow the user to simply issue this query as:

```
SELECT * FROM employee
```

In **vertical fragmentation**, subsets of the columns of a table are stored at different locations in the DDBS. All of the records from the table are stored at every location, but only some of the columns. Since only a subset of columns is stored at a location, it is important to include the primary key from the table as one of the columns in each vertical fragment. To reconstruct the complete table, all of the fragments have to be *joined* together, using the primary key as the join condition.

Figure F.3 shows an example of a vertically fragmented table. In this example, the following query would create a *join* of two fragments and thereby reconstruct the complete table:

```
SELECT a.empid, a.empname, b.empgender,
       a.empphone, b.empbdate
FROM   employee_location_a a, employee_location_b b
WHERE  a.empid = b.empid;
```

The distribution transparency property of the DDBS would allow the user to simply issue this query as:

```
SELECT * FROM employee
```

EMPLOYEE (Not Fragmented)

EmpID	EmpName	EmpGender	EmpPhone	EmpBdate
0001	Joe	M	x234	1/11/1985
0002	Sue	F	x345	2/7/1983
0003	Amy	F	x456	8/4/1990
0004	Pat	F	x567	3/8/1971
0005	Mike	M	x678	5/5/1965

EMPLOYEE (Vertically Fragmented - Location A)

EmpID	EmpName	EmpPhone
0001	Joe	x234
0002	Sue	x345
0003	Amy	x456
0004	Pat	x567
0005	Mike	x678

EMPLOYEE (Vertically Fragmented - Location B)

EmpID	EmpGender	EmpBdate
0001	M	1/11/1985
0002	F	2/7/1983
0003	F	8/4/1990
0004	F	3/8/1971
0005	M	5/5/1965

FIGURE F.3   An example of vertical fragmentation.

EMPLOYEE (Not Fragmented)

EmpID	EmpName	EmpGender	EmpPhone	EmpBdate
0001	Joe	M	x234	1/11/1985
0002	Sue	F	x345	2/7/1983
0003	Amy	F	x456	8/4/1990
0004	Pat	F	x567	3/8/1971
0005	Mike	M	x678	5/5/1965

EMPLOYEE (Location A)

EmpID	EmpName	EmpPhone
0001	Joe	x234
0002	Sue	x345
0003	Amy	x456

EMPLOYEE (Location B)

EmpID	EmpName	EmpPhone
0001	Joe	x234
0004	Pat	x567
0005	Mike	x678

EMPLOYEE (Location C)

EmpID	EmpGender	EmpBdate
0001	M	1/11/1985
0002	F	2/7/1983
0003	F	8/4/1990
0004	F	3/8/1971
0005	M	5/5/1965

FIGURE F.4 An example of mixed fragmentation.

It is possible to combine both horizontal and vertical fragmentation strategies within the same table. Combining horizontal and vertical fragmentation is referred to as **mixed fragmentation**. Figure F.4 shows an example of a table fragmented using mixed fragmentation.

In this example, the following query would reconstruct the complete table:

```
SELECT a.empid, a.empname, c.empgender,
       a.empphone, c.empbdate
FROM   employee_location_a a, employee_location_c c
WHERE  a.empid = c.empid
UNION
SELECT b.empid, b.empname, c.empgender,
       b.empphone, c.empbdate
FROM   employee_location_b b, employee_location_c c
WHERE  b.empid = c.empid;
```

The distribution transparency property of the DDBS would allow the user to simply issue this query as:

```
SELECT * FROM employee
```

Data replication occurs when more than one copy of the data is stored at different locations in a distributed database. When the entire database is replicated at each location in the distributed system, it is called a **fully replicated distributed database**. A type of replication in which some of the data is replicated at multiple locations while other parts are not is called **partial replication**.

The main advantage of data replication is the quicker performance of queries (more data can be processed locally) and the availability of data even when a computer that is a part of a DDBS is not functioning (as long as another computer contains the same data that is stored on the nonfunctioning computer). While data replication can increase query performance and availability of the data, it can also complicate the update process. When one copy of the data is updated, a strategy must be in place to make sure all of the other copies are updated as well. In one update strategy, one of the copies of the data is designated as a "distinguished" copy, whose location is responsible for coordinating updates to all other copies. Updated data cannot be accessed until the coordinator ensures that all copies have been successfully updated. Another update strategy, called "quorum" or "voting," does not have a coordinator, but instead requires a majority of the copies to be updated before that data can be accessed.

A **federated database** is a type of distributed database system that comprises a collection of preexisting databases that are connected into one system. The preexisting databases remain autonomous, but agree to cooperate and share data in order to form a new database. One example is a federated library database that comprises the library databases at different universities across the country. While each library has its own database containing information about books stored in that library, the libraries agree to form a federated database. Users can then access information from all of the university libraries that are in the federated database. Federated databases do not necessarily provide transparency. A federated database requires a global view of the federation that can be used when accessing the entire system, since each database in the federation has its own schema.

PARALLEL DATABASES

The computers in a **parallel database** system work on the same task and perform the same operations simultaneously on different portions of the same data set. In other words, the computers work in parallel. Modern parallel databases utilize **massively parallel processing (MPP)** technology. MPP is an industry term referring to a large number of separate computer processors running in parallel to execute a single program. There are various architectural approaches to parallel computing that differ in whether computer processors share or maintain their own disk storage and memory. Depending on the approach, the computer processors in a parallel system may share disk storage and memory or have their own memory and share disk storage. A parallel system in which each processor has its own memory and disk storage is referred to as a **shared-nothing MPP architecture**.

The parallelization of database operations can improve performance greatly when dealing with large amounts of data. That is why many data warehouse systems are implemented using parallel RDBMS systems, such as Teradata or Greenplum.

In Appendix J, we illustrate the use of parallel computation for the implementation of the MapReduce method for dealing with unstructured data. Parallel computations are also very common in **cloud computing systems**, which use the Internet to deliver data storage and processing services hosted by a service provider.

CLOUD COMPUTING

Cloud systems have emerged as a computing model as well as a business model, providing computing resources to users upon request and allowing users to increase or decrease the amount of resources requested based on their needs. The computing resources provided can range from computer software to computer hardware, and can even be a particular computing platform. By utilizing a cloud, an organization does not have to invest in computer hardware and support an IT staff.

Some of the characteristics of a cloud are its on-demand access to computing resources, pay-per-use model, elasticity, virtualization, and distributed/highly-parallel approach.

Clouds provide resources on-demand to customers as they are requested. Customers pay per use, because they are only charged for the resources they use. Since a customer can request resources as they are needed, he or she does not have the cost of maintaining unneeded resources. For example, promotions, sales, festivals, and special occasions in a consumer market can create a large spike in the workload of data applications. Deployment of available resources to handle that spike could be the wrong strategic decision for any company, because those resources are unused during the rest of the year.

Cloud service providers tend to offer services that can be grouped into three categories: infrastructure as a service, platform as a service, and software as a service.

Infrastructure as a service (IaaS) provides hardware as standardized services over the network. Customers can rent resources, such as server space, network equipment, memory, processing cycles, and storage space.

Platform as a service (PaaS) supplies all of the resources required by a customer to build applications. It encapsulates a layer of software to create a platform by integrating an operating system, middleware, application software, and a development environment. The customer can interact with the platform through an interface, and the platform performs actions to maintain and scale itself according to the customer's needs.

Software as a service (SaaS) features an application offered as a service on-demand, which is hosted and operated over the Internet for use by customers. A single instance of the software running on the cloud can be used simultaneously by multiple clients (multitenant).

Database as a service (DaaS) is another specialized version of SaaS that is specifically developed for database management in clouds.

As the amount of data being stored is increasing dramatically, cloud architectures can solve some of the key difficulties faced in large-scale data processing. A cloud computing environment can allow databases to auto-scale up and down based on dynamic workloads. Clouds are viewed as well suited for analytical data management applications, which handle historical data from multiple operational databases and require few or no updates. Operational databases present more challenges when deployed in a cloud. Unlike analytical databases, operational databases require updates to the data. Maintaining consistent values when data is updated can become complex and can affect performance when data is replicated over a wide geographic area.

Clouds are described as "elastic" because they can accommodate an increase in demand for resources as well as a decrease in demand. Clouds use virtualization to allow multiple tenants to use the same equipment at the same time. A single server in a cloud can provide multiple operating instances so that more than one client can run an application using a different operating system on the same machine. The virtualization software can emulate many physical machines and platforms for the customer. For example, a customer can choose a particular operating system on which to run his application.

Clouds are typically distributed and can comprise multiple data centers distributed across large geographical areas. Solving problems in parallel exploits the advantages of a cloud, as multiple machines can be used to solve a problem quickly in parallel. Instead of expensive servers, many clouds comprise commodity or off-the-shelf computers. The possibility of failure of any component of a cloud is built into the computing model of a cloud. Processes can be replicated so that any processing failure can result in a quick recovery. Similarly, data reliability and availability are usually achieved by creating a certain number of replicas of the data distributed over different geographical areas.

There are certain security and privacy issues associated with storing data in a cloud. Moving data off the premises and storing it in a third-party vendor's servers potentiality increases security risks. Storing an enterprise's data in a cloud requires trust in the host. In a cloud, data can be stored in any location around the globe. Different countries have different rules and regulations regarding the rightful access to data. Any government can force access to data stored in that country by law, in which case data may be handed over without any notification to the owner of the data. Accountability issues related to incorrect billing or nonpayment of bills may also arise. In spite of these challenges, cloud computing is a growing trend and is being adopted by an increasing number of companies and organizations worldwide.

APPENDIX G
Data Mining

Data mining is broadly defined as the process of discovering novel and interesting patterns in large amounts of data. Data mining techniques and algorithms originate in many different fields, such as mathematics, statistics, machine learning, and databases. While there is no clear distinction between standard data analysis (such as regression analysis and OLAP) and data mining, the latter often involves a very large number of possible findings, with only a few being discovered as valid.

These findings can be surprising, previously unknown, and sometimes counterintuitive. For example, finding the top-selling products for a large supermarket chain is certainly not considered data mining, while finding products that commonly sell together is one of the most studied and well-known data mining problems.

The data warehouse is one of the primary data sources for data mining. Since it provides high-quality, integrated, enterprise-wide data, it can be used to answer questions and find new and interesting patterns in many aspects of business.

One of the most typical and widespread classes of data mining applications is called **predictive analytics** and involves using past data to predict future events. Examples include using past credit history to determine the creditworthiness of new loan applicants, deriving usage patterns from typical credit card transactions and comparing new purchases against these patterns to flag potential instances of fraud, and predicting the likelihood of certain diseases for patients using genetic and environmental information. There are many techniques that can be used to build predictive models, such as *classification*, *clustering*, and *regression*.

Describing details of various data mining methods is beyond the scope of this book. However, in order to provide an illustration of the mechanisms and application of a data mining method, we will give an overview of one of the most applied methods, association rule mining.

ASSOCIATION RULE MINING

Association rule mining, also known as **market basket analysis**, is considered the flagship of data mining from a database perspective. This method originated in database research in the early 1990s. It is particularly applicable to data warehouses and data marts built using dimensional modeling (resulting in star schemas). The simplest definition of association rule mining is finding groups of items that tend to appear together in transactions. The term "market basket analysis" stems from the fact that the initial data for this type of mining was supermarket checkout data. The goal was to find products that tend to be purchased together more often than you would expect if everything were purchased at random. While some mining results are not surprising (such as *hot dogs and ketchup are often purchased together* or *cereal and milk are often purchased together*), the canonical unexpected result cited in the academic literature is *beer and diapers are often purchased together*. This example had been in turn debunked and then reestablished several times by different researchers, but the important point is that association rule mining can discover *nonobvious patterns* that can be used by marketers to boost sales and increase profits.

ASSOCIATION RULE MINING EXAMPLE

Association rule mining discovers correlations among items within transactions. The correlations are expressed in the following form:

Transactions that contain X are likely to contain Y as well.

This is noted as association rule X→Y, where X and Y represent sets of transaction items. The prototypical example of utilizing association rule mining determines what products are found together in a basket at a checkout register at the supermarket, where correlations are represented in the form of a rule:

Customers buying X are likely to buy Y during the same purchase transaction.

There are two important quantities measured for every association rule: support and confidence. The support for rule $X \rightarrow Y$ is the fraction of all transactions that contain both item X and item Y:

support = (number of transactions containing X and Y)/(number of all
transactions)

The confidence for rule X→Y is the fraction of transactions containing items X, which also contain items Y:

confidence = (number of transactions containing X and Y)/(number of
transactions containing X)

Intuitively, the support measures the significance of the rule, so we are interested in rules with relatively high support. The confidence measures the strength of the correlation, so rules with low confidence are not meaningful, even if their support is high. A meaningful rule, in this context, is the relationship among transaction items with high (above certain thresholds) support and confidence, where the thresholds are determined by the analyst.

To illustrate how support and confidence measures facilitate association rule mining, consider the following simplified example:

The ZAGI Retail Company retail chain sells hundreds of different products including Item A, Item B, and Item C.

Suppose we are looking for association rules with at least 0.5 percent support and 50 percent confidence. Normally, these thresholds are determined by the analyst, and they can be revised in subsequent iterations of the data mining process. Table G.1 shows the number of transactions involving:

- Item A
- Item B
- Item C
- Item A and Item B together
- Item A and Item C together
- Item B and Item C together
- Item A, Item B, and Item C together

There are 500,000 total transactions: 10,000 involve Item A; 7,000 involve Item B; 11,000 involve Item C; 4,000 involve both Item A and Item B; and so on. Note that the transactions that involve both Item A and Item B are a subset of the transactions that involve A.

The support of the pair Item A, Item B is 0.80 percent (support for $A \rightarrow B$ and for $B \rightarrow A$ is the same: 4/500 = 0.80%, because the support is always the same for both rules involving the same pair of items). There are 10,000 transactions that involve item A, and 7,000 transactions that involve item B. Therefore, the confidence of $A \rightarrow B$ is 40.00 percent and the confidence of $B \rightarrow A$ is 57.14 percent (confidence for $A \rightarrow B$ is 4/10 = 40% and for $B \rightarrow A$ is 4/7 = 57.14%). Support and confidence for all possible rules in this example are shown in Table G.2.

TABLE G.1 Transaction Statistics (in thousands)

Total	A	B	C	A&B	A&C	B&C	A&B&C
500	10	7	11	4	5	2	1

TABLE G.2	Support and Confidence Values	
Rule	**Support**	**Confidence**
A → B	0.80%	40.00%
B → A	0.80%	57.14%
A → C	1.00%	50.00%
C → A	1.00%	45.45%
B → C	0.40%	28.57%
C → B	0.40%	18.18%
A, B → C	0.20%	25.00%
C → A, B	0.20%	9.09%
A, C → B	0.20%	20.00%
B → A, C	0.20%	14.29%
B, C → A	0.20%	50.00%
A → B, C	0.20%	10.00%

Of the 11 possible rules shown in Table G.2, only the following two satisfy the required threshold of at least 0.5% support and 50% confidence:

Item B → Item A (sup=0.80%, conf=57%)

Item A → Item C (sup=1.00%, conf=50%)

Setting the thresholds for the support and confidence values enables analysts involved in market basket analysis to discover the most meaningful rules among all of the possible rules. Once those discoveries are made, they can be used to influence business decisions. For example, retailers that discover that two products sell particularly well together can use this discovery in several ways. They can stock these two products together, providing a convenient shopping experience. Or they can stock them apart, driving the customers who want to buy both products to be exposed to many other products in the store. Retailers can also run a sale on one of the products and raise the price of the other. None of these options for changing the existing business practice would have been recognized by retailers had they not first engaged in the data mining of the data they own.

APPENDIX H
XML

MARKUP LANGUAGES

A **markup language** is a language to annotate (i.e., to "mark-up") text in a document, where annotations add functionalities to the text. Depending on the type of the markup language, the annotations can be used for various purposes, such as indicating how the annotated text in the document is to be formatted, presented, structured, and so on.

Hypertext markup language (HTML) is an example of a markup language. HTML provides functionality for describing how to display the information contained in Web pages. The purpose of HTML is strictly to facilitate the display of data.

Consider the HTML code shown in Figure H.1, which is stored in a file titled HTMLExample.html. The code contains text annotated by the HTML tags. For example, the text annotated by the start tag <p> and end tag</p> is marked up as text to be displayed as a separate paragraph, and the text annotated by the start tag <b> and end tag </b> is annotated as text to be to be displayed in bold font.

HTMLExample.html, containing the HTML code shown in Figure H.1, will be retrieved by a Web browser as the Web page shown in Figure H.2.

XML

Extensible markup language (XML) is a markup language for adding structure and semantics to a document. One of the common usages of XML is to facilitate data exchange from databases in e-business applications. In such scenarios, data is extracted from databases, formatted as XML documents, and transported to and displayed on

```
<html>
   <head>
      <title> Web page EXAMPLE</title>
   </head>
   <body>
      <p>This is an example of a HTML Web page.</p>
      <p><b>This part is in bold font.</b></p>
      <p><i>This part is in italic font.</i></p>
   </body>
</html>
```

FIGURE H.1   An example of HTML code.

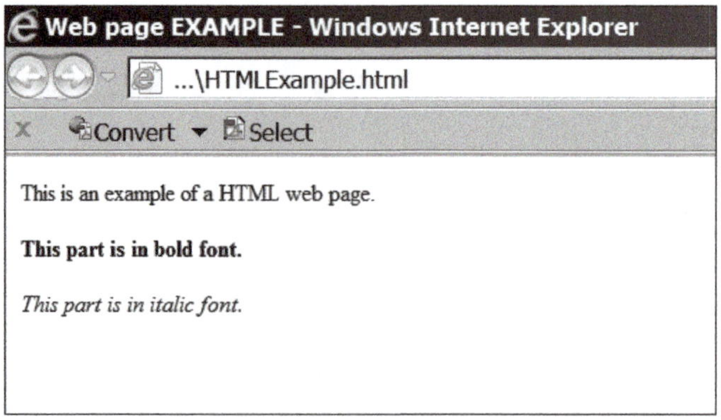

FIGURE H.2   An example of a Web page.

Web pages using HTML. The following is a brief overview of some of the most basic functionalities of XML.

The basic building block of an XML document is called an "element." An XML document is composed of the "root element," which contains all other elements in the document. Elements in an XML document are identified by a start tag <element_name> and an end tag </element_name>. "Simple elements" are the actual data values (e.g., an integer or a character value). "Complex elements" are elements that contain other elements.

Consider the XML code shown in Figure H.3. The first line of this code is the XML declaration.[1] The rest of this XML code is based on a subset of data in the HAFH database (used in Chapters 3 and 5) that depicts buildings, apartments, and corporate clients.

In this simple example, the root of the tree is the *HAFH* complex element that contains *Building* elements. Each *Building* element is a complex element that contains two simple elements *BuildingID* and *BNoOfFloors*, and one or more *Apartment* elements. Each *Apartment* element is a complex element that has two simple elements *AptNo* and *ANoOfBedrooms*. In addition, some *Apartment* elements contain *CorporateClient* elements. Each *CorporateClient* element is a complex element that has two simple elements *CCID* and *CCName*.

In XML, all elements are hierarchically organized. The terms "parent element," "child element," "descendant element," and "sibling element" are used to describe the hierarchical relationship between the elements. For example, *Building* is a parent element of child elements *BuildingID*, *BNoOfFloors*, and *Apartment*, while *Apartment* is a parent element of child elements *AptNo*, *ANoOfBedrooms*, and *CorporateClient*. At the same time, *BuildingID*, *BNoOfFloors*, *Apartment*, *AptNo*, *ANoOfBedrooms*, *CorporateClient*, *CCID*, and *CCName* are all descendent elements of *Building*. Sibling elements are elements that share the same parent. For example, *BuildingID* and *BNoOfFloors* are sibling elements.

```
<?xml version="1.0" ?>
<HAFH>
<Building>
          <BuildingID>B1</BuildingID>
          <BNoOfFloors>5</BNoOfFloors>
          <Apartment>
                    <AptNo>21</AptNo>
                    <ANoOfBedrooms>1</ANoOfBedrooms>
          </Apartment>
          <Apartment>
                    <AptNo>41</AptNo>
                    <ANoOfBedrooms>1</ANoOfBedrooms>
                    <CorporateClient>
                            <CCID>C111</CCID>
                            <CCName>BlingNotes</CCName>
                    </CorporateClient>
          </Apartment>
</Building>
<Building>
          <BuildingID>B2</BuildingID>
          <BNoOfFloors>6</BNoOfFloors>
          ...
          ...
</HAFH>
```

FIGURE H.3   An example of XML code.

---

[1]XML declaration identifies the document as being XML and specifies the version of the XML standard (in this case 1.0).

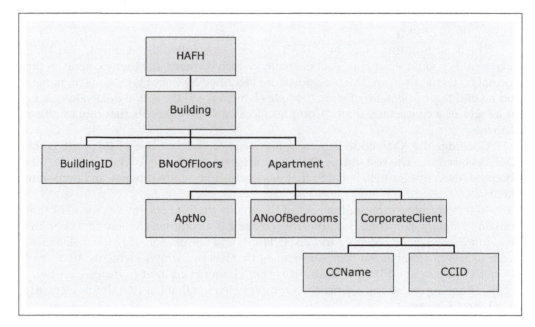

FIGURE H.4 The schema of the XML data shown in Figure H.3.

Since the XML data is hierarchical, the schema of XML data is described by a tree. Figure H.4 depicts the schema of the HAFHInfo.xml document shown in Figure H.3.

As illustrated by Figure H.3, the data extracted from a database can be captured in an XML document. In addition, an XML document itself can be stored in a database. There are different ways to store XML documents in a database. XML documents can be stored as text in a database system, which requires the DBMS to have a module for document processing. Alternatively, the XML document contents can be stored as data elements, if all the documents have the same structure. In such cases, the XML schemas must then be mapped to a database schema. It is also possible to create XML documents from a preexisting relational database and store them back into a database. Special DBMS called "native XML databases" have been designed specifically for storing and processing XML data. Native XML databases have an XML document as the basic unit of storage. Many DBMS have built-in functions that will present the data in XML elements in a typical relational format, as rows of a table.

XML QUERIES

XML is often used for exchanging data between a database and an application. In such cases, XML documents can contain fairly complex structures of elements. Thus, it is necessary to have a mechanism for traversing the tree structure of XML elements and for extracting information contained within.

XML Path Language (XPath) is a simple language that utilizes the tree representation of an XML document, allowing the user to travel around the tree. XPath expressions return a collection of element nodes from the tree that satisfy patterns specified in an expression. Separators / and // are used to specify the children or descendants of a tag as described by the following:

```
/    means the tag must appear as the immediate descendant (i.e., child) of
     a previous parent tag
//   means the tag can appear as a descendant of a previous tag at any level
```

For example, to access the buildings in the HAFH database, the following statement would be issued:

```
/HAFH/building
```

As another example, consider the following statement that accesses the apartment numbers of apartments with more than 1 bedroom:

```
//apartment [ANoOfBedrooms > 1]/AptNo
```

XQuery is a language used for more wide-ranging queries on XML documents. XQuery provides functionalities for querying XML documents similar to SQL functionalities for querying relational tables. XQuery uses XPath expressions within a "FLWOR" (*For Let Where Order by Return*) expression, which is similar to the SELECT… FROM…WHERE expressions of SQL. The *For* part extracts elements from an XML document. The *Let* part allows the creation of a variable and assignment of a value to it. The *Where* part filters the elements based on a logical expression. The *Order by* part sorts the result. The *Return* part specifies what is to be returned as a result. The *For* and *Let* in the FLWOR expression can appear any number of times or in any order. The *Let*, *Where,* and *Order by* are optional, while the *For* and *Return* are always needed. To illustrate these expressions, consider the following example, which assumes that the XML document shown in Figure H.3 is saved into a document titled *hafhinfo.xml* and stored on the web server *www.hafhrealty.com:*

```
FOR $x in doc(www.hafhrealty.com/hafhinfo.xml)
RETURN <res> $x/CorpClient/ccname, $x/CorpClient/ccid </res>
```

This XQuery is requesting a list of the names and IDs of corporate clients. Now consider the expanded example, requesting a list of the names and IDs of corporate clients who are renting apartments that have more than one bedroom, sorted by IDs of corporate clients:

```
FOR $x in doc(www.hafh.com/hafhinfo.xml)
LET $minbedroms := 2
WHERE $x/ANoOfBedrooms >= $minbedroms
ORDER BY $x/CorpClient/ccid
RETURN <res> $x/CorpClient/ccname, $x/CorpClient/ccid </res>
```

Apart from having efficient mechanisms for extracting specific elements and data from an XML document, there is also the need for efficient means for automated construction of XML documents, based on the data queried from a database. Many of the dominant database management systems today incorporate XML by including **SQL/XML**, which is an extension of SQL that specifies the combined use of SQL and XML. The following is a simple example that illustrates one of the particular functionalities of SQL/XML.

Consider SQL query *QueryA,* which retrieves the content of the table INSPECTOR in the HAFH database:

SQL Query A

```
SELECT   i.insid, i.insname
FROM     inspector i;
```

SQL query *QueryA* results in the following output:

SQL Query A Result

insid	insname
I11	Jane
I22	Niko
I33	MIck

SQL/XML query *QueryAX* utilizes SQL/XML function xmlelement() to create an XML element.

SQL/XML Query AX

```
SELECT   xmlelement(name "inspector",
         xmlelement(name "insid", i.insid),
         xmlelement(name "insname", i.insname))
FROM     inspector i;
```

SQL/XML query *QueryAX* results in the following output:

SQL/XML Query AX Result

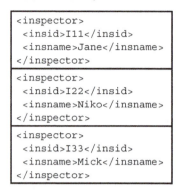

```
<inspector>
 <insid>I11</insid>
 <insname>Jane</insname>
</inspector>

<inspector>
 <insid>I22</insid>
 <insname>Niko</insname>
</inspector>

<inspector>
 <insid>I33</insid>
 <insname>Mick</insname>
</inspector>
```

Whereas the SQL query *QueryA* produced rows and columns of data from the table INSPECTOR, the SQL/XML query *QueryAX* produced XML elements based on the data in the table INSPECTOR.

One of the typical uses of XML is as a means for presenting database content on Web pages. One of the ways to present the XML elements retrieved from the database in a Web page is by using **Extensible Stylesheet Language (XSL).**

Consider the XML file *inspectors.xml* shown in Figure H.5. The first line of code is the XML declaration. The second line of code specifies that an XSL file *insptoweb1.xsl* (shown in Figure H.6) will be used to describe how the file *inspector.xml* should be displayed as a Web page. The remainder of the code in the XML file *inspectors.xml* contains the content from the table INSPECTOR retrieved by *QueryAX*.

XSL file *insptoweb1.xsl* shown in Figure H.6 describes how the file *inspector.xml* will be displayed as a Web page.

The first four lines and the last two lines of the code in Figure H.6 contain the necessary utilitarian information for XSL documents. The tags <html>, <title>, <body>, <b>, and <p> used after the first four lines of the code are standard HTML tags illustrated by the example shown in Figures H.1 and H.2. The code in the center, shown in bold font, uses the XSL element <xsl:for-each> to select (in the XML file referencing this XSL file) every XML tree element identified by the XPath expression buildinginspectors/inspector. When the XML file *inspectors.xml* is opened by a Web browser, it is displayed as shown in Figure H.7.

```
<?xml version="1.0" ?>
<?xml-stylesheet type="text/xsl" href="insptoweb1.xsl"?>


<buildinginspectors>
        <inspector>
                <insid>I11</insid>
                <insname>Jane</insname>
        </inspector>
        <inspector>
                <insid>I22</insid>
                <insname>Niko</insname>
        </inspector>
        <inspector>
                <insid>I33</insid>
                <insname>Mick</insname>
        </inspector>
</buildinginspectors>
```

FIGURE H.5 The XML file *inspectors.xml* (to be displayed as a Web page).

```
<?xml version="1.0" ?>
<xsl:stylesheet version="1.0"
xmlns:xsl="http://www.w3.org/1999/XSL/Transform">
<xsl:template match="/">

  <html>
  <head>
  <title> Web page XML EXAMPLE1</title>
  </head>
  <body>
    <b>Building Inspectors</b>
     <xsl:for-each select="buildinginspectors/inspector">
       <p> --- </p>
       <p>Inspector ID: <xsl:value-of select="insid" /></p>
       <p>Inspector Name: <xsl:value-of select="insname" /></p>
     </xsl:for-each>
  </body>
  </html>

</xsl:template>
</xsl:stylesheet>
```

FIGURE H.6   The XSL file *insptoweb1.xsl* (formats *inspectors.xml* as a Web page).

To illustrate how the same XML elements can be formatted differently, Figure H.8 shows the file *insptoweb2.xsl,* which contains a different version of the XSL code for the file *inspectors.xml.* This code uses HTML tags for coloring and table formatting. For example, tag <tr bgcolor="#808080"> specifies the use of a gray background color in the header of the table.

Assume that the XML file *inspectors.xml* now refers to the XSL file *insptoweb2.xsl* instead of the XSL file *insptoweb1.xsl.* In that case, the XML file *inspectors.xml* will be displayed as shown in Figure H.9 when opened by a Web browser.

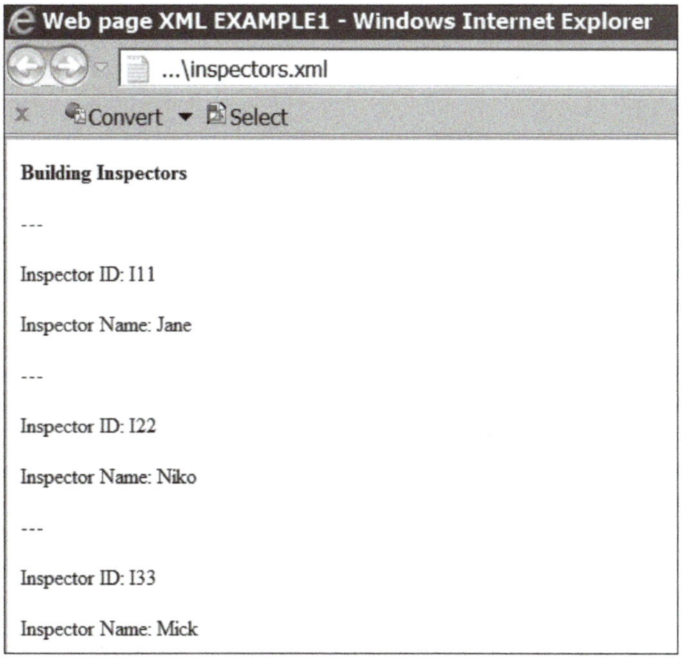

FIGURE H.7 The XML file *inspectors.xml* (displayed as a Web page).

```
<?xml version="1.0" ?>
<xsl:stylesheet version="1.0"
xmlns:xsl="http://www.w3.org/1999/XSL/Transform">
<xsl:template match="/">

  <html>
  <head>
  <title> Web page XML EXAMPLE2</title>
  </head>
  <body>
    <b>Building Inspectors</b>
    <table border="1">
      <tr bgcolor="#BBFFFF">
        <th>Inspector ID</th>
        <th>Inspector Name</th>
      </tr>
      <xsl:for-each select="buildinginspectors/inspector">
      <tr>
        <td><xsl:value-of select="insid" /></td>
        <td><xsl:value-of select="insname" /></td>
      </tr>
      </xsl:for-each>
    </table>
  </body>
  </html>

</xsl:template>
</xsl:stylesheet>
```

FIGURE H.8 The XSL file *insptoweb2.xsl* (formats *inspectors.xml* as a Web page).

FIGURE H.9 The XML file *inspectors.xml* (displayed as another Web page).

As we just illustrated, the extracted database content annotated by the XML tags in an XML document can be transported to various destinations and arranged, formatted, and presented in various ways.

This appendix represented a brief illustration of some of the most fundamental XML concepts, focusing on the XML functionalities relevant to database-related topics.

APPENDIX I
NOSQL Databases

As a broad term, a **NoSQL database** describes a database that is not based on the relational model and does not use SQL as a query language. In addition to not being based on RDBMS technologies, one of the main differentiating features of a NoSQL database is its flexible and extensible data model. In relational databases, database schema in advance capture the semantics of the elements in the database. In NoSQL databases, data does not have to be stored in structures described by an organized database schema. For example, data in many NoSQL databases is organized into simple key–value pairs. In a key–value pair, the instance of data that is stored in the database is a value that is given a key to be used for data retrieval. Whether the values are simple (e.g., one word or number) or arbitrarily complex structures with their own semantics, the values are processed by applications outside the database system and not the database system itself.

We will illustrate the data model, query language, and extensibility of NoSQL databases using a simple example of a hotel-business related database in one of the most popular NoSQL databases, MongoDB.

NOSQL DATABASE EXAMPLE: MONGODB

MongoDB is a so-called *document-oriented* NoSQL database organized around collections of documents. The term *collections* corresponds to the notion of a table in a RDBMS, whereas *documents* corresponds to the notion of rows in a RDBMS. The collections can be created at run-time; the structure of the documents in any particular collection is not required to be the same, although in most cases, the structures are similar.

Consider the following example of an online company that collects information about lodgings, such as hotels, motels, bed and breakfasts, rooms in private houses, camping sites, etc. The data collected and presented on its Web site contains lodging information, such as rates, room types, and amenities. Designing a relational schema for such a diverse set of objects is not impossible, but would involve significant modeling effort and may result in a schema that would evolve over time.

In MongoDB, such a collection of hotel documents can be built incrementally without having to modify any schema, since there is no general schema.

For example, a document can contain the most basic hotel info, such as name, address, and numeric rating. The statements below show the creation of three documents that are saved in the database:

```
h1 = {name: "Metro Blu", address: "Chicago, IL", rating: 3.5}
db.hotels.save(h1)
h2 = {name: "Experiential", address: "New York, NY", rating: 4}
db.hotels.save(h2)
h3 = {name: "Zazu Hotel", address: "San Francisco, CA", rating: 4.5}
db.hotels.save(h3)
```

At this point, the database contains a collection called *hotels* with three documents. All such documents can be found in the database by issuing the following query (equivalent to the "SELECT * " statement in SQL):

```
db.hotels.find()
```

Note that the *hotels* collection, or the schema of the documents in it, did not have to be declared or defined. In order to add a new hotel with an unknown rating, a new document without the rating feature can be created as follows:

```
h4 = {name: "Solace", address: "Los Angeles, CA"}
db.hotels.save(h4)
```

All hotels in California can be found by querying *hotels*:

```
db.hotels.find( { address : { $regex : "CA" } } );
```

The query uses a regular expression to find any document with an address that contains the "CA" string (similar to the "SELECT * FROM Hotels WHERE address LIKE '%CA%'" query in SQL).

If the company decides to add additional information about some hotels, the updates can be applied to each hotel document, as depicted by the following statements:

```
db.hotels.update( { name:"Zazu Hotel" }, { $set : {wifi: "free"} } )
db.hotels.update( { name:"Zazu Hotel" }, { $set : {parking: 45} } )
```

These statements added new features to the *Zazu Hotel* entry, namely the availability of Wi-Fi (*free*) and the price of parking (*$45*). There is no need to change a schema and migrate the data to the new schema, as would be the case for a relational database.

Of course, such flexibility comes at the cost of limited querying capability. In particular, the joining of documents is not directly supported by MongoDB. The developer must implement such functionality using a general programing language (JavaScript, in MongoDB's case). Such implementation involves nested loops over the collections that are being joined. Any performance optimizations, such as use of indexing and taking advantage of the physical layout of the documents within each collection, would have to be implemented by the developer. This creates a high burden on the developer when contrasted with the ease of writing a JOIN query over two tables when using SQL.

NOSQL DATABASES VERSUS RELATIONAL DATABASES

NoSQL and relational databases differ in a number of characteristics. Here, we will summarize some of the most basic differences.

There is no fixed schema in NoSQL databases. As we illustrated with the example above, this provides more flexibility in comparison with relational databases, but can also make the development of queries substantially more complex.

Another common characteristic of NoSQL databases is that they are distributed and "horizontally scalable." NoSQL databases are typically designed as a distributed data store for handling massive amounts of data (for example, the name MongoDB is derived from the term "humongous"). A NoSQL database can be run on a large number of relatively inexpensive (commodity) servers. Their power and ability to handle large amounts of data can be increased by adding more commodity servers, as needed. This property is referred to as *horizontal scalability*. This is in contrast to the *vertical scalability* of centralized relational databases, where the ability to handle large amounts of data is increased by adding more computing power to the central server. (However, relational databases can also be configured to take advantage of distributed and parallel computing, as described in Appendix F.) NoSQL databases cannot be used straightforwardly for all database operations (e.g., see the discussion above about the lack of a JOIN operation in NoSQL databases), but there is a category of relatively simple database tasks for which they are well suited (e.g., storage and retrieval of a massive amount of simple text files, such as tweets). For such tasks, achieving horizontal scalability by distributing the data and processing is typically simpler and more affordable with NoSQL databases than with relational databases.

Another difference between NoSQL databases and relational databases is in the way they handle database transactions. RDBMS ensures so-called *ACID properties* of database transactions in relational databases. The acronym ACID stands for atomicity, consistency, isolation, and durability. The *atomicity* of a transaction ensures that a database transaction is either completely executed or not executed at all. For example, a bank-transfer transaction from account A to account B that includes the withdrawal from account A and deposit to account B will either be fully executed or not executed at all. *Consistency* ensures that every transaction leaves a database in a valid state, where all the constraints, business rules, and so on, are observed. *Isolation* ensures that each transaction is free from interference by another transaction. *Durability* ensures that the effects of a transaction on a database are permanent. On the other hand, a NoSQL database transaction often exhibits *BASE properties* (BASE stands for "basically available soft-state eventual consistency") instead of ACID properties. In such NoSQL databases, additions and modifications are not always immediately available to the users, but are eventually properly reflected in the system. Not adhering to the ACID properties allows for simpler and less costly scalability.

The ACID properties are usually important for many corporate databases, such as financial, accounting, and supply-chain databases, as they assure the uniform accuracy and time lines of the data necessary for properly conducting business. However, in other situations, such as Web databases handling user postings or tweets, BASE properties are sufficient. For example, a situation in which a critical user does not have immediate access to the result of a financial transaction can have grave business consequences. On the other hand, having to wait a brief amount of time for the most recently issued tweet to appear in the system is typically not of earth-shattering consequence.

An additional difference between relational and NoSQL databases lies in the fact that SQL is a standard language for RDBMS, whereas there is nothing standard or uniform in the variety of languages and methods utilized by the NoSQL databases.

In the current state of corporate computing, relational databases implemented with RDBMS are used in a large majority of business scenarios. However, NoSQL databases provide an attractive and efficient alternative in certain cases, such as the ones illustrated by the examples and discussion above.

APPENDIX J
Big Data

The amount of data generated by commercial, scientific, governmental, and other organizations continues to grow at an ever-increasing rate. The rate of growth has been particularly accelerated by the proliferation of various sensors and smart devices. Examples of such devices generating large amounts of data include the following:

- smartphones that broadcast their location every few seconds
- chips built into cars that perform thousands of diagnostic tests per second
- cameras that are continuously recording public and private spaces
- radio-frequency identification (RFID) tags that send a wireless signal that is read at various points as the carts of merchandise to which the RFID tags are attached travel in the supply-chain from the manufacturer to the customer

Big data is a broad term that refers to the massive volumes of diverse and rapidly growing data that are not formally modeled. Big data is mostly unstructured[1] and, as such, not straightforwardly organized into tables with rows and columns. Big data is characterized not only by its lack of structure and massive size, but also by its heterogeneity. In a typical large corporation, big data can include various kinds of data originating from smart devices, Web logs, public records, social media, and numerous other types of data outlets.

Enterprises that have already recognized the undeniable value of data and have built operational databases and data warehouses to deal with the formally modeled operational and analytical data are now considering how to take advantage of this less structured data, which is much larger in volume and grows at a much faster pace. Standard database and data warehousing techniques, such as relational modeling and dimensional modeling, cannot adequately capture the diversity and heterogeneity of big data. Furthermore, relational DBMSs often cannot achieve satisfactory performance in order to handle complex queries over big data.

Thus, several new ideas have emerged in order to deal with such data, including:

- the MapReduce framework (described in this appendix) first introduced by Google in 2004
- NoSQL databases that do not impose a relational structure on the managed data (described in Appendix I)
- extensions of relational database technology, such as massively parallel processing architecture for RDBMS (described in Appendix F) and columnar storage, where data is stored physically in columns rather than rows, providing performance advantages for certain types of queries, such as aggregates on columns

MAPREDUCE

To illustrate an approach to dealing with big data, we will give a brief discussion of the *MapReduce* computation framework and present a simple example that illustrates this method.

One of the typical big data examples is a large volume of unstructured text, such as articles, reviews, tweets, and so on. In order to manage such data in a standard data warehouse, organizations need to decide on a fixed ETL. However, with such data diversity and the continuous possibility of adding new sources, it is impossible to determine how to transform the data without losing some information, so the data is best left in its original form. For example, given a written review of a product or a service, it may not be clear which particular features found in the review should be extracted and which should be discarded, so it is better to keep the review intact.

---

[1]"Mostly unstructured data," "semi-structured data," "low-structure data," and "lightly structured data" are various terms that describe data with little or no formal metadata.

Consequently, processing such data is not possible using traditional database and data warehousing techniques. Even though reviews could be stored in columns of TEXT data type, computing over hundreds of millions of large entries in such columns would be very slow, since regular databases and data warehouses are not designed to deal with such data efficiently at a massive scale.

The MapReduce framework invented by Google in 2004 is one of the approaches that addressed the issue of computing over big data. The MapReduce framework uses a cluster of nodes (separate computers) performing tasks in parallel. A MapReduce computation has two phases: the "map phase" and the "reduce phase."

During the map phase, every record in the original data (e.g., text containing a product review) is mapped by a program (usually written in Java or another general purpose language) to zero or more key-value pairs. A key can be a single value, such as an integer or a URL, or a more complex value. For example, given a product review, a map function can output several pairs, where each pair consists of a key composed of a *product and feature combination,* and a value that is a *numeric rating* for that product and feature. Since the output of each pair depends on a single input record, the input data and the work of creating output pairs can be distributed among many compute nodes. All the results from the map function performed on different nodes are collected by the framework.

The next step is the reduce step. This involves collecting all records with the same key and generating a single output record for every key. The reduce step can also be distributed, based on the keys, among many compute nodes. Consider the following example.

An Example of MapReduce

Convert the set of written tennis racket reviews to quantitative ratings of certain features. The output is the average of all numeric ratings of the tennis racket feature.

Review 1: The X tennis racket is very flexible, with ample power, but provides average control.

Review 2: The Y tennis stick provides medium power and outstanding control.

Review 3: Using the Y racket gives you great control, but you have to generate most of your power. The frame is not very flexible.

Map Function Output:

```
map(R1) -> (<X, flexibility>, 9), (<X, power>, 8), (<X, control>, 5)
map(R2) -> (<Y, power>, 5), (<Y, control>, 10)
map(R3) -> (<Y, control>, 9), (<Y, power>, 3), (<Y, flexibility>, 2),
```

The map function applied to R1 returns three key-value pairs, the first of which has the key <X, *flexibility*> and the value 9. The second key-value pair has the key <X, *power*> and the value 8, while the third key-value pair has the key <X, *control*> and the value 5.

Note that separate reviews could have been processed, and map function outputs could have been created by separate nodes, as illustrated by Figure J.1. The results of the map functions would then be consolidated by the framework.

Next, the reduce step for each individual key (tennis racket, feature) can be distributed again to various nodes.

Reduce Function Result:

```
reduce((<X, flexibility>)) -> (<X, flexibility>, 9)
reduce((<X, power>)) -> (<X, power>, 8)
reduce((<X, control>)) -> (<X, control>, 5)
reduce((<Y, power>)) -> (<Y, power>, 4)
reduce((<Y, control>)) -> (<Y, control>, 9.5)
reduce((<Y, flexibility>)) -> (<Y, flexibility>, 2)
```

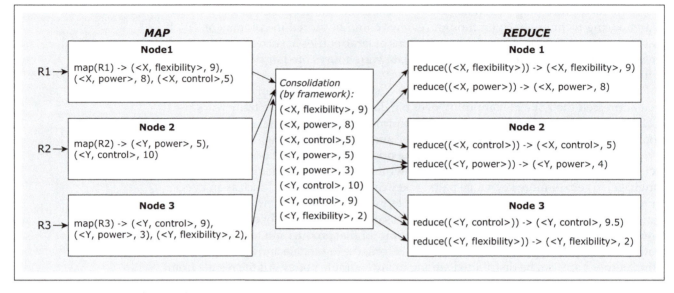

FIGURE J.1 An example of MapReduce.

For example, the reduce step for *<Y, power>* could have been performed on one node by combining map function outputs *(<Y, power>, 5) and (<Y, power>, 3)* and calculating the average numeric power rating, producing the reduce result *(<Y, power>, 4)*. Meanwhile, the reduce step for *<Y, control>* could have been performed on a different node by combining map function outputs *(<Y, control>, 10) and (<Y, control>, 9)* and calculating the average numeric control rating, producing the reduce result *(<Y, control>, 9.5)*. This is illustrated by Figure J.1.

The results of the map reduce steps shown in Figure J.1 can be presented and/or stored in a table, as shown in Figure J.2.

Given the map and reduce functions and input data set, the MapReduce framework[2] determines how to distribute the data among the nodes performing the map and reduce phase in a way that assures efficient performance. For example, if all nodes are performing identically, the work will be evenly distributed. If one of the nodes fails, its work will be distributed to other nodes.

It is important to note that the programmer only has to write the map and reduce functions. The rest of the work—such as starting up compute nodes, distributing the data among them, collecting the output of the map phase, sorting it and distributing it among the compute nodes, and executing the reduce phase—is done by the framework. Even though map and reduce functions can be fairly complex, typically they are

Racket	Feature	Rating
X	flexibilty	9
X	power	8
X	control	5
Y	flexibilty	2
Y	power	4
Y	control	9.5

FIGURE J.2 The result of the MapReduce example shown in Figure J.1.

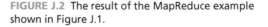

[2]The Apache Hadoop is the most popular (and open-source) implementation of the MapReduce framework.

as simple (if not simpler) as the ones shown in the example above. In a sense, the relative ease of development is similar to writing an SQL query for processing relational data. Within a RDBMS, the SQL query does not need to specify how the tables will be accessed or what particular algorithm to use to perform a join operation. In MapReduce, the programmer need not be concerned with the underlying details, such as data distribution, node failures, and sorting algorithms. Thus, in both cases, the programmer's task is significantly simplified by using the RDBMS and MapReduce implementations (such as Apache Hadoop), respectively.

As illustrated by the example, processing this unstructured data results in an organized and readable data set that can be reported directly to the user or stored in a spreadsheet, database, data mart, or data warehouse. Note that the original set (collection of written tennis racket reviews) is still intact and available for additional types of analyses.

Big data techniques increase the ability to analyze the data that an organization owns or to which it has access. Big data methods, such as MapReduce, do not replace database and data warehousing approaches developed for managing and utilizing formally modeled data assets. Instead, they allow organizations to analyze and get insight from the kinds of data that are not suited for regular database and data warehouse technologies.

GLOSSARY

Access privileges Assigned to the database user account to determine which actions (SELECT, UPDATE, ALTER, DELETE, INSERT) the is user allowed to perform on a particular database object.

Accidental misuse Misuse of a database system during data entry as a result of an accident rather than a deliberate malicious attempt.

Accuracy (Data quality) The extent to which data correctly reflects the real-world instances that the data is supposed to depict.

Active data warehouses Data warehouses with loads that occur continuously in micro batches, ensuring that the data in the data warehouse is updated close to real time (enabling analysis of the latest data).

Aggregate functions SQL functions used for calculating and summarizing values in queries; includes COUNT, SUM, AVG, MIN, and MAX functions.

Aggregated data Data representing summarization of multiple instances of data.

Aggregated fact tables Fact tables in which each record summarizes multiple facts.

Alias An alternative and usually shorter name that can be used anywhere within a query instead of the full relation name; columns can also have aliases but their use is more restricted within a query.

Alpha release Internal deployment of a system to the members of the development team for initial testing of its functionalities.

ALTER TABLE (SQL) Used to change the structure of the relation, once the relation is already created.

Analytical databases Databases that contain analytical information.

Analytical information Information collected and used in support of analytical tasks; it is based on operational (transactional) information.

Application development component It provides functionalities to the developers of front-end applications. In some DBMS packages, this component is a part of the DBMS; for others, it is available as an add-on.

Application-oriented Supporting an application serving one or more business operations and processes.

Assertion A mechanism for specifying user-defined constraints.

Association rule mining Data mining method that finds groups of items that tend to appear together in transactions.

Associative entity An ER diagram construct used as an alternative way of depicting M:N relationships.

Attribute (of an entity) Depiction of a characteristic of an entity.

Attribute (of a relation) A column of a relation.

Augmented functional dependencies Functional dependencies that contain an existing functional dependency; they do not add new information to what is already described by the existing functional dependency and therefore can be omitted.

Authentication Verification of the user's identity through the use of the user's account identifiers and passwords for a login procedure.

Authorization matrix Matrix (provided by the DBMS and available for manipulation by the DBA) in which the rows and columns represent database subjects and objects; entry in the matrix indicates the particular privilege assigned to a user for a particular object.

Autonumber data type A data type that automatically generates consecutive numeric data values in a column.

AVG see *aggregate functions.*

Backup Saving additional physical copies of the data, in addition to the original copy.

Beta release The system release (following the alpha releases), in which the system is deployed to a selected group of users to test the usability of the system.

Big data A broad term that refers to the massive volumes of diverse and rapidly growing data that is not formally modeled.

Binary relationship An ER diagram relationship that involves two entities; also known as a relationship of degree 2.

Binary search A search method that takes advantage of sorted lists.

Boyce-Codd normal form (BCNF) A table is in BCNF if it contains no functional dependencies other than full key functional dependencies (where only the primary key or other candidate keys fully determine other columns).

Bridge relation The relation that represents an M:N relationship.

Business intelligence (BI) tools See *online analytical processing (OLAP) tools.*

Business rules A category of user-designed database constraints that specify restrictions on resulting databases that are not a part of the standard notation for creating ER diagrams.

Candidate key When an entity has more than one unique attribute, each unique attribute is also called a candidate key.

Cardinality constraints ER diagram relationship symbols that depict how many instances of one entity are associated with instances of another entity.

Catalog The data dictionary created by the DBMS.

CHECK (SQL) used to specify a constraint on a particular col-umn of a relation.

Checkpoints Part of a recovery log. When a checkpoint is created, all updates recorded in the recovery log—and as a result any updates to data stored in memory—are written to the database in the data file on the disk.

Circular foreign key dependency Occurs when Table A has a foreign key referring to the primary key of Table B, and Table B has a foreign key referring to the primary key of Table A.

Class An object-oriented concept referring to a grouping of objects that share the same structure and operations.

Class hierarchy (specialization hierarchy) A hierarchy within an object-oriented model that contains a superclass and its subclasses connected by their "IS-A" relationships.

Class instances Objects of a particular class.

Cloud computing systems Systems which use the Internet to deliver data storage and processing services hosted by a service provider.

Column See *attribute (of a relation).*

COMMIT (SQL) A TCL command that causes all updates to be to recorded to the database.

Complete mirrored backup A separate complete physical copy of the database that is continuously updated so that it fully corresponds to the original database.

Completeness (Data quality) The degree to which all the required data is present in the data.

Composite attribute An entity attribute that is composed of several attributes.

Composite primary key A primary key of a relation that is composed of multiple columns.

Composite unique attribute An entity attribute that is composed of several attributes and whose value is different for each entity instance.

Conceptual database model Visualization of the database requirements, independent of the logic on which a particular DBMS is based.

Conformed dimensions Standardized dimensions created before development of star schemas; typically used with multiple fact tables.

Conformity (Data quality) The extent to which the data conforms to its specified format.

Consistency (Data quality) The extent to which the data properly conforms to and matches up with the other data.

Constellation (galaxy) of stars Star schema containing multiple fact tables.

Corrective data quality actions Actions taken to correct the data quality problems.

Correlated subquery The inner query (nested query) that uses columns from the relations listed in the SELECT part of the outer query.

COUNT See *aggregate functions.*

CREATE TABLE (SQL) Used to create and connect relational database tables.

CREATE VIEW (SQL) Used to create views.

Creating ETL infrastructure Creating necessary procedures and code for ETL.

Creating the data warehouse Using a DBMS to implement the data warehouse model as an actual data warehouse.

Cubes Multidimensional database repositories; can be used to store dimensionally modeled data.

Data Facts that are recorded and can be accessed.

Data cleansing (scrubbing) The detection and correction of low-quality data.

Data control language (DCL) Part of the SQL language used in processes related to database maintenance and administrative use; DCL commands facilitate the process of data access control.

Data custodian Person responsible for the technical aspects of data management and use, such as protection, transport, and storage of data.

Data definition component A DBMS component used by database designers to create the structural components of the database, such as database tables and referential integrity constraints connecting the created tables.

Data definition language (DDL) Part of the SQL language used to create and modify the structure of the database.

Data dictionary A repository of the metadata of the database.

Data duplication Result of a uniqueness data quality problem; occurs when a real-world instance is represented more than once in the same data collection.

Data governance A broad term describing a set of initiatives within an organization aimed at formally regulating how, when, and by whom the organizational data and metadata is created, stored, updated (inserted, modified, deleted), and archived.

Data manipulation component A DBMS component that enables end users to insert, read, update, and delete information in a database.

Data manipulation language (DML) Part of the SQL language used to manipulate the data within the database; includes the commands for inserting, modifying, deleting, and retrieving the data in the database.

Data mart A data store based on the same principles as a data warehouse, but with a more limited scope; while a data warehouse contains data about multiple subjects of analysis retrieved from operational databases across an entire organization, a data mart is typically smaller, containing data about one subject, and does not necessarily have an enterprise-wide focus.

Data mining The process of discovering novel and interesting patterns in large amounts of data.

Data quality Defined by a number of different data properties including accuracy, uniqueness, completeness, consistency, timeliness, and conformity.

Data replication Storing more than one copy of the data at different locations in a distributed database.

Data steward Person who undertakes tasks related to data governance; responsible for the proper use of the data in databases.

Data warehouse A structured repository of integrated, subject-oriented, enterprise-wide, historical, and time-variant data; the purpose of the data warehouse is the retrieval of analytical information; a data warehouse can store detailed and/or summarized data.

Data warehouse administration and maintenance Performing activities that support the data warehouse end user, including dealing with technical issues, such as providing security for the information contained in the data warehouse; ensuring sufficient hard-drive space for the data warehouse content; or imple-menting the backup and recovery procedures.

Data warehouse deployment Releasing the data warehouse and its front-end applications for use to the end users.

Data warehouse modeling The creation of data warehouse models that are implementable by the DBMS software; the first step following the requirements collection, definition, and visualization stage of a data warehousing project.

Data warehouse use Retrieval of the data warehouse data by end users.

Database A structured collection of related data stored on computer media; its purpose is to organize data in a way that facilitates efficient access to the information captured in the data.

Database administration and maintenance Performing activities that support the database end user, including dealing with technical issues, such as providing security for the information contained in the database, ensuring sufficient hard-drive space for the database content, or implementing the backup and recoveryprocedures.

Database administration component A DBMS component used to perform the technical, administrative, and maintenance tasks, such as ensuring security, optimizing performance, and providing backup and recovery.

Database administrators (DBA) People who manage issues related to security (e.g., creating and issuing user names and passwords, granting privileges to access data, etc.), handle backup and recovery of database systems, monitor use and add-ing storage space as needed, and perform other tasks related to the proper technical functioning of the database system.

Database analysts People involved in the requirements collection, definition, and visualization stage of a database project.

Database as a service (DaaS) Specialized version of SaaS developed for database management in clouds.

Database deployment The release of the database system (i.e., the database and its front-end applications) for use to the end users.

Database designers (database modelers or architects) People involved in the database modeling stage of a database project.

Database developers People in charge of implementing the database model (as a functioning database) using the DBMS software.

Database fragmentation A strategy for distributing the data across different locations in a distributed database.

Database front-end A component of a database system used to provide access to the database in a way that does not involve the user writing commands (i.e., indirect use).

Database implementation The use of a DBMS to implement the database model as an actual database.

Database management system (DBMS) Software used to create databases; to insert, store, retrieve, update, and delete the data in the database; and to maintain databases.

Database metadata The data about the data; the database content that is not the data itself (e.g., table name, column name).

Database modeling (logical database modeling) The creation of database models that are implementable by the DBMS software; the first step following requirements collection, definition, and visualization.

Database policies and standards Policies and standards used in the development, use, and administration of the database. A common purpose for all database policies and standards is to reflect and support the business processes and business logic.

Database requirements Statements that define the details and constraints of the data and metadata for the database that is being developed. Database requirements state what the future database will keep track of and in what fashion.

Database system A computer-based system whose purpose is to enable efficient interaction between the users and the information captured in a database.

Database use The insertion, modification, deletion, and retrieval of the data contained within the database system by end users.

Decryption key Algorithm that reverts the encrypted information back to its original state.

Degenerate dimension An event identifier included within the fact table (rather than having its own separate dimension).

Degree of a relationship The number that reflects how many entities are involved in the relationship.

Delete cascade A referential integrity constraint option that allows a record to be deleted if its primary key value is referred to by a foreign key value of a record in another relation; all the records whose foreign key value refers to the primary key value of the record that is being deleted are also deleted.

Delete operation A database operation used for removing data from the relation.

Delete restrict A referential integrity constraint option that does not allow a record to be deleted if its primary key value is referred to by a foreign key value of a record in another relation.

Delete set-to-default A referential integrity constraint option that allows a record to be deleted if its primary key value is referred to by a foreign key value of a record in another relation; in all of the records where the foreign key value refers to the primary key of the record that is being deleted, the value of the foreign key is set to a predetermined default value.

Delete set-to-null A referential integrity constraint option that allows a record to be deleted if its primary key value is referred to by a foreign key value of a record in another relation; in all of the records whose foreign key value refers to the primary key of the record that is being deleted, the value of the foreign key is set to null.

DELETE (SQL) Used to delete the data stored in database relations.

Deletion anomaly An update anomaly that occurs when a user who wants to delete data about a real-world entity is forced to delete data about another real-world entity.

Denormalization Reversing the effect of normalization by joining normalized relations into a relation that is not normalized.

Dependent data mart A data mart that does not have its own source systems; instead, its data comes from the data warehouse.

Derived attribute An entity attribute whose values are calculated and not permanently stored in a database.

Designer-added entities (tables) Entitles not called for by the original requirements, added by the database designer; they result in designer-added tables.

Designer-added keys Primary keys of designer-added tables, created by the database designer.

Designer-created primary key Primary key column, not called for by the original requirements, added to a table by the data-base designer.

Detailed data Data composed of single instances of data.

Detailed fact tables A fact table in which each record refers to a single fact.

Developing front-end applications The design and creation of applications for indirect database use by the end user.

Dimension tables (dimensions) Tables in a dimensional model that contain descriptions of the business, organization, or enterprise to which the subject of analysis belongs and contain a primary key and attributes that are used for analysis of the measures in the fact tables.

Dimensional modeling A data design methodology used for designing subject-oriented analytical databases, i.e., data warehouses or data marts.

Dimensionally modeled data warehouse Data warehouse modeled using dimensional modeling.

Direct interaction An interaction between the end user and the database in which the end user communicates with the DBMS directly.

Disjointed subclasses Subclass entities that do not have common instances, sharing the same superclass entity.

DISTINCT (SQL) Used in conjunction with the SELECT statement; eliminates duplicate values from a query result.

Distributed database system (DDBS) A database system where the database is distributed among separate computers.

Distribution transparency The property of a DDBS that ensures that the end users can use the distributed database in the same fashion as if the database is not distributed (i.e., without knowing the details of the distribution of the data or even if the data is distributed).

Domain constraint A relational database restriction that states that, within a relation, all values in each column must be from the same predefined domain.

Drill down An OLAP operation for making the granularity of the data in the query result finer.

Drill up An OLAP operation for making the granularity of the data in the query result coarser.

DROP TABLE (SQL) Used to remove a table from the database.

DROP VIEW (SQL) Used to remove a view.

Encryption Changing information using a scrambling algorithm so that the information becomes unreadable to anyone who does not have a decryption key.

Encryption key A scrambling algorithm used to make data unreadable to anyone who does not have a decryption key.

End users (business users) People who use a database system to support their work- or life-related tasks and processes.

Enhanced ER (EER) An expanded ER notation that depicts additional concepts beyond standard ER modeling.

Enterprise resources planning (ERP) system A pre-made, integrated (multi-functional) corporate information system.

Entity An ER diagram construct that represents what the database keeps track of.

Entity instances (entity members) Occurrences of an entity.

Entity integrity constraint A relational database rule that states that all primary key columns must have values.

Entity-relationship (ER) modeling A widely used conceptual database modeling method that enables the structuring and organizing of the requirements collection process and provides a way to graphically represent the requirements.

Equivalent functional dependencies Occur when two columns (or sets of columns) that functionally determine each other determine other columns; if one of the equivalent functional dependencies is depicted, the other equivalent functional dependency does not have to be depicted.

ER diagram (ERD) A graphical representation of database requirements; contains entities and relationships.

Exact minimum and/or maximum cardinality Minimum and/or maximum cardinality (of a relationship) that is known in advance.

EXCEPT See *MINUS*.

Executive dashboard A front-end application that contains an organized, easy-to-read display of critically important queries describing the performance of the organization.

EXISTS (SQL) Used to check if the result of the inner query is empty.

Extensible markup language (XML) A markup language for adding structure and semantics to a document.

Extensible stylesheet language (XSL) Language used to present the XML elements in a Web page.

Extraction-transformation-load (ETL) The process of extracting analytically useful data from the operational data sources; transforming such data so that it conforms to the structure of the subject-oriented target data warehouse model while ensuring the quality of the transformed data; and loading the transformed and quality assured data into the target data warehouse.

Fact tables Tables in a dimensional model that contain measures related to the subject of analysis and foreign keys that connect the fact table to the dimension tables.

Federated database A type of distributed database system that comprises a collection of preexisting databases that are connected into one system.

Field See *column*.

First load The initial data warehouse load populating the empty data warehouse.

First normal form (1NF) A table is in 1NF if each row is unique and no column in any row contains multiple values from the column's domain.

Foreign key A column in a relation that refers to a primary key column in another (referred) relation.

Form A database front-end component whose purpose is to enable data input and retrieval for end users.

Fourth normal form (4NF) A table is in fourth normal form if it is in BCNF and does not contain multivalued dependencies. Consequently, a relation is not in 4NF if it contains multivalued dependencies.

Front-end applications Applications created to provide a mechanism for interaction between the users and the DBMS.

Front-end applications analysts People in charge of collecting and defining requirements for front-end applications.

Front-end applications developers People in charge of creating the front-end applications.

Full key functional dependency Occurs when a primary key functionally determines the column of a relation and no separate component of the primary key partially determines the same column.

FULL OUTER JOIN See *OUTER JOIN statement*.

Fully replicated distributed database A type of replication where the entire database is replicated at each location in the distributed system.

Functional dependency Occurs when the value of one (or more) column(s) in each record of a relation uniquely determines the value of another column in that same record of the relation.

GRANT (SQL) A statement used to grant an access privilege.

Granularity Describes what is depicted by one row in the fact table.

GROUP BY (SQL) Enables summarizations across the groups of related data within tables.

HAVING (SQL) Determines which groups will be displayed in the result of a query and consequently which groups will not be displayed in the result of the query.

Heterogeneous DDBS A DDBS architecture where different DBMS can run on different computers.

Homogeneous DDBS A DDBS architecture where all the computers run the same DBMS.

Horizontal fragmentation A fragmentation where subsets of the records from a table are stored at different locations in the DDBS.

Hybrid online analytical processing (HOLAP) An OLAP architecture that combines MOLAP and ROLAP approaches.

Hypertext markup language (HTML) A markup language that provides the functionalities for describing how to display the information contained in Web pages.

Identifying relationship A relationship between a weak entity and its owner entity in an ER diagram.

Implicit constraints The implicit relational database model rules that a relational database must satisfy in order to be valid.

IN (SQL) Used to compare a value with a set of values.

Independent data mart A stand-alone data mart with its own source systems and ETL infrastructure; it has a single subject and (when compared to the data warehouse) fewer data sources, smaller size, shorter implementation, and often a narrower focus.

Index A database mechanism for increasing the speed of data search and data retrieval on tables with a large number of records.

Indirect interaction The type of interaction between the end user and the database that involves the use of front-end applications.

Information Data that is accessed by a user for some particular use and purpose.

Infrastructure as a service (IaaS) Computer hardware provided as standardized services over the network.

Inner query See *nested query*.

INSERT INTO (SQL) Used to populate the created relations with data.

Insert operation A database operation used for entering new data in the relation.

Insertion anomaly An update anomaly that occurs when a user who wants to insert data about one real-world entity is forced to enter data about another real-world entity.

Insertion, modification, deletion, and retrieval The operations through which end users use the data contained within the database system.

INTERSECT (SQL) Operator used to combine the results of two SELECT statements that are union compatible by listing every row that appears in the result of both of the SELECT statements.

IS NULL (SQL) Used in queries that contain comparisons with an empty value in a column of a record.

JOIN (SQL) Used to facilitate the querying of multiple tables.

LEFT OUTER JOIN See *OUTER JOIN statement*.

LIKE (SQL) Used for retrieval of records whose values partially match a certain criteria.

Linear (sequential) search A search method that finds a particular value in a list by checking elements sequentially one at a time until the searched-for value is found.

Line-item detailed fact table A fact table in which each record represents a line item of a particular transaction.

Logical database model (implementational database model) Database model that is implementable by the DBMS software.

Many-to-many relationship (M:N) A relationship in the ER diagram whose maximum cardinality is "many" on both sides.

Market basket analysis See *association rule mining*.

Markup language A language used to annotate (i.e., to "markup") text in a document, where annotations add functionalities to the text.

Massively parallel processing (MPP) An approach that uses a large number of separate computer processors running in parallel to execute a single program.

Master data Contains an authenticated quality version of the key data that provides a common point of reference for the organization's information systems.

Master data management (MDM) Creating and maintaining a collection of quality master data tables and ensuring that the use of master data is embedded across the operational information systems in the organization.

Master data registry Contains a list of keys that is used to connect and coordinate the actual master data that resides in operational systems; allows information systems to access master data from other information systems to align and supplement its own master data.

MAX See *aggregate functions*.

Maximum cardinality—one or many The part of the cardinality constraint symbol closer to the entity rectangle; depicts the maximum number of instances of an entity that can be associated with one instance of the other entity.

Metadata Data that describes the structure and the properties of the data.

MIN See *aggregate functions*.

Minimum Cardinality (participation)—optional or mandatory The part of the cardinality constraint symbol farther away from the entity rectangle; depicts the minimum number of in-stances of an entity that can be associated with one instance of the other entity.

MINUS (SQL) Operator used to combine the results of two SELECT statements that are union compatible by listing every row from the result of the first SELECT statement that does not appear in the result of the other SELECT statement.

Mixed fragmentation A combination of horizontal and vertical fragmentation.

Modification anomaly An update anomaly that occurs when, in order to modify one real-world value, the same modification has to be made multiple times; one of three types of update anomalies.

Modify operation A database operation used for changing the existing data in the relation.

Multidimensional database model A model for implementation of dimensionally modeled data in which the database is implemented as a collection of cubes.

Multidimensional online analytical processing (MOLAP) An OLAP architecture that stores data in multidimensional cubes.

Multiuser system Database system in which the data manipulation component can be used by multiple users at the same time.

Multivalued attribute An entity attribute for which instances of an entity can have multiple values for the same attribute.

Multivalued dependency Occurs when separate columns of the same relation contain unrelated values; i.e., when the same relation represents separate relationships of cardinality greater than 1.

Necessary redundancy A term that refers to multiple appearances of foreign key values in the 3NF set of relational tables; essential for connecting the tables in a relational database.

Nested object Occurs when an object is contained in another object.

Nested query Query that is used within another query, also known as inner query.

Nonkey column A column in a relation that is neither a primary nor a candidate key column.

NoSQL database A broad term describing a database that is not based on the relational model and does not use SQL as a query language.

Normal forms A term representing a set of particular conditions (whose purpose is reducing data redundancy) that a table has to satisfy; from a lower to a higher normal form, these conditions are increasingly stricter and leave less possibility for redundant data.

Normalization A process used to improve the design of relational databases that contain redundant data, and are, therefore, prone to update anomalies.

Normalized data warehouse A data warehouse modeled by using the traditional database modeling techniques of ER modeling, relational modeling, and/or normalization, resulting in a normalized set of tables.

NOT (SQL) Used in conjunction with the condition comparison statements returning the Boolean values TRUE when the specified condition is FALSE, and returning the Boolean values FALSE when the specified condition is TRUE.

Object An object-oriented concept that corresponds to a real world object in the same sense as the entity in ER modeling corresponds to a real object in the real world.

Object attributes Object elements describing characteristics of an object; equivalent to the attributes of an entity.

Object identifier (OID) Identifier of an object; its value is automatically assigned by the OODBS and is immutable.

Object operations Object elements describing functions of an object.

Object-oriented database (OODB) A database based on object-oriented concepts.

Object-relational database Relational database that contains object-oriented features.

OLAP/BI Tools See *online analytical processing (OLAP) tools*.

One-to-many relationship (1:M) A relationship in the ER diagram whose maximum cardinality on one of the sides is "many" and on the other side is "one."

One-to-one relationship (1:1) A relationship in the ER diagram whose maximum cardinality is "one" on both sides.

Online analytical processing (OLAP) Querying and presenting data from data warehouses and/or data marts for analytical purposes.

Online analytical processing (OLAP) tools Tools enabling end users to engage in an ad-hoc analytical querying of data warehouses.

Online transaction processing (OLTP) Updating (i.e., inserting, modifying, and deleting), querying, and presenting data from databases for operational purposes.

Operational databases Databases that collect and present operational information in support of daily operational processes.

Operational information (transactional information) The information collected and used in support of the day-to-day operational needs in businesses and other organizations.

Optional attribute An entity attribute that is allowed to not have a value.

ORDER BY (SQL) A clause within the SELECT query used to sort the results of the query by one or more columns (or expressions).

OUTER JOIN (SQL) Variations of the JOIN operation, which include LEFT, RIGHT, and FULL, that supplement the results with the records from one relation (that is being joined) that have no match in the other relation (that is being joined).

Outer query A query that uses the nested (inner) query.

Overlapping subclasses Subclass entities (sharing the same superclass entity) that have common instances.

Owner entity An entity whose unique attribute provides a mechanism for identifying instances of a weak entity.

Parallel database A database using multiple computers to work on the same task and perform the same operations simultaneously on different portions of the same data set.

Partial functional dependency Occurs when a column of a relation is functionally dependent on a component of a primary key.

Partial key An attribute of a weak entity that combined with the unique attribute of the owner entity uniquely identifies the weak entity's instances.

Partial replication A type of replication where some of the data is replicated at multiple locations while other parts of the data are not replicated.

Partial specialization Occurs when one or more instances of a superclass entity is not an instance of any of its subclass entities.

Pivot (rotate) An OLAP operation that reorganizes the values displayed in the original query result by moving values of a dimension column from one axis to another.

Platform as a Service (PaaS) Resources required for building applications provided as standardized services over a network.

Predictive analytics Using past data to predict future events.

Preventive data quality actions Actions taken to preclude the data quality problems.

Primary key A column (or a set of columns) in a relation whose value is unique for each row; in case there are multiple candidates, a designer chooses one of the candidates to be the primary key.

Primary key constraint A relational database rule stating that each relation must have a primary key.

Production release The actual deployment of a functioning system.

Query A data retrieval expression.

Query cost The time length of query execution.

Query hints Suggestions for overriding the default behavior of the query optimizer; only intended to be used by experienced database administrators for fine-tuning.

Query optimization Examining multiple ways of executing the same query and choosing the fastest option.

Query optimizer A feature in the DBMS that determines how to execute an SQL statement in an efficient manner.

Read operation The data retrieval operation used for reading the data from relations.

Record A row of data within a relation.

Recovery Recovering the content of the database after a failure.

Recovery log A file recorded to the disk that logs database updates, ensuring that, even if the update performed on the data in memory is somehow lost before it is written to the disk, the information about the update will still be captured.

Redundant data Multiple instances of the data (stored in a database) referring to the same occurrence.

Reference object Occurs when an object is referenced by another object.

Referential integrity constraint A relational database rule stating that in each row of a relation containing a foreign key, the value of the foreign key either matches one of the values in the primary key column of the referred relation or the value of the foreign key is null.

Referential integrity constraint lines The lines in a relational schema connecting the relations by pointing from the foreign keys to the corresponding primary keys.

Refresh cycle The frequency with which the data warehouse is reloaded with new data.

Refresh load Every subsequent load after the first load.

Related multivalued columns Columns in a table that refer to the same real-world concept (entity) and can have multiple values per record.

Relation A table in a relational database; contains rows and columns.

Relational database A database that is modeled using the relational database model; a collection of related relations within which each relation has a unique name.

Relational DBMS (RDBMS) Relational DBMS software, based on the relational database model and used to implement relational databases.

Relational database model The most commonly used logical database model; represents a database as a collection of related tables.

Relational online analytical processing (ROLAP) An OLAP architecture that stores data in relational tables.

Relational schema A visual depiction of the relational database model.

Relational table See *relation*.

Relationship An ER modeling construct depicting how entities are related. Within an ER diagram, each entity must be related to at least one other entity via this construct.

Relationship attributes Attributes of a relationship, applicable to M:N relationships.

Relationship instances Occur when an instance of one entity is related to an instance of another entity via a relationship.

Relationship role Additional syntax that can be used in ER diagrams at the discretion of a data modeler to clarify the role of each entity in a relationship.

Report A database front-end component whose purpose is to present the data and calculations on the data from one or more tables from the database in a formatted way.

Requirements collection, definition, and visualization The first and most critical step in the development of the database (or data warehouse); it results in the requirements specifying which data the future database (or data warehousing) system will hold and in what fashion, and what the capabilities and functionalities of the database (or data warehousing) system will be.

REVOKE (SQL) A statement used to revoke an access privilege.

RIGHT OUTER JOIN See *OUTER JOIN statement*.

Role-based access control A database access control method that allows creating groups that contain multiple users and assigning access privileges to those groups.

ROLLBACK (SQL) A command that rolls back all the updates since the last COMMIT.

Row See *record*.

Row indicator A column that provides a quick indicator of whether the record is currently valid.

Second normal form (2NF) A table is in 2NF if it is in 1NF and does not contain partial functional dependencies.

SELECT (SQL) The most commonly issued SQL statement; used for the retrieval of data from the database relations.

Self-JOIN A join statement that includes a relation that contains a foreign key referring to itself, and joins a relation with itself in a query.

Set operators Operators union, intersection, and difference, which are used to combine the union compatible results of two or more SELECT statements.

Shared-nothing MPP architecture A parallel system in which each processor has its own memory and disk storage.

Single-user system Database system in which the data manipulation component can be used by one user at a time.

Slice and dice An OLAP operation that adds, replaces, or eliminates specified dimension attributes (or particular values of the dimension attributes) from the already displayed result.

Slowly changing dimensions A dimension that contains attributes whose values can change.

Snowflake models A star schema that contains the dimensions that are normalized.

Software as a Service (SaaS) Computer applications offered as a service on demand, hosted and operated over the Internet.

Source systems Operational databases and other sets of data used for operational purposes that provide analytically useful information for the data warehouse's subjects of analysis.

SQL data types Data types for columns of tables created in SQL.

SQL standard Standard created and agreed upon by standardization organizations specifying SQL's logical framework and central elements as well as specifications on how SQL is to work with other programming languages, external data, and multimedia, in addition to a growing range of other capabilities.

SQL/XML An extension of SQL that specifies the combined use of SQL and XML.

Star schema Schema containing fact tables and dimensions.

Structured Query Language (SQL) A language used to query a database; create a database; add, modify, and delete database structures; and insert, delete, and modify records in the database.

Subclass A class that has its own attributes and operations, and it also inherits attributes and operations from its superclass.

Subclass entity An entity that has two types of attributes: its own attributes and attributes inherited from its superclass entity. All subclass entities that share the same superclass entity share the same attributes inherited from their superclass. Instances of a subclass entity are at the same time instances of its superclass entity.

SUM See *aggregate functions*.

Superclass A class that contains other classes (subclasses).

Superclass entity An entity whose attributes are inherited by its subclass entities.

Subject-oriented Created for the analysis of one or more specific business subject areas.

Surrogate key A noncomposite system-generated key assigned to each dimension of a star schema.

Table See *relation*.

Ternary relationship An ER diagram relationship involving three entities; also known as a relationship of degree 3.

Third normal form (3NF) A table is in 3NF if it is in 2NF and does not contain transitive functional dependencies.

Timeliness (Data quality) The degree to which the data is aligned with the proper time window in its representation of the real world.

Timestamps Columns in tables that indicate the time interval for which the values in the records are applicable.

Total specialization Occurs when every instance of a superclass entity is at the same time an instance of at least one of its subclass entities.

Transaction control language (TCL) Part of the SQL language used in various processes related to database maintenance and administrative use. TCL is used to manage database transactions.

Transaction identifier A column representing the transaction id.

Transaction time A column representing the time of the transaction.

Transaction-level detailed fact table A fact table in which each row represents a particular transaction.

Transitive functional dependency Occurs when nonkey columns functionally determine other nonkey columns of a relation.

Trigger A rule written using SQL that is activated by a deletion of a record, insertion of a record, or modification (update) of a record in a relation.

Trivial functional dependencies Occur when an attribute (or a set of attributes) functionally determines itself or its subset.

Tuple See *row*.

Type 1 approach The approach to handling slowly changing dimensions based on overwriting values in records of dimensions; it is used mostly when a change in a dimension is the result of an error.

Type 2 approach An approach to handling slowly changing dimensions that is used in cases when history should be preserved; it creates a new additional dimension record using a new value for the surrogate key every time a value in a dimension record changes.

Type 3 approach An approach to handling slowly changing dimensions used in cases when there is a fixed number of changes possible per column of a dimension, or in cases when only a limited history is recorded; it creates a "previous" and "current" column in the dimension table, for each column where the changes are anticipated.

Unary relationship (recursive relationship) A relationship in the ER diagram that involves one entity in a relationship with itself; also known as a relationship of degree 1.

Unauthorized malicious data updates Misuse of a database system during data entry as a result of a deliberate malicious attempt.

UNION (SQL) Operator used to combine the union compatible results of two SELECT statements by listing all rows from the result of the first SELECT statement and all rows from the result of

the other SELECT statement; if two or more rows are identical only one of them is shown (duplicates are eliminated from the result).

Unique attribute An entity attribute whose value is different for each entity instance.

Uniqueness (Data quality) Requires each real-world instance to be represented only once in the data collection.

Update anomalies Anomalies in relations that contain redundant data, caused by update operations; see *deletion anomaly*, *insertion anomaly*, and *modification anomaly*.

Update cascade A referential integrity constraint option that allows the primary key value of a record to be changed if its primary key value is referred to by a foreign key value of a record in another relation, all the foreign key values that refer to the primary key being changed are also changed.

Update failure Failure of a database system during an update operation.

Update operations Three operations for updating the data content in a relation; see *delete operation*, *insert operation*, and *modify operation*.

Update restrict A referential integrity constraint option that does not allow the primary key value of a record to be changed if its primary key value is referred to by a foreign key value of a record in another relation.

Update set-to-default A referential integrity constraint option that allows a record to be changed if its primary key value is referred to by a foreign key value of a record in another relation; in all of the records whose foreign key value refers to the primary key being changed, the value of the foreign key is set to a predetermined default value.

Update set-to-null A referential integrity constraint option that allows a record to be changed if its primary key value is referred to by a foreign key value of a record in another relation; in all of the records whose foreign key value refers to the primary key being changed, the value of the foreign key is set to null.

UPDATE (SQL) Used for modifying the data stored in database tables.

User-defined constraints Database constraints that are added by the database designer.

User-defined type (UDT) A class created by a user used as a data type in another class.

Vertical fragmentation A fragmentation where subsets of the columns of a table are stored at different locations in the DDBS.

View A mechanism in SQL that allows a query to be saved in the RDBMS; also known as a virtual table. When invoked, a view shows the table resulting from executing the saved query.

View materialization Saving a view as an actual physical table.

Weak entity An ER diagram construct used to depict entities that do not have a unique attribute of their own.

WHERE (SQL) Determines which rows should be retrieved and consequently which rows should not be retrieved.

Write operations See *update operations*.

XML Path Language (XPath) Language that utilizes the tree representation of an XML document, allowing the user to travel around the tree; XPath expressions return a collection of element nodes from the tree, which satisfy patterns specified in an expression.

XQuery Language that provides functionalities for querying XML documents similar to SQL functionalities for querying relational tables.

INDEX